James Dean, An International Scrapbook

978-1-9997231-5-6

Introduction, design and annotations
© Paul Sutton, 2018

Paul Sutton is identified as the author of this book. The moral rights of the author have been asserted by him in accordance with sections 77 and 78 of the Copyright, Designs and Patents Act, 1988.

Published by Buffalo Books
camerajournal@hotmail.com

For educational use
and for preservation and publicity purposes

All rights reserved. No part of this publication may be reproduced, stored in a retrieval system or transmitted in any form or by any means electronic, mechanical, print on demand or otherwise, without the prior written permission of the author. This book shall not, by way of trade or otherwise, be lent, re-sold, hired out or otherwise circulated without the publisher's prior consent in any form of binding or cover other than that in which it is published.

Also by Buffalo Books

Paul Dufficey: The Art of Collage
The Art of the Horror Film Press Advert
Remaking Heaven (Sam's First Day)
Understanding Gary Numan
Gary Numan, an International Scrapbook
Talking About Ken Russell
The Lemon Popsicle Book
The Moving Picture Boy Gallery
The Moving Picture Girl Gallery
Becoming Ken Russell
Charlie Ellis and the Day Trip to Mars
Six English Filmmakers
Falling Upwards *by Tim Dry*
Ken Russell's Dracula
To Each His Own Dolce Vita,
by John Francis Lane

All illustrations from *East of Eden, Rebel Without a Cause, Giant* © Warner Brothers, all rights reserved.

All other images and articles are the copyright of the James Dean Estate and the original writers and photographers.

© Roy Schatt

Standing in the field he once worked, Jimmy seemed more like the troubled actor than a simple youth from a midwestern farm.

While never enthusiastic about farming, Jimmy always liked animals. Amid his uncle's cows, he seemed almost as contented as they.

© Dennis Stock/ Magnum

It starts and ends in the countryside

In Anton Corbijn's quietly excellent film *Life* (2015), the Dutch pop culture photographer looks at the rising phenomenon of James Dean through the eyes of Dennis Stock, one of a trio of masterful photographers (with Roy Schatt and Sanford Roth) on whose art would be built the most lasting memorial to a young man who died before his time. The film opens on the eve of the release of *East of Eden*, Elia Kazan's interpretation of John Steinbeck's novel about a new generation of country folk who went West to make a new start (they make fortunes in sex and war), and which starts with the troubled young Cal (James Dean) out looking for his long absent mother and throwing stones at a whore house. In life, James Dean went West to find his father, study for a degree and become a film star (after completing his first and only term as an undergraduate he appeared in an advert for Pepsi Cola. It is available on-line). He was hired into the very top tier of the acting business when Kazan saw him on Broadway in *The Immoralist*, a challenging (im)morality play adapted from a novel by the French Nobel Prize winner, André Gide (Dean quit the play on the opening night). But the crux of Corbijn's film, the journey into the heart of the artist that was James Dean, takes place on the Indiana ranch where, at the age of nine-years-old, the motherless boy was shaped into the man he became. A man whose shoulders were broad enough to carry the projections, hopes and dreams of his own generation, and of successive generations of misunderstood youth as each discovers the three James Dean feature films and the photographs of Stock, Schatt and Roth.

The importance of James Dean's rural upbringing on a working farm cannot be overstated if one is to understand who James Dean was, and what made him so different from all other young actors. On the farm he learned to connect with Nature, that's not nature in the *abstract* but Nature in the *absolute*. It means a daily immersion into the seasons and the earth and the fruits of the earth. It means ploughing and sewing and raising and butchering. It means sweeping and mending, hammering and sawing. Cattle and dogs. It means winter cold and summer heat. It means discipline and the almost constant thinking of things beyond oneself. For there are animals and crops to care for, over and above the duties of a full and firm Quaker schooling and an horizon-opening friendship with a Methodist priest. There are the rhythms of the full day to master.

From there James Dean went Full West and then Full East where he honed his art in the famous Actors Studio in the skyscraper city of New York. He learned sculpture too and photography and dance, three arts that cultivate an understanding of physical space. Then back to the hot lands of Hollywood. Thus his was a talent built across the whole span of the United States. His was not an urban childhood of talent agencies and feeder schools. He didn't grow wrapped in cotton wool.

I was in Wyoming with the great American filmmaker John McTiernan. We were on his ranch watching Sergio Leone's mighty film, *Once Upon a Time in the West*. John hadn't seen the film before and was thrilled with it. He liked everything about it. But the thing that impressed him most, the one scene that truly stood out to him as a film director, was when

Charles Bronson marks out the floor boundaries of a new building in the new town, striding out much in the manner of James Dean marking his inherited land in *Giant*. Bronson hammers heavy iron markers into the ground all the while carrying on a conversation. McTiernan said to me: "It's impossible to do a scene like that now. There aren't the actors who can do it. There are no actors now with *pioneer skills*. You don't have the time to teach an actor the skills of manual labour. You can't pretend physical expertise." Charles Bronson was hewed from Pennsylvanian mining stock. He had authentic working class, or pioneering class, physicality and skills, but it took him so long to reach the Hollywood heights that he was obliged by his agents to deduct six years from his actual age, and was late middle-aged when his star struck.

Look at the first farm scene in *East of Eden*. Cal's father is buying a hayloft warehouse full of ice. James Dean runs up the rickety tumbledown outside chute of the warehouse and into the upper floor like he'd been doing it all of his life. Because he had been. In a fit of temper he rams a spike into the ice blocks and hurls them down the chute with more efficiency than a machine. It's like he's been hurling ice blocks or hay bales for all of his life. And he had. He had the physical life skills that filmmakers cannot teach. The skills allowed him to go deeper into the role.

Contrast those pioneer skills, that dexterity and awareness of physical space, with a complaint by a popular young actress that made the main news channels in the MeToo era. When making *Kill Bill*, Quentin Tarantino told Uma Thurman to drive an open-top car down a dirt road at sufficient speed to get her hair blowing in the wind. A fair thing to ask of an adult with a driving license. She asked for a stunt driver. Tarantino turned down the request, saying it wasn't a stunt it was driving. Thurman lost control of the car on a gentle bend, crashed into a tree and damaged her legs. I'm not making light of the accident, I'm using it as an illustration of how far the expected life skills of star actors had fallen from the days when a director knew they could run up rickety chutes and hammer in iron markers for the building of a house. They sure don't make 'em like they used to.

In light of that anecdote, it's ironic of course that the dexterous James Dean lost his life in the almost open countryside north of Los Angeles after suffering a fatal accident with his hands at the wheel of an open-top car. Fate does have a way of biting one on the backside. Dean lived fast. Died young. And had a horrible horrible corpse. His was a death that broke a million hearts. And onto his shoulders came the hopes and dreams of generations.

But James Dean's ascendancy in death to something akin to a patron Saint of misunderstood youth, did not come about because of his pioneer skill-set, though his keen understanding of physical space, and the way he held and moved his hands and his body, is a cornerstone of his mastery of the acting art. It was his ability as an actor to communicate. He communicated frustration and disappointment and hope. He communicated pain and joy. His wild joy as he lies on the earth in *East of Eden,* watching the green shoots of his fortune in beans take hold, sets him dancing so wildly that the faces of the farmer's children shine with happiness. In *Rebel Without a Cause* he gives his warm wind-cheater jacket to the needy young Plato (Sal Mineo) and it makes the cold and damaged boy shiver with sensual pleasure. But the thing Dean communicates best, and most consistently across the three films, is an impassioned stand against the values of the older generation. In *East of Eden*, Dean's character challenges the prevalent adult vice of hiding behind the virtues of The Big Black Book. His good father's love for The Word of The Lord has prevented the father from loving his own wife and sons. Such blind conformity takes the world into war. By putting Cal (Dean) at the heart of the adaptation, Kazan's *East of Eden* becomes a film about immaturity. It's a film about a teenager's cry for parental love. And this is the twist, Kazan isn't criticising or commenting on the natural immaturity of the child, he's attacking the endemic immaturity of the adults. James Dean's loveless Cal is understandably morose, partly symptomatic of his young age, but, with the exceptions of a good businessman who teams up with Cal, and one very good and strong lawmaker (Burl Ives), Cal is the most mature person in the film. He is the one trying to understand the reason why his father's marriage failed (why he lost his mother). His is the successful solution to his father's financial failure. There is a goodness behind even the most wrongful of his actions. The other characters in the film are pedantic, selfish and weak.

Rebel Without a Cause is also a film about immaturity; a mostly nocturnal urban film about the immature wayward children of immature middle class parents. Dean's character, Jim Stark, is again one of only three mature people in the film and, again, one of them is on the payroll of the law; the third is a maid hired to look after Plato. Again the young people are hurting and failing because they lack parental love. Actually, Dean's Stark isn't all that mature. People who make noises at planetarium shows can't be classified as adult. He's just the most mature of the younger folk. But in *Rebel*, first in a suit, then with blue jeans, white T-shirt, boots and a red jacket, James Dean as Jim Stark strides more fully into the Kingdom of Cool than any loveless dungaree-wearing Monterey farm boy could muster. In *East of Eden*, Dean's character looked down more often than he looked up. In *Rebel Without a Cause*, James Dean is now man enough to look the enemy full into the eye - first the fallen father (fallen in that he fails to live up to the younger man's definition of masculinity, i.e. standing up to a bullying wife). Then Dean stands up to the bullying leader of the gang (Corey Allen, a most improbable High School boy): "And I'm cute too," says Dean. The gang leader soon professes his like for Jim before dying in a car crash of spectacular stupidity. In real life, Nick Adams, one of *Rebel*'s gang boys at the deadly Chickie Run, was hired to overdub the car-dead Dean in Dean's last scene in *Giant*. For Dean's character's drunkenness lapsed too close to incoherence. Yes, James Dean starts his second film drunk and ends his third film drunk. A short career framed by drunkenness will always frighten the chattering classes and challenge my claims for his maturity.

In *Giant*, Dean as Jett Rink rebels against his employer, a Texan aristocrat who made his fortune the way of all aristocrats - by stealing land. Jett Rink becomes the state's Kingpin with the Queen, the daughter of his rancher rival, waving to her own surprised parents from the back of his car. His is not a wholly sympathetic character. When good fortune strikes, Jett Rink attempts to better himself by learning to read and to write, and by reviving the English tea customs of his forefathers, but he doesn't attempt to erase the old endemic racism of the white American adult. It rightly pulls him down.

Giant is a multi-generational life film about a strong woman who sacrifices many of her own desires and needs to the love of a Texan husband and their children. A 20th Century role beautifully played by Elizabeth Taylor. It's a film about maturity. Having co-stars of the stature of Elizabeth Taylor and Rock Hudson enabled James Dean to raise his own game. He's mesmeric. *Giant* is the only feature film in which James Dean played a character close to his own age of the early-middle twenties. In *Eden* and *Rebel* he plays characters one third younger than himself. Miscast? Only in the way that, for example, Laurence Olivier and Orson Welles were miscast as The Moor in *Othello*. Dean was too old to authentically play Cal and Jim Stark but his were performances that went beyond authenticity. They sought for and reached the peak called Myth. Could a real schoolboy ever look that cool?

In *Giant*, the myth-making is completed not in the latter part of the film when Dean plays a drunken man of fifty as if he's eighty-nine, and that's the director's fault, but in the early scenes, particularly when he doesn't speak, when he's just leaning on a fence, or sitting in an open top Rolls Royce and looking like a ranch hand as carved by God. If *Giant* didn't drizzle out slightly in overdoing the anti-racist theme that overbalances the final quarter (turning a *character* film into an *issues* project) then it could have been right up there on Classics Hill on the right-hand side of *Gone With the Wind*. It's a damn good film. *East of Eden* is a damn good film. *Rebel Without a Cause* has the emotional punch and, in James Dean's performance, the iconography of a great one.

The spur to making this book was to preserve a host of yellowing magazine articles that are more than half a century old, some of which have been in my collection for decades, and which are starting to decline rapidly. I wanted too to curate an international collection that gave a multi-decade look at a three continents representation of James Dean's unwavering appeal, and of the great work he did for Warner Brothers and with Stock, Schatt and Roth.

I have included some articles published in contemporary American magazines by people who knew James Dean. They contain detail missing from even the best biographies. I've included too the cream of the analytical pieces published in the British journals. The best of these come from *Films and Filming*. The articles are reprinted by the permission of Gerald Jones and the journal's custodian, Britain's first international film correspondent, John Francis Lane. But for the most part, in making the selection, I have erred on the side of the pictorial. The images speak.

I like the differing approaches to style and design found in the American, Japanese, British and German magazines. I spend my annual holiday in Germany, at the traditional old Schauburg Kino in Karlsruhe, where the popcorn packets still carry James Dean's image. I did intend to translate the German articles but they're mostly pitched to 1980s teenagers and rarely do more than tell the plots of the films and the life story of James Dean. Anyone who picks up this book will know those already, and the book does include the English-language equivalents. Translating the Japanese text is beyond my abilities. I have endeavoured to identify the sources of the cuttings but many were taken by me in boyhood when such things were unimportant.

Paul Sutton
Cambridge 2018

© Warner Brothers, all rights reserved

Contents

East of Eden, 14

Rebel Without a Cause, 56

Giant, 120

Childhood, 158

New York City, 165

The Television Films, 169

General cuttings, 178

Magazine covers, 301

EAST of EDEN

LOUELLA PARSONS in hollywood

I nominate for stardom: JAMES DEAN

■ This twenty-three-year-old actor from Broadway, I guarantee you, will be the rave of the season after he is seen in *East Of Eden*.

You probably place young Dean as the actor Pier Angeli was supposedly madly in love with just before she announced her engagement to Vic Damone.

Dean has had much publicity about being "another Marlon Brando," the sweatshirt, motorcycle-riding, grumpy young sophisticate in tennis shoes.

It's true that his off-screen behavior seems to be a sort of cross between Brando and Montgomery Clift. But, it isn't really important how he behaves off screen (that is, if it's nothing disgraceful).

It is what James projects on the screen that makes him my pick among the new actors for stardom in 1955. He is a great young actor.

Before a Warner Brothers scout discovered him in *The Immoralist* on the New York stage, James had been just a kid struggling for a break and accepting what bits were handed out to him on TV or radio. His performance in *The Immoralist* was so telling that he won the Antoinette Perry award for the best supporting actor on Broadway.

He was born in Fairmount, Indiana, a blond boy with intense blue eyes. I predict a long and brilliant career for this screen newcomer. (Now come on, young Mr. Dean, how about forgetting the Brando bit?)

JAMES DEAN: This boy would rather race through the streets in a sports car all by himself than stroll down a lovers' lane with the prettiest girl in the world. Fact is that Warners has been having fits over their newest star's predilection for racing cars, and is secretly delighted that his pet machine caught fire and burned up. Any affection Dean has left over after he's been through admiring oil filters he's been spending on Marilyn Morrison, Louise De Carlo, Lili Kardell and Marisa Pavan. Jim's due to be drafted any day now.

Modern Screen (USA), March 1955

new faces

james dean

born: in Fairmount, Indiana
formerly: stage actor
eye-appeal: 5'10", 155 lbs., blue eyes, blond hair.

Screen Album, November 1955

■ When James Dean was given the starring role in Elia Kazan's *East of Eden* he swore he wouldn't become a "Hollywood character." If *not* becoming a character means buying a Palomino the first week in town, running around in a beat-up leather jacket and blue jeans, driving a souped-up MG, insulting Hedda Hopper and playing the bongo-drums at 3 a.m. then Jimmy is sticking to his vows. Orphaned as a baby and raised on a farm by an aunt and uncle, he dabbed in academic dramatics for two years at U.C.L.A. At the advice of James Whitmore he went to New York and made his stage debut in *See The Jaguar.* A role in *The Immoralist* led to films.

CINEMATOGRAPH EXHIBITORS' ASSOCIATION
OF GREAT BRITAIN AND IRELAND

REGISTERED FILMS LIST

CINEMATOGRAPH FILMS ACT ★ Films Registered by the Board of Trade from **17th June, 1961** to **15th September, 1961** ★ **No. 122**

「エ

アカデミイ賞
新作「エデンの
心とともに彼の
ネスコ・スクリ
彼は一言にして

＊ていない。普通の映画と同じようにクローズ・アップもどしどし使うし、激しい感情を表わすためにはゆがんだアングルも使っている。その一種無造作な手法が、これまでのシネスコ作品のマンネリズムを破る結果になり、さきの「スタア誕生」のジョージ・キューカーの演出とともにシネスコの将来に新しい希望をもたせる。俳優ではジェームス・ディーンがすばらしいデビュー振りで特に印象的である。相手役のジュリー・ハリス、老けのレイモンド・マッシーもいい。（野口久光）

JOHN STEINBECK'S
ワーナー映画シネマスコオプ作品

East of Eden
エデンの東の鑑賞

双葉十三郎

解説梗概

既に本誌に紹介されたダイジェストで、スタインベックの原作の概要はご存じの方が多いと思うが、映画ではその終り三分の一の部分を、カレブを中心にして描いている。「ミニヴァー夫人」や「ジェニーの肖像」など、文芸作品の脚色に定評のあるポール・オスボーンの脚色は極めて巧みであるし、エリア・カザンの演出は、彼の最初のシネマスコオプ作品という ハンディキャップにも拘らず、「波止場」の快調を持続して、却ってシネマスコオプという形式に新しい生命を吹き込んだとさえ、云われている。起用された新人達もカザンの演出で、素晴らしい個性を発揮しているが就中、ジェイムズ・ディーンの評判は既に読者諸君もご存じの通りである。相手の少女役をやるジュリー・ハリスは「結婚式の一員」という劇の舞台女優として評判になった舞台女優である。

映画では、アダムの息子カレブが既に、と云う名で、カレブ達が住むサリナスから十五哩離れた漁港モントレイで、娼家を営んでいる事を知り、銀行の帰りのケイトを尾行する所から始まる。カレブは、いぶかしがって出て来た召使いに「あの人に嫌いだと云ってくれ」と云い乗って、貨物列車に飛び乗って、サリナスに帰る。この辺の風景描写はジョン・ヒューストンの名作「黄金」でリアルな味を見せたカメラマン、テッド・マッコードが素晴らしい画調を見せる。サリナスに帰ると、カレブ

こう。まずカザンは、こってりした色絵というよりは淡い水彩画のような色調、ハアフトンを豊かに生かした画面、ひろびろとした画面のなかに人物を配した絵画的な美しい構図によって、ぼくたちの心を奪うが、その遠景ショットとクロオス・ショットを組み合せて、おなじようなリズムを創りだす。緑色の服を着て深くヴェイルをたれたケイト（ジョオ・ヴァン・フリイト）が銀行で預金をして往来へ出ると、店のガラス窓の中から町のおしゃべり女たちが眺めてささやきをかわしている。そのガラス窓のなかのショットも映っている。「日本人の勲章」でもケイトが入ってゆくのをみとどけ、その邸宅の前でうろうろしはじめる。ケイトはボオチを掃除していたが、カザンの場合はこれとおなじ方法をこころみたが、シネマスコオプの画面に近いショットで、シネマスコオプの画面を一杯に生かしている。若いカレブ（シェイムズ・ディーン）は彼女のあとを尾け、すこしはなれた邸宅のぞきからすこしはなれた邸宅の、彼女が入っていくのをみとどけ、その邸宅の前でうろうろしはじめる。ケイトはボオチを掃除していた少女アン（ロイス・スミス）をよび、窓のカアテンのかげからのぞきしめる。カアテンのかげから石を投げる。出てきたジョオは、あまり害悪もなさそうな若者なのをみて、殴りつけたりせず、おだやかに話しはじめる。このジョオとカレブのひろびろとしたショットに、カアテンのかげからのぞいているケイトのクロオス・アップがカット・インされる。これはいままでのシネマス

コオプにみられなかった大胆な手法であるとともに、いままで得られなかったリズミックな美しい効果でもある。

やがてカレブは双生児のアーロン（リチャアド・ダヴァロス）とその恋人エブラ・アダム（レイモンド・マッセイ）にさそわれて、父親アダム（レイモンド・マッセイ）にさそわれ、父親からようやくカレブがブラック・シイブで、しく買いとった氷室へゆく。このあたりから父親からとまれているのとがわかってくるが、氷室のなかで、氷の塊からアーロンとエブラの様子をうかがうカレブに用いられたクロオス・アップがまたシネマスコオプ画面のサイズを一杯に生かして非常に効果的である。そして夜のわが家の居間。アダムはカレブに聖書を読ませる。カレブは拗ねた態度を示す。二人の争いをみたくないらしいアーロンは、エブラと部屋を出る。残ったカレブは父親に去った母のことをしつこく訊く。この室内

カレブに扮するジェイムズ・ディーン

のシイクェンスで、カザンは最初から斜の構図を用いる。右あがりの斜のショットで、アダムとカレブのクロオス・ショットを切りかえす。この構図で、アダムは高い位置にありカレブが低い位置にあるように印象づける。そして父親に威圧された低い位置からカレブが逆襲的に問いつめてゆくという心理的な葛藤が、ドラマ的な迫力を加える。この居間のシインは後にもあらわれるが、カザンは必ず斜の構図をとっている。この居間のシインはあとにもあらわれる。この居間のシインは後にもあらわれるが、外景とちがい居間では電灯の位置からでもあろう斜の構図を強調するのに役立つからでも天井からつるされた電灯の線とか斜の構図を強調するのに役立つわけである。従ってアダムとカレブが対立しないほかの場面では、水平ショットが用いられている。

カレブはふたたびモントレイへゆき、アンの手びきでケイトが経営する酒場に入り、アンの手びき

レブはアダムの旧友で保安官のサム（民謡歌手として有名なバアル・アイヴスが扮している）に助けられて家に送られる。やがて、アダムは、レタスを氷詰めにしてニューヨークへ送る事業を始め、カレブは誰よりも熱心に働くが、却って妙な気持をいだかせた事でアダムに叱られてしまう。発送したレタスは、列車が雪崩で立往生した為に、殆ど無一文になる。カレブは父の損害をつぐなおうと、事業家のウィルと共同で、大豆の買占めをしていたエブラに心のやすらぎと親しさを感じる。発送したレタスは、列車が雪崩で立往生した為に、殆ど無一文になる。カレブは父の損害をつぐなおうと、事業家のウィルと共同で、大豆の買占めをしてすっかり親しさを感じる。この時の語り合いで、それまでアーロンの善良さに何か心の距りを感じていたエブラは、カレブに心からすらすら親しさを感じる。発送したレタスは、列車が雪崩で立往生した為に、殆ど無一文になる。カレブは父の損害をつぐなおうと、事業家のウィルと共同で、大豆の買占めをしてすっかり親しさを感じる。この時の語り合いで、それまでアーロンの善良さに何か心の距りを感じていたエブラは、カレブに心からすらすら親しさを感じる。ケイトは事の皮肉の無心にがら小切手を書く。これは原作には全くない件りだが、スタインベック自身も感心しただろうと思うほど、巧みな着想である。米国は参戦し、カレブは父の損害を補う為けの大金を儲ける。ここで参戦に伴うお祭騒ぎや、ドイツ系市民の迫害が、鋭く描かれる。遊園地のワゴンホイールに乗って、カレブとエブラは初めてキスを交わす。

「アーロンを愛してるのよ。本当に愛してるのよ」——エブラは自分の心に云いきかすように、叫んで泣き伏す。

クリスマスの晩、カレブはエブラの手伝いで、部屋を飾り立て、そう父を迎える。父はアーロンと一緒にカレブは一万五千

Elia Kazan's East of Eden

第一に話題になるのは第一ヴァイオリンのジェイムズ・ディーンである。彼はあちらの評判によると第二のマアロン・ブランドだということだったが、スクリインで実際に見ると、容貌はグレゴリイ・ペックの寸を詰めたような感じといったほうが適切で、個性からみてもブランドのようにひねくれたふてぶてしさは感じられず、非常に感受性がつよく、適量の甘さがある。比較なしに一言でいえばすこぶるハンサムであり、将来タフなすね者の役をあたえられても、この感受性と甘さがものを云うのではないかと想像される。カレブとしての彼は、ちょっと阿呆みたいな表情や動作をするところが気にかかるが、これはカザンの解釈と演出であろう。その点をのぞけば、笑い顔の魅力といい、しゃべり方（これだけはブランドに似ている）の魅力といい、若者らしく変りやすい気分のたくみな表現といい、ぼくたちの二枚目顔だけにはおかない。彼の出現で二枚目顔色なしということになろう。

ジュリイ・ハリスは、見る機会を逸した「結婚式の一員」でさわがれたが、今度の作品でもすでに三十歳の年齢をカヴァする演技はたいしたもので、その演技から生みだされるやわらかくパセティクなムウドは、この悲劇の緩衝地帯を構成し、水彩画的な美しさを強調する役割を果している。

レイモンド・マッセイ久々の好演もみとめたい。彼はいままでにずいぶん変てこな役をやらせられているが、本格的な演技をみるのは「摩天楼」以来のことである。し

かも「摩天楼」よりはるかに深味を要求される役で、狂信的になる一歩二歩手前でぐっとおさえ、過去の苦汁を内心にかくした謹厳な人間を、立体的にポオトレイトしている。

これら三人に比べると、やはりリチャド・ダヴァロスは弱い。おつき合いの二枚目的傍役とちがい、腰がすわっているのはカザンの指導のおかげであろうが、他の三人があまりにもあざやかにうかびあがっているのか、影がうすくなっている。しかしクワルテットのハアモニイという点からみれば、立派に成功である。

その他の人々では、母親ケイトをやるジョ・ヴァン・フリイトが、役もいいがたいへん印象的で、つよい演技でもある。バアル・アイヴスの保安官サムは柄がうまく生かされ、少女アンのロイス・スミスは、出場がすくないが特異な個性（とくにそのしゃべり方）が心にのこる。

以上、この一篇は演出と演技のアンサンブルにおいて出色のアメリカ作品と結論してよく、イリヤ・カザンにとっては、「波止場」とともに今日までの彼の代表作品の双璧をなすものといえよう。「波止場」で述べたようにカザンはこの作品で、生粋の映画育ちの監督を映画的に追い越したと感じた。シネマスコオプというあたらしい媒体が、カザンにその機会をつかませたとも云える。広く云えば、シネマスコオプはカザンによってまた一段の進歩をとげたのである。

〔おことわり〕編集部との打合せで、この一文にはストオリイがくわしく書いてあません。はなしのわかりにくいところは別項の梗概を読んでください。——双葉生

る。が、父親には彼の気持がわからない。はじめから母親に似た奔放な性質だと思いこんでいるからである。最後の努力も空しく、父親の愛情と理解を得られなかったカレブは、ついに爆発する。母親が生きているというこの真相は、真面目で心いかがわしい商売をしているという真相は、真面目で心からのヘソくれた一突きをもってしたいさな世界にとじこもっていたアーロンは、まともにゆけば、これは恐ろしい肉親相剋の悲劇である。ところがカザンは、この強烈なるべき悲劇を、人間的な理解に富んだ眼でながめ、田園詩的なムウドで描いているのである。カレブは父親とアーロンの水準からみればえない不良であるが、ぼくたちからみれば父親やアーロンよりはるかに自然で人間的な若者である。そしてエブラの在り方もカレブと共通している。だから彼女は、カレブたちが理解し共感できるように、カレブを理解し共感する。その結果、気の毒なのはむしろアダムとアーロンという印象が生れる。アダムとアーロンは二人とも悪い人間ではない。アーロンにも若者らしい正義感や悩みがある。それはアメリカの参戦

のお祭りさわぎに浅らす彼の言葉や、ドイツ人をかばおうとする努力にもあらわれている。が、父親とともに、その心はせまい場所にとじこめられている。そこに悲劇が起因する。これは宿命の悲劇であり性格の悲劇でもある。同時に、観客が彼らを理解することによって成立する悲劇である。従って、この作品には「波止場」のように善玉と悪玉の対立などはない。それぞれの立場からの悲劇を、理解し得ぬとかはこの悲劇を、冷酷につき放してとらえずに、同情的な眼でながめている。そしてカザンの作品になっている理由は、ここにあるように思う。

しかし一つの問題がある。それはカレブに同情の重量がかかりすぎていないか、ということである。彼は神の御前を去ってエデンの東に移り住む必要もなく、父親の愛情をかちえるという満足な結果をもって終るのが、彼よりもともかく真面目で立派な若者であるアーロンが、背中の一突きで参ってしまったままであることは、神の御前でおこなわれた事件としては、いささか不公平ではないか。ジェイムズ・ディーンがすてきな青年で主役であり、リチャド・

ダヴァロスは傍役だから適当に片づければいい、というハリウッド的処理法のあらわれとは考えたくないが、おそらくこういう不公平に不満を感じるひとも多いのではないかと思う。しかしもうすこし考えてみれば、いわば甘やかされたお父さん子で、いささか愛情にあまえた御機嫌とりの態度をもうかがわれる。そのような若者が、ひとつのショックに会うと、ひとたまりもなく崩れてしまう。カザンはそうした性格的な悲劇を描いているのである。とすれば不公平でもなんでもない。

筆が横道にそれかけたが、ともかくカザンはこのような扱い方を根底に、一篇の田園詩劇を創りあげた。すでに挙げた場面のほか、後半においても頼るべき数々の場面がある。カレブはお金を借りようとする場面を訪れる途中、道ばたで彼女に会う。一面に霧をはいた軟調の道の風景。カレブを邸に連れてはいったケイトは、鏡に向かう彼女とともにとらえたショットで話す。その鏡の中のケイトとカレブは、シネマスコオプの広い画面のゆとりによって、普通版映画よりもはるかにゆたかな雰囲気が盛りあがる。天井のあかりがあるので、ショットは、とのショットをさらにいきいきとさせている。

豆の豊作をよろこんで畑をころげまわるカレブ。遊園地の観覧車の上でのカレブとエブラのラヴ・シイン。折角こしらえてたお金を父親に拒絶されたカレブが、庭の柳の蔭にかくれて泣く場面。アーロンを酒場の母親のもとに残して帰ってきたカレブが、ブランコに乗る場面。その画面はブランコのゆれるにつれてゆれる。こういう演

出方法で画面をゆらしたシネマスコオプは、いままでに輸入されたシネマスコオプ作品では最初にシインやショットの魅力について云いだしたら際限がないが、結論すれば、これはカザンのシネマスコオプ演出の勝利をたたうべき作品である。

カザンの演技指導によって生きいきとした演技陣

が、讃るべきはそれだけではない。この作品の成功は演技指導の領分に入る理の成功であり、これだけの演技と人物処理の成功であり、これだけの演技と個性を示した俳優にも、独立して賞讃の辞がおくらるべきである。「タイム」誌はこの演技陣を絃楽四重奏にたとえ、ジュリイ・ハリスがヴィオラ、レイモンド・マッセイがチェロ、ジェイムズ・ディーンが第一ヴァイオリン、リチァド・ダヴァロスが第二ヴァイオリンと想定している。が、なんといってもまったく同感である。

アダムに扮するレイモンド・マッセイ

でケイトの部屋へゆく。このシイクェンスは陰翳のふかい照明が注目されるが、とくにケイトの部屋へ通じる廊下のショットが、逆光線を使ってみごとに窓ごしにあけたドアの間からみえるだらしなく椅子にすわったケイトの両手がねじりあわされるクロオス・アップが、ショックに似た効果をあげている。

カレブは用心棒のジョオになぐられてほうりだされるが、保安官サム（パアル・アイヴス）からケイトが母であることをたしかめる。彼女がここでこんな商売をしていることは父親アダムもアーロンも知らない。帰宅したにケイトの部屋からみえるだらしない様子のアダムがポオチから窓ごしに冷凍レタスをのぞいているところをのぞく。このショットにおけるカレブの微笑で、彼が父親に愛情を抱いていることがはっきりする。そして、その愛情が次のシインでアーロンの収穫に張り切って働いていくカレブがアーロンのためにランチを持ってくる。ここでこの作品の最も牧歌的な美しい場面が展開される。カレブがメキシコ系らしい雇いの娘を追いのけて木蔭でパンをかじっているところへ、エブラがかたわらにすわって話しはじめるのであるが、バックには風にそよぐ黄色い花と白い花。花というも、そのやわらかな色調を生かした場面はあまりないと思うが、前景のカレブとエブラのムウドがよくマッチして、快いハアモニィをかなでる。エブラのジュリイ・ハリスの髪のかたちや顔だちが、ルノワアルの名画に似ているせいもあるが、カザンは「波止場」の屋上のシインにまさるともおとらぬ情景描写に成功しているわけである。

「エデンの東」の主題 それははげしい主題であるが情緒的である

カザンはこの作品で「波止場」よりもはるかに情緒的であり、感傷的でさえある。「タイム」誌は、スタインベックの原作小説とこの映画を比較して、スタインベックの指の爪の泥をきれいにおとし云々と、たいへんうまい表現をしているが、たしかにカザンはこのカインとアベルの聖書物語の現代化を、一種の古風な悲劇的ムウドで清潔に扱い、父と子の相剋をドラマとしてまともに強調するよりも、美しい階調のうちにうかびあがらせるという方法をとっているようである。アダムは聖書にこりかたまった清廉潔白な人物であり悪人ではない。アーロンも父親に信頼され愛されている。が、カレブは最初から不良と思いこまれ、父親の愛情に浴することがゆるされない。彼のほうでは父親を愛しているのだが、その愛情は酬いられない。彼が母親ケイトから五千ドル借りて豆の収穫に出資して儲けたのは、レタスを冷凍して輸送する計画が失敗して損をした父親の埋め合わせをするためである。それ以前、レタスの収穫に精を出してはたらくのも、父親の仕事を成功させたいためで

ドルの大金を美しい紙に包んで、アダムにアーロンにプレゼントする。それを見てアーロンも、エブラとの婚約を発表する。この間の兄弟の食い違う感情の表現の的確さは見事である。アダムは余りの大金に驚いて、その出所を問い正し、それは戦争を道具に農民を搾取した金だ、徴兵委員をやっている自分には受取れないと云い、却ってアーロンとエブラの婚約を祝福する。父の愛を買おうとした最後の努力にさえ裏切られたカレブは泣き出す。ここはカットバックを全然使わずに、見事に効果を出している。「欲望という名の電車」に於ける下品クソなクロオス・アップの用法から見ると、カザンの成長がよく判る。

その夜、カレブは怒りに任せて、アーロンを連れて初めてケイトに会わす。アーロンは狂ったように叫んで、そこを飛び出してしまう。保安官サムの知らせで駅で卒中を起して倒れる。自分の罪を悟ったカレブは失踪しようとしたが、エブラに連れ戻されて、父の病床の傍らに立つ。エブラの少年らしい愛を示す。この泥酔した挙句、軍隊に志願してしまう。保安官サムの知らせで駅で卒中を起して倒れる。自分の罪を悟ったカレブは失踪しようとしたが、エブラに連れ戻されて、父の病床の傍らに立つ。エブラの少年らしい愛を示す。この「ぼくに看護してくれだって。このぼくにだよ」——カレブの顔に最後のたみ込みは、息もつかせない。力作であり、名作である。一九五五年度作品。一時間五五分。

エブラに扮するジュリイ・ハリス

イリア・カザンの新作「エデンの東」に主演する ジェームス・ディーン

ジョン・スタインベックが一九五二年に発表した二十五番目の小説「エデンの東」に主人公カル・トラスクを演ずるジェームス・ディーンは、いまや"第二のマーロン・ブランド"といわれるニュー・センセーション。

インディアナ州の農園に育った彼はロスのカリフォルニア大學で二年演劇を學んだ後、単身ニューヨークへ進出。一年ほど周旋屋の頭をたたきまわったのち「ジャガーを見よ」の端役でブロードウェイ・デビュ。次のアンドレ・ジイドの「背徳者」で一九五四年度デイヴィッド・ブラム賞の"最も有望なる新人賞"を得た。

この舞臺を見てすっかり惚れこんだのがイリア・カザン。さっそく「エデン」に連れこんで手脚にかけ、この完成後ワーナーと契約成った彼はいよいよハリウッドに根を下ろすもよう。その魅力は野性的にしてかつセンサイ、まったく新鮮なる新人である、と諸家絶讃のありさま。当年二十三歳ながら、少年のような右ページの二枚はいずれも「エデンの東」から、共演は「結婚式のメンバー」の若手名女優ジューリー・ハリス。

JAMES Dean

31

歌なという事実は、やはり偶然そのもの、不慮の災難と考えるほかはない。ほかに考えられる事といったら、ジミーが強度の近眼だったこと、孤独な人間にありがちな子供のような突飛なはしゃぎ性と生来のスポーティな性分を持っていたことなどで、人をも神をも憎むことの出来ない原因があるばかりだ。たゞ一つ我々の心に懸る永解しがたき謎は、この災難が「エデン」の舞台たるサリナスの地へ行く途上におこったということ、故郷の先祖代々の墓地には「エデン」で彼が演じたキャルCalという名と同一の名が曾祖父の墓に刻まれていたということ、彼を初めて一躍世界に輝かしめた映画「エデンの東」が何やらこの彗星の光明と消滅を運命づけているらしいという暗示的事実である。

自動車競走ばかりでなく投縄や斗牛まで夢中になった青年、ボンゴ・ドラムを叩き、レコード蒐集の傍ら作曲までやろうとしたり、多方面の難しい書籍に読みふけったり、キャメラに凝った青年、フェアモント・ハイ・スクールからカリフォーニア大学法科に学んだが自然の精気と巨人的天分に恵まれたこの青年にとつては、有り余る才能が百方に湧き出て、趣味は多岐にわたり、その趣味がいつしか享受親實の域を越えて創造的作業になろうとするという有様で、自分自身でも制御できぬ生に幾つか天才的いとぐちをつかみかけていたようである。そしてその中で一番早く天才の天才たる力倆を見せた二つ、演技道とスピード競争がジェイムズ・ディーンをこの世に出さしめこの世から去らしめたのである。

スタインベックと「エデンの東」

大久保康雄

一

現代アメリカ文学の特長を、すくなくとも二つもつている。一つは地方主義的傾向であり、一つは社会意識である。たとえばコールドウェルは、南部ジョージア州を舞台にして、その地方の貧しい白人の生活をとりあげているし、スタインベックは、カリフォーニアを背景にして、時代にとり残された人々を描いている。

しかし、スタインベックの場合、その社会意識は、作品によって、かならずしも露骨には出ていない。出世作と目されている「トーティア・フラット」(一九三五)にしても、劇になったり映画になったりして評判の高い「廿日鼠と男たち」(一九三七)にしても、作者の社会意識は作品の底に沈んでいて表面には出ていない。前者は、カリフォーニアの海岸沿いの山間に住むパイサノという特殊な民族の生活を、ダニイという男を中心にして描いたものであるが、放埒、無頼、無道徳で、無知で、狡猾しかも心の底に愛すべき誠実と善意とをひめた彼らの日常生活は、ときには野放図な笑いをともなって、またときには深い人間的なペーソスをたたえて、読むものの胸に、ふしぎとあたたかい、しみじみとした感動をよび起さずにはおかない。粗野で、開放的で、底ぬけの明るさと哀愁のいりまじった、アメリカン・ユーモアの一つの典型を、私たちはこの作品に見ることができる。後者は、農場から農場へと渡りあるく貧しい移住労働者の奇妙な友情を描き、前者におとらぬ効果をあげている。

戦時中に発表した「罐詰横丁」も、この系列にぞくする作品である。この小説の舞台は「トーティア・フラット」と同じモントレイの町の、海岸近い罐詰工場街であり、この横丁に住む魚貝実験所のドックという酒好きの男、町の顔役のマック、それをとりまく少年たち、あいまい屋のおかみ、雑

East of Eden とその原作者

Jenseits von Eden
(EAST OF EDEN)

Nach dem gleichnamigen Roman von John Steinbeck, in Deutschland erschienen im Diana-Verlag, Konstanz-Stuttgart (760 Seiten, Ganzleinen 19,80). Zu beziehen durch jede Buchhandlung.

Regie: Elia Kazan **Manuskript:** Paul Osborn
Kamera: Ted McCord, A.S.C. **Musik:** Leonard Rosenman

Ein CinemaScope Film in Warnercolor

DARSTELLER:
Abra	Julie Harris
Cal Trask	James Dean
Adam Trask	Raymond Massey
Sam	Burl Ives
Aron Trask	Richard Davalos
Kate	Jo Van Fleet
Will	Albert Dekker
Ann	Lois Smith
Mr. Albrecht	Harold Gordon
Joe	Timothy Carey
Piscora	Mario Siletti
Roy	Lonny Chapman
Rantany	Nick Dennis

Eine Elia-Kazan-Prod. im Verleih der Warner Bros.

Wir schreiben das Jahr 1917. Die drohende Gefahr des Eintritts Amerikas in den Krieg beschäftigt die Gemüter allerorten. Auch der biedere Farmer Adam Trask (Raymond Massey) macht sich ernsthafte Gedanken, was nun aus seinen beiden Söhnen werden soll: Aron (Richard Davalos) hilft ihm, sein Projekt zu verwirklichen, Gemüse mit Hilfe von Eis transportfähig zu erhalten, aber auf Cal (James Dean) ist kein rechter Verlaß. Jedenfalls hält ihn Vater Trask — im Gegensatz zu seinem folgsamen Zwillingsbruder — für einen Taugenichts, dem er jeden Wunsch von den Augen abliest — für den Taugenichts, ohne zu bemerken, wie sich Cal nach der Vaterliebe sehnt, ohne zu erkennen, daß erst diese fehlende Zuneigung ihn „böse" gemacht hat. Und Cal leidet ganz besonders unter der offensichtlichen Bevorzugung seines Bruders, zumal er sich ebenso verzweifelt wie offenbar aussichtslos darum bemüht, die Liebe des Vaters zu gewinnen. Die Mutter hat Cal nie gekannt — sie war nach den Erzählungen des Vaters kurz nach der Geburt gestorben. Aber eines Tages erfährt er durch einen Zufall, daß sie gar nicht tot, sondern in Wirklichkeit die wohlhabende Besitzerin eines übelbeleumundeten Hauses im Nachbarort ist. In dieser erschreckenden Entdeckung glaubt er die Erklärung für seine „bösen" Charaktereigenschaften gefunden zu haben. Aber er gibt dennoch nicht die Hoffnung auf, und als der Vater durch das Scheitern seines geplanten Unternehmens sein gesamtes Vermögen verliert, sieht er seine große Chance, ihm zu helfen und dadurch auch seine Liebe zu gewinnen. Zu diesem Zwecke leiht sich Cal von seiner Mutter, die ihre Wesenszüge in ihm wiederfindet, eine größere

---

AB 8. FEBRUAR
Jenseits von Eden

Kinoklassiker mit dem unsterblichen Daueridol James Dean. Nach dem Roman von John Steinbeck entstand diese immer

Die Liebe ist ein seltsames Spiel: Nur Abra hält zu Cal

noch moderne Version der Kain-und-Abel-Geschichte aus Kalifornien. Dean spielt den jungen Cal, der vergeblich um die Liebe seines Vaters kämpft. Der bärbeißige Alte zieht jedoch immer Cals Bruder Aron vor. Mit Julie Harris und Burl Ives.
USA 1954, 115 Min.
ARD: 8.2., 23.50 Uhr

Lesen Sie regelmäßig das film JOURNAL
Bei jedem Zeitschriftenhändler für nur 70 Pfg. erhältlich

Summe und beteiligt sich an einer Spekulation, die auf Grund der Zeitverhältnisse einen großen Gewinn verspricht. Cal findet plötzlich auch Hilfe und Verständnis bei der jungen Abra (Julie Harris), die seinen Bruder zu lieben glaubt. Sorgfältig bereiten Cal und Abra gemeinsam die Geburtstagsfeier des Vaters vor, bei der Cal das wiedergewonnene Geld überreichen will und damit endlich die lang ersehnte Anerkennung und Aussöhnung herbeizuführen gedenkt. Aber es kommt anders. Sein Bruder Aron erklärt als „Geburtstagsüberraschung" seine Verlobung mit Abra, und der Vater erweist das Geld, das auf Kosten vieler Söhne des Landes erworben wurde, voller Verachtung zurück. Innerlich aufs tiefste getroffen und enttäuscht darüber, daß auch seine letzte Hoffnung zunichte wurde, verläßt Cal haßerfüllt das Haus. Um sich an der vermeintlichen Ungerechtigkeit der Welt zu rächen, stürzt er sich auf das Objekt seiner stets unterdrückten Eifersucht; er zeigt seinem „guten" Bruder Aron die nackte und ungeschminkte Wahrheit über ihre Mutter. Stunden später erleidet Vater Trask einen schweren Schlaganfall, als er erfährt, daß sich sein Lieblingssohn vor Entsetzen über seine Mutter sinnlos betrunken und in seinem Rausch freiwillig gemeldet hat. Durch die Hilfe Abras, die inzwischen ihre wahre Zugehörigkeit zu Cal erkannt hat, erringt der „verlorene Sohn" nun endlich die ersehnte Liebe seines Vaters.

Für mehr als 3 500 Filme (deutsche und ausländische) lt. Verzeichnis ist die ILLUSTRIERTE FILM-BÜHNE lieferbar
Sammelmappe mit Klemmvorrichtung für 100 Filmprogramme gegen Voreinsendung von DM 3,00 zuzügl. 50 Dpf. Versandspesen beim Verlag erhältlich

Gegen Voreinsendung des Rückportos und des Rechnungsbetrages auf unser Postscheckkonto München 27 92 erhalten unsere Sammlerfreunde jedes gewünschte Filmprogramm (4-seitig 10 Dpf., 8-seitig 20 Dpf.) und unser Filmprogrammverzeichnis (40 Dpf.). Vereinigte Verlagsgesellschaften Franke & Co. KG., München 2, Sendlinger-Tor-Platz 1, Telefon 55 59 41. Druck: Druckhaus Tempelhof, Berlin. Nachdruck (auch auszugsweise) nur mit Erlaubnis gestattet. Erfüllungsort und Gerichtsstand München. Vertrieb für die Schweiz: Illustrierte Film-Bühne, Basel 18, Postfach; Verkaufspreis 4-seitig 20 Rp., 8-seitig 30 Rp.

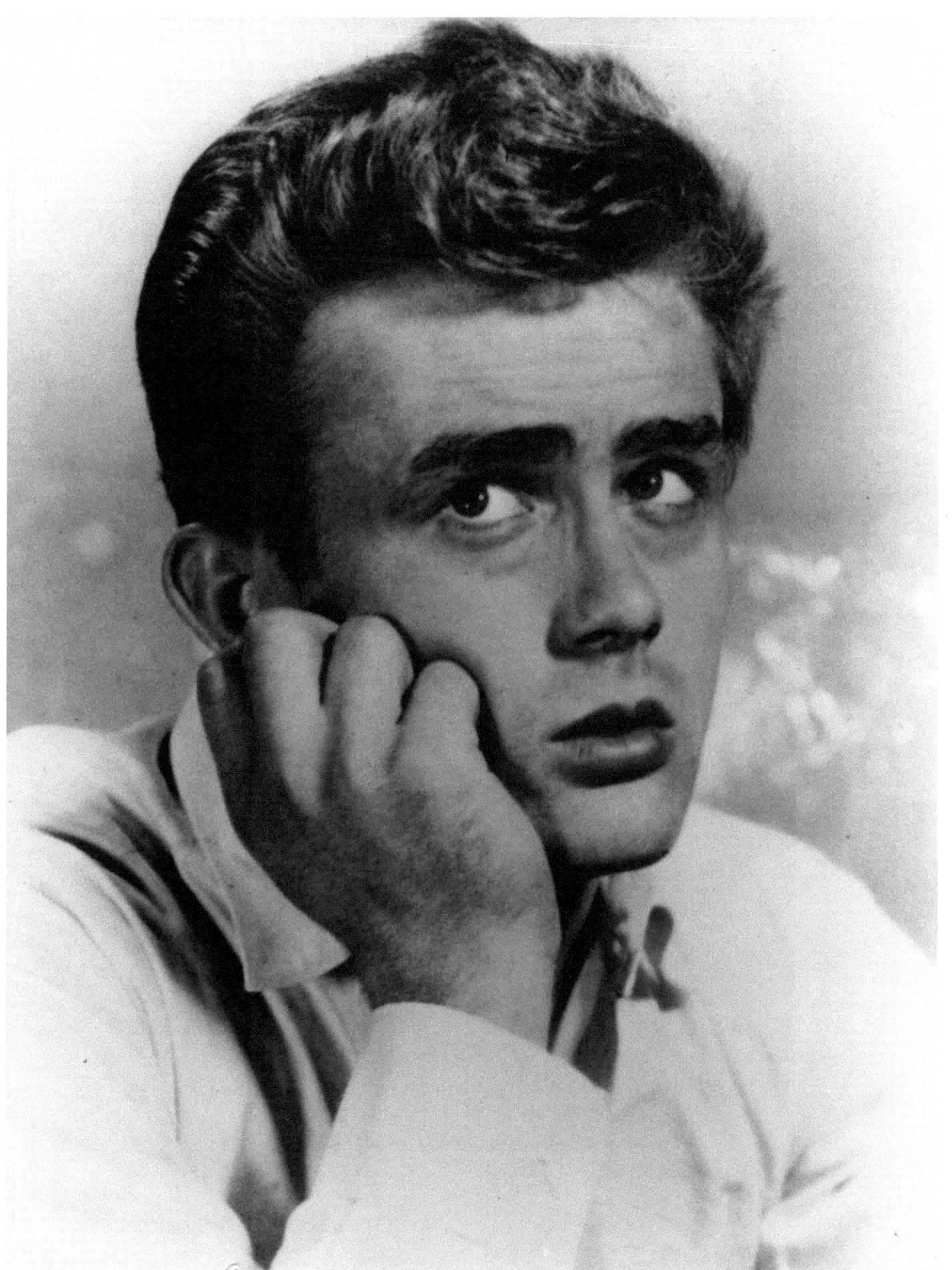

BRAVO-Serie: Das war James Dean — Teil 3

Die stärksten Szenen aus den Dreharbeiten hinter den

"The strongest scenes from the film, and what happened behind the scenes during the filming."

Jenseits von Eden

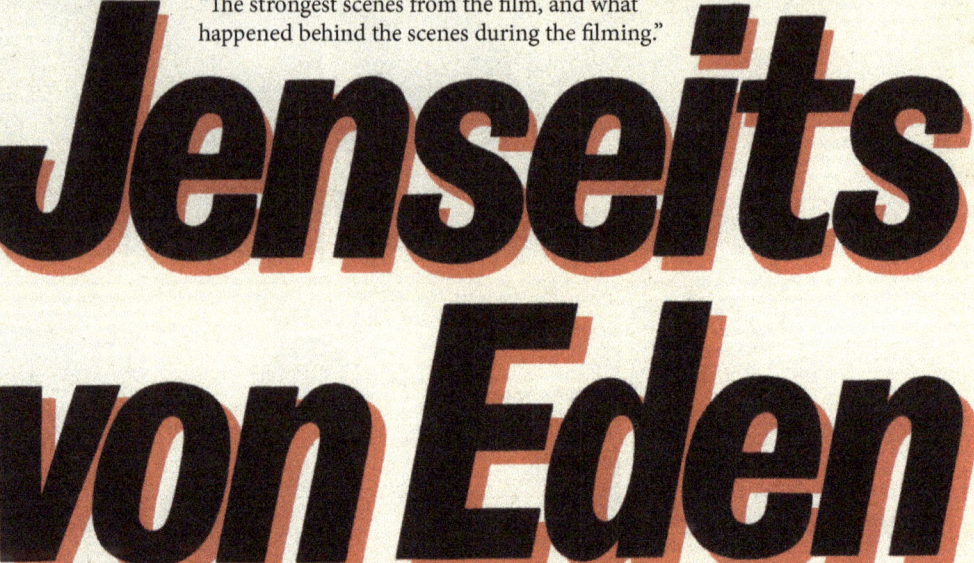

Nach der Ankunft in Los Angeles 1954 blieben Dean noch ungefähr zwei Wochen, bis die Tests und Proben zu „Jenseits von Eden" anfingen.

Trotz seiner Vorbehalte gegen Hollywood genoß Dean anfangs das süße Leben, das den Erfolg begleitet. Dick Clayton, der Agent, der sich in Hollywood um Deans Interessen kümmerte, verschaffte ihm bei Warner einen Vorschuß auf seine 20 000-Dollar-Gage. Und bald sah man Kazans neueste Entdeckung in einem roten MG-Sportwagen auf dem Sunset Boulevard oder in Begleitung hübscher junger Starlets in den traditionellen Nachtlokalen.

Der einzige Hinweis auf seinen schlechten Ruf in der Film-Branche waren die verwaschenen Jeans, die ihn von den eleganteren Clubs und Restaurants ausschlossen. Dean legte sich bald ein neues Motorrad zu, obwohl ihm der Vertrag mit Warner das Motorradfahren ausdrücklich für die Dauer der Dreharbeiten untersagte. Als Ersatz kaufte er ein Pferd, das er auf einer Ranch nahe der Stadt hielt. Dort ritt er stundenlang oder lehnte am Gatter und betrachtete es.

Auf Kazans Rat lebten Dean und Richard Davalos, die in „Eden" die beiden ungleichen Brüder spielen sollten, während der Vorbereitungen und Proben zusammen. Sie hatten ein kleines Apartment gegenüber den Warner-Studios und lebten die Haßliebe ihrer Rollen aus.

Das klappte ausgezeichnet. Sie fühlten sich wie Brüder und halfen sich gegenseitig, entwickelten dabei aber einen gesunden Konkurrenzkampf um Sympathie und Anerkennung. Als die Dreharbeiten begannen, funkelten die Spannungen.

„Jenseits von Eden" spielt zur Zeit des Ersten Weltkriegs im Tal von Salinas in Kalifornien. James Dean spielt Cal, den jüngeren von zwei mutterlosen Söhnen, die von ihrem strengen Vater (Raymond Massey) beherrscht werden und ganz offensichtlich den biblischen Figuren Kain und Abel entsprechen. Der ältere Bruder Aron (Richard Davalos) ist ein Mustersohn, Vaters Augapfel. Cal – der Kain – wird vom Vater abgelehnt.

Cal findet heraus, daß seine angeblich tote Mutter in der Hafenstadt Monterey ein Bordell führt. Zwischen Aron, dessen Freundin Abra (Julie Harris) und Cal sammelt sich inzwischen Zündstoff, weil sich bei Abra und Cal etwas anbahnt. Auch Cals verzweifelte Versuche, sich mit seinem Vater anzufreunden, scheitern. Als Cal in einem eifersüchtigen Wutanfall Aron mit seiner Mutter im Bordell konfrontiert, stürzt dessen heile Welt vollends ein. Er zieht, obwohl Kriegsgegner, ins Feld. Sein Vater wird daraufhin schwer krank. Cal und Abra pflegen ihn; erst dadurch kommen sich Vater und Sohn etwas näher.

Die Anfangs-Sequenzen des Films bauen Jimmys starke körperliche Ausdruckskraft und das jugendliche Gehemmtsein auf. Man sieht Dean als Cal gebückt auf einem hölzernen Gehsteig sitzen, Zweifel und Unglauben im Gesicht, während er versucht, nicht hinter sich auf die kleine Dame in Schwarz zu schauen, die vorbeigeht – die Puffmutter der Stadt. Kate, die, wie sich später herausstellt, seine totgeglaubte Mutter ist. Aufgeregt und linkisch folgt er ihr. Dann steht er unter den

Bitte umblättern

So reagiert Cal seine Wut ab: Nachdem er seinen Bruder Aron und Freundin Abra im Kühlhaus-Speicher beim Rendezvous belauscht hat, läßt er die Eisblöcke die Rampe runterpoltern

Cals verzweifelter Versuch, beim Vater ein bißchen Anerkennung und Wärme zu finden

dem Film, und was bei Kulissen passierte

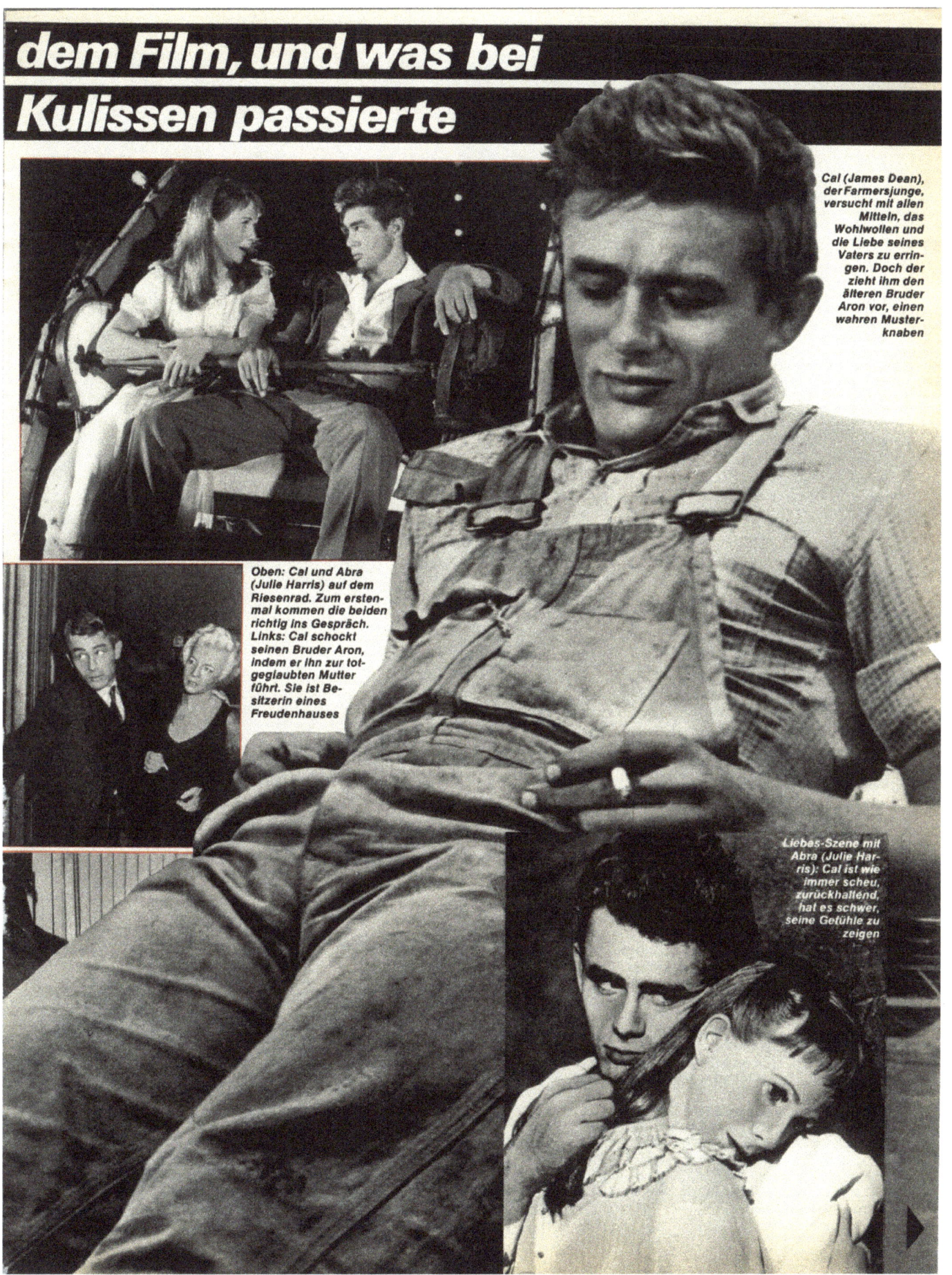

Cal (James Dean), der Farmersjunge, versucht mit allen Mitteln, das Wohlwollen und die Liebe seines Vaters zu erringen. Doch der zieht ihm den älteren Bruder Aron vor, einen wahren Musterknaben

Oben: Cal und Abra (Julie Harris) auf dem Riesenrad. Zum erstenmal kommen die beiden richtig ins Gespräch. Links: Cal schockt seinen Bruder Aron, indem er ihn zur totgeglaubten Mutter führt. Sie ist Besitzerin eines Freudenhauses

Liebes-Szene mit Abra (Julie Harris): Cal ist wie immer scheu, zurückhaltend, hat es schwer, seine Gefühle zu zeigen

JAMES DEAN

Am 8.2. wäre er 60 Jahre alt geworden

Am 8. Februar diesen Jahres wäre James Dean 60 Jahre alt geworden. An diesem Tag strahlt die ARD um 23.50 Uhr (warum eigentlich erst zu dieser späten Stunde???) den aufrüttelnden Streifen „Jenseits von Eden" (1954 gedreht) aus. Es ist die Geschichte des Farmers Adam Trask, der mit seinen Söhnen Cal (James Dean) und Aron (Richard Davalos) im kalifornischen Salinas-Tal lebt. Die Liebe des Vaters gehört Aron, während Cal für ihn ein mißratener Taugenichts ist. Cal findet eines Tages seine totgeglaubte Mutter als Chefin eines Bordells. Er glaubt, von ihr seine „bösen Eigenschaften" geerbt zu haben. Cal gibt die Hoffnung nicht auf, doch noch die Liebe seines Vaters zu gewinnen. Am 22. Februar wird „Denn sie wissen nicht, was sie tun" ausgestrahlt. „Giganten", der letzte Film von Dean (er verunglückte kurz vor der Premiere tödlich) wurde bereits im letzten Herbst gesendet.

Diese drei Filme haben James Dean unsterblich gemacht. Er wurde zum Mythos, wahre Geschichten und noch mehr Gerüchte gibt es über ihn, denn wirklich gekannt hat diesen James Dean niemand. Er war der jugendliche Rebell auf der Kinoleinwand, Millionen wollten so sein wie er. Er starb jung, mit 24, aber wäre ein James Dean überhaupt mit einem normalen Leben fertig geworden?

Szenen aus seinem ersten Film „Jenseits von Eden"

So niedlich sah Jimmy mit zwei Jahren aus

Jimmy als Fünfjähriger, von seiner Ma fotografiert

Jimmy als Student der Rechtswissenschaften

Lässig mit acht Jahren – Links sein Geburtshaus in Marion, Indiana

Jimmy mit Sal Mineo in „Denn sie wissen nicht, was sie tun"

Bleiben wir bei seinem Tod: Es war in der Abenddämmerung des 30. September 1955, als Jimmy mit seinem silbergrauen Porsche Spider auf der 466. Straße von Hollywood nach Salinas raste. Da bog von einer Nebenstraße ein Ford in die Hauptstraße ein. Der Fahrer, der 23jährige Donald Turnupseed, hatte den Porsche übersehen. Um 17.45 Uhr war James Byron Dean tot.

James hieß der Arzt mit Vornamen, der am 8. Februar 1931 in der kleinen Industriestadt Marion, Indiana, den kleinen Dean zur Welt brachte. Byron war der Lieblingsdichter von Mutter Mildred. Daher also die beiden Vornamen für ihren Sohn. Vater Winton arbeitete als Zahntechniker bei der Bundesbehörde.

Die Mutter vereinnahmte den Sohn völlig für sich. Sie las ihm Gedichte vor, spielte für ihn Klavier, gemeinsam bastelten sie aus Pappkartons ein Spielzeugtheater. Jimmy mußte Violin- und Steptanz-Unterricht nehmen. Allerdings ohne Erfolg. Die Nachbarkinder zogen Jimmy auf, weil er ein richtiges Muttersöhnchen war. Jimmy fühlte sich isoliert, wurde in der Schule zum Außenseiter. Diesen Außenseiter verkörperte er später auch in seinen Filmen.

Die Familie war 1935 nach Santa Monica, einem Vorort von Los Angeles, gezogen. Eine Lehrerin erinnert sich: „Im Unterricht war er intelligent und kapierte schnell, aber im Umgang mit fremden Menschen war er scheu und zurückhaltend." Als Jimmy neun Jahre alt war, starb die geliebte Mutter an Krebs. Jimmy kam zu den Großeltern.

Nach der Schule schrieb sich Jimmy für das Studium der Rechtswissenschaften ein. Gleichzeitig belegte er auch Theaterkurse. Das Studium brach Jimmy, zum Leidwesen des Vaters, bald ab. Dafür schaffte er den Sprung in die berühmte Lee-Strasberg-Schauspielschule in New York. Mit 21 Jahren war er einer der jüngsten Schauspielschüler. Seinen Lebensunterhalt verdiente er sich als Tellerwäscher, Taxifahrer und Hafenarbeiter.

Die erste größere Rolle spielte Jimmy in dem Theaterstück „See the Jaguar". Der renommierte Regisseur Elia Kazan sah dieses Stück und engagierte Jimmy sofort für „Jenseits von Eden". Jimmy wurde zum Idol der amerikanischen Jugend.

Die Einsamkeit des James Byron Dean symbolisiert jener Satz, den er einst zu Elizabeth Taylor (Partnerin aus „Giganten") sagte: „Ich liebe die Tiere, weil sie mich so akzeptieren, wie ich bin."

Peter Raschner

He would never forgive his mother as he could never forgive himself. Her crime was his and her badness was born again in him. And yet, some strange force drew him further and further toward the evil.

Cal's father was a stranger to his son. No matter how hard he tried, the boy could not please him . . . he didn't know how. But he loved him as only an outcast son can love his father.

Picture Show & FILM PICTORIAL

THE PAPER FOR PEOPLE WHO GO TO THE PICTURES

October 15th, 1955
Vol. 65 No. 1698 Every Tuesday
3D

DORIS DAY'S Blouse or Rhinestone Earrings *CAN BE YOURS!*

Doris Day wears the Striped Silk Blouse and the Rhinestone Earrings in "Love Me or Leave Me"

SEE INSIDE *(Page 4)*

JULIE HARRIS & JAMES DEAN IN "East of Eden"

Cal and Aron are the sons of Adam Trask, a God-fearing lettuce farmer in Salinas, California. Aron is a likeable lad, interested in his father's farm and in his girl, Abra. Cal is neurotic, blindly striving for love and understanding. His devotion to his brother struggles with his resentment at their father's seeming preference for Aron. The two boys have always been told that their mother, Kate, had died when they were babies. A neighbour tells Cal that Kate had left Adam because she couldn't stand the dreariness of her quiet life on the ranch. She longed for life and company
Richard Davalos (*Aron*), **Julie Harris** (*Abra*), **James Dean** (*Cal*)

Not even the coming of her two boys was enough to make Kate happy and when she had disappeared after a quarrel, Adam had been too proud to search for her. Cal also learns that she is still alive, living in the neighbouring town of Monterey where she keeps a prosperous house of questionable respectability. He makes himself known to her and finding her interested in him he borrows money from her to start a business of his own
Jo Van Fleet (*Kate*) **James Dean**

East of Eden

Only Abra understands Cal's loneliness, desire for affection and terrible inner conflict. She gives him the sympathy he needs so desperately and learns of his scheme to grow beans for soldiers' food should America be drawn into the war. In this way, Cal tells Abra, he will be able to show his father that he can be of real help to him on the ranch. Abra's sympathy fires Cal to look around and put every ounce of his strength into furthering the work on the ranch
Julie Harris, James Dean

Cal takes a big interest in a plan his father has to preserve his lettuces so that they arrive at the market in a fresh condition. It was Cal's idea to "borrow" a chute from a neighbouring coal dealer so that the work of loading the fragile lettuces should be easier and save valuable time
Adam, who has never had much faith in his younger son, is pleased in the way in which the boy works to save his threatened crops but a freezing scheme he has put all his money into, goes awry and he is threatened with ruin
Burl Ives (*Sam*), **James Dean**, **Raymond Massey** (*Adam Trask*)

East of Eden

Cal goes to Will whose idea it was of the bean growing business and who is in partnership with him in this venture. He joyfully learns that there has been a bumper crop and the books show a good profit. Excitedly he trades his share for ready money. On the day of Aron's birthday Abra helps Cal to organise a surprise party where the boy can present the money to his father. At the party Aron, jealous of Abra's interest in Cal, announces that he and Abra are engaged. Cal's gift is overlooked in the excitement and the boy is bitter and hurt
James Dean, Albert Dekker (Will)

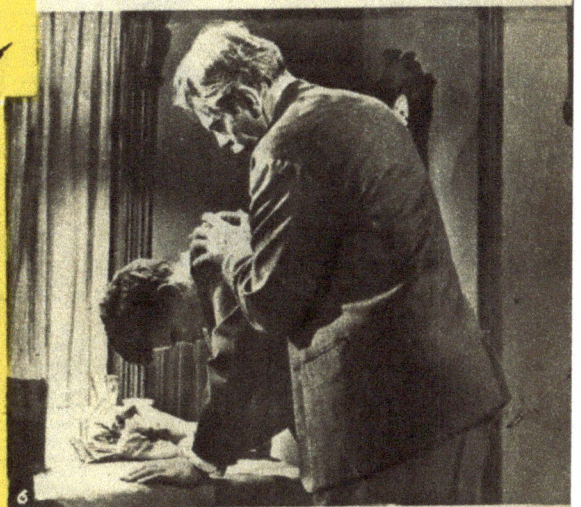

In this mood he follows his father and shows his disappointment at the way he has received his gift. He sobs as he tells him to what lengths he has gone to save this money. Then Adam, when he learns how the money has been made, refuses to accept it, calling it profits made from the food which soldiers eat. For the year is 1917 and America is now in the first world war and Adam is a member of the local draft board and is suffering deeply by having to refuse exemption to the sons of many of his friends and neighbours
James Dean, Raymond Massey

A quarrel ensues, made all the more bitter because Cal is so very hurt at his father's misunderstanding of the motives which had caused him to strive so hard to be able to help his father in his need. Cal, half demented with grief and disappointment, searches for a way to hurt back. He decides to do this through his father's love for Aron; to reveal the secret of his mother to him
James Dean, Raymond Massey

Cal forces his brother to come with him to their mother's house, on the journey telling him her story. Aron is so shocked and horrified at this meeting that he runs out of the house and gets drunk. Then he rushes off and volunteers for the army. News that Aron is about to board a train with other volunteers reaches Adam who rushes out to prevent him from leaving. The exertion is too much for Adam and he suffers a stroke
Richard Davalos, James Dean, Jo Van Fleet

Adam is brought home totally paralysed. Outside his bedroom door, with this added guilt on his conscience, Cal waits with Abra for news from the doctor. He tells Cal that he is all that Adam has now to help him in his tragic condition. Abra now knowing it is Cal she wants to marry, pleads with Adam for some sign of his forgiveness and using all his strength, Adam lifts his hand and lets it fall on his son's head in blessing
James Dean, Julie Harris

Abra (Julie Harris) ist die einzige, die – in „Jenseits von Eden" – für den schwierigen Cal (James Dean) Verständnis hat. – Der Ort der Film-Handlung ist Salinas, die Gegend, in der James Dean tödlich verunglückte …

Zoff mit dem Vater Verliebt in die Freundin des Bruders

Unvergessen: James Dean als jugendlicher Rebell

JENSEITS VON EDEN

SAT1 9.8. 22.05 Uhr

Er drehte nur drei große Filme, aber James Dean wird immer unvergessen bleiben. Er wurde zum Idol einer Generation. In „Jenseits von Eden" (gedreht 1955) verkörpert er einen sensiblen, rebellischen Außenseiter, der den Heranwachsenden der damaligen Zeit aus der Seele sprach. Cal und Aron sind Zwillinge. Cal ist das „schwarze Schaf", sein Vater hält ihn für einen Taugenichts. Vergeblich kämpft er um dessen Zuneigung. Eskalation, als Cal herausfindet, daß seine totgeglaubte Mutter im Nachbarort ein Bordell betreibt. Dann verliebt sich Cal auch noch in die Freundin seines Zwillingsbruders. Eine Katastrophe bahnt sich an. Anschließend an den Film wird eine 59minütige James Dean-Dokumentation gezeigt.

Great Films of the Century
EAST

No appreciation of the cinema of the postwar years can afford to neglect the work of Elia Kazan. But it is difficult to pick on any of his works up to *The Anatolian Smile* (formerly titled *America, America*, under which it was released in the US) and say that this is a 'Great' film: individual, powerful, stylist, compelling, yes. Kazan expresses a preference for *Viva Zapata!*, the critics mainly associate him with *On the Waterfront*, personally I have a deep affection for *Wild River*. So as mediator we settled on deciding what was his most *influential* work, that which has provided a lesson for directors and actors to learn from, rather than copy as in the case of *Waterfront*. As an intense, penetrating analysis of the time in which it was made (it said more of the mood of the 'fifties than any other film of its time, even though set in 1917); as an object lesson in the use of film as a visual medium and on economy of dialogue; and in it's imaginative use of a new medium, Cinemascope, the choice fell on *East of Eden*.

Year of production: 1954. Directed and produced by Elia Kazan. Screenplay by Paul Osborn from the novel by John Steinbeck. Director of photography, Ted McCord. Editor, Owen Marks. Music written and conducted by Leonard Rosenman. Art directors, James Basevi and Malcolm Bert. A Warner Bros production. American. Cinemascope. Warnercolor. British Board of Film Censors 'A' certificate. Running time: 115 minutes.

CAST: *Abra*, JULIE HARRIS; *Cal Trask*, JAMES DEAN; *Adam Trask*, RAYMOND MASSEY; *Sam*, BURL IVES; *Kate*, JO VAN FLEET; *Aron Trask*, RICHARD DAVALOS; *Will Hamilton*, ALBERT DEKKER; *Ann*, LOIS SMITH; *Mr Albrecht*, HAROLD GORDON; *Joe*, TIMOTHY CAREY; *Piscora*, MARIO SILETTI; *Roy*, LONNY CHAPMAN; and *Rantani*, NICK DENNIS.

Plot Outline: California, 1917. Adam Trask, a farmer in Salinas, is the epitome of goodness and self-righteousness. He has led his twin sons, Aron and Cal, to believe that their mother, Kate, died when they were born. Aron he has made his favourite

Films and Filming, May 1964

One of the dramatic climaxes from 'East of Eden': Cal (James Dean), having failed to 'buy' the love of his father (Raymond Massey) tries to embrace him

ROBIN BEAN

OF EDEN

son, seeing in him all the virtues he believes in; while Cal he fails to understand, disliking his moodiness, not realising that Cal is desperately seeking his affection, resenting that lavished on his brother.

In his roaming around, Cal discovers that in fact his mother is alive, running a saloon/brothel on the other side of the mountains at Monteray. But when he tries to get in to see her, he is thrown out. Adam, always thinking of ways in which he can ' do some little thing for progress ' invests all his money in taking frozen lettuces by rail to the big cities. But his first assignment is held up by an avalanche, the ice melts, he faces bankruptcy. Cal, determined to make enough more to pay back to his father what he lost, approaches his mother again. A certain affinity grows between them, and she agrees to lend the money so he can go into the cultivation of beans—Cal has his eye on the impending American entry into the war which will make the price soar.

War comes, and while Adam and Aron are in town working on the drafting of soldiers, Cal uses the ranch for his crops. Cal, though, finds himself falling in love with his brother's girl friend, Abra, which leads to further antagonism between the brothers culminating in a fight in which Cal knocks Aron down, bitterly reproaches himself for it and gets drunk. He draws out all the money he has made in beans, determined to surprise his father with it on his birthday. But Adam rejects it—' I sign my name and men go out, and some get killed, and some lie helpless without arms or legs. not one will come back untorn. Do you think I could take a profit on that? ' Cal, after trying to embrace his father, rushes from the house. When Aron warns him to stay away from Abra, Cal challenges him to face the truth about their father and takes him to see their mother. Aron is appalled at the meeting, gets drunk and enlists in the army.

When Cal returns home, Adam challenges him about his brother's whereabouts Cal retorts—' I don't know, I'm not my brother's keeper ' then pours out his pent up feelings about his parents . . . ' I know why she left you. Couldn't stand it, 'cause of your goodness and your rightness, you didn't love her any more than you do me. You never gave either one of us an inch for what you thought was right. You kept on forgivin' us, you didn't really love us, and I know why you didn't love me, 'cause I'm like my mother and you never forgave yourself for having loved her. . . . I took Aron there tonight because I was jealous, I've been jealous all my life, so jealous I couldn't even stand it. Tonight I even tried to buy your love, but now I don't want it anymore, I can't use it any more.' Adam rushes down to the station to try to stop Aron leaving, but Aron only laughs in his face, and Adam collapses in Cal's arms from a stroke. Adam, critically ill, is attended by a nurse with a rasping voice and belief that she won't have the job for long ' just my luck I always seem to get them when they're old and ready to die off '. Adams friend Sam quotes to Cal ' "And Cain rose up against his brother Abel and slew him and Cain went away and dwelt in the land of Nod on the east of Eden." Why don't you go away someplace? '

Abra pleads with Adam to give Cal some sign that he loves him: when Cal bawls out the nurse for disturbing them Adam smiles and manages to stutter out that he would prefer Cal to stay with him and look after him.

Biographical :

ELIA KAZAN : After seeing his *The Anatolian Smile*, which he directed from his own original screenplay, one realises even more that the dominant force in all his films of the past ten years has been Kazan, even to the muting of the Inge sexual frustration in *Splendour in the Grass*. This is because he presents his characters and ideas in an intense, personal way, to such an extent that one can trace the growing, perhaps more enlightened, philosophy through each of his films. Each has more to say about the time in which he made it, rather than specifically with the period the story is set in. Each is, in a way, a furtherance of an understanding of life. As with Antonioni, Truffaut and now Frankenheimer, each film is a progressive step in the development of cinema as an interpretative medium. He has in the past ten years been able to do what he has wanted to, and been successful, placing himself in a powerful enough position to be able to make a three hour film, set in Greece, with no ' name ' star, for a major production company (Warner Brothers) . . . ' I couldn't do it unless I had made money somewhere along the line . . . but I've made enough films that have made money like *East of Eden, On the Waterfront, Splendour in the Grass*. As long as I can go on making what I want to I will do so, and when I can't I'll simply cut costs and go on doing it anyway! '. The producers feel about me that every two or three pictures " He's going to do one that's going to make us some money ".'

Kazan was born in Istanbul, September 7, 1909. When he was two his family moved to Berlin, but as business was bad there they moved back to Turkey. His father then emigrated to New York to see if he could set up as an importer and then sent for his family, Kazan was then four. There he attended school and later college, with no interest in dramatics. On graduation he enrolled in Yale's drama school, more to extend his education as he wanted to delay any connection with ' something called work '. His instructor told him he didn't impress anyone as an actor, but he was given a job as errand and prop boy for the Group Theater in the evenings after his daily work as a bookkeeper. He was promoted to assistant stage manager. His first assignment as ASM was for Sidney Kingsley's play *Men in White*. He began his career as an actor in *Waiting for Lefty* as the cab driver Agate Keller, each night, running up to the stage from the audience. He had important rôles in Odets' *Paradise Lost, Golden Boy* and *Night Music*, and in Irwin Shaw's *The Gentle People*. Among the people at the Theater then were John

37

Opening scene: Cal waits for an opportunity to discover whether Kate (Jo van Fleet) is his mother

Cal joins his brother (Richard Davalos) and Abra (Julie Harris) to look at their father's new ice house

Garfield, Lee J Cobb, Franchot Tone and Sam Jaffe (Kazan believes it was Tone who invented his nickname of Gadget, since shortened to 'Gadge'). From 1935-41 he 'couldn't avoid acting', 'For an odd-looking guy I did all right.' He directed his first play in 1934 with an off-Broadway group, Theatre of Action. Subsequently he directed Robert Ardrey's *Casey Jones* and *Thunderock*, Wilder's *The Skin of Our Teeth*, *One Touch of Venus* (musical with Mary Martin), *Jacobowsky and the Colonel*, Williams' *A Streetcar Named Desire* and *Camino Real*. In 1947 he organised the Actors Studio with Lee Strasberg and Cheryl Crawford. and with a cast entirely of its members staged Bessie Brewer's *Sundown Beach*. In the theatre he has since directed, among others, *All My Sons*, *Death of a Salesman*, *Tea and Sympathy*, and *Cat on a Hot Tin Roof*.

At the age of 34 he directed his first film, *A Tree Grows in Brooklyn*, having been granted his two 'freedoms', okay over material, and a schedule of only one picture a year. He then did *Boomerang*, *Gentleman's Agreement* (Academy Award for best direction), *Pinky*, *Panic in the Streets*, *Sea of Grass*, *Streetcar Named Desire* and *Viva Zapata*. (An excellent analysis of Kazan's work up to 1956, written by Eugene Archer, appeared in *films and filming* Dec 56/Jan 57.) Since then 'I've initiated all my own subjects, good, bad or indifferent, success or failure, anything that is wrong with my films since 1952 is my fault . . . I've interested a writer in a subject, created a script; it's a much longer process but for me it's a much more satisfying way of living in films'. He won another Oscar for his direction of *On the Waterfront* (1954), and has since done *East of Eden* (1954), *Baby Doll* (1956, with cast wholly of members of the Actors Studio; Malden, Wallach, Carroll Baker, Mildred Dunnock), *A Face in the Crowd* (1957), *Wild River* (1960), *Splendour in the Grass* and *The Anatolian Smile*. 'In order to get better films, it is important to bring good writers to them and also to write directly for the screen. I've done more of that than any other American producer'— *Viva Zapata* (Steinbeck), *On the Waterfront* (published subsequently as a book), *East of Eden* was virtually an original taking only a part of Steinbeck's long novel, *Face in the Crowd*, *Wild River*, *Splendour* and now *The Anatolian Smile* (*America, America*) which marks Kazan's own début as a writer.

'The screen doesn't need a long story, it needs a single strong incident that is explored, expanded by penetration and suspense. The whole sense of writing about contemporary issues, whether the story's in the past or not, the issue is contemporary, is my own temperament.'

Kazan is generally acknowledged to be the leading theatre director in America: in films he has been one of a small nucleus that has kept American cinema alive. He has often been criticised by American critics for exposing the less glamorous aspects of American life, which probably accounts for some of the over ecstatic reviews of his latest work which symbolises America as the great freedom country . . . but boy I can't wait for the sequel, I should think they're in for a shock. According to *Newsweek*, we are in fact due for two more films following his uncle's life in America, the sequel is being written by Kazan who hopes to work on a third part. If this materialises, as I hope it will, then we may be in for the most stunning trilogy made.

But while Kazan may not be American cinema's most talented technician, there is no doubt that there is no other director better with actors: maybe this has its disadvantages in that each time he takes an unknown for a leading rôle the expectations are so great of them that not always are they able to live up to it, eg, Andy Griffith. It created a 'star' of Warren Beatty before he had been seen in the cinemas, while Stathis Giallelis was already the 'new James Dean' while *The Anatolian Smile* was still shooting. Many actors owe a great debt to him: Brando, Clift, Malden, Wallach, Beatty, Jo van Fleet, Julie Harris, Patricia Neal . . . and Dean.

JAMES DEAN: 'I was never very appreciative of Jimmy Dean becoming an idol, he's not an idol of mine, and I didn't particularly like what he was . . . I think I told the truth about him in *East of Eden*, or rather a character like that, but I didn't like the result which was to blame your parents for everything, to blame the way you were brought up and say "I'm bad because . . ." I don't go for that, if your parents raised you wrong you should realise it as soon as possible and go your own way. Why be obsessed with the whole thing?' This reflection on Dean by Kazan during an interview I did with him two years ago might seem a pretty unappreciative remark for a director to make of an actor who indirectly had helped to boost Kazan's name. He further said that in all probability had Dean lived he would never have worked with him again. Why then did he choose him? In an interview after Dean's death, Kazan had said he chose him 'because he *was* Cal Trask. There was no point in attempting to cast it better or nicer. Jimmy was it. He had a grudge against all fathers. He was vengeful; he had a sense of aloneness and of being persecuted. And he was suspicious. In addition, he was tremendously talented'.

Just how talented Dean was has been a much debated topic, and don't forget that most of what has been written about him was done so *after* his death (in fact none of his films had been generally released in Britain at the time of his death.) So most of the evaluations or criticisms were mixed with sentimentality or antagonism. George Stevens, whose work Dean admired more than Kazan's, described his acting as 'a mixture of technique, intelligence and hard work. He gave the impression of being completely natural and of improvising as he went along. But no single detail was ever impromtu. He had everything figured out and could do a scene in exactly the same manner time after time. An actor, working on inspiration alone, couldn't do this. . . . He had his own approach to acting, it was something elusive that nobody else tried on the screen'. Part of this rather contradicts what Carroll Baker said 'He was unpredictable in his acting, but he always acted with a fresh flavour . . . we did the nightclub scene about 30 times, but he never did it the same . . .'

  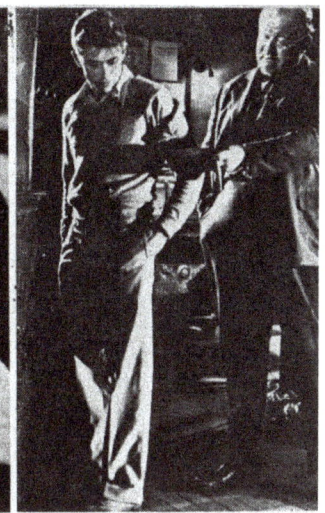

In Kate's bar, Cal gains the sympathy and help of Ann (Lois Smith)

Cal is dragged from Kate's room by Joe (Timothy Carey) and knocked out

The Sheriff (Burl Ives) confirms Cal's belief that Kate is his mother

Much has been written about the myth of the Dean cult, and why an actor should become popular after his death. But one must remember that he did very much reflect the mood of youth at the time (and it was *Rebel Without a Cause* which really had the first impact, *East of Eden* subsequently made much of its money in re-runs) when growing up and accepting responsibility had no appeal to youngsters; authority, whether parental or civil, was weak and uncertain in the fluctuating post-war years — and Dean more than anything else resembled a permanent embodiment and symbol of their frustrations and uncertainties in life, and like Peter Pan, never grew old. He also stood for the rejection of psychiatric and technical forces that were slowly putting a stranglehold on the adult world. Basically too, it was a search for a simple love that had ceased to exist between generations, there was a barrier between that both wanted to penetrate but which society had made impregnable. Sociologists have had a field day with Dean, but the only comment I'll record here is one from Truffaut (*Arts*, 26 September 1956) — 'In James Dean, today's youth discovers itself. Less for the reasons usually advanced: violence, sadism, hysteria, pessimism, cruelty, and filth, than for others infinitely more simple and commonplace: modesty of feeling, continual fantasy life, moral purity without relation to everyday morality but all the more rigorous, eternal adolescent love of tests and trials, intoxication, pride and regret at feeling " outside " society, refusal and desire to became integrated and, finally, acceptance—or refusal—of the world as it is.'

As for Dean himself, he did several TV productions, appeared in two plays and in six films (three in bit parts). He was born in Marion, Indiana on February 8 1931. His mother was a farmer's daughter, his father a dentist. When he was eight, his mother died of cancer, and his father, unable to look after him, sent him to live on his uncle's farm in Fairmont. At high school he won a contest with his reading of Dickens' *The Madman*. At 18, he went to California to study at Santa Monica, after school working as an usher and as an extra in films and TV commercials (he appeared in *Somebody Stole My Gal, Sailor Beware*—as a second to Jerry Lewis —and in *Fixed Bayonets*). He enrolled at UCLA where he joined a theatre group run by James Whitmore, who later advised him to ' Go see Elia Kazan at the Actors Studio! ' There he auditioned for Lee Strasberg (' He made an excellent impression at the audition, but he never again performed as well for us as at the audition '). Although he had a few rôles on TV, he found parts scarce and took a job as a crewman. The skipper happened to have a friend who was a casting agent: and Dean landed his first Broadway play, Richard Nash's *See the Jaguar* with Arthur Kennedy. Although it only ran five nights, he received excellent reviews which led to several TV plays and Billy Rose's production of Genet's *The Immoralist* (as the young homosexual Arab). But he left the cast a week after its Broadway opening following a dispute (his part had been severely cut down in size) with the director (Daniel Mann) and producer although he did win an award for the most promising newcomer of the year. Kazan then signed him for *East of Eden* (filmed on a closed set). Then came *Rebel Without a Cause* (original by Stewart Stern) for Nicholas Ray—' Jimmy knew how to use himself with truth and without compromise. I levelled with him all the time and made him feel a part of the entire project. He wanted to belong and I made him feel that he did '. He convinced George Stevens he could mature from sullen cowhand to middle-aged oil-tycoon, and landed the part of Jett Rink in *Giant*. By now Dean, whom Warners was offering 100,000 dollars a film in future, had plans to direct. The weekend after *Giant* finished, he was killed in a car crash while driving to a sports car meeting, September 30 1955. Had he lived he would have next played in *Somebody Up There Likes Me*— Robert Wise confirmed this when he was in London recently although he was not keen on him as his build was anything but that of a boxer's . . . but he was becoming a ' name '.

Apart from directing, his ambitions were to play Billy the Kid, and Hamlet. On Hamlet, he told Hedda Hopper, ' Only a young man can play him as he was—with the naivete. Laurence Olivier played it safe. Something is lost when the older men play him. They anticipate his answers. You don't feel that Hamlet is thinking— just declaiming. Sonority of voice and and technique the older men have. But this kind of Hamlet isn't the stumbling, feeling, reaching, searching boy that he really was '.

Cal rings the firebell to clear the gym, then uses a rope to swing him across the room, so he can catch Will Hamilton (Albert Dekker) to talk him into going into business together

The Trasks are visited by the local German (Harold Gordon) who is the victim of local hate: later Cal's intervention causes a riot to break out in the German's garden

applied for a walk on part at a Broadway theatre in *It's a Gift*, which she got. But after four days of rehearsal she lost the job because of inexperience — ' it worked both ways, as a matter of fact, I thought the producer was a fool, and he knew what I thought '. She joined a New York amateur group, the Comedy Club, and appeared in *The Devil's Disciple* and *The Idiot*. Following some work with a professional stock company, she was given walk-on parts with the Old Vic during their American tour. After more experience in stock she enrolled at the Actors' Studio, her Method period she regards as gruelling, ' psycho-analytical, but invaluable '. She then appeared in several plays culminating with *Member of the Wedding* which she played in for a year and a half before being signed for Zinnemann's adaptation of the play in 1952. She played on the stage in *I Am a Camera* (which she later repeated on film with Laurence Harvey) and then was taken by Kazan for *East of Eden*. She did Anouilh's *The Lark* on stage and on TV, and appeared in two British films, *The Trouble with Women* and *Sally's Irish Rogue*. She won the TV Emmy for her portrayal of Queen Elizabeth. Her most recent films: Ralph Nelson's *Requiem for a Heavyweight* and Robert Wise's *The Haunting*.

JO VAN FLEET: born Oakland, California, December 30. An actress of remarkable range, she has only appeared in six films, each time playing women older than herself. Several actors have asserted that, contrary to the figures she portrays on screen she is still a comparatively young and good-looking woman. *East of Eden* was her first film, for which she won the Oscar as best supporting actress.

She started as a character actress while at school. She won a scholarship to the Neighborhood Playhouse in New York. Her first professional appearance was in the road company of *Uncle Harry* which starred Luther Adler. She then appeared on Broadway in *The Winter's Tale* and subsequently in *The Whole World Over, The Closing Door, King Lear, Flight into Egypt* and *Camino Real* (directed by Kazan). In films she appeared with Lancaster and Magnani in *The Rose Tattoo*, as Susan Hayward's mother in *I'll Cry Tomorrow*, as Big Nose Kate in *Gunfight at the OK Corral* and as gun-toting mother in *The King and Four Queens*. In her second film for Kazan, *Wild River*, she played the 80 year old widow who refuses to leave her home which has been acquired by the TVA.

The Critics:
East of Eden was reviewed by the British critics twice: in July 1955 and on its reissue August 1961. On the first occasion, it arrived having been awarded the ' best dramatic film ' award at Cannes, which had met with a strong left-wing antagonism at the festival. The critics were widely divided at the time, and many of the more serious ones paid little attention to Dean (whereas on the film's reissue they gave their whole attention to him). While C A Lejeune (*Observer*, July 10 1955) claimed it ' has much of the odd excitement we found in the early Orson Welles films and in the theatre with *Dark of the Moon*', Penelope Houston (*Spectator*, July 8 1955) found it ' elaborate, infinitely showy and ultimately unsatisfying that often results when a film has been " directed " to within an inch of its life '. But the *Times* critic found that ' Kazan has not abused the freedom gained to simplify the story but has taken advantage of it to supply a background which allows him to link the fortunes of the various characters even more effectively than Steinbeck did with the written word '. Gavin Lambert found it ' dedicated to display, that mistakes mannerisms for style, artifice for art '.

Dilys Powell, on holiday when the film opened in 1955, enlarged on ' the brief (and, come to that, laudatory) comments I made from Cannes' in *The Sunday Times*, August 6 1961, although dwelling more on Dean's performance than anything else . . . ' Brando is all power: power sometimes pinioned, or trapped, or degraded. James Dean was sentenced by physique to stand for defencelessness ; and some instinct, far more than the actor's technique, taught him how to suggest, behind the mask of rebelliousness, a different being, shrinking, fragile, not quite fully grown. As long as he stuck to that he had no equal ; and looking again at this first film I am astounded by his performance. It is even better than I had thought: more truly anguished, more delicately poised between the awkward, sulky scapegoat and the young creature exploding with love . . . this half-trained young man was perfectly capable of conveying emotion, as he showed in the exchanges with the girl he secretly loves (Julie Harris); perfectly capable of standing up to experienced stage players, as he showed in the scene with the errant mother, so finely played by Jo Van Fleet '.

The critics of the popular papers in 1955, also dealt mainly with Dean, then shackled to the term of ' the new Brando '. Brandoism was neatly described by Fred Majdalany (*Daily Mail*, July 6 1955) as ' the portrayal of a character not recognisably human by an actor not recognisably acting '. But he decided that Kazan ' has made a fine job of this one pictorially and cinematically. For the first time we have a glimpse of the maturer use that can be made of Cinemascope . . . The new man James Dean can obviously act—but I shall want to see him again before sharing the enthusiasm which precedes him here . . . Brandoism is much in evidence with a great deal of capricious jumping about and a Richard Widmark giggle thrown in '.

Production and re-evaluation:
Kazan has never liked working in the Cinemascope ratio, which may account to a large extent for his extra efforts to use the ratio itself to dramatic purpose, as in his use of the tilted camera to emphasize the emotional up-hill conflict, or to give greater depth to his compositions. ' I think

I did do one good thing with Cinemascope, I did solve the problem by interior framing. In other words, I'd had the frame of Cinemascope and inside I'd often put a strong object in the foreground' (for instance, the heavy lamp over the table, during the Bible reading scene between Dean and Massey) 'and therefore confine the action to one side or the other ; I'd frame it so that you weren't constantly aware of the same shape, that ribbon, all the time . . . I did also push it beyond its means, I didn't care if it was a little blurry or out of focus, or I'd have a big close-up'. Many of these things are now quite commonplace now that Cinemascope has become such a dominant ratio. Remember that in 1954 it was in its infancy and directors were in the main largely content to play out scenes as if photographing a stage play, being scared to get within six feet of the actors.

But nevertheless within that framework he obtained some wonderful compositions, which say so much in themselves that dialogue seems an unnecessary crutch (and which he dispensed with in many scenes). Take, for instance, the opening sequence of Kate walking along by the shore towards the bank, then past the huddled figure of Cal on the sidewalk. He hears her pass behind him, then slowly in hesitant movements, as a curious boy might as though afraid of being discovered, looks up at her retreating figure. Immediately Kazan has established the mood and feeling of the film. Cal's complete picture of curiosity questioning innocence, of a little boy lost looking for an explanation, contrasts with the strong, businesslike bearing of Kate. When Cal launches a stone at her front door, and the henchman comes running out, the latter is baffled by Cal's refusal or inability to give an explanation and by his mysterious curiosity. His action here, as in the subsequent scene when he hurls ice down the chute at his father's ranch, Cal cannot explain—it's an act of resentment, maybe of a small boy attracting attention that he cannot get otherwise. His father digs for an explanation in coldly domineering fashion that only causes Cal to withdraw further into his shell—and to antagonise his father—' I wanted to see it slide down the chute'. When later he manages to draw his father into conversation about his mother, Adam falters and drifts into silence. Cal cries out to him painfully, 'Talk to me, father. I've got to know who I am, I've got to know what I'm like, I've got to know . . . Where is she?—' I'm telling you truthfully, after she left the ranch I never heard from her again'. Cal, with an expression now nearer contempt, walks out of the room.

One could spend hours musing over each scene of this film, for every moment of *East of Eden* is an exhilarating essay in the complete integration of elements into an idea ; emotionally it is on an ever fluctuating level, switching instantly from anger to hesitant curiosity. In many of his scenes, Kazan has two or three focal points in shot (one of the most outstanding

○ ○ ○ ○ ○ ○ ○ ○
○ *see for yourself* . . . ○
● **This is the twenty-eighth in a unique series. You can actually see the films discussed by the experts. If you want to see** *East of Eden* **you can borrow a print from 16 mm Department, Warner-Pathe Distributors, Warner-Pathe House, Wardour-st, London, W1. Write for details today, mentioning** *films and filming.*

is after the riot in the garden of the local German whom the residents are taking their hate out on, when Abra is in the foreground clutching Cal's coat, Aron is getting his breath on the left, Sam is greeting everyone in a friendly way as if nothing had happened, and Cal is sprawled on the porch steps on the right—the voice of reason within a vicious triangle).

There is a wonderful cohesion of performances, and not even one of the bit part players ever jars. On paper each of the main characters now appears to be rather simplified : the father the figurehead of 'society'; the brothers, one the image of what every parent wants his son to be, the other trying to come to grips with life, searching, questioning, wanting a justification. The girl, understanding, trying to live up with what is expected of her. The mother, self-made, dominant, ruthless. While the emotional range of Cal tends to push the others into the background, one of the main strengths of the film comes from the solid, deep characterisations of the others. Certainly we have here the best performances on screen from Raymond Massey, Julie Harris, Jo van Fleet (who is such a dynamic actress that one feels she has been much neglected) and Burl Ives. Still, the film succeeds or fails entirely on the portrayal of the central character, Cal (who appears in virtually every scene), and without doubt James Dean's performance is the most astonishing ever drawn from an actor in his first film.

One is inclined to agree that it came more out of an affinity of Dean with the character, and out of his personal questioning on life, than out of acting technique itself. Only Montgomery Clift has attained this great depth of delicate sensitivity: and even Kazan could never have 'directed' an actor to such a natural degree. You can never anticipate his reactions, yet never fail to understand them. In society terms he is bad : but he is likeable, moody, morose yet sympathetic. He didn't represent, but rather lived the feeling of youth at that time : of distrust of an adult world that had led to a world war, that was concerned only with keeping a very right appearance and seeking only security : it was a time when parents set themselves up as arbitrators and judges, the war and consolidation years having blunted their feeling of youth. Like Cal many were seeking a genuine love from their parents, a toleration and understanding. Not finding it, their energies were directed elsewhere, covering up their bruised emotions with defiance and de-

light in agitation of their elders; 'living for kicks' didn't provide them with a satisfactory alternative, but it did consume their energies and provide a barrier behind which they could develop an individuality home life didn't encourage. Like Dean, many were suffering from split homes, of divorces, foster-parents, or members of the family playing off against each other. In the rebellion, the half smiles, the hysterical giggle, the intense expression in his face of pain, curiosity or delight, of Dean they found someone who reflected their feelings of frustration, of insecure independence, of rejection. It certainly wasn't out of a morbid attachment to a dead man, even though there was a strong attitude of 'What have we to live for ?'

Now most youngsters realise at an early age that the world is a very superficial one, in which they have learned to live without 'being accepted'. Certainly it is not possible to compare the idolising of Dean with that of the Beatles : one was a deep personal attachment, the other a sort of 'growing pain' that has manifested itself in this 'mass hysteria' and general knocking of convention. I disagree with Kazan when he says the result of the film was to blame your parents for everything; this became a cliché excuse behind which they hid. It was just the beginning of one generation alienating itself from another, the rift has widened the more the elders try their 'enlightened policies', the distrust has grown. Maybe just once they came closer together, with the assassination of Kennedy, for a brief period there was a feeling of remorse. But society is harsh, no place for emotion (and when it is shown it is mistrusted) and youth has learned to live with it. It is regrettable, but once the illusions of love and respect are destroyed what hope is there ?

Yes, maybe *East of Eden* is a great film: for it reflected so many ideals that have been crushed by cynicism and a mutual exploitation of one generation of another. Kazan will probably never be critically accepted as a Great *film-maker* because he is too intensely personal in his work and when you work entirely from within yourself you are bound to antagonise various elements, particularly the film purists ! His success or failure depends on whether he manages to penetrate you personally ; and this he has always done with me. I know, when coldly considering his work, that this is not his best film, for he improves so greatly with each subsequent work ; but it worked and I know that it has left a great impression on many people, particularly actors who regard many of its qualities as distant, intangible things they would love to equal, unconsciously emulate, but rarely achieve.

Bibliography :
Interview with Kazan, *films and filming* March 1962.
Analysis of Kazan's earlier film by Eugene Archer, *films and filming* December 1956, January 1957.

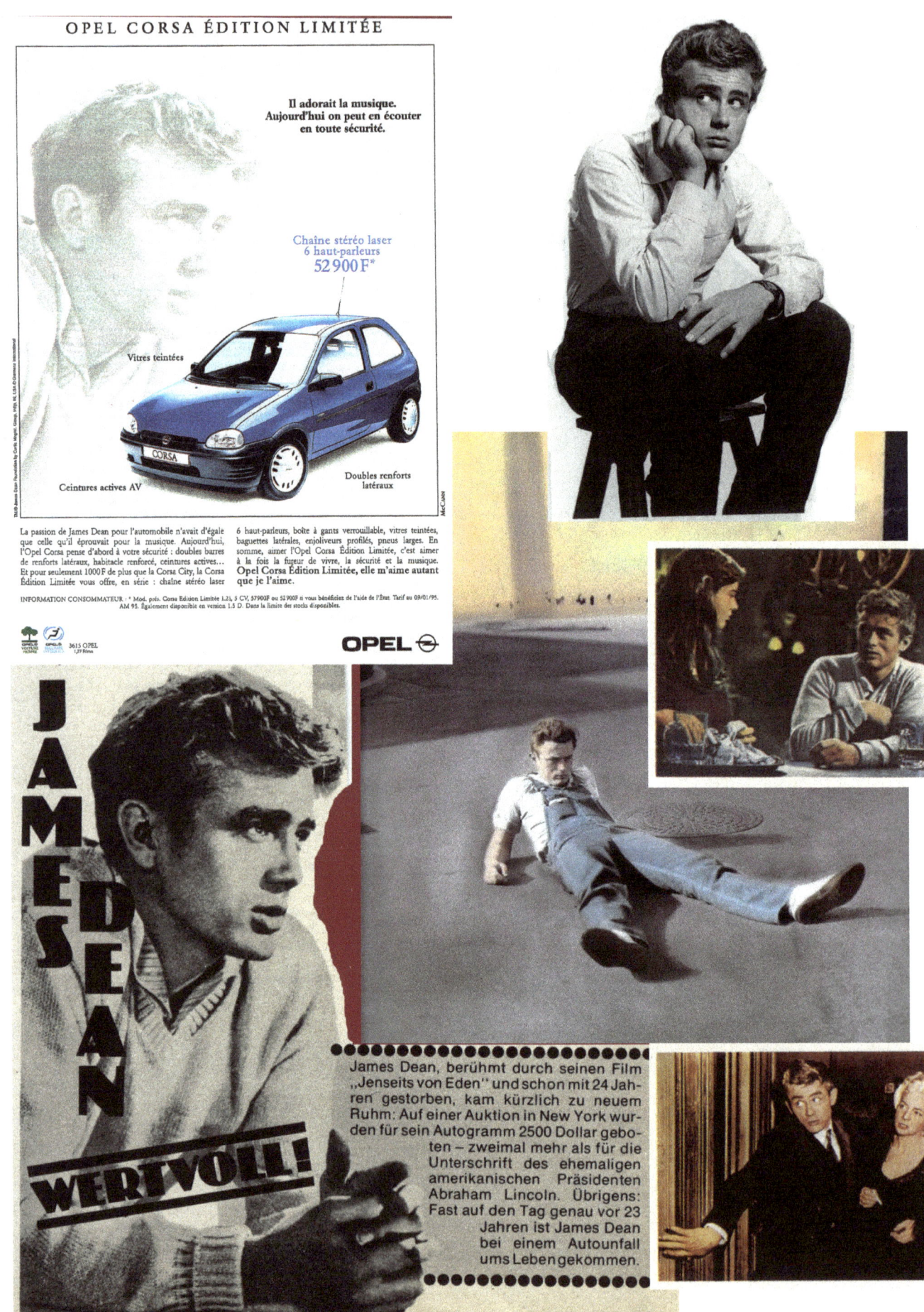

REBEL WITHOUT A CAUSE

理由なき反抗

異常なまでの青春の抗議を絶叫に描き抜いた狂奔巨篇！

JAMES DEAN in "REBEL WITHOUT A CAUSE"
CinemaScope
シネマスコープ総天然色
ニコラス・レイ監督作品

ジェイムズ・ディーン　ナタリイ・ウッド主演

ワーナー・ブラザース映画配給

Jimmy Dean in

REBEL without a cause

story begins on next page →

REBEL without a cause

All he longed for in his tortured youth was that someone would help him bear his heart's loneliness.

Buzz jerked Jim's head back and viciously cracked him across the face with the palm of his hand. The others watched; this was merely customary in testing a newcomer.

(above) After the crash there was silence. Then, far below, flames crackled.
(below) He told them what had happened, then said he wanted to go to the police.

Judy loved her brother, but she couldn't understand why her father refused to show any affection for her.

Cast of "Rebel Without A Cause"
Jim Stark.....................James Dean
Judy..........................Natalie Wood
Mr. Stark.....................Jim Backus
Mrs. Stark....................Ann Doran
Plato.........................Sal Mineo
Buzz..........................Corey Allen
Ray Framek....................Edward Platt

Adapted from the WARNER BROTHERS CINEMASCOPE Production—Produced by DAVID WEISBART—Directed by NICHOLAS RAY—Screenplay by STEWART STERN —Color by WARNERCOLOR

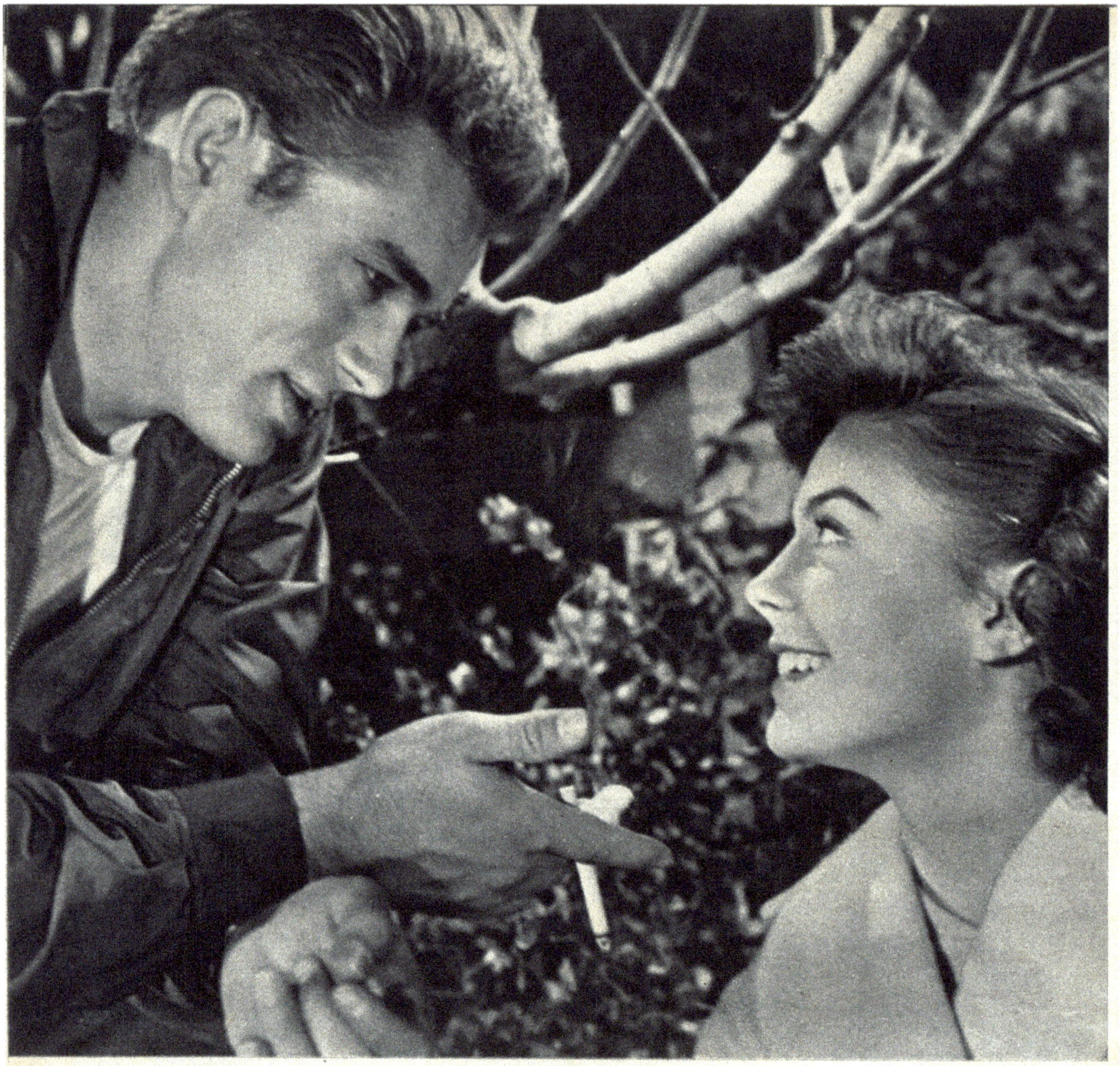

思わぬ自動車事故のため急逝した**ジェイムス・ディーン**が二本の遺作をのこしてくれたことは、ファンにとつてはせめてもの贈物といえるであろう。**「理由なき反抗」**はジョージ・スティーヴンスの大作「巨人」に先立つて撮影を完了していたウォーナー作品で、**スチュアート・スターン**の脚本により、**ニコラス・レイ**監督のシネマスコープ映画である。

ジェイムス・ディーンは「エデンの東」が公開される前から、イリア・カザンが發見した第二のマーロン・ブランドォという噂がたかかつたが、この「理由なき反抗」は、「乱暴者」のマーロン・ブランドォの線を狙つてえらばれたストォリイのようにおもわれる。

彼の演ずるジムというハイ・スクールに通つている若者は氣まずくなつている兩親の家庭の冷たさにぐれかけているが眞實をもとめようとしている氣持のよりどころを必死になつてもとめている。そのために不良仲間にもはいるが、つねに何かの生き甲斐をもとめようとして、かえつて危機にとびこんでゆく、それが思わざる事件の渦中に捲きこまれることになる。こうした劇的焦點は「乱暴者」よりもさらに一歩すすめた社會性があるようだ。もともと、この映画のストォリイはフロイド派の精神分析學者が、實際におこつた特異な事件の心理的な原因をさぐつた學究的著書にヒントを得て書かれたものだといわれている。物語の環境は「暴力教室」をおもわせるものもあるが青少年の心理をより深刻にえぐつたところに一層のリアリティが存在しているのではないかと見られる。

そしてまた「エデンの東」に見せた心理的陰影の濃いディーンの演技がこの映画に厚味を加えていることは豫想に難くない

監督のニコラス・レイは「追われる男」「太平洋作戦」「大砂塵」などで紹介されているが、彼の傑作のきこえたかい「彼等は夜生きる」「どの扉でも叩け」などが輸入されていないため過少評價されているきらいなしとしないが、社會的な主題をとらえたとき、鋭角的な切れ味のよい演出力が評價されている。きつとこの作品でもよい仕事をしているだろう。

なお、**ナタリイ・ウッド、ジム・バッカス、アン・ドーラン、サル・ミネオ、コーリイ・アレン**が共演している。

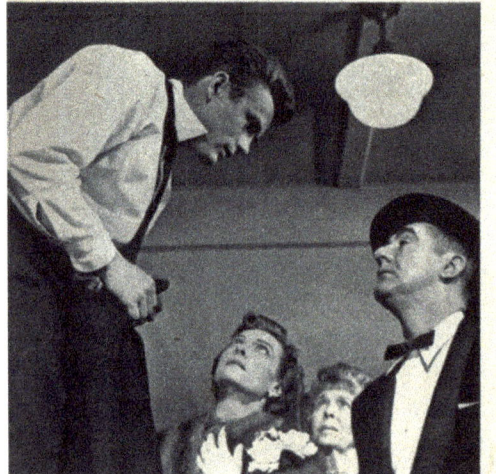

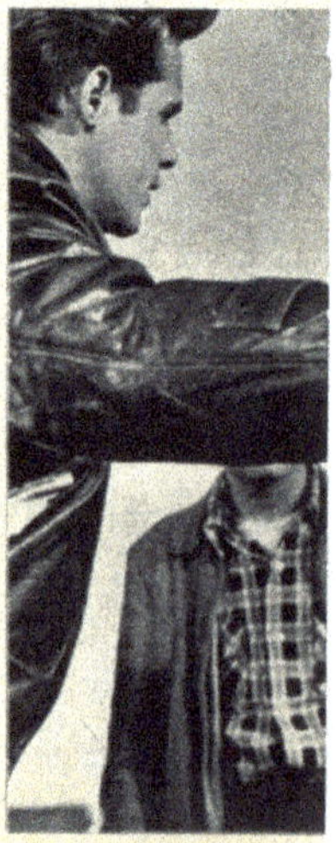

めに、そうしたことではわからなくともその理解以上には激しい共感だけが傳わって来る。
この年代を互に支えているものは「何故か」を持たない限り動物的な共感なのだ。スタート寸前、ジムがつけた煙草をバズが横からひったくって唇にくわえる、羞恥に顔をしかめてしまう笑いの内にぶつきら棒に「俺はお前が好きなんだ、嘘じゃない——」と言って横を向いてしまう、あの粗暴な友情の表現には理解を超えた狂暴なまでに激しい共感が溢れていた。
僕はあの映画で一番感動したシーンはあそこだった。
もわかる。あのジムにバズが感じ、幾度も一人で俺にはわかるんだ〞と言わなくして激しく理解しようとする自分同様黙っていた筈だ。だから二人はそれっ切りもわかれずあの稚拙で粗暴に見え切った一番新しい共感の情表外にはなかった。彼等が古い価値世界をぶちまけた二人は又寸刻後バズの死によって切り離されなくてはならない。ジムが呆れたようにジュディの手を握りながら延ばしたレジ否した彼等にとって果して妥当かどうかは誰にもわからないのだ。答はもっと後になって出て来るだろう。と
かくあれは唯一の遊びではない。現実傷ついているのは決して彼らの無意識の内に目ざしているものにとっての末梢的な残酷な事件が起きるとジャーナリズムは何時も慌てて一人勝手な判断を下すことだろう。大人はこれを観、又この映画の實感はそれだけ通用するだろうか、言葉の上ですると言われても若い世代の実情はそれを信じはしない。屍にジャンパーをかけた息子を見て、ジムとバズが出會いに行うナイフゲームはカットされていた。「暴力教室」と言う映画にしても一體何故ああいう騒がれ方をするのであろうか。たまたまその後若い世代に映画の内容に似た事件が起きるとジャーナリズムは必ず発するだろう。古びた価値と情操として固まり、爆発する時、僕らの世代としても實る答だ。それは言わば同胞に対する共感でしかない。この共感が、とうした映画や文學作品を通して一世の親たち、大人たちの理解を暗示したつもりだろうが、そうすると全くお笑いである。あのラストにいたって僕は彼等はあそこで何を理解したのだろうか。そして何を大切なものをひとつ奪われただけではなかったか。僕は氣に入ったのはプラネタリユウムの中で學生たちに天體の誕生を説明する教授の言葉と彼等の生態のコントラストだった。「星は暗黒から生れて育つ。我々人間も暗黒の内より生れ、その星の光が未だこの地上にとどかぬ前に又暗黒の内に消えて行くのだ——」
が所詮人間がどのようにちっぽけなものであろうと、若い世代の自身の価値と真実に支えられた新しい狂暴な宇宙を造って行くだろう。
この映画には曖昧な描寫が随分

この作品では僕は矢張りジムとバズの交渉に一番惹かれた。大人からすれば訳のわからぬ、全く出鱈目とも思われる彼等の行動を、この映画はそのまま余計なつて良いと思う。大人はこの行動を体どれだけ通用するだろうか、言葉の上ですると言われても若い世代の實感はそれだけ通用するだろうか、言葉の上ですると言われても若い世代の實感はそれを信じはしない。屍にジャンパーをかけた息子を見て、演出家は両親はすでに悲しみに取り扱い、その夢から醒めて慌てて大きな悲しさにとうして大きな声を上げていることにもならない。一體彼等はあそこで何を理解したのだろうか。そして何を大切なものをひとつ奪われただけではなかったか。僕は氣に入ったのはプラネタリユウムの中で學生たちに天體の誕生を説明する教授の言葉と彼等の生態のコントラストだった。「星は暗黒から生れて育つ。我々人間も暗黒の内より生れ、その星の光が未だこの地上にとどかぬ前に又暗黒の内に消えて行くのだ——」
が所詮人間がどのようにちっぽけなものであろうと、若い世代の自身の価値と真実に支えられた新しい狂暴な宇宙を造って行くだろう。
この映画には曖昧な描寫が随分

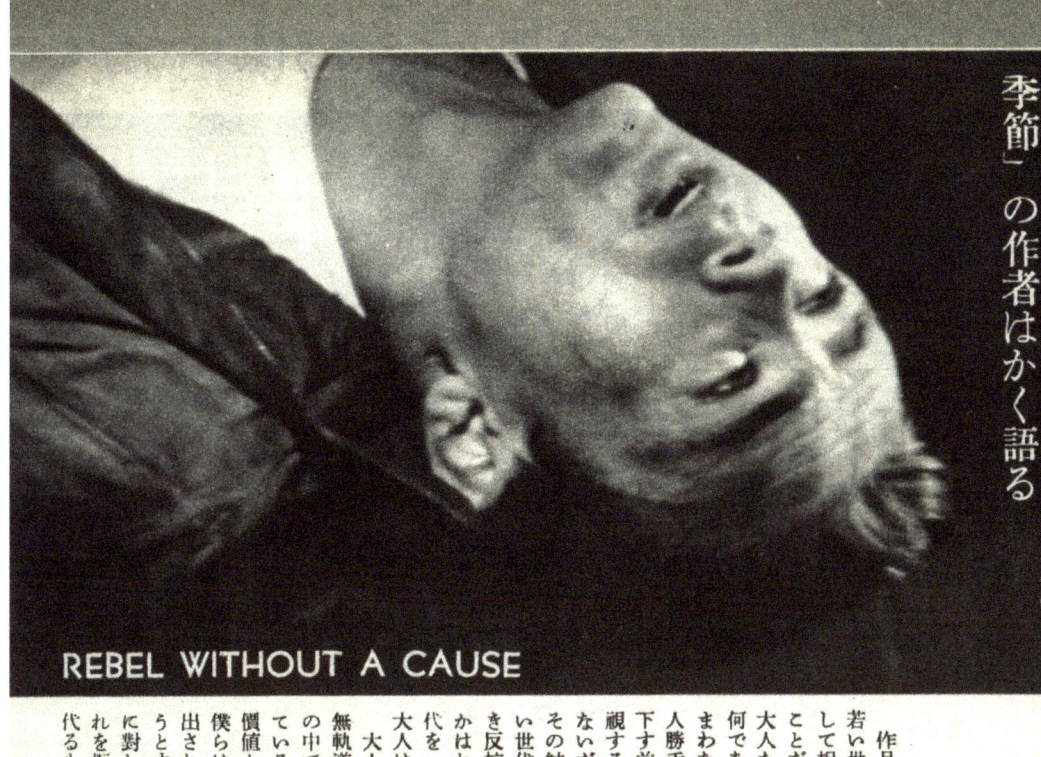

REBEL WITHOUT A CAUSE

あらゆる世代の注目を浴びた芥川賞「太陽の季節」の作者はかく語る

『理由なき反抗』を見て

石原愼太郎 Shintaro Ishiwara

作品自體の出来栄えは別として若い世代をこの内容のように直視して捉えようとした試みは正しいことだと思う。直視した後に来るべての行動の内にもある筈だ。そして大人たちの價値判断が何であろうとそれはかまわない。とにかく一人勝手に早急な判斷を下す前にこの世代を直視することが大切ではないだろうか。

その結果大人たちの今していることに若い世代のしていることに「理由なき反抗」と言う曖昧なレッテルをかれはしないのだ。結局この世代を「理解」するべき何ものをも大人は持ち合わしてはいない。

大人からすればヒステリックで無軌道としか思えぬああした行動の中で、彼らが無意識の内に求めているものは一番新しい人間的な價値と眞實なのだ。彼らは、いや僕らは始めから何も持たずに投げ出された。大人が一方的に與えようとする古い觀念世界の既成價値に對し、僕らが唯、嫌惡を感じそれを拒否する限り、僕らはそれに代るものを自らの手でいかなる手

段においても捉まなくてはならない。その手がかりは、最初から僕らの一人勝手な、言わば悲愴な自惚れに過ぎない。大人はすでに僕らに反抗され得るものを持ってはいないのだ。「理由なき反抗」とは僕らに反抗しているいわば操作自體が無駄ではないかとそうした操作自體が無駄ではないかと言うだけの。必要なものは理解ではない、要るものは共感か嫌惡のどちらかだけだ。再言すれば、僕らを理解する基となる新しい價値と言う奴は未だ僕らにも見つからないのだ。それを探すために手さぐりで傷つきながら進んでいるのではないか

僕よりも前にこの映画を観たある人から、あのチキンラン(断崖に車を疾走させ、どちらが先きに恐れて飛び下りるか競争する)のシーンだけはどうしても理解しついて行けないと言われた。何故、一體何のために彼らはあれをしなくてはならないのかどうしてもわからぬと言うのだ。が僕にも何故と言うことはわからなかった。恐らくジムにもバズにもわかりはしまい。しかし彼らをあそこまで驅り立てて行くものは何か、何故か、何のた

石原愼太郎氏

つきり感じるのだ。この實感があるだけではそれが捉えられないと言うことだけは知っている、と言うよりは考えるして僕らは

反抗とは大人を對象として言い得る限り僕らはあくまで求めているものを、動いて、この體を張ってしなくてはならない。

がこれが果して大人の言うように抵抗であり、反抗であろうか。僕らは實際に反抗の對象を持ちたい。僕らだけで動き廻り傷だらけになりながら、自身の新しい價値を探しているのだ。この映画の中で、ジムやバズがやつの反抗ではない。少くとも彼らは決してそんな意識はない筈だ。反抗されていると思うのは無關心

に取り殘されようとしている大人の一人勝手な、言わば悲愴な自惚れに過ぎない。大人はすでに僕らに反抗され得るものを持ってはいないのだ。「理由なき反抗」とは僕らに反抗しているいわば操作自體が無駄ではないかとそうした操作自體が無駄ではないかと言うだけの。必要なものは理解ではない、要るものは共感か嫌惡のどちらかだけだ。再言すれば、僕らを理解する基となる新しい價値と言う奴は未だ僕らにも見つからないのだ。それを探すために手さぐりで傷つきながら進んでいるのではないか

『理由なき反抗』

話題のジェイムス・ディーンの第二作をニコラス・レイ監督はどう演出して見せたか

登川直樹
Naoki Togawa

REBEL WITHOUT A CAUSE

「エデンの東」をみたおそらくすべての人がそうであるように、私もまた、**ジェイムス・ディーン**の第二作という、ただそれだけの理由で、この映画に大きな期待をもってのぞんだ。一瞬の閃光を放って永遠の闇に消えたとえばたしかに偉大な存在であった。私たちの期待も当然である。けれどもあのとき、ディーンは、エリア・カザンのために彼の藝術的な生命のすべてを燃燒しつくしたのではなかったかという不安も、一方にはあった。

街路に匍いつくばって、玩具にたわむれるタイトル・バックのジェイムス・ディーンに、あどけなさのうちに孤獨の痛ましさがあった。世代の暗い谷間に墮ちこんだ若者だけが抱く心痛で、これは「エデンの東」の繰り返しを思わせる。實は、ディーンのパースナリティがそっくり「エデンの東」のものであったのか、それともニコラス・レイがそのようにしか捉えなかったのか、いずれであるか判らない。が、どちらにしても私は、このタイトル・バックだけで、この映画に「別のジェイムス・ディーン」を期待してはならないことを豫感しはじめたのである。

物語は深夜の警察にはじまる。したたか醉っぱらったジム（ジェイムス・ディーン）が連行されて來た。その日は、取調べをうける未成年者の集團が事件でも起したものか、ほかにも若い男女が取調べをうけている。ジュディ（**ナタリイ・ウッド**）は深夜の街をひとりで徘徊していたという理由だが、彼女もまた、裕福ではあるが自分が求めるようには愛されない家庭に住んでいる。さらに年少のプレイトー（**サル・ミネオ**）の場合も同様だ。坊主刈りの補導係レイ（**エドワード・プラット**）の職業的な冷たさがいい。

ジムはジュディの置き忘れたコンパクトを手にいれ、ふるえるプレイトーに上衣をかけてやろうとするが、それらはあとのからみ合いの伏線でもあり、果してこの三人が最後までこの物語の中心人物となる。一見はなはだ圖式的な仕組みだが、そうと判っても苦にならぬのは、全體がこの調子の痛烈ではあってもロマンティックな構成のためであろう。

ラス・レイがそのようにしか捉えなかったのか、早くも映画はこの青年のシチュエイションを語りつくす。轉々と住居をかえてここに移り住んだばかりだが、何とかよい友達を見つけて健やかに育ってほしいと思う親心にも拘らずジムが孤獨で偏執的なのは、好きなものは何でも買い與えるほど裕福であっても、男勝りという以上に時には狂暴でさえある母親（**アン・ドーラン**）と、始終彼女にびくびくしている弱氣な父親（**ジム・バッカス**）のいびつな家庭のせいらしい。

最初のシーンで主要人物をすべて登場させ、そのシチュエイションを紹介してしまった映画の構成が、賢明な作法であったことは、翌朝の登校で、ジムとジュディが又しても顏を合わせる近所に住まいを同じ高校にとじこめた三人の強引さを度外視すれば、いずれはくり返し行動するうちに、設定された性格に從って行物が、あとはただ、これらの人られ、問題は自ら社會的なひろがりを帯びてくるからだ。

轉校の新参者を迎える生意氣盛りの高校生の眼は冷い。ましてジェイムス・ディーンの見るからに繊細な風貌と、ひとりで自家用車をのり廻すぜいたくさがあれば、「ひよこ」と綽名してからかうのも當り前だ。いきおいジムの方にひきいれ

た不良学生のグループ雰囲気は鮮やかだ。段取りはすべて順調に運んで、不良仲間の首領格バズ（コーリイ・アーレン）とジムが断崖に車を走らせて最後の刹那に飛び降りるのも常然だろう。プラネタリウムの見学で、講師の解説が宇宙の未来に地球の爆発をとともに映してみせたりするが、鼻持ちならぬ哲學的なセリフを吐くのは、安直に死ぬ間際の男が必ずもらす類型的な不良高校生の押出しで凄味をきかせるグマを演じたアーレンが、典型的な不良だが、土壇場になってジムに、白状するがお前が好きになったと、奇嬌な勝負方法となる。バスを並べて映画にレジスタンスを感じるのだろう。

これまでは、ジムが主人公であったこれまでは、ジムが主人公でありながらジムと共に新しい舞臺にもそこで映画の主人公をすり変えるのである。

襲われる。ジムの危険を知ったプレイトーはピストルを擬してジムを守りに來たわけであった。しかしジムとジュディの間に、不良たちに襲われたプレイトーは、ピストルを放ち、ジムを詰りながら、近くのプラネタリウムに逃げこみ、圖らずも警官隊がとりまく大捕物と化する。責任を感じたジムが單身乗り込み、プレイトーを説き伏せて連れ出し、た苦心のエ作にも拘らず、喰い違いはプレイトーを警官の彈丸の犠牲にしてしまうのだ。

映画の並んだ自動車の群が一齊にヘッドライトを照らし、その間を二豪の車が疾驅して、あっという間にドアのハンドルに手をとられたバズが、車もろとも斷崖から海に落ちこむまでのカットの積み重ねは迫力が漲る。しかしこの前後、西側に並んだ自動車の群が一齊にヘッドライトを照らし、その間を二豪の果も傷ましく、それの輕蔑をしりぞけることに成功したジムは、ジュディとの愛情も深めた。しかしジュディとの愛情も深めた。

つぶらな演技をつびとみせてやるジュディのからみ合いがなければ持ちたくないところだ。最期的なセリフを吐いたバスは案の定失敗する。しかしこの前後、西側に並んだ自動車の群が一齊にヘッドライトを照らし、その間を二豪の車が疾驅して、

出けずに負傷ったのが彼らの勘にさわり、顔見知りのレイが不在だったばかりに自首を思い止まり、タイヤにジャック・ナイフをつき立てられた挑戦に応じて渡り合う殺気立った三人が、この古い館で、子供のようにはしゃぎ廻る一場の情景は、そこでプレイトーに出遭う破綻の多いこの映画のなかでいくれるバスの手下たちに

傷ましい勝利をかちとったジムは、事實を知って狂気のように止める両親をふりきって警察へ出頭する。かねてからジムに憧れていたレイの弟分になっていたプレイトーは、ジムの自首をおそろしいおそれる
この悲惨な結末によって、作者は何を語ろうとするのか。とにかくには、経済的には豊かでも、精神的には不毛の地に等しい

『理由なき反抗』を見て同じ世代の子を持つ母の感想

十代の群像が描かれた。彼らを理解する術を全く知らない家庭も描かれた。もし「暴力教室」が現代アメリカの病巣をあばいたと言うなら、この映画はまた、同じ企てをやってのけたのではなかったか。

もしこの場合、貧困と汚濁が生活を暗く塗りつぶしているブルックリンの貧民街でなく、カルフォルニアは明るい太陽のもと、裕福で清潔な生活のなかにこの悲劇が生まれたところに、さらに奥深い問題があるといえよう。

ニコラス・レイはこの問題を、どちらかといえば青年の立場に同情をこめて描いている。ジムの偏執は明らかに母親の血をひいているのだろう。母が父の小心翼々たる擧動に我慢がならぬように、ジムもまたこの父親に我慢がならないのだ。エプロンをかけて祖母に食膳を運ぶ父の姿に、作者はいささかのカリカチュアもなく、ひそんでいる現代社會のいびつな親子關係の家庭に根深くの問題をぶちまけているのであろ。

ジュディにしても、十六歳になったからといって接吻を許さない父親が、いきなり荒々しく口紅を拭きとる父親でもあるということはあまりにも仕組まれたドラマに耐えられないのだ。大人とも子供とも扱ってくれないことは、まさしく世代の谷間に落ちこんでいる證據なのである。さらにプレイトーに至っては、たった一度の面會のために、遠くはなれた親元から仕送りをうける生活なのだ。黒人女中にかしずかれる一人住いが、どさに事大主義的な身構えも感じられるのだ。これには、いさましい犠牲者をつくりあげた作者のたくらみに従うして不安をうける十代を守る健全な家庭と言えるだろうか。十代の悲劇の展開し、くり返して世代の谷間のオリジナル・アイデアがそこに焦點を合わせていたとすればスるからであろう。ニコラス・レイて發展させナタリイ・ウッドのジュナンスがあるが、後ディも自半大役のサル・ミネオのプレイは起るべくして起ったにすぎないし、問題はナな末端だけで捉えていで、もっと描き込んでよかった人物である。レオナード・ローゼンマンの鋭い雰圍氣音樂もこの映画の情感を高めていた。

ペシミステイックな生活感情を大寫しにしながら、こじつけに従うほかはなかったに違いない。技巧的なレイの演出から容易に推察されることである。

それにしても技術的には流麗な作品である。ジェームス・ディーンの扱いは「エデンの東」のそれを一歩ぬきんでるものではなかったが、この纖細可憐な美青年の痛々しさはそのまま再現された。強烈なパースナリテイではあるが、ユニークな個性が拾いものの環境が背景から正體をのぞかせる代りに、振幅の大きな末端だけで捉えていた代りに、振幅の大きな末端だけで捉えていた人物である。

チュアート・スターンの脚色もアーヴィング・シャーマンの潤色も、

思いあたることが澤山あります

山本紀子（四十七歳）

二十三歳の長男をかしらに四人の息子と十三歳の娘が一人おりますが、あの映画を見ると隨分思いあたることがございます。あの映画に出て來るような子供たちは、新制中學の三年ごろから高校の一、二年といったところのようです。この年ごろは、男の子では一番元氣がありました。四男が今年十四歳でちよう

どその年代にかゝっていますが、休日には登戸のスケート場へスケートをしにまいります。それも、とんでもない程朝早くから起きて出てまいります。母もうかうかしておられません。その年頃が、あの映画で見られるような危險がはらんだ年代なのですから。親たちはそういう子供たちのやり場のないエネルギーを、何かで發散させることを考えてやらなければならないのでしよう。幸いなことに私どもの子供たち

は、男の子では一番元氣がありました四男が今年十四歳で、ちよう譯なくあんな仕ぐさを、よくしましたが、うちの子供たちも叩き割ろうとするようなところがありますが、うちの子供たちも、はらんだ年代なのですから。親たちはそういう子供たちのやり場のないエネルギーを、何かで發散させることを考えてやらなければならないのでしよう。幸いなことに私どもの子供たち

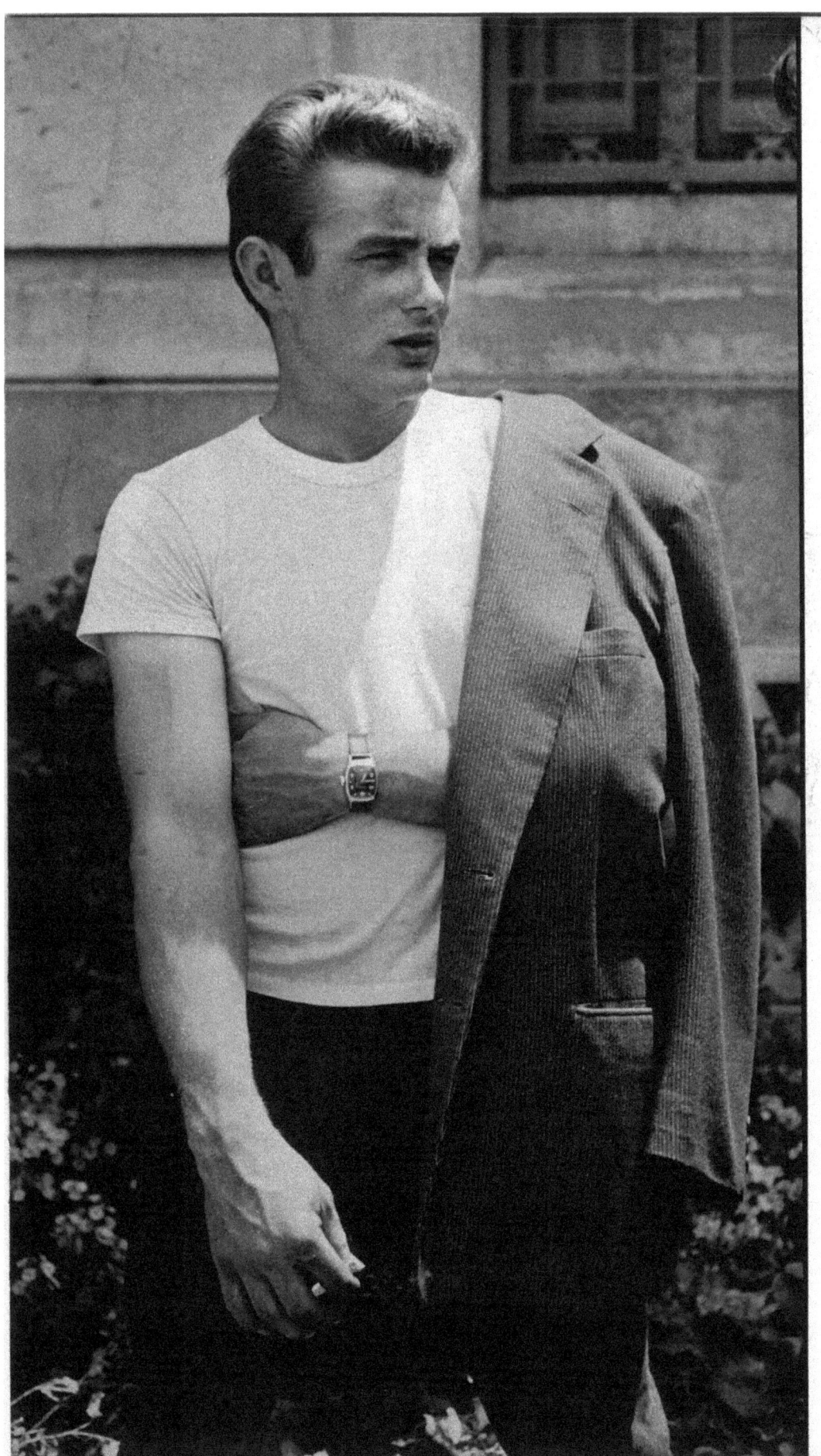

ディーン逝って三年

まだディーンをつぐスタアは現れないか

夏の光に別れを告げ秋の寂しさと共にジミー・ディーンへの哀悼の情を迎える——そんな悲しい慣わしが世のファンにひろがって今年は三年目。改めて彼の風貌を熟視し、併せてジミー・ディーン派ともいうべき人々を見るグラフ特集を贈る。

Rebel without a Cause

STAFF:
Produced by	David Weisbart
Directed by	Nicholas Ray
Screenplay by	Stewart Stern
Adaptation by	Irring Shulman
Story by	Nicholas Ray
Director of Photography	Ernest Haller
Music by	Leonard Rosenman

CAST:
Jim	James Dean
Judy	Natalie Wood
Jim's Father	Jim Backus
Jim's Mother	Ann Doran
Judy's Mother	Rochelle Hudson
Judy's Father	William Hopper
Plato	Sal Mineo
Buzz	Corey Allen
Goon	Dennis Hopper
Ray	Edward Platt
Moose	Nick Adams
Chick	Jack Grinnage
Crunch	Frank Mazzola
Cookie	Jack Simmons
Harry	Tom Bernard

顔馴染のプラトオ（サル・ミネオ）と相知った。彼女は深夜街を俳徊していたため保護されたのだったが、複雑な家庭環境にある鰥宅の後嫌疑が晴れて帰された。二人は説諭の後鰥宅を許され、プラトオは仔犬を射つたため保護されたのだったが、複雑な家庭環境にある鰥宅の後嫌疑が晴れて帰された。ジムの家庭は父（ジム・バッカス）にかわって男勝りの母（アン・ドーラン）がきりまわし、時々と住居を変えて最近この街へ移って来たばかりだった。翌朝新しい學校ドウスン・ハイスクールに通うことになったジムは再びジュディに會った。彼女は不良學生のバズ（コーリイ・アーレン）ムーズ（ニック・アダムス）ハリイ（トム・バーナード）クッキー（ジャック・シモンズ）クランチ（フランク・マゾーラ）グーン（デニス・ホッパー）等と一緒だった。午後星の勉強にプラネタリウム舘へ皆は出掛けたがバズの一派は講義を野次り、ジムも輕口を飛ばしたがそれが反感を買い、終ってからバズはジムに挑んで来た。ナイフを手にした二人は互にシャツを染め合う格闘をしたが守衛の出現にバズは今晩チッキイ・ランをやろうと捨てセリフを殘して立去った。その夜二人は吹き晒しの崖ぶちで落合った。チッキイ・ランとはそれぞれボロ自動車を崖ぶちに向って走らせ初めに車から飛出した方が年臆者の刻印を押されるのである。不良仲間が見守るうち二豪の車は崖に向って驀進したが、バズは飛出す時ジャンパーの袖口を把手にひっかけた寫車諸共死の谷底へ落ちた。警官のサイレンにプラトオとジュディを連れ帰った。警察に届出る

この空邸も二人にとっては殿堂だった。數刻後ジムを探すムーズ、グーン、クランチの三人はこの邸に来て、プラトオを發見、突然の恐怖に襲われたプラトオは拳銃を取上げようとしたが、新けつけたクランチは彈を拔けつけたクランチは彈を拔けつけたクランチは彈を拔けつけたクランチは彈を拔け出はプラネタリウムへ逃げ込んだ。警官隊の大掛りな警備網の中を彼が子の姿を見て心から慰めた、彼等は初めて互に理解し合うことが出来たジムを連れ帰った。

不良學生をふり切ってジムは警察へ出向いたが生憎少年保護係レイ（エドワード・プラット）は不在だった。ムーズとクランチはジムを脅して事件の暴露を恐れプラトオを脅してジムの住所を知った。プラトオは怒って父親の拳銃を持出すと暗闇を驅け出した。その頃ジムは秘かにジュディに會っていた。しばしの間二人の心は近くプラネタリウムの近くの空家へ行こうと相談が決まった。空家でプラトオと出逢った時、轟然一發警官の銃彈でプラトオは斃れた。ジムはプラトオに寄りすがると大聲で泣き叫んだ。ジムの両親は憐れな我が子の姿を見て心から慰めた、彼等は初めて互に理解し合うことが出来たのだった。

COMING NEW PICTURE

理由なき反抗

今は亡き不世出の天才俳優ジェームズ・ディーンの遺作登場！

解説

今は亡きジェイムズ・ディーンが「エデンの東」に次いで主演する思春期の世代の混乱と悩みを描いた一篇。

製作は「コマンド」のデイヴィッド・ウィズバート、「追われる男」のニコラス・レイの原作をスチュアート・スターンが脚色し、アーヴィング・シャーマンが潤色、原作者のニコラス・レイが監督した。撮影監督は「ダラス」のアーネスト・ホーラー、美術監督にウィリアム・ホッパー等が共演。十六歳の舞豪俳優サル・ミネオが重要な役で登場している。

ジェイムズ・ディーンをめぐっては「銀の盃」のナタリー・ウッドがヒロインに抜擢され、その他テレビで活躍中のジム・バッカス、「マッコーネル物語」のアン・ドーラン、「紅の翼」のエドワード・プラット、「肉の蝋人形」のヴァージニア・ブリサック、それ「スタア誕生」のマルコム・パート、音楽は「エデンの東」のレオナード・ローゼンマンが担当。一九五五年度作品。一時間五十一分。(米・ワーナー映画、ワーナーカラー・シネマスコープ作品)

梗概

酔いしれた十七歳の少年ジム(ジェイムズ・ディーン)がその晩起した集団暴行事件の容疑者として署に連行されそこで可憐なジュディ(ナタリー・ウッド)と紅

未完の傑作 ジェイムズ・ディーン

高 季彦

ジェイムズ・ディーンが昨日自動車事故で死んだと聞いて、狐につままれたような気がした。冗談じゃないか、ついこないだ「エデンの東」の彼に目を睜り、輝かしいスタアの誕生にお祝いの言葉を綴ったばかりなのに、そのペンを拭うヒマもないうちに早くも彼の弔辞を書かなければならないとは、あんまりではないか。死んでもらって一向差支えのない有象無象が多い世の中で、よりにもよっ

てこんな貴重な若い人材が突如葬られてしまうとは、あんまりヒドいではないか。"彗星の如く現われた、とはまさしく彼のことだが、この彗星は清らかな一瞬の光を放ったと見る間に怨ち天上の闇の彼方へ永遠に消えてしまったのだ。

ディーンを失ったことである。最初の一作でこれほどのセンセイションを惹きおこし、前途を嘱望させた新人男優も珍しいが、彼はたしかにこのような実質を具えていたのである。彼の死によって蒙ったアメリカ映画の損失は、おそらく何びとによっても当分は償えないものであろう。

「エデンの東」の演技の成果は、もとよりエリア・カザンのきびしい指導を得てはじめて達せられたものではあるが、またディーン自身のパアスナリティやすぐれた才能を離れては考えられないものである。

僕は、演出者と俳優の関係は、演奏者と楽器の関係に等しいなどと考えたこともあったが、それはどうやらちがうらしい。例えば、いかに名器ストラディヴァリウスを使わなくともティボオの弾くアルベニスの美しさに変りはあるまいが、ディーンのかわりにロバアト・ワグナア君を使っても、いくらカザンの演出力をもってしても「エデンの東」のキャルのなまなましい悲劇性は表現できなかったにちがいない。演出家は、自分の用いる楽器の個有の音色によって屡々インスピレイションを享

けるのであり、それを条件とした演奏効果を狙うのであり、ときには特定の名器によってしか演奏し得ないような楽想が彼を誘惑することさえあるのだ。「エデンの東」の場合がそれであったと云えよう。

カザンは、主人公キャルの性格をディーンを借りて表現しようと試みたというよりも、ディーンというい個性のうちにスタインベックの人物を見出したのである。カザンのはじまる前の、オーケストラに調子をためすひとときのあの期待に満ちたざわめきを思い出させる。

ディーンの若さは、青春の多感な生命につきものの、あの光栄ある混沌を蔵していた。亡びに向う混沌ではなく、生れ出ようとする混沌だ。それは拾も、さまざまな可能を孕んだ豊かな混沌の人物の・各楽器がてんでに表現すべき人物の感情に身を委ねて演技する。彼の演ずるキャルが泣き顔や力ない笑顔ばかりでなく、背すじや肩が彼の孤独を伝え、すぼめた胸が愛の喜びを語りもするのである。ケイトの家に石を投ずる腕の怒りや悶えは全身を震わせ、豆畑に腹ばいになって芽生えを喜ぶ

彼の笑顔は足の爪先にまで伝わるのだ。その流儀は、権威あるいかなる先輩の真似でもない。彼は、いわば自分自身にある野性や反逆や孤独や渴望や愛の心の自由な表現にキャルの人物をすり替えたのだ。本能にも等しいこの流儀が、彼の八方破れとも見える芸の構えにキャルの人物をすり替えたのだ。本能にも等しいこの流儀が、彼の八方破れとも見える芸の構えに鮮な個性や表現をなまなましく表現でこの新しい演技精神の傑作が、未完のまま終ったことは、まことに痛恨に堪えない。

それからさき、美男の新人はいくらでも出て来ようし、ツムジ曲りのタイプも続々見つかるだろう。しかし、ディーンのような、自然児の清潔な情熱と都会人のセンシティヴな憂愁を兼ね備えた新鮮な個性や表現をなまなましく表現できる新人は、容易に現われそうには思われない。

死んでしまったディーン、君を讃える喝采とアンコオルの拍手に何もかも見せてしまった人のように姿を消したディーン。僕には、「エデンの東」をもう一度見るのがおそろしいような気さえもする。の一作こそ君の短い生涯の頂点であり、君の全生命がそこに結晶しているかと思えば、あまりに傷ましいからだ。

ジェイムズ・ディーンの霊よ、君の生命はカザンの名作とともにいつまでも地上に輝いて、幾多の若い無名の俊才を導いて行くだろう。（十月一日）

ジェイムズ・ディーンの死

双葉十三郎

 事故は突然おこるものとはいえ、あまりにも突然な計報だった。「エデンの東」の感動がまだなまなましいときだけにショックは大きい。彼はこの映画で、ハリウッドで最も有望な若手として大変な評判になった。人生の無常を痛感せずにはいられない。伝えられるところによれば自動車事故だそうである。が、自動車狂が自動車で死を招いたのもなにか宿命的である。非常なスピード狂で、ゴシップなどではオートバイをさかんに乗りまわしているというのが、彼の危険きわまる遊びにひやひやしていたが、当人はやめようとしなかった。ついで「理由なき反抗」に出演したが、その撮影中も、土曜日の仕事がやくすむとすぐレース場へかけつけるという有様でパルム・スプリングスとベイカアスフィールドの大会に出場し、両方とも優勝したのだ。この道に年期を入れた或るヴェテラン選手は、「彼はまったく恐怖を知らぬ若者でまるで死神からお前は絶対に殺されぬという約束を貰っているみたいにすっ飛ばす」と評しているが、その死神に約束を破られてしまったわけである。

 彼は「エデンの東」に出演し評判された。いつもジャンパアで仕事着のズボンをはき、マアロン・ブランドのイミテイションなどといわれたが、自分ではマアロンなどの手伝いをしたりして、やつとプロードウェイに機会をつかみ、テレビの近くに住むジェイムズ・ホイトモアにすすめられて俳優になる決心をきめ、ニュウ・ヨークへ向い、テレビに出たりヨットの手伝いをしたりして、やつとプロードウェイに機会をつかみ、テレビでも重要な役をもらうようになり、舞台の「背徳者」でデヴィッド・ブラム賞をもらい、師のカザンに招かれて「エデンの東」でハリウッド・デビューした、というくわしい経歴はここにくりかえすまでもないだろうが、前評判にちがわず、映画の彼は決してマアロン・ブランドではなく二代目マアロン・ブランドだつたらしいハリウッド・スタアになりきろうという気持はなかったらしい。「エデンの東」の撮影が終るとすぐニュウ・ヨークへ帰り、イリヤ・カザンの《仕事場》で演技の勉強をつづけたが、すこぶる多趣味で、彼はフェアモント・ハイスクウル時代には野球や陸上競技や篭球の選手だったという。あちらのファン雑誌にでているスナップには、近視なのだろう、眼鏡をかけているのが多いが、そう強くはない筈である。強かったら自動車を襲来したりも無理はない。馬も好きだし、ピアノをひき、ボンゴをたたき、二頭ほど牧場にあずけてあった。なにによらず牧場にあずけてあった。その眼は永遠に閉じてしまったのだから。

 ニュウ・ヨーク時代のアパアトの同室でレナアド・ロオゼンマンに作曲を教わったりしていた。「エデンの東」の音楽を担当しているのは彼だ。カザリン・ダンハムについて舞踏を学んだり、ニュウ・ヨオクの彼のアパアトに近いとカザン独得の演出で、両手をふらつかせたりしてからで全体に大いに売られたが、容貌はまるでちがい、ロマンテックな甘さがあり、彼の表情をあらわしたハリウッドは彼ういう性格の持主だつたらしい。イロン・デインという名前にふさわしいやつとロマンテックな冒険家であったように、ジェイムズも多角多彩飛躍が予想されていた。エリザベス・テイラアと共演の「巨人」が完成されたらしいが、ブランドを乗りきった新しい彼が発見されるにちがいない。たしかにディーンの新しさはおそれていた悲劇が、ついに実現してしまった。それも若々しいいた生涯かもしれないが、やっとのばされた芽をばさりと刈りとつてしまう運命の残酷さを、ぼくは嘆き呪いたい。享年二十四歳。一九三一年二月八日インディアナ州フェアモントに生れ、一九五五年九月三十日カリフォルニア州パソ・ロープルスに死す。

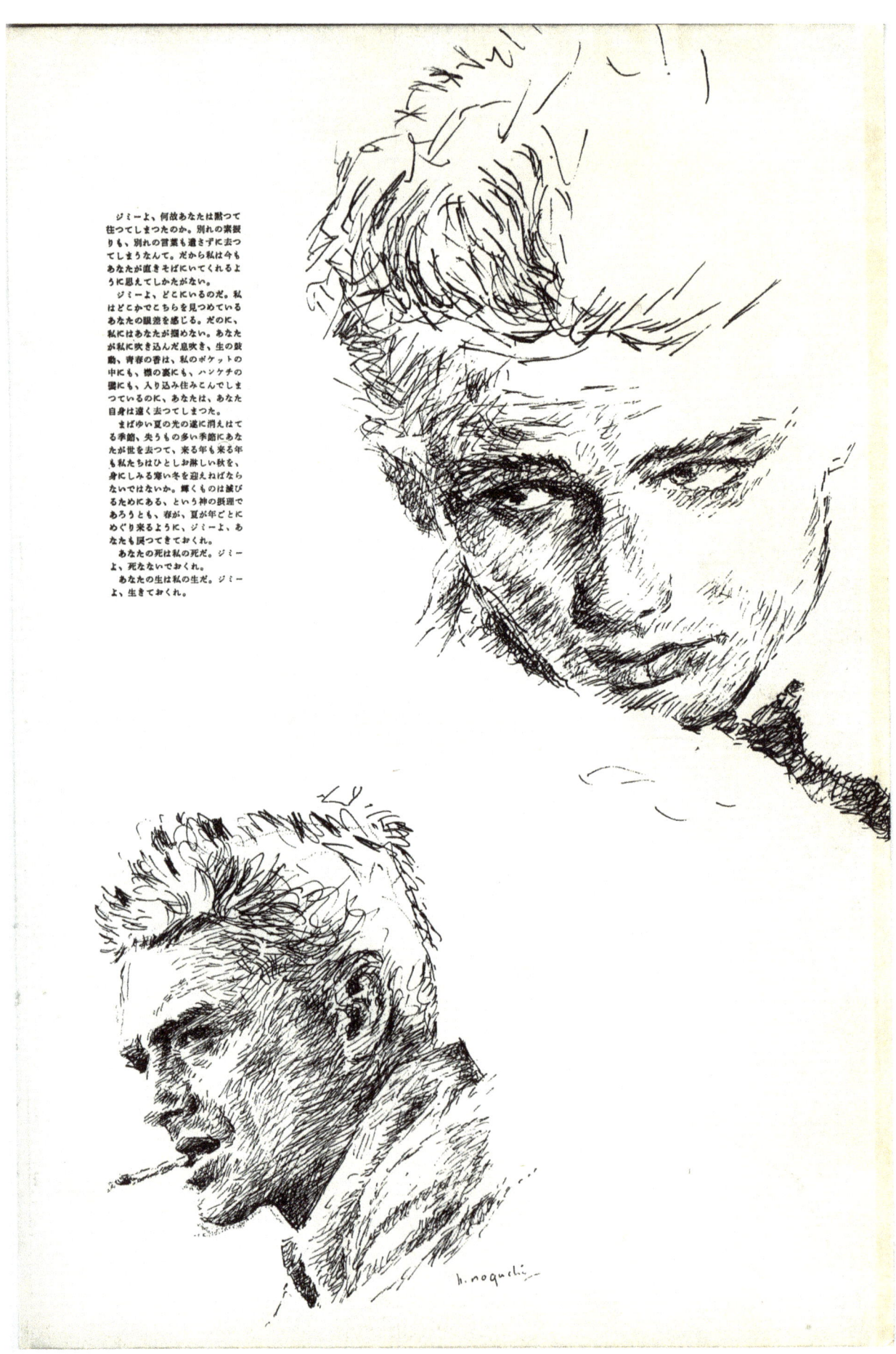

ジミーよ、何故あなたは黙って往ってしまったのか。別れの素振りも、別れの言葉も遺さずに去ってしまうなんて。だから私は今もあなたが直きそばにいてくれるように思えてしかたがない。

ジミーよ、どこにいるのだ。私はどこかでこちらを見つめているあなたの眼差を感じる。だのに、私にはあなたが掴めない。あなたが私に吹き込んだ息吹き、生の鼓動、青春の香は、私のポケットの中にも、襟の裏にも、ハンケチの襞にも、入り込み住みこんでしまっているのに、あなたは、あなた自身は遠く去ってしまった。

まばゆい夏の光の遽に消えはてる季節、失うもの多い季節にあなたが世を去って、来る年も来る年も私たちはひとしお淋しい秋を、身にしみる寒い冬を迎えねばならないではないか。輝くものは滅びるためにある、という神の摂理であろうとも、春が、夏が年ごとにめぐり来るように、ジミーよ、あなたも戻ってきておくれ。

あなたの死は私の死だ。ジミーよ、死なないでおくれ。

あなたの生は私の生だ。ジミーよ、生きておくれ。

ジェームス・ディーン特集

JAMES DEAN

直木久蓉画
この原画は本月號懸賞の特
賞とします。(134頁参照)

The boy who refuses to DIE

James Dean

今は亡き若く偉大なりし彗星！

ジェイムズ・ディーンはブランドーとクリフトの後に出るべくして出てきた万人渇仰の星だつた。モンロー、ヘプバァンの後にグレイス・ケリーあるが如くに。

エリア・カザン監督の「エデンの東」で大きくデビューし、ジョオジ・スティーヴンス監督の"Giant"（巨人）及びワーナー作品"Rebel Without Cause"（理由なき反抗）に出演という活躍が続々はじまらんとした矢先、9月末日交通事故によつて彼は永遠に還らぬ人となつてしまつた。惜しみてもなお余りある彗星の昇天である。

Official James Dean Anniversary Book 1956

Jimmy Dean in
REBEL
without a cause

● "Your eggs are on the table, dear," Jim's mother said. Jim, standing at the window, did not move. "Sit down and eat," his mother said. "You'll be late."

Deliberately Jim let another long minute pass before he turned. They were all seated around the table now, their eyes on him: his grandmother's —bright, malicious, dominating the room; his mother's—sullen, aggrieved, staring at him from beneath carefully plucked brows; his father's—gentle, vague, and (as always when he looked at his seventeen-year-old son) just a little bewildered.

Jim sat down. But the taste of last night's liquor was still dark and furry in his mouth, and he shoved back his plate. "It'd stick in my throat, Mom," he muttered. "I'm nervous or something."

His father darted a glance at Jim's grandmother. "My first day of school," he recalled sympathetically, "Mother'd make me eat, and by golly, I could never even swallow till recess."

"Well, drink your milk anyhow," Jim's mother snapped. "There's nothing to be nervous about." She held out a brown paper bag. "Here's peanut butter and meat loaf."

Jim made a derisive noise. His grandmother laughed unpleasantly. "What did I tell you?" she sneered. "Peanut butter!"

Her daughter-in-law's voice sharpened defensively. "Well, there's a thermos of orange juice," she said, "and some applesauce cake in the wax paper to wash it down."

Jim snatched the bag and ran, eager to be away from them, out of reach of their wrangling and the sight of his father caught between them, their meek, unprotesting victim. They make mush out of him, Jim thought bitterly. Just mush. One thing I know, he told himself, I never want to be like him.

Standing on the back steps in the pale winter sunshine, Jim was remembering the night before. The drinking and the dark street, and then the sirens and the precinct police station and the shocked faces of his family, summoned to take him home. Even there it had been the same—the barbed recriminations of both his mother

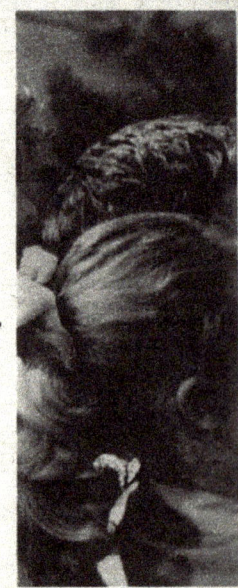

They jerked his head back, and someone cracked him across the face.

54

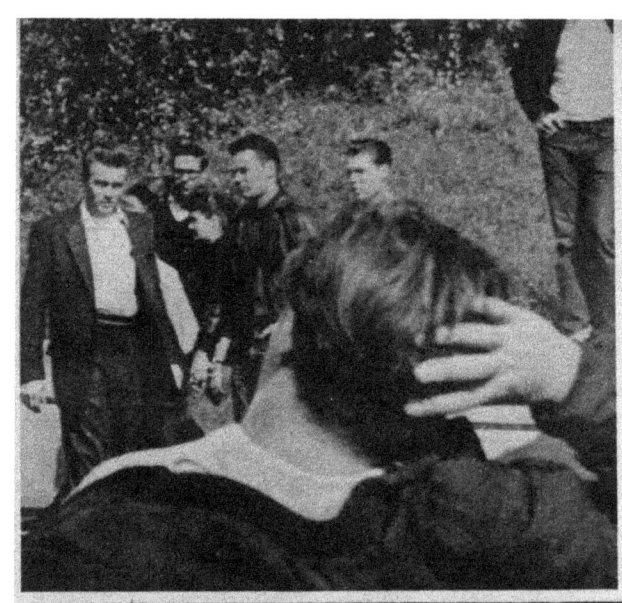

Jim's first day at school, none of the kids were friendly.

"This is the test," Buzz said. "Just sticking—jab real cool."

continued

Jimmy Dean in
REBEL
without a cause

"We got to do *something*," Buzz had said. In one moment he and Jim would drive their cars to the edge of the cliff—last one out the winner. Judy wished them good luck.

and grandmother, the groping, fumbling voice of his father. "I want to understand you," he'd pleaded. "Why'd you get drunk? There must have been a reason." But the reason lay deeper within him than any words he knew could reach; suffering and inarticulate, he could not explain why even to himself.

There had been one man at the police station, Jim remembered gratefully, who had not needed an explanation; Ray, they'd called him—Jim never heard the rest of his name, but his title, he knew, was Juvenile Officer. Ray had understood. He'd seen beneath Jim's drunken bravado the confusion of a boy struggling to become a man, needing a man to show him how; he'd seen the despair of a boy whose father had never learned to be a man himself. "Will you do something for me?" Ray had said at the end. "If the pot starts boiling again will you come and see me before you get yourself in a jam? Even if you just want to talk —come in and shoot the breeze. It's easier sometimes," he'd added gently, "than talking to your folks."

Jim smiled a little, remembering that, remembering the sure, kind eyes in Ray's creased, sunburned face; Ray was a friend. This was another new town, another new school—how many of them there'd been in the last few years!—but maybe it would be different this time. This time he had a friend.

56

This was a happy moment for Plato (Sal Mineo). He had found two people whom he could love...

Natalie Wood and Jimmy Dean, young co-stars in "Rebel Without a Cause"

You haven't heard the half about JIMMY!

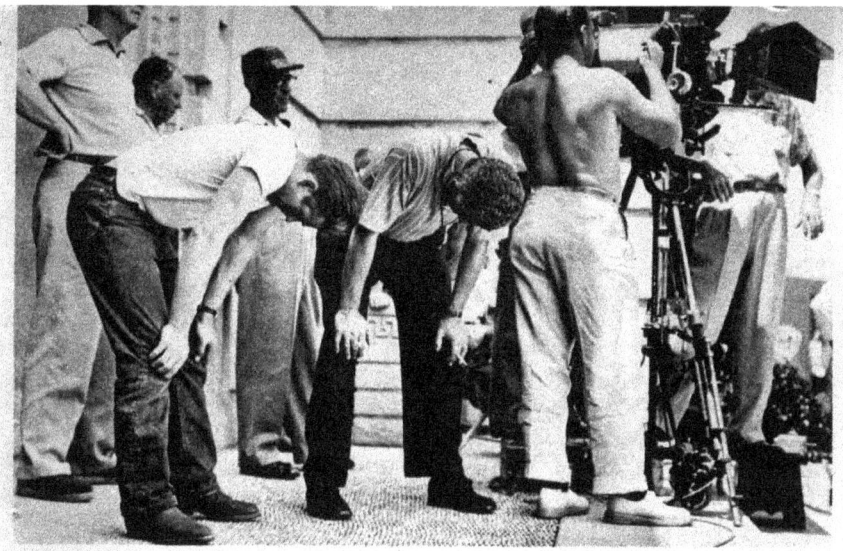

"Before a scene, he'll stand by the camera, jumping or swinging his arms. He says it relaxes him"

With director George Stevens. "When Jimmy works, he concentrates, uses tape recorder to rehearse"

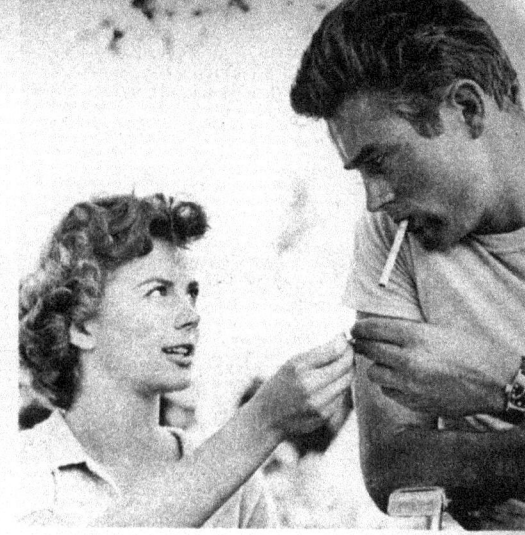

Natalie, working with Jim above, far left, expected a real "gloom." "Was I surprised!"

"Jimmy's always friendly to fans. He really gets a bang out of posing for photographs"

Jimmy Dean is also in "Giant"

The writer worked with Jimmy Dean— and she's all steamed up. But we'll let her tell you why!

BY NATALIE WOOD

● James Dean and I sat in his plush white Porsche, sipping a Coke at Hamburger Hamlet on the Sunset Strip. We'd just finished a long hard day on the set of "Rebel Without a Cause" and were in that delightful state of silence that only comes when the air is slightly tangy, the company really companionable and you've had a terrific day at the studio.

"Hi, Jimmy," said a man who appeared to be a little older than either of us. Jimmy flushed slightly and said apologetically, "I'm sorry, I don't think I know your name." It was not only an apology to the man but to me, too.

The man gave Jimmy his name, and I could tell by the expression on Jimmy's face that this recalled nothing and with *(Continued on page 82)*

You Haven't Heard the Half About Jimmy!

(*Continued from page 55*)

very good reason—he'd never met him before. Jimmy listened politely as the man explained he'd been sitting in the drive-in when we arrived and couldn't help hoping that a fellow actor, who'd succeeded, would give him a few tips on how to get his foot in a studio door.

With that quick sympathy Jimmy has for a person trying, they were soon off comparing notes. I sat and listened and, as I did, I grinned all over. I thought, What a whale of a lot of things people don't know about James Dean.

Jimmy, an oddball? Jimmy, weird? Jimmy, sullen?

The first time we met was while Jimmy was making "East of Eden" and I was working on an adjoining sound stage where he had several pals. We were introduced when he came over for a visit. He was nicely dressed in well-pressed slacks and a sport shirt, was polite and intelligently interesting. There was nothing strange about him.

Six months later, in an old abandoned theatre in Los Angeles, the two of us were working on a television script that was to be my first grown-up role. I had been cast opposite James Dean and, like everyone else in Hollywood, I had heard the stories. I was, frankly, afraid of him. During the morning absolutely nothing out of the ordinary happened. The two of us worked, took our breaks when the director called them and finally lunchtime rolled around.

It had been a long time since I'd walked in this particular neighborhood, so I made my way through the crowds, hoping I'd see a little restaurant. There was no roaring motorcycle with brakes screeching to a stop to announce the fact that James Dean was following me. He simply caught up to me and asked, "Mind sharing lunch?" We found a cafe and, like actors, gabbed about the script we were working on and the show. During the four days we worked together, I brought my portable radio, tuned to the classical music Jimmy likes, and he brought hamburgers —which I like.

"Eden" made Jimmy Dean into a juvenile delinquent. I shudder to think what "Rebel Without a Cause" is going to do. In one terrific scene Jimmy, carried away by rage, knocks his father down the steps into the living room and almost kills him. Poor Jim Bachus—who plays his dad— really thought he was going to finish him.

In "Rebel," both Jimmy and I play disturbed teenagers who go wrong from lack of sympathetic understanding and turn to each other for comfort. But there's no sense diagnosing Dean a delinquent and explaining his symptoms in unloved terms.

"I had a happy childhood," Jimmy will tell you. After his mother died—he was nine—his dad sent him out to live with his sister and her husband in Iowa. They were thoughtful, religious folks—Quakers, I believe—and owned a farm. It was a fine place to grow up, to go to school. Although Jimmy never had any aspirations for farming, the only rebelling he ever did was to skip cleaning the chicken coops once in a while. In school, he was an A student in art, an easy mixer, the class athlete.

After graduating from high school, Jimmy headed west to California and Santa Monica College for a degree in Physical Education and, he hoped, later a basketball coach's job. He'd won the Indiana State Dramatic Contest as the best high-school actor and this started him thinking. When a junior, he switched to UCLA and law. One day, he says, he finally faced facts. He quit school to tackle Hollywood. This was no cinch.

Hollywood didn't exactly welcome Jimmy Dean with open arms. He managed to get an usher's job at CBS-TV, landed a one-minute TV commercial for a soft drink (Jimmy danced around a juke box, sang the ad—for $30). An agent helped him get a few bit parts, but that was all. In one Rock Hudson film, he had two lines. (I bet Rock was surprised when Jimmy reminded him when they met for "Giant.")

Realizing he wasn't the Hollywood matinee-idol type and lead roles were not destined to come to him fast, Jimmy pocketed his last few dollars and climbed aboard a cross-country bus for New York. Arriving in New York, he made the round of Broadway producers, getting nowhere in a hurry. Finally, he turned to TV agencies, wangled jobs as an extra. At one time, he was a stand-in for contestants on "Beat the Bank." They tested the consistency of custard pies—later to be thrown in jest at contestants—by throwing them first at Jimmy.

Jimmy says there were plenty of nights he'd walk up and down Broadway, alone and pretty despondent, sure he'd never make it. Plenty of times, too, when he didn't have the rent or food money. Temporary jobs—and a series of little miracles —helped tide him over.

His first break on Broadway came in a rather peculiar way. He was told one evening of a job opened for a crewhand on a sloop—and he needed a job. Besides, the skipper knew someone who knew someone who might arrange a tryout. What could he lose, Jimmy decided. He took the job, got the tryout, won the role —and the play, "See the Jaguar," was a flop. It did one thing for Jimmy though— it brought TV leads, gave him money for good drama coaches. With his top performance in the hit play, "The Immoralist," he received rave notices, won the David Blum award for the most promising newcomer of 1954 and caught Hollywood's eye. Not easy? Jimmy's the last one to tell you it was. I doubt whether he'll ever forget those days or the people who had faith in him.

Believe it or not, Jimmy's a sentimentalist. I remember a hot afternoon, soon after we started shooting "Rebel." We were sitting around, killing time, while the lights were being adjusted and readied. I hardly knew Jimmy then, so I busied myself with a manicure. I think he was reading a book—on astronomy or bullfighting, I don't remember which. Neither of us said a word. There was only the constant hum of voices, directions and moving apparatus in the background. Then, quite by accident, I looked up. Jimmy was sitting with the widest grin.

"Penny for your thoughts?" I said, curious.

"Aw, guess," he teased.

"Thinking about your new sports car," I offered.

"Nope."

"Your new stallion?" I guessed, knowing Jimmy was forever running down to Santa Barbara after work to ride and exercise Cisco.

"Nope," he answered, arching his eyebrows in that funny way he does when teasing.

"I got it," I fairly screamed, delighted because I felt I'd outwitted him. "Your new sixteen millimeter movie camera." Jimmy had bought it only yesterday. It cost two hundred dollars with special lenses and I knew he had saved up for it.

"Nope," he said quietly, in his softspoken way. "Remember that scroll? The one I got from the folks back in Grant County? I was just sitting and thinking how nice it was for those three thousand people to sign the scroll, to tell me they liked my acting."

Jimmy's proud to be an actor, don't ever doubt that. But it's not for the fame, the glamour, the money. It's the sense of achievement, the thrill of doing a good job. "I'm an actor not a personality," he'll complain, sometimes giving the wrong impression, getting labeled non-cooperative, ungrateful.

I had plenty of opportunity to see how grateful Jimmy Dean is to his fans. "Rebel" was shot all over Los Angeles and we had a chance to meet a lot of people. For one sequence we used the Planetarium and some high-school students. I had a late call the first morning so I arrived at the Planetarium after Jimmy.

Rushing to makeup, I turned the corner full speed, came to a dead stop! Sitting in a big old trash can was the star of "Rebel"—Hollywood's newest, brightest, most talented boy actor—James Dean. Crumbled up in an awkward ball, he busily signed autographs, exchanged stories —very obviously unaware that he'd been pushed there, and equally unaware of his position or dignity!

Photographers have been reported to complain that Dean is uncooperative. If so, that doesn't explain the twenty minutes I had to wait for him to go to lunch. Everything was humming along smooth-
(*Continued on page 84*)

WHO ARE YOUR FAVORITES?

Send your votes for the stars you want to see in PHOTOPLAY

In color I want to see: ACTOR:

(1)_____
(2)_____

ACTRESS:

(1)_____
(2)_____

I want to read stories about:

(1)_____
(2)_____
(3)_____
(4)_____

The features I like best in this issue of PHOTOPLAY are:

(1)_____
(2)_____
(3)_____
(4)_____
(5)_____
(6)_____

NAME_____
ADDRESS_____AGE_____

Paste this ballot on a postal card and send it to Readers' Poll Editor, Box 1374, Grand Central Station, N. Y. 17, N. Y.

(Continued from page 82)
ly and we all found ourselves working a little longer than usual one morning. When lunch was mentioned, we realized we'd have to cut it short, so I hustled my belongings together, plus Mr. Dean, and we started for the commissary. I hadn't noticed, but Jimmy, in his uncanny ability to sense people's needs and problems, did. Standing off by the camera were three women, one shyly pushed her companion toward us.

"Can I do something for you?" Jimmy asked.

"Would you mind—posing for a picture for us—" she hesitantly inquired.

"Sure," obliged Jimmy.

He hammed it up with me, stood on one foot, clowned around, posed and postulated until their hearts were content. A shutter bug himself, he offered composition suggestions, pointed out camera angles and gave tips on lighting—while I starved.

When I badgered him, in a deathlike whisper, about my hunger, he looked surprised. Then, like a little boy, said, "Aw, we're having fun."

Despite stories, Jimmy Dean does have fun. Acting can be fun. In "Rebel" I play my first grown-up film role and I also get my first kiss—from Jimmy. There's no sense denying it, I was a little nervous.

"You look green," Jimmy complimented me while we waited for the signal to begin the love scene. "And you know how green photographs in color."

I managed a grin, I think. I really can't remember. I felt like a fighter before a match—let's go in and get it over with. Jimmy was saying something, but all I could think of was, "Is this the way—should I do it the way I rehearsed? Maybe that was too smooth. Maybe I should fumble a little."

"Come on," coaxed Jimmy. Suddenly I realized we were on. Complete silence. Then—"Roll," shouted the director and the camera began clicking.

It was Jimmy's move. I listened to him and felt almost inspired. He played it so gently, he brought out the best in me—under the circumstances. Then came the kiss. I heard the director call "Cut," but the cameras seemed to be grinding away. I didn't exactly know what to do, but I had no choice. Jimmy held and held and held. Might as well enjoy it, he kidded afterwards as I turned from green to red. But the nervous spell was broken. His kidding did it; I relaxed and the rest of the shooting went like a breeze!

Comes a big dramatic scene, Jimmy's the opposite. Boy, is he intent. I didn't know what he was going through the first time he prepared for an important scene.

"Hi, Jimmy, what are you doing?" I asked. He mumbled something—and completely unlike him—made it plain he wanted no conversation. He was kind of working himself into the role. Flaying his arms about, going through a bicycle-type movement with his legs. "I'm concentrating," is all he said.

"By doing that?" I asked, sure that he'd be worn out before he began the scene. Patiently, he put up with me. "It gets me in form."

I left him. By the time the cameras rolled, he was no longer Jimmy Dean. He was the confused, rebellious, unwanted *Jim* of "Rebel."

Something went wrong, lights or camera position, and the director called cut to the scene. Jimmy stood where he left off, motionless. Then—and I remember this clearly—one of the fellows went up to him and started to kid. Wow! Was Jimmy furious. He made it clear, between breaks, no talk. He has to stay in "character." This is true even when it takes a whole day to complete a scene.

Later that afternoon, Jimmy was scheduled to finish the sequence. It was hot, the cast had worked hard all day and most of us were exhausted. I had one idea—shared by the rest of the cast and crew—let's go home. "For those who aren't in the last scene, scram," came the welcome reprieve.

For some reason, we hung around for a few minutes—and I'll never forget this experience. Cameras rolled, the set quieted and Jimmy began—to go into one of the most tragic, heartbreaking scenes I've ever seen. One by one, members of the cast returned and stood, gripped by the tremendous emotional impact of the moment. We were carried away. At the end, not one of us could honestly confess there weren't tears in our eyes. It was electrifying.

Director Nick Ray asserts Jimmy is the finest actor for his age he's ever directed, also adds that, contrary to reports, he's a breeze to handle. For his fine work and cooperation, the production staff gifted Jimmy with a bicycle. As for me, I'm greatly indebted to him for his stimulation and help. There's no question, Dean's great talent.

For the future, Jimmy hopes to direct. For the present, he hopes to act, to vary his roles, to grow as an individual, learn as a professional. He studies acting techniques, writing, photography and the stock market! To direct and produce, he grins slyly, you need money, too. With his new Warners contract, he'll do nine films in the next six years. He'd like to return to the stage, maybe try *Hamlet* some day. This year, he may wind up playing *Romeo* for a color featurette for Warners. Talks about doing the life of Harry Greb, the middleweight fighter of years ago, too. He and stand-in Mush Callahan, the champion ex-fighter, were forever "getting into shape," for the role.

Jimmy's 5 foot 10 and looks short ("because I slump," he says), but he's amazingly strong. Always a good athlete, he keeps in trim by swimming, playing volleyball, sailing and deep-sea diving. Ask, "Tennis anyone—boxing, riding, baseball or basketball"—and you've got a partner. But his chief love, I think, is bullfighting. Someday he wants to get into the ring himself.

I don't mean to imply that Jimmy isn't a character. He is—but a pretty interesting one. He'll hardly say a word in a crowd until someone mentions architecture, hi-fi, sports-car racing or music. Then try and stop him. Question him about himself, he'll answer straight. Show some ulterior motive, he'll clam up even if you're a V.P. in charge of world news. He can talk about carburetors in one breath, discuss William James' pragmatic philosophy in another and be off on the subject of design two minutes later. If he has a free moment, chances are you'll find him behind a serious book or buried underneath a pile of travel folders. Mention music and he'll go mad—over native African rhythms, Beethoven's Ninth or progressive jazz. Take a drive with him, and you'll be tuned in to classical music. Jimmy studied violin as a child, has picked up his studies again with Leonard Rosenman, who was his roommate in New York and is now a Warners composer. Invite him to Sunday dinner, he'll accept. What's more, he'll win your parents over with charm and intelligence.

An oddball, did you ask? Yes, if you call talent odd. A weirdy? Maybe, if you don't like individualists. Sullen? Never! Jimmy Dean's too busy living to sulk.

THE END

Jim (James Dean, l.) ist neu in der Stadt und legt sich gleich mit dem Anführer (Corey Allan) einer Jugendbande an („...denn sie wissen nicht, was sie tun", SAT.1, 22.10 Uhr)

'Rebel without a Cause'

● **James Dean** To commemorate the 50th anniversary of Dean's death the Proud Central gallery in London is exhibiting a collection of rare and unseen pictures of the iconic actor by photographer Phil Stern, from 29 April to 24 June. The National Film Theatre is showing all three of his features, including an extended run of 'Rebel without a Cause', which will then travel to cinemas nationwide from 6 to 28 May

„...denn sie wissen nicht, was sie tun" (1955). James Deans Outfit beeinflußte eine ganze Generation (unten).

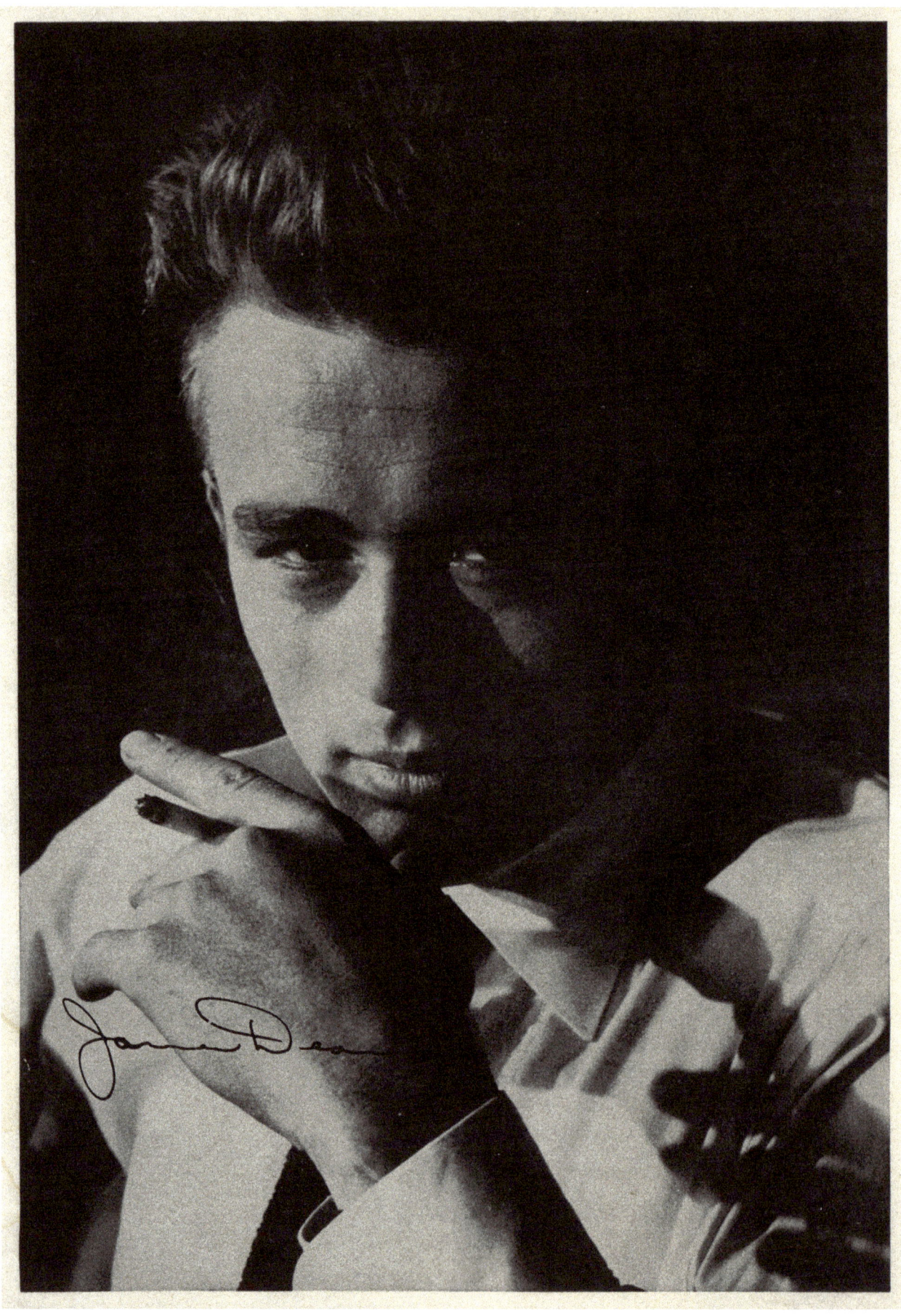

Cult movies
REBEL WITHOUT A CAUSE

DOUGLAS McVAY

THE GREATEST ART transcends its era, and rises above the ephemerality of fashion. This is especially true of the cinema, despite the frequent accusation that films 'date' more quickly and embarrassingly than works in any other medium. In fact, the finest movies since, at any rate, the coming of sound continue to seem fresh and vitally relevant today. Certainly that is the case where the first two pictures starring the late James Dean—*East of Eden* and, above all, *Rebel Without A Cause*—are concerned. Although Dean remains conceivably the archetype of the 'cult idol', his cult has diminished since the end of the 1950s, because the more stoical, cynical or apathetic attitudes to living and conduct which have dominated the '60s and '70s (and have been mirrored by the playing techniques of most male film actors) are alien to the brand of uninhibited emotion which, in his first two movies in particular, he so electrifyingly incarnated. Yet, whilst he may now be far less of a cult-figure, his performances in *Eden* and *Rebel* seem in 1977 even more unmistakably the performances of a great screen artist than they did back in the mid-1950s. His Method mannerisms may long since have lost their novelty, as have Brando's: but these mannerisms, like Brando's, were always just the top-dressing of his histrionic talent; beneath them lay a virtuosity of cinematic nuances and timing, together with an authentic ability to communicate the heights and depths and subtleties of a wide range of feelings. And both *East of Eden* and *Rebel Without A Cause* (companion-pieces to some extent, in their study of a young man's struggles to escape from the constrictions of his family and to find his identity via a sexual fulfilment) effortlessly rise above the limitations of '50s censorship, to emerge in the late '70s as intensely gripping and moving dramas, stylistically audacious and inventive, with superlative portrayals from their casts. *Eden* is arguably Elia Kazan's finest work as a director. And *Rebel* is surely Nicholas Ray's masterpiece.

The film's themes, style and tone are established visually and verbally right from the credit-title scene, in which Jim Stark (James Dean) tipsily composes himself in sleep in the nocturnal street beside a dropped toy monkey, solicitously covering the toy with a sheet of paper, then drowsily tucking his hands between his legs in an automatic gesture of self-protection and desire for physical comfort: these opening moments, in addition to their delicate psychological observation, immediately display a bold feeling for the use of colour and CinemaScope framing; low-key lighting and close-shot grouping instantly achieve a 'masking' of parts of the wide screen in order to make it a dramatic medium; the rest of the movie is frequently to reflect the same pictorial approach (with the characteristically sombre palette of Warner Color assisting in the fulfilment of this intention).

The subsequent scene at the police-station 'Juvenile Hall' forms a masterly example of exposition: the dilemmas of Jim, his next-door neighbour Judy, and the rather younger boy Plato (all three of them students at Dawson High), are cogently stated by a powerful blending of imagery and dialogue: whilst the trio are from the outset significantly connected, not only by visual composition and camera-movement, but by pieces of business and gesture. Judy's sense of alienation from people in general and her father in particular (deriving from her father's unease at her sexual development and his lurking attraction towards her, which drives him to adopt a harshly puritanical stance of disapproval and rejection when she makes overtures of daughterly affection) is crystallised by her bitter murmur of 'I'll never get close to anyone', her isolation accentuated by a close-up. Her cry from the heart is meaningfully echoed by Plato's 'Nobody can help me': his own separation from his parents, and especially from the uncaring wealthy father whom he vainly idolises, is increasingly prompting him to commit ominous acts of violence (such as killing puppies). Jim shows concern for Plato by lending him his crimson jacket, and erotic interest in Judy by secretly retaining her dropped powder-compact: both the jacket and the compact are to become motifs in the film's intricate visual texture.

Jim's own personality (its dangerous elements as well as its sympathetic aspects), together with his own domestic difficulties and strain in all human relationships, are explored during this lengthy episode at Juvenile Hall through a rich variety of means. His tendency towards mischievousness is mirrored in his imitation of the police-car siren and his shadow-boxing of an irate cop (this mime also conveying his capacity for a swift physical motion). His tipsy condition is communicated by his giggling, and by his wild rubbing of a finger against his nose in a drunk's uncontrolled manner. His underlying seriousness and loneliness surface when he clutches the toy monkey and pleads 'Can I keep it?': while the suffocating influence of his family is

Youngsters from unhappy homes, victims of the 'fifties generation gap: Jim (James Dean) and Judy (Natalie Wood) find comfort and consolation in each others company

Films & Filming, August 1977

> The eleventh in an occasional series on the films that may not be included on the 'all-time greats' lists, but nevertheless have a cult following, and are held in nostalgic esteem; as well as being essential terms of reference

apparent from the moment that his father, mother and maternal grandmother arrive to bail him out, as the two women henpeck his Dad and possessively fawn over Jim himself. Jim reveals his awareness of his father's complacent, weak side, as he eyes him in his evening dress and quietly asks 'Were you having a ball, Dad?'. A little later, he reduces his grandmother to a scowl by remarking to her with deceptive gentleness, 'Tell one more lie, and you'll be turned to stone'. And the three adults' petty friction is encapsulated at one stage in the framing of the mean, reproving face of Jim's grandma between his bickering parents. The violence within Jim erupts first in an abortive physical attack upon the no-nonsense but not unfriendly police officer in charge of his case, and then in his taking-out of his bottled ferocity on the officer's desk at the cop's suggestion: Jim's mixture of thoughtfulness, self-mocking humour and genuinely neurotic ferocity is strongly underlined, as he contemplates the desk in pensive amusement before punching it furiously several times and finally wringing his hand in anguish. After this outburst, however, he is able to explain his domestic situation in calm and considered terms which win from the officer an understanding response.

Jim's sense of being stifled by the conflicts and demands of the three grownups in his home receives further crisp illustration in the sequence which follows when, the next morning, he prepares to leave his house for his first day at a new school. His chance encounter with Judy, their walk together and talk together, finds Nicholas Ray, cameraman Ernest Haller, and players James Dean and Natalie Wood enhancing Stewart Stern's perceptive script, achieving a crucial development in the friendship which tentatively flowers between the couple, and providing the movie with one of its most spontaneous-seeming yet carefully realised dialogue scenes. In contrast to the opening nocturnal exterior episode and the rather grim interior lighting at the police station (or, come to that, the slightly oppressive comfort of the Stark household interior as shown during the breakfast-time sequence), this walk to school possesses a liberating feeling of air and light and greenery, of matching hope and even gaiety in the behaviour of Jim and Judy: this mood is perfectly captured by one image of Judy bending

James Dean: the hero figure for lonely youth in the 'fifties, symbolising the hurt and frustration, the pent-up emotions, the misunderstandings, the need for love that many grew to live without. On screen, Dean had many affinities with The Little Prince *(a book which, not surprisingly, was one of Dean's favourites), seeking that which 'is invisible to the eye'*

her head to light a cigarette, her green-dressed figure to the left of the frame, the delicately-hued street and trees stretching away behind her to occupy the remainder of the screen. Yet this impression of visual freedom and brightness is soon to prove illusory: and indeed, the cheerful banter between Judy and Jim as they stroll is quickly mingled with hints of their continuing pessimism and inner tensions.

Ray establishes a marvellous pictorial equivalent of the banter, as Jim leaps up momentarily behind a wall and then, equally momentarily drops down again (while trying to attract Judy's attention): or as Judy affects to ignore Jim and starts to walk away right off the frame's left-hand edge; or as the camera reverse-tracks gently when the pair at length saunter down the street towards the lens. Their dialogue is partly concerned with marked by a steady accumulation of revelatory small detail, as well as by a growing dramatic intensity. Plato re-enters the action, strengthening his friendship with Jim (the younger boy's need for an older male figure to hero-worship being unobtrusively emphasised by the photo of Alan Ladd pinned up in his locker). The lecture at the planetarium allows the film to make clear to us, and (painfully) to Jim, the close relationship which apparently exists between Judy and her fellow-pupil Buzz: Jim, seated behind the couple, notices their side-by-side proximity and the way in which Buzz casually touches her. And the script's preoccupation with metaphysics recurs with heightened force, in the starry images and the lecturer's phrases, which place the youngsters and their problems *sub specie aeternitatis* as 'an episode of little consequence'. Yet, whilst the listen- over this vision of planetary disintegration, followed by Plato's bitter question to him (apropos the lecturer's sententious commentary), 'What does *he* know of "Man alone"?' . . .

The subsequent persecution of Jim by Buzz and his friends outside the planetarium is lent urgency and sinisterly restless suspense by the way Ray deploys his camera to prowl with the characters, cutting on movement, and varying the angle to encompass overhead shots. This tense, hovering camera technique (achieving an impression of taut, impending violence, by combining staccato editing with pans, tracks and tilts) is supported by Rosenman's nervy, dissonant, rapid, minatorily thumping and rumbling sound-track music. The director also supplies some eloquent corporeal and gestural detail. Judy is yanked, at one point, by Buzz to stand with him and his gang,

The outsider trying to fit into a new high school in a new neighbourhood, the victim of his parents' paranoias: James Dean caught between takes for the early sequence at the Planetarium, which causes him to take part in a 'chicken-run'

previous events: there is an abrupt, jolting close-up of Judy's disconcerted face in mid-walk when Jim tells her that he has seen her before (he is referring to their presence at Juvenile Hall, but he doesn't say so, and she didn't recall him at the police station). In the main, though, their chat is made up of colloquial, adolescent existentialism and metaphysics, with the jaunty, mock-carefree teenage slang and joshing epigrams betraying their interior uncertainty and disturbance: 'Who lives?'; 'Life can be beautiful'; 'Stop the world!'; 'Life is crushing in on me'. When Judy teases him with 'You know, I bet you're a real yo-yo', Jim as they part mutters (a shade sourly, but half-seriously and with unconscious prophecy) 'I love you too' . . .

The film's evocation of the school atmosphere and pupils forms the next extended section of the narrative, and is ing, watching students may wryly acknowledge their mortal transience, still they know that life must go on (and 'can be beautiful'), and that their emotional yearnings, though 'of little consequence' in the long view of time, have a relevance and importance to them here and now. So Jim endeavours to win laughter and friends in his new peer-group by his mooing impersonation of Taurus the bull (only winning, to his disenchantment, the students' derision and potential hostility instead). The explosion in lurid red light which forms the lecture's climax, whilst the most vivid chromatic effect in the movie, is scarcely intended by its vividness to convey any optimism. The swelling, thundering chords of Rosenman's score during this climax reflect the true, apocalyptic flavour of the imagery. And cosmic and personal fates intertwine, in the close-up of Jim's face as he broods her face unsure in its half-assumed expression of hard, bright mischief as she appears to join the others in taunting Jim. Her legs dangle enticingly in close-shot now, while Buzz knifes Jim's car-tyres: her body thus reminds us alluringly and tantalisingly—as it reminds Jim—that she is currently Buzz's girl. Jim stretches slowly, like an uncoiling spring, as he realises what Buzz has done: he reacts, too, by criticising Judy in a harsh murmur about the bad company she is keeping. The outcome is the 'sticking game' and then the fight with blades between himself and Buzz, with Buzz challenging him to a 'chicken-run' (Jim assuring him with fake-nonchalant, throwaway confidence, 'It's all I ever do'). As the gang disperses, the film's fondness for mimicry is again evident (in the imitation of Hitler by one of the gang-members, as he ribs an adult who breaks up the group quarrel): and

Jim's typical self-deprecating irony crops up once more (along with his penchant for shadow-boxing), as he inquires 'Say, Plato—what *is* this chicken-run?', whereupon the sequence ends.

The staging of the knife-duel between Jim and Buzz out-of-doors is yet another instance of the way, throughout the picture, in which ostensibly liberating space and light turn out to be merely elements in relentlessly confining feuds. And, just as the interior of Jim's home has only a faintly claustrophobic air of respectability and relative affluence, so Plato's home is shown to have an atmosphere of significantly impersonal, 'unlived-in' (and, by extension, 'unloved-in') luxury, to which the presence of the anxiously lamenting maidservant—in the absence of the much-needed parents—simply contributes further. Similarly, Judy's home, if slightly brighter, is far about 'a question of honour' (the upcoming chicken-run). And the phrase 'stand up' is to be another key motif in the film's dramatisation and resolution of its tensions.

The chicken-run, a car-race between Jim and Buzz towards a cliff-edge, with the first driver to leap to safety being branded as coward or 'chicken', is arguably the movie's summit, and one of the greatest sequences of the American cinema. It begins with a long-shot of the cars gathering on the bluff at dusk, their headlamps fitfully gleaming, Rosenman's music trumpeting at once excitingly and forbiddingly. Subsequent overhead images of the adolescents gazing down into the dark waters from the bluff-edge reinforce the sombre, menacing majesty of the scene: and a symbolic, again metaphysical quality informs their remarks about the drop ('It's the edge . . . the end'). The and Judy butterfly-kiss quickly three times, after Judy has given Buzz mud to smear on his hands in order to gain a firm grip: Jim—secretly stroking her powder-compact—asks her 'Me too?', rapidly reassuring her that it's only mud he wants; a brief, half-amused, half-attracted pause between them nevertheless ensues after she obliges his request . . .

These preliminaries culminate in the brilliant theatricality and ritual of the cars all 'hitting their lights', to lend the location a kind of arc-lit staginess (enhanced, once more, by Leonard Rosenman's trumpetingly annunciatory musical flourishes, like an orchestra heralding a variety act). The thrill of the event is epitomised, perhaps, in five shots of Judy, as she stands in the midst of the encircling cars and prepares to give Buzz and Jim the signal to go. First the camera

Moose (Nick Adams) trails Jim around the corridors of the Planetarium

Judy and Jim, drawn to each other more by mutual alienation from their parents; the consolation they find from each others company gives them the strength to understand 'the older generation'

from chic: and her personal predicament is shrewdly stressed in several ways, from glimpses of childhood toys, and the touching love displayed for her by her young brother, to a confrontation with her father that synthesises their relationship within a single image, in a three-shot of Judy trying to caress her Dad affectionately as she stands by him at the meal-table, while he resists the buried incestuous temptation which she has come to hold for him, by ignoring her and determinedly concentrating his verbal and physical affections on the 'safe' figure of her brother; when she persists in her daughterly overtures, he angrily slaps her face. Jim's own relationship with his father is sharply elaborated on by the script as he reacts in inarticulate shame to the sight of his aproned Dad kneeling to retrieve spilt crockery, murmuring to him to stand up, and asking his advice preliminaries to the run are memorable. There's the poignant irony in the exchanges between Jim and Buzz: the way Buzz casually stretches out his hand to clasp Jim's, while announcing 'I'm Buzz Gunderson'; Buzz's 'You know something? I *like* you', Jim's reply 'Then why are we doing this?', and Buzz's existentialist answer 'You got to do *something!*' There is Jim's nimble tumble out of his car-door in a 'trial run': Judy and Plato watch, and Judy hesitantly sounds out Plato as to what Jim is like; Plato fantasises that Jim plans to take him hunting, and then tells her that Jim is 'sincere', to which she responds thoughtfully 'That's the main thing'. (Later in the film, she comments of her own family that 'Nobody's sincere'). Then there is the little piece of dead-pan erotic rivalry and mutually acknowledged, charming humour, as Jim wistfully watches Buzz tracks quickly back from her; then cuts to a long-shot of her; then gives us a high-angle shot of her jumping up in the air as she swings down her arms to make the 'off' signal; then another long-shot of her. And lastly, in a classic image of hysteria and exhilaration, the camera rushes towards her with the advancing cars, as she stands poised and facing them in medium-shot, her features exultant, before the vehicles sweep past her and the lens; and she—as soon as the autos have zoomed by on either side of her—turns her back on the camera and rushes away in their wake towards the bluff-edge, skirt swirling, arms frantically pumping . . .

Intercut close-ups now follow: Buzz vainly grinning and flamboyantly combing his hair; Jim looking across at him; Buzz piratically sticking the comb between his teeth; Buzz's coat-belt catch-

19

ing in the door-handle; his face reacting in terror; Jim responding to the bluff's approach, flipping his cigarette over the edge of the car and hurtling out of the door; the comb falling from Buzz's mouth as he screams; a view of the drop taken from behind his shoulder, the rocks and water rising up to meet him as his jalopy plunges downwards; a long-shot of Buzz's car hitting and exploding (all to the jagged discords and fast rhythms of Rosenman's soundtrack scoring, which ideally complements Ray's montage). The aftermath is in stunning contrast: Jim's giggling, gasping, unknowing arrival amongst the other teenagers who are gazing down in numbed horror at the crashed automobile; his query of 'Where's Buzz?', and silent shock when he learns the truth; the close-shots of Judy looking over the edge in horror, Jim beside her but slightly apart from her, then Jim slowly stretching out his hand, she slowly stretching out hers, the other adolescents melting away at this hushed moment of final emotional commitment between the pair; their finger-tips meet, and she turns, to meet his gaze, which mingles contrition with an attempt at helpless self-exculpation and a tacit reminder to her that it is futile to go on staring down at the wreck; he shepherds her away from the precipice—while Plato, who has stood watching in the background of the image, follows the couple. The three youthful protagonists, their destinies and presences linked by chance, connected from the film's opening sequence, have now at last come fully together, to snatch a fleeting shared warmth of affection, and to play out their tragic drama to the finish.

The movie sustains its control right to the end: whether in tiny touches such as the moment after Jim drives Judy home from the bluff, when he pulls her slightly towards him, figuratively as well as literally, by holding the ends of her head-scarf as she gets out of the car, in a gently masterful gesture of attraction and protection, before he asks her if she's all right; or in the full-scale showdown between Jim and his parents. The latter sequence, which itself includes such telling, credible behavioural flashes as Jim's rubbing of a milk-bottle against his exhausted face, also powerfully develops the 'stand up' motif in the relationship between Jim and his father: when his affectingly quiet plea for moral guidance and help, 'Dad—stand up for me', meets with no response, Jim reacts with a near-impassive and irresolute pause, then whirls on his physically subjugated Dad, yanking him upright, then flinging him down with the repeated cry 'Stand-UP!' . . . This scene climaxes, though, in the only moment in the entire picture which strikes me as over-contrived: Jim just happens to see a painting with its back towards him, turns it round, finds that it's a portrait of his mother, and shoves his foot through it. The act has an undeniable shock-effect, and is certainly relevant to the movie's indictment of matriarchal excesses in general and transatlantic Momism in particular. Yet for me it has a too explicit, rigged symbolism.

The sequence between Jim and Judy when he drives up to her home and finds her seated outside is, on the other hand, distinguished by a moving delicacy, in his brief light kiss to her, her whispered 'Why did you do that?', and his muttered rejoinder (not looking at her) of 'I felt like it'. Her wondering murmur, 'Your lips are soft', has the self-consciousness of an appropriate compliment learned from romantic magazine stories—but is none the less touching for that. Ray films in two-shot as Jim suggests that they go to Plato's discovered, deserted mansion: on the right of the frame, gazing inwards at her, Jim assures her, aware of the sexual possibilities in their plan and of her probable qualms, 'You can trust me, Judy'; on the left of the frame, in profile, gazing inwards at him, she willingly acknowledges her trust.

In the long episode at the mansion, with the couple soon joined by Plato himself, the improvisatory techniques in writing, acting and direction, which have so often rewardingly characterised *Rebel Without A Cause*, perhaps reach their peak. The script's liking for mimicry is put to witty but underlyingly astringent service. The trio mock their parents' pretensions, with Judy adopting an accent and manner which parody Katharine Hepburn, whilst Jim does a vocal impression of Mr Magoo (as Magoo is 'voiced' on the soundtrack of the UPA cartoons by none other than Jim Backus, who plays Jim's father in *Rebel* . . .). There is a curious, painful little echo, in Jim's Magoo-accented remark that the way for parents to treat kids is to 'drown 'em like puppies', of the cop's early question to Plato at the police-station ('Why did you kill those puppies?'). In this mimicry, the three children not only satirise pompous adults who despair of and mistreat their offspring, but half-consciously comment on their own respective domestic misfortunes and generation-gap frictions (Judy yelps in her lampoon, clinching the argument flippantly yet mordantly, 'Parents don't *talk* to their children—they just *tell* them!'). The discussion of parents also extends, if only by implication at first, to the quasi-parental position which Judy and Jim now find themselves in with regard to Plato: as well, of course, as the burgeoning *Romeo and Juliet*-style love between Jim and Judy *apart from* Plato. This sense of classical love-idyll is beautifully felt when Plato himself lights and lifts a candelabrum, and looks up (the camera tilting) to see the couple standing close together: their pose has a distinct air of 'star-cross'd lovers' formalisation about it; Plato, viewing the pair not as lovers but as substitute parents, derives great pleasure from the tableau.

The ripening passion between Judy and Jim is even more skilfully conveyed, however, after they leave the sleeping Plato and explore the rest of the house. Ray holds the couple in a close two-shot

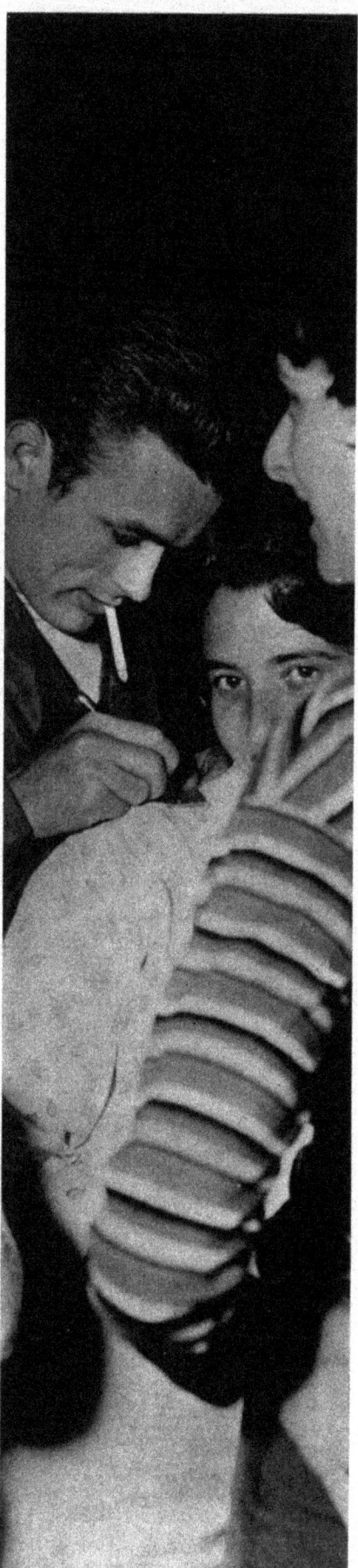

The Idol: James Dean signing autographs

as they lie side by side, and Judy is driven to ask (impelled by this relaxed, quasi-domestic closeness to Jim) 'Is this what it's like to be in love?', going on to whisper, 'I love somebody. All this time I've been looking for someone to love *me*—and now I love somebody, and it's so easy. Why is it easy now?'. (At this moment of amorous avowal, one recalls Dixon Steele's comparable confession to Laurel Gray in Ray's 1950 film *In A Lonely Place*, which begins 'All my life I've been searching for someone . . .'). Jim can't answer her very coherently, and indeed doesn't try to, because he doesn't wish to: he realises that this moment of mutual giving is too rare and precious to be marred by needless, pointless over-verbalisation. Instead, after simply murmuring 'It's easy for me too', he accepts her hesitant mouth's questing overtures, passively yet with a gentle strength, in a slow and loving open-lipped kiss, with Leonard Rosenman's exquisite main-title melody furnishing the dimension of emotion which words cannot communicate. Both the music and the playing here remind us of James Dean as Cal and Julie Harris as Abra, in their similarly hushed and languorous love-scenes to another seductive Rosenman main-theme in the earlier Kazan *East of Eden*.

This image of consummated happiness is, alas, all too transitory: the spirit of menace, exemplified in the nightmare shock-image when Jim's father (drawn to his front door by the taunting voices of members of Buzz's gang) finds a live chicken hanging squawking upside-down from the lintel, now disrupts the lovers' idyll, as the kiss between Judy and Jim is bleakly succeeded by a visual transition to the clinking chains in the hands of Buzz's cronies as they stand over Plato's wakening form. Ray employs a hectically mobile camera and staccato editing, with Rosenman's score providing an appositely frenetic accompaniment, as Plato snatches up a long hose-pipe and wields it like a lash, swinging it at his attackers in the empty swimming-pool of the mansion.

Jim's torment at the film's finale is made doubly poignant by the finesse with which, a little earlier, he has coaxed Plato into giving up the revolver which the boy possesses: he doesn't immediately return the weapon to Plato after covertly removing the ammunition; instead he uses it to lure Plato towards safety, abruptly seeming to remember his promise to give it back and handing it to him with an 'Oh—here' only after he sees that the lure is working. Ray employs one further convulsive judder of the lens when, after Jim's desperate dive for the fleeing Plato's ankles has failed, Plato is shot down by the misguided police in the glare of the police-car headlights (*cf* the use of headlamps in the chicken-run sequence), and staggers in the foreground of the image whilst beyond him Jim and Judy look on aghast. All Jim's agony is articulated in his scream to the cops of 'I got the

The Loner: walking on the streets in New York

The Hero: both for Judy and the love-seeking Plato (Sal Mineo)

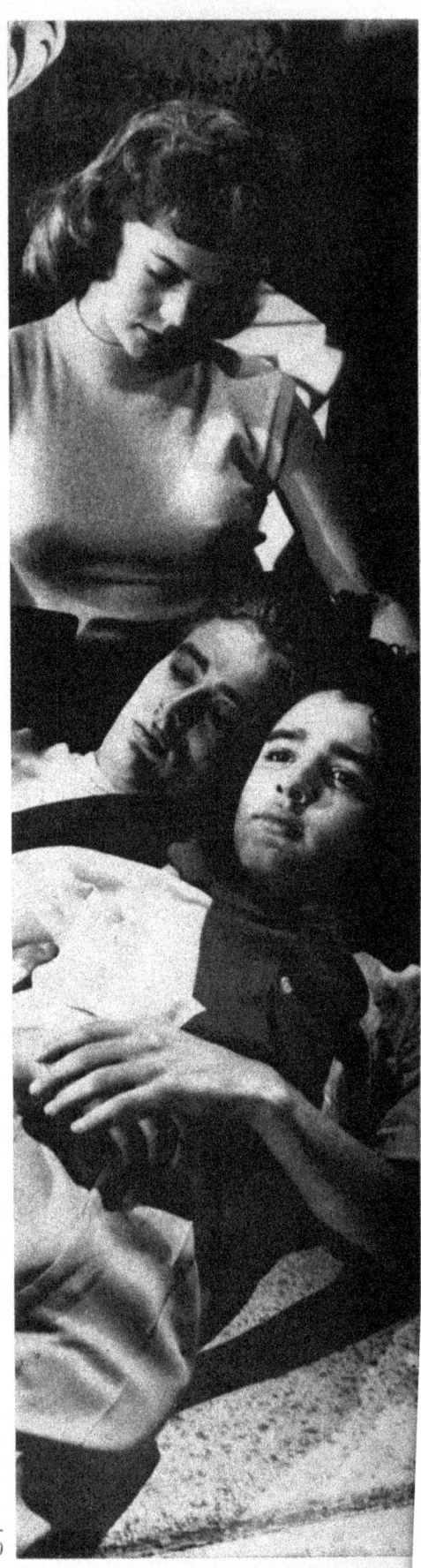

Plato shows Jim and Judy around the deserted mansion that has become his emergency retreat: mocking parental pretensions whilst seeking an almost idyllic lifestyle that is an ironic parallel of what they are rejecting

bullets!', as he flings open his arms and unclenches his hand to show the ammunition in his palm: and in his sinking to his knees, sobbing, by Plato's corpse, his head turned away from both the body and the camera. The tragic irony is subtly strengthened by visual and aural echoes: in, for example, Jim's hysterically tearful, bereaved renewal of his previous laughter, as he notices again that Plato had absent-mindedly put on one red sock and one blue. ('*I've* done that, haven't you?', he had earlier remarked to Judy in the mansion, during their shared, kindly mirth as they looked down at the sleeping boy: and she had equally kindly accepted the fact).

A more substantial and complicated pictorial echo occurs, also, as Jim zips up the red jacket which he had lent to Plato at the police-station, making a gift of the windcheater to his dead friend ('He was always so cold . . .', he murmurs). In this pervasively dark-toned movie, even the crimson jerkin, though it several times affords a splash of superficial brightness, ultimately acquires inextricable overtones of violence, blood and death, both by its gory tint and its eventual shrouding of Plato's cadaver. There is, too, a sensitive visual analogy when Jim's father drapes his own jacket around his son's shoulders: just as Jim expressed his concern and generosity towards Plato from the film's start by giving him the windcheater, so this similar gesture by Frank Stark supports his verbal promise to Jim as he helps him to stand up ('I'll stand up with you—I'll try to be as strong as you want me to be'), and completes the script's 'stand up' motif on a note of tentative affirmation. Jim's mother watches this cementing of the father-and-son bond with a residual trace of the resentment which has always marked her battle with her husband for Jim's affection. But on her face now, put there by the tension, the tragedy, and her relief that Jim has survived, there dawns a reluctant but definite acceptance of the new reconciliation between her son and her spouse.

Whilst the ensuing exchange of beaming smiles between the parents (as they do a double-take on learning that at long last their loner son has got himself a girlfriend) is a shade too readily forgetful of Plato's recent death and Jim's grief, this shot should not be criticised as a facile, upbeat ending, but taken simply as one more pictorial index to the psychology of Jim's mother and father. In any case, the movie's concluding images reassert the preceding, pervading mood of loss, of a classical tragedy: the anguished features of the maidservant mourning Plato; the camera shifting to an overhead position to emphasise the tone of formally measured, inexorable catharsis; the high-angle view of the fateful location, with the slowly departing line of police cars acting as a sort of funeral cortège, and the stone façade of the planetarium amalgamating visual impressions—of temple and church and even morgue; the final glimpse of a solitary man walking in the opposite direction to the file of cars (as if to restore order to the scene of chaos, and to achieve thereby a complete and proper purging by pity and terror). And Rosenman's secondary theme in his score (a solemn, dragging, fate-filled, dirge-like refrain) rounds out this purgative sensation. One comes away from any re-viewing of this masterpiece feeling emotionally drained but aesthetically uplifted: in the cinema, only a small handful of movies from any country can be said to produce such an impact. *Rebel Without A Cause* must be ranked, in this respect, only with *East of Eden*, Cukor's *A Star is Born*, and Chaplin's *Limelight*, amongst the American films of the 1950s that I have seen.

REBEL WITHOUT A CAUSE
1955

Production Company, Warner Bros. Produced by David Weisbart. Directed by Nicholas Ray. Screenplay by Stewart Stern, from an adaptation by Irving Shulman of a story by Nicholas Ray. Director of photography, Ernest Haller (Warner Color; CinemaScope). Music by Leonard Rosenman. Art director, Malcolm Bert. Editor, William Ziegler. 111 mins.

Cast: JAMES DEAN (Jim Stark), NATALIE WOOD (Judy), SAL MINEO (Plato), JIM BACKUS (Jim's Father), ANN DORAN (Jim's Mother), COREY ALLEN (Buzz), WILLIAM HOPPER (Judy's Father), ROCHELLE HUDSON (Judy's Mother), VIRGINIA BRISSAC (Jim's Grandmother), NICK ADAMS (Moose), DENNIS HOPPER (Goon), JACK SIMMONS (Cookie), MARIETTA CANTY (Plato's Maid), JACK GRINNAGE (Chick), BEVERLY LONG (Helen), STEFFI SIDNEY (Mil), FRANK MAZZOLA (Crunch), TOM BERNARD (Harry), CLIFFORD MORRIS (Cliff), IAN WOLFE (Lecturer), EDWARD PLATT (Ray).

'You're tearing me apart': Jim berates his parents (Jim Backus and Ann Doran) for continually bickering with each other after he has been arrested on a drunken charge

THE OUTSIDER: 'I'M AN INTENSE LITTLE DEVIL'

James Dean in the Porsche which took him into immortality

NATALIE WOOD:
almost a sweetheart
....almost a sister

■ When Natalie Wood told us how she met Jimmy Dean, we decided that here was one story that needed no editing. In her own words, Natalie relates the strange yet meaningful incident which marked the beginning of their friendship. Natalie was neither a sweetheart nor a sister to Jimmy. She was a little of both . . . and something more.

Later in this book, in a revealing story by Nick Adams, you will read how Natalie took the terrible news of Jimmy's crash, and how her great courage allowed her to stifle her grief long enough to meet a responsibility to an audience of forty million Americans.

"The rehearsal for a television play we were in together, was held in an old theatre in downtown Los Angeles, a rarely visited area for film stars. Everyone arrived on time except Jimmy.

"The longer we waited, the more frightened I became. And as I went through the script, I found that he was going to make love to me.

"After a half hour with everyone watching the door for Dean's arrival, Jimmy came in—through a large window of the building.

"He came in and all I could think of was 'He sure knows how to make an entrance!' He was dressed in a dirty torn sport shirt and he had a large safety pin across the front of his pants—jeans, of course. He jumped down to the floor, looked around, picked up a script from the table and sat in a corner. The director said, 'C'mon, Jimmy, sit next to Natalie. You're going to have to make love to this girl.'

"Jimmy didn't even look up. He just grunted. After we rehearsed for a while, Jimmy suddenly got up and came over to sit next to me.

"At noon, we broke for lunch, but since that area of town was strange to us, everyone wandered off in different directions.

"I hadn't gone more than a block when I realized someone was following me. I turned and there was Jimmy. He didn't even look at me but kept walking—right by me. He got ahead of me a little and then turned and said, 'Well, are you coming or not?' We found a little diner and Jimmy was silent for a while and then in the middle of his sandwich he said, 'I know you. You're a child actor.' I said that was true, but it's a lot better than acting like a child. He didn't get it for a moment. Then he started to laugh. Then I started to laugh and that's how our wonderful friendship began."

James Dean Anniversary Book, 1956 (Dell)

JAMES DEAN

"Well, here I is! In the grand old city of New York.... Wish you folks were here to see this town."

JAMES DEAN

◀ **POUT TIME:** Jimmy always looked good in black leather, wearing it in an age in which it was always associated with delinquency.

A page from George Perry's enjoyable book from 2005. It's packed with photographs from the Dean family's collection © Dorling Kindersley

Jim (Foto James Dean) kommt mit seinen Eltern nicht zurecht. Er schließt sich einer Bande an, bei der er gefährliche Mutproben bestehen muß („... denn sie wissen nicht, was sie tun", ARD, 20.15 Uhr)

Films Illustrated January '76

Letters to the Editor

JAMES DEAN'S DURABILITY

I would like to reply to the letter of Caroline Carmody (November) on the subject of James Dean.

I agree with her completely that Dean would have evolved out of the role of actor and into the broader role of director-actor. The evidence for this is not overwhelming since he died so young, but it is clearly there, as I have tried to show in my book *From "Blind Run" to James Dean: The Filming of "Rebel Without a Cause"*. In the book, I analyse a sequence from *Rebel* and show how Dean constructed the *mise en scene* and how he changed all the dialogue in the shooting script, to make it more authentic and more of a tool to enable himself to act it in a more convincing manner. Where he didn't take charge of the dialogue, the film is a bit wooden, verbally. This bit of evidence shows that he knew how to create cinematic authenticity, the essence of direction.

As for Paul Newman, yes, Newman did gain from Dean's demise, but there was room enough in Hollywood at that time for newer actors. It would be unjust to say that Newman walked in over Dean's body. Actually, the great loss to Hollywood was the trio of Garfield, Dean and Clift, all of whom would have survived, even when the next generation of actors moved in.

Finally, the list of actors influenced by Dean in specific ways would fill a page. Foremost among them: Bruce Dern, Dennis Hopper, Jack Nicholson. There is also the great boost that Dean gave to Natalie Wood's career.

I would argue that Dean convincingly showed his durability.

John Kreidl

'For the first time in the history of mankind the teenager was liberated. After seeing "Rebel Without a Cause" I went out and bought Levis and a red windcheater, and so did thousands of others' — Adam Faith

James Dean

Beloved Rebel

Films Illustrated June '76

THERE are common points of reference, memory junctions, in every generation. Every adult in the western world can remember precisely what he was doing when the news of the Kennedy assassination broke. And those of us who grew up in the austere aftermath of World War II — perhaps the last generation to accept filmgoing as part of a staple diet — we all remember when first we saw *Rebel Without a Cause*. In the best traditions of film advertising, the film is now "back for a whole new generation to see." With the new key artwork of Dean's frowing stare from the open window of the stolen car (replacing the more aggressive juvenile delinquent slouch of the original), the campaign suggests that, "When he died, a legend was born."

The truth of that is self-evident. Had it not been for Dean's fatal car crash on September 30, 1955 *Rebel Without a Cause* might never have been shown in this country. Warner Brothers had submitted the film to the British Board of Film Censors who were originally inclined to refuse it a certificate altogether. The distributors and the censors, sharing a common opinion that the film was meretricious rubbish, argued in fits and starts. Multiple cuts were suggested to bring the film in line for the relatively infant X certificate and Warners, acutely aware of the impact that Dean's death had had on the teenagers of America, argued that these reducations would, in fact, bring the film in line for the commercially more advantageous A certificate. In the '50s, the X was open to sixteen and over: the A prohibited no-one, but insisted on parental accompaniment, a structure that was almost impossible to enforce.

For an A certificate, the British Board of Film Censors asked for further cuts that would totally have emasculated the film. Any suggestion of parent culpability was to be cut, the chicken run was to be omitted (the knife fight at the planetarium was already outlawed for an X) and the whole bias of the film would have been shifted. But, as the morbid Dean cult gained momentum, Warners saw the dangers of procrastination and settled for the X. It was to be more than twenty years before company executives thought to re-submit the film, for exactly the same commercial consideration (accessibility to the teenage market). When the film went to the British Board of Film Censors in the spring of this year, it was classified AA and opened successfully in London during late April. A national re-release is now planned.

As Warners have struck new prints for this re-issue (amazing how interest has revived in a film that was, only months ago, due for junking), the new classification covers the material the Board had previously demanded be cut for X. Therefore, although director Nicholas Ray was kept aware of the British censorship cuts being imposed on his film in 1955 (he actually wrote to the Board to thank them for their thoughtful consideration), the version currently on release is the closest ever seen in cinemas in this country to Ray's final cut.

The film opens with Dean lying drunk in the street as the credits superimpose. He is curled into a foetal position, playing with a toy monkey in the gutter. The monkey was a hangover from a false start

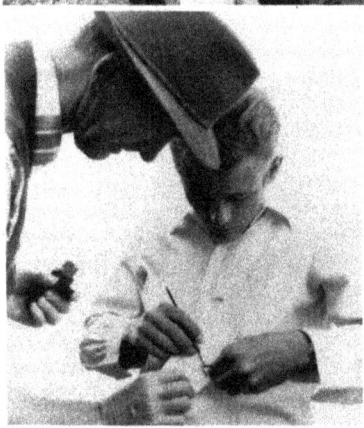

Preparing the make-up (above) for the knife-fight sequence, now restored. Metamorphosis from middle-class teenager (top) into juvenile delinquent (right)

that Ray made on the film. They were some days into shooting (in black and white) when the studio decided to take a larger gamble and go for a colour production. In the monochrome version, a gang of teenagers attacked an old man and set fire to the parcels he was carrying. The monkey was all that was left when Dean (not himself a participant in the attack) came on the scene. The prologue was dropped in re-shooting, but it is improbable that the British Board of Film Censors would have found it acceptable, since the whole notion of juvenile violence and elders being menaced or held up to ridicule was a subject of serious concern.

For the mooted A certificate, the Board would have required some intricate cross-cutting in the police station to reduce the bickering between Dean's parents when they call to collect their son. On view for the first time here is the scene in which Dean is taken into a separate room by the police officer, attempts to strike him and finally vents his spleen by punching and kicking the desk. In the cut version, this scene was reduced to suggest that the episode was merely one of conversational respite.

The other new material is in the knife fight itself. In the British version, the scene ended with Dean saying to Buzz (Corey Allen): "I'll meet you some place, but not with those." The reference was to the flick-knives and although the exchange of dialogue came after Dean had defeated Allen in a knife fight, the censored version made it look as though the chicken run was an *alternative* to this fight instead of an addition. In the chicken run itself, the Board asked for a lot of the dialogue to be trimmed. Before the race that ends in Allen's death, Dean asks: "What are we doing this for?" Allen replies: "We've got to do something, haven't we?" This exchange was considered unacceptable, as was the evident relation of Judy (Natalie Wood) in starting the race. When Allen's car goes over the edge of the bluff, it was asked that his scream should be cut.

Even though the Board were prepared to allow a certain amount of parental criticism in the X version, they demanded a reduction in the scene in which Dean grasps and tries to throttle his father (Jim Backus), provoking the cry from his mother (Ann Doran): "Stop it, you'll kill him! Do you want to kill your own father!"

Social attitudes (to say nothing of those in film censorship) have changed so much since the submission of *Rebel Without a Cause* in 1955 that many of these requests for abridgment or omission look foolish by today's lights. But the X certificate was only four years old and X films were the exception rather than the rule. And, in the '50s, juvenile delinquency was a hot topic, only one serious film on the subject (*Blackwood Jungle*) having been passed previously. But the signal difference between the two films was that *Rebel Without a Cause* shows the problem from the juvenile point of view. Identification is with Dean and Natalie Wood (and to a lesser degree with Sal Mineo, who played Plato, a character whose latent homosexuality worried the Board not at all, if even it dawned on them). Dean begins the film as an ordinary, unexceptional middle-class kid. He wears a fleck sports coat and baggy slacks, drives to school in his old jalopy with a lunch pack. It isn't until he has been systematically failed, or actually rejected, by his elders, that he breaks away from stereotype. The T-shirt, red windcheater and Levis that Adam Faith recalls so vividly marked the transformation from passive, trusting patience into more direct, volatile action.

"When you first see Dean in his red

jacket against the black car, it isn't just a pose. It's a warning, a sign," said Ray.

A sign of what? Faith recalls interpreting it as a sign of affluence after austerity. This may well have been generally true for British audiences, but the Americans (on whom the film had its first impact) had experienced no such post-war austerity. More, it was the signpost to the teenagers' group power, the enfranchisement of a group that had long been without a voice. As Ray Connolly noted in his fine documentary, *James Dean: The First American Teenager*, Dean was the first actor to give the teenager a status, and *Rebel Without a Cause* (certainly more than *East of Eden* or *Giant*) communicated directly with a young mass audience.

When Connolly's film was shown on television on the twentieth anniversary of the actor's death, the feature film around which all the interest centred remained prohibited to teenagers by the twenty year-old X certificate. (In fact, since the age limit for the X had been raised to eighteen in the interim, it could be argued that the situation was even *more* restrictive.) The onus is obviously on the distributor to re-submit his film, but the Board have made the exercise more feasible by halving their costs for films made before 1965 (and halving them yet again for foreign language films that are wholly sub-titled). Thus, for instance, Bergman's *Smiles of a Summer Night* (again originally cut for X) could be presented for reclassification at a quarter of the normal fee.

In a recent survey of the eighty-three films showing in commercial London cinemas, eighty-one had been passed by the Board. (The remaining two, rejected by the Board, had been passed by the Greater London Council.) Of this eighty-one, fifty films had been passed as submitted and the remaining thirty passed only after cuts. The thirty broke down into sixteen low-budget sex films; three *kung-fu* films, cut for violence; four recent X films, cut for legal reasons; three films cut at the request of their distributors, seeking a particular certificate; and four old non-British films that were still circulating with the cuts demanded for their original certificates. This last category includes not only *Smiles of a Summer Night*, but the version of *Gone With the Wind* that needed trimming for a 1939 A.

Can the cut material be reinstated? Have the film companies in question kept tabs on the footage that could now be restored to finish a long-incomplete jigsaw? Would they in many cases bother to re-submit their films, even at the Board's discount rates? The questions are larely rhetorical, but the renewed interest in the restored version of *Rebel Without a Cause* may yet make distributors re-think their attitude as custodians.

Inflexibility is a charge frequently levelled at the British Board of Film Censors. In this instance, at least, the shoe is on the other foot.

Left: "It isn't just a pose. It's a warning, a sign."

393

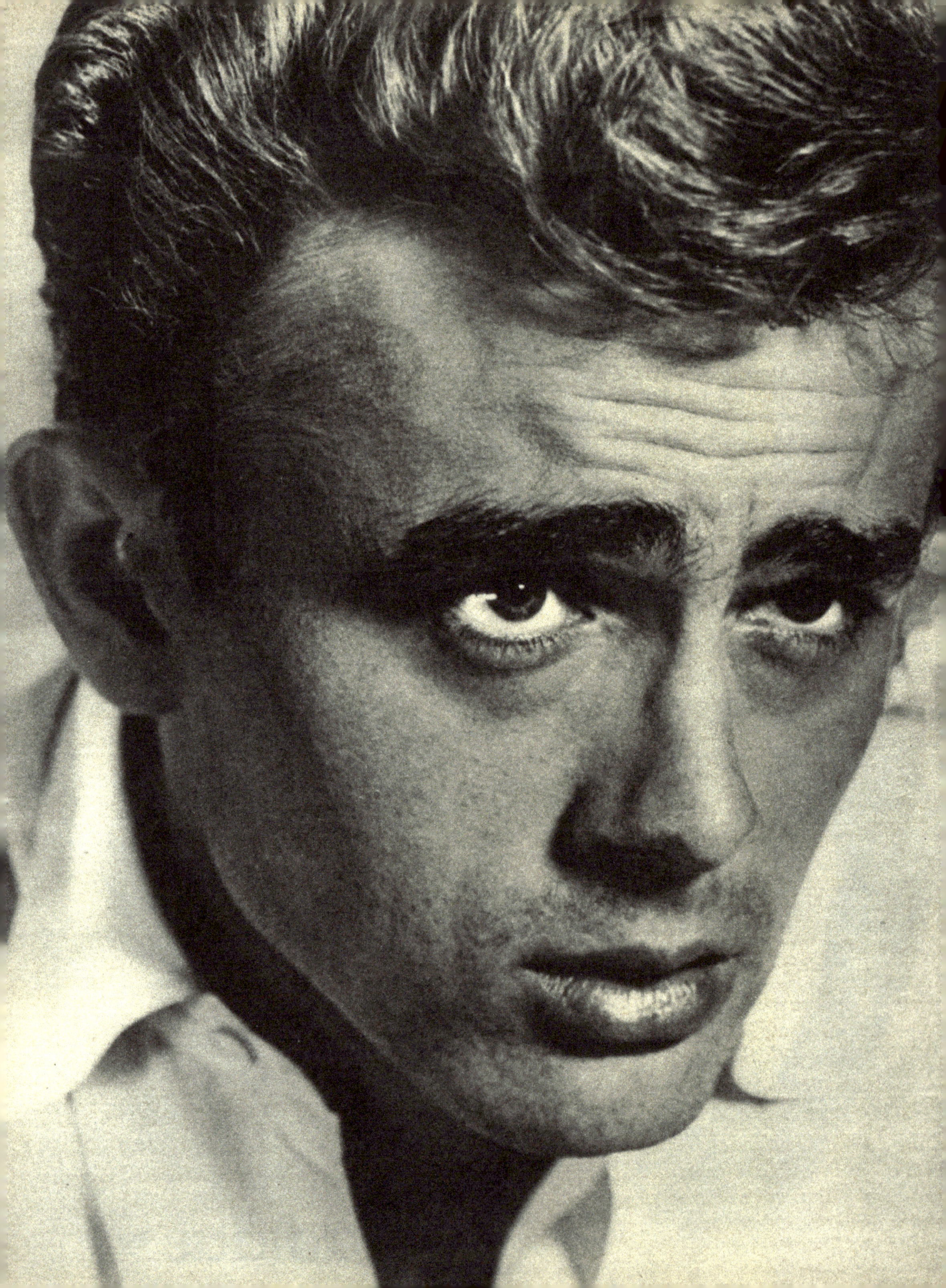

Film-maker Richard Glatzer on 'Rebel Without a Cause'

Daddy cool

Living in Hollywood, I play host to a lot of visitors from out of town, but I'm not much of a tour guide – guests are free to explore Disneyland and Universal City on their own. They might convince me to stop by the Chinese Theatre, but the only places I really enjoy showing visitors are movie locations: the wrought-iron heaven of the Bradbury building as seen in *Blade Runner* or the mad Tower Drive apartment Elliot Gould inhabited in Altman's *The Long Goodbye*.

However, the one don't-miss stop for me is the Griffith Observatory. There you can gaze out over the city, smog permitting, or watch men cruising in the park below. The real romance of the place, though, derives from Nicholas Ray's *Rebel Without a Cause*, as it is here that his teenagers rumbled, confronted death and contemplated eternity under phoney stars. It is amazing the resonance the place has, not just for me, but for everyone I show it to. For who has not fallen in love with the semi-tough kids of Ray's masterpiece, the youth movie that invented the genre?

Rebel is a film shrouded in Hollywood legend, not just because of the premature deaths of so many of its actors (how can Dennis Hopper still be alive?), but because of the infinite promise they all showed. James Dean, Natalie Wood, Sal Mineo – they were so young in 1955, yet they would never show such charisma again. Their charisma derives at least in part from the genius of Ray's casting, which is so perfect that it's hard not to confuse fact with fiction. Wasn't James Dean really Jim, the conflicted high school student proving his masculinity by racing fast cars? It's a shock to remember that this film was released after Dean's death, for the Dean myth couldn't exist without it. However brilliant the actor was in *East of Eden* and *Giant*, this is the film in which he defined his persona. To see the film again is to realise how contemporary Dean's persona remains. Unlike Clift, who had a post-war maturity about him, or Brando with his mumbling machismo, Dean is all youthful intensity. For the first time, an actor shows us the geek in the teenage heartthrob, and shows how hipness can derive from timidity. To watch Dean curl up in the foetal position with a mechanical monkey, to hear his *Beavis & Butthead* laugh, is to see a whole new screen body language being born. Club kids today (and every young actor from Alexis Arquette to Christian Slater) strive for the glamour of Dean's Jim.

Rebel is as much about juvenile delinquency as Ray's *Bigger Than Life* is about the drug cortisone. How could *Rebel*'s protagonists – so searching, so well-meaning – ever be perceived as a threat to society? True, they fight and 'chicky' race, they even play with guns, but compared to the Los Angeles gangs of the 90s they seem downright cuddly. Ray chooses to show us not how fearsome his teenagers are, but how desperate. They are rebels in an Emersonian sense, trying to build themselves a world outside of a corrupt society. Yet they can never completely sever the links with that society – they can never eliminate the traces of it within themselves.

A timid hero: James Dean with Sal Mineo at the Griffith Observatory

Rebel offers us three teenagers, each living in a dysfunctional family. Judy can't understand why her father calls her a tramp, why he slaps her when she tries to kiss him. Plato, the film's most friable character, spends more time with the maid than with his elusive rich parents. Jim keeps brawling with other kids.

It's incredible how much Ray invests himself in the teenagers – most particularly in Jim, whose quest seems to become the film-makers' own. As we follow Jim through his first day in a new town, we gradually realise what he is searching for: a model of masculine behaviour that he can emulate. His father (played by Mr Magoo, Jim Backus) is a roast capon of a dad, fussing about in an apron, cowering before his shrewish wife. Jim pleads with his father to be strong, but the poor old sissy just doesn't have it in him. Jim's outrage over his father's weakness builds ominously until in a fit of rage he throttles his father and almost murders him.

One can easily imagine Jim turning into a fag-basher, a white supremacist, or some other crypto-fascist. Instead, he becomes the moral centre of the film, forming a romantic bond with Judy, looking after the desperate Plato, and going to the police when a rival teenager is accidentally killed. As Jim learns moral lesson after moral lesson, the film is in danger of becoming pat. Yet Ray doesn't inflate the characters' epiphanies. Nor does he suggest that right action can avert tragedy. However good Jim's intentions are, he cannot save Plato, who is shot down on the observatory steps.

It is easy to feel knowing about the characters' inchoate sexuality. Plato is obviously in love with Jim, Jim's probably a closet gay, and Judy will find out soon enough why Jim's kisses are just pecks. Ultimately, though, the film is less about sex than about how we form makeshift families to compensate for the failure of blood ties. This is the real reason for the inclusion of Plato in the Jim and Judy relationship. It is also why the film still exerts such a pull. Had it resolved itself into a simple boy-girl romance, *Rebel* would not have the same resonance as it does. Instead, Ray offers us his three main characters, alone in a deserted mansion, trying to recreate the bonds of family.

There's something strangely moving about Jim's need to protect Plato. Ray invents a beautiful bit of symbolism to convey Jim's paternal impulse. Twice Jim offers the shivering Plato his jacket, once at the police station in the film's opening and again in the final sequence at the observatory. It is only the second time that Plato accepts Jim's offer. Moments later he is gunned down. Jim watches silently as the paramedics load Plato's corpse onto a stretcher. He bends down to zip up the jacket. It bothers him that Plato was always cold.

The accumulation of details such as these gives the film its power, but the thing that really makes it stay in the mind is its evocative settings. There are the more mundane spaces, such as Jim's home and the police station, which Ray renders so beautifully with his dense use of CinemaScope. Then there are the more symbolic locations – the observatory, the palisades and the deserted mansion – all suggestive of the vastness of eternity and the need for shelter.

Who can count the number of films spawned by *Rebel Without a Cause*? The more recent examples range from *Natural Born Killers* to *True Romance* to the upcoming Antonia Bird disappointment *Mad Love*. Most of these offspring feature a soundtrack instead of a narrative, fast cutting in place of imaginative visuals. It's painful to think how uninspired Hollywood film-making has become since the days of Nicholas Ray. But it's a revelation to look at his masterpiece again and witness it truly growing younger with the years.

'Rebel Without a Cause' is released on the Elite Collection

Er rebellierte gegen die Verständnislosigkeit der Erwachsenen

JAMES DEAN in „Denn sie wissen nicht was sie tun"

Sal Mineo als Plato

„Sei endlich mal ein Mann, Vater", rüttelt Jim den Pantoffelhelden durch

Jim (James Dean) und sein Rivale Buzz

Ein Liebespaar: Judy (N. Wood) und Jim

Gespenstische Szene auf dem Felsen von Millertown: Mit geklauten Autos haben Buzz und seine Bande in der Dunkelheit eine Gasse bis zum steilen Abgrund gebildet.

Im Scheinwerferlicht sieht man die Autos der beiden Rivalen am Start. Scheinbar lässig sitzt Jim Stark (James Dean) in seinem knallroten Blouson und mit einer Zigarette im Mundwinkel im Wagen. Das „Hasenfuß-Rennen", diese aberwitzige Mutprobe, soll darüber entscheiden, ob Jim von den anderen akzeptiert oder weiter ein Außenseiter bleiben wird.

Neben ihm läßt Buzz den Motor aufheulen. Quietschende Reifen, Vollgas, Start! Die Wagen rasen auf den Abgrund zu, stürzen in die Tiefe. Ein Aufschrei: Wo ist Buzz? Jim hat sich – wie vereinbart – in letzter Sekunde aus dem fahrenden Wagen fallen lassen. Buzz hat die Tür nicht aufbekommen, weil sich sein Ärmel im Türgriff verfangen hatte. Fassungslos blickt die Bande auf die zerschellten Autos und gerät in Panik: Das „Hasenfuß-Rennen", die Mutprobe, ist tödlich ausgegangen...

Am Abend zuvor war Jim völlig besoffen von der Polizei aufgegriffen worden. Seine Eltern waren mal wieder mit ihm umgezogen, weil er, der Einzelgänger, nirgends Anschluß fand.

Auf der Wache trifft Jimmy auf Judy und Plato, die ebenfalls aus kaputten Familien stammen. Sie alle drei sind auf der Suche nach Nestwärme und Geborgenheit, finden bei ihren Eltern aber kein Gehör für ihre Probleme.

Jims Vater ist ein Pantoffelheld, der sich von der keifenden Mutter ständig demütigen läßt, was Jim wiederum anwidert.

Am ersten Schultag in der neuen Stadt schlägt Jim, dem scheuen Einzelgänger, wieder die Ablehnung der anderen entgegen. Der Unterricht findet in einem Planetarium statt, wo ein Lehrer genüßlich den Untergang der Welt ausmalt.

Nach der Schule kommt es auf der Terrasse des Planetariums zum Zusammenstoß zwischen Buzz und Jim. Buzz will den Neuen antesten. Er läßt sein Klappmesser aufspringen und hüpft wie ein Torero vor Jim rum, um ihn zu reizen. Der nimmt die Herausforderung zunächst nicht an. Erst als Buzz den Weißwandreifen von Jims Auto zersticht, sieht Jim rot: Er stellt sich Buzz zum Messerkampf und entwaffnet ihn. Sein Ansehen in der Bande steigt.

Das „Hasenfuß-Rennen" auf der Klippe soll endgültig darüber entscheiden, ob er von den anderen respektiert wird oder nicht. Nach Buzz' Tod ist Jim verzweifelt. Er fühlt sich mitschuldig, will sich der Polizei stellen. Seine Eltern reden ab, wollen nicht, daß er sein Leben ruiniert. Da ist auch die Angst vor Buzz' Kumpeln, die hinter ihm her sind, weil sie denken, er würde sie verraten.

Jim weiß keinen Ausweg. Er sucht das Gespräch mit seinem Vater: „Paps, sie haben mich Feigling genannt. Hörst du: Feigling! Ich mußte hingehen. Wenn ich's nicht getan hätte, hätte ich diesen Jungs nie wieder in die Augen sehen können." Doch wieder hört er vom Vater und von der zeternden Mutter nichts als leere Phrasen. Außer sich packt er seinen Vater am Kragen: „Paps, steh für mich gerade!" Seine Mutter schreit: „Jimmy, du bringst ihn ja um."

Nach diesem Krach verläßt Jim das Haus. Er trifft auf Judy, die ebenfalls Zoff mit ihrem Vater hatte, und auf Plato, der mit der Pistole seiner Mutter von daheim weg ist, nachdem Buzz' Leute zu Hause nach ihm gefragt hatten.

Die drei verstecken sich in einer verlassenen Villa in der Nähe des Planetariums. Zwischen Jim und Judy entwickelt sich eine zarte Liebesgeschichte. Sie verziehen sich in ein anderes Stockwerk.

Unterdessen hat die Polizei die Spur der drei aufgenommen. Aber noch kurz vorher treffen Buzz' Leute vor der Villa ein und stoßen auf Plato. Der schießt einen nieder. Dann beleuchten Polizeischeinwerfer die Szenerie. Jim läßt sich von Plato die Pistole geben und entfernt heimlich die Patronen. Als Plato ins Freie tritt, blitzt seine Pistole auf. Ein nervöser Polizist zieht seine Waffe und tötet Plato. Weinend kriecht Jim um die Leiche herum. Der irre Zwang, sich selbst und anderen etwas beweisen zu müssen, um anerkannt zu werden, ist von ihm gewichen...

The German title is: "Because they do not know what they are doing."

Teil 4
BRAVO-Serie
Das war James Dean

Jimmy in seiner stärk
der in eine Jugendba

....DENN

Die Eröffnungs-Szene: Der betrunkene Jim Stark (James Dean) findet einen Spielzeugaffen

Wegen Trunkenheit wird Jim von der Polizei festgenommer

sten Filmrolle: Als Halbstarker mit Schulproblemen,
nde gerät und sich auf gefährliche Mutproben einläßt

SIE WISSEN NICHT, WAS SIE TUN

Ende des Zweiten Weltkriegs hatte ein gewisser Dr. Robert Lindner ein Buch mit dem Titel „Rebel Without a Cause" (Rebell ohne Grund) geschrieben, eine Fallstudie über einen jungen Mann, der durch sein Anderssein mit sich und der Umwelt nicht klarkommt. 1946 kauften Warner Brothers zwar die Filmrechte, verwerteten sie aber nicht.

Sieben Jahre später erst fischte Nicholas Ray das Buch aus den Regalen von Warner und bekam grünes Licht für eine Billig-Produktion mit dem Film-Titel „Denn sie wissen nicht, was sie tun". Am 27. September 1954 bezog Ray dann ein Büro bei Warner und begann mit der Arbeit am Drehbuch. Von der Besetzung der Hauptrolle des Jim Stark hatte er bald eine feste Vorstellung; er wollte dafür unbedingt James Dean haben.

An sich wäre es eine gute Zeit gewesen, um Dean für ein neues Projekt zu interessieren. Denn seit der Hochzeit von Pier Angeli (Jimmys großer Liebe) und Vic Damone im Dezember 1954 hockte er trübsinnig und mutlos in seiner Bude in Sherman Oaks.

Doch Ray selbst hatte Zweifel, ob Warner ihren neuen Star in einem düsteren Film, der mit niedrigem Budget und in Schwarz-Weiß gedreht werden sollte, einsetzen würden. Der Erfolg der Testvorführungen von „Jenseits von Eden" sprach dagegen. Er mußte eine klare Zusage von Dean haben, um die Film-Gesellschaft überreden zu können, ihn in „Denn sie wissen nicht, was sie tun" spielen zu lassen.

Als Dean im selben Monat nach New York flog, folgte ihm Ray ein paar Tage später mit einem Teil des Drehbuchs von etwa 30 Seiten. Ray und Dean trafen sich oft in New York, aßen meist am Abend zusammen, gingen dann auf Partys oder ins Kino. Sie brauchten lange, um miteinander warm zu werden. Dafür aber verstanden sie sich dann um so prächtiger. Trotzdem blieb Dean lange Zeit unentschlossen, was die angebotene Rolle betraf. Erst am Abend, bevor Ray nach Hollywood zurückflog, sagte Jimmy zu, den Film zu machen.

Jetzt ließ Jane Deacy, Deans Agentin, Warner wissen, wie sehr sich ihr Klient für die Rolle des Jim Stark interessiere. Am 4. Januar 1955 wurde bekanntgegeben, daß James Dean die Rolle spielen werde.

Während in Hollywood die Vorbereitungen für den Film bereits auf Hochtouren liefen, entdeckte Jimmy eine neue Leidenschaft: Er legte sich einen Porsche-Sportwagen zu, besorgte einen Mechaniker und meldete sich mit dem Porsche für zwei Rennen in Pacific Palisades und Pasadena an. Nick Ray sah es mit einiger Besorgnis. Doch weder jetzt noch bei den Dreharbeiten versuchte er, ein Machtwort zu sprechen.

Die Hollywood-Journalisten taten Jimmys Renn-Ehrgeiz als Werbe-Trick ab. Doch er bewies ihnen, daß sie damit falsch lagen. Dean gewann beide Rennen in Palisades und Pasadena. Und bevor Warner ihm das Rennenfahren verbot, machte er bei drei weiteren Veranstaltungen mit: in Bakersfield, Palm Springs, und Santa Barbara. Innerhalb von ein paar Wochen stieg er damit zu einem

Bitte umblättern

Nach der Mutprobe: Jims Rivale ist mit seinem Wagen ins Meer gestürzt. Das hat Jim nicht gewollt...

Jim und sein Vater: Er ist ein Pantoffelheld, der mit dem aufsässigen Jungen nicht fertig wird und ihm keinen Halt bieten kann

Jim startet zum Autorennen mit Buzz. Judy wünscht ihm Glück bei dieser Mutprobe

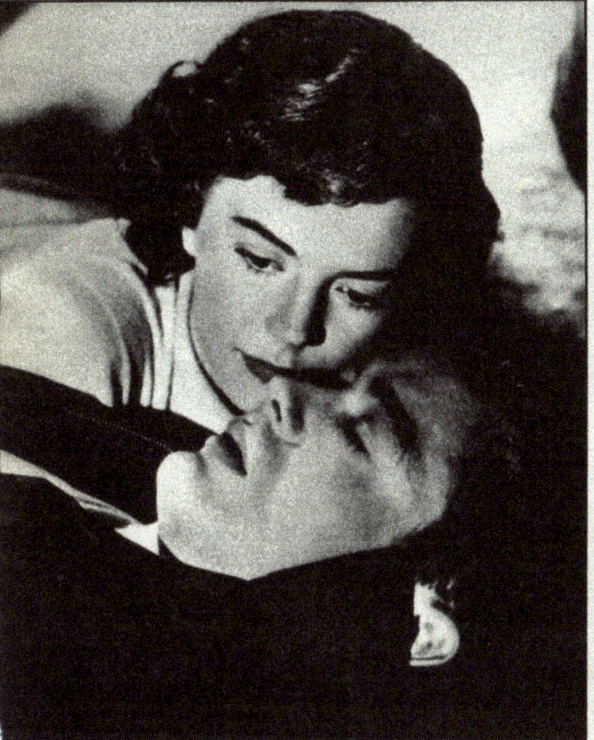

Judy (Natalie Wood) ist die Freundin des Bandenchefs Buzz. Sie verliebt sich in Jim. Aber es gibt doch kein Happy-End

Jims einziger Freund ist Plato (Sal Mineo, l.), ein Außenseiter wie er selbst

Films & Filming, Sep59

POST-WAR YOUTH: *The late James Dean as the Rebel Without a Cause (1955), Nicholas Ray's startling portrait of post-war adolescence and delinquency. Corey Allen (right) has since specialised in criminal roles (Party Girl, etc.).*
Above Photo: National Film Archive

TWO REBELS

Warner Brothers is taking the lead in star building. Two of its latest candidates are Dennis Hopper and Natalie Wood. Hopper graduated from High School in June 1954, and appeared on TV as an epileptic in the NBC Medic programme. Warner immediately signed him and put him in Jagged Edge, Rebel Without a Cause and Giant.

Natalie Wood has been a child actor since 1944, making her début as Orson Welles' daughter in Tomorrow Is Forever. Her first important rôle was in Rebel Without a Cause: and she is now making The Searchers. Watch her, she has a great future. Photo: Warner

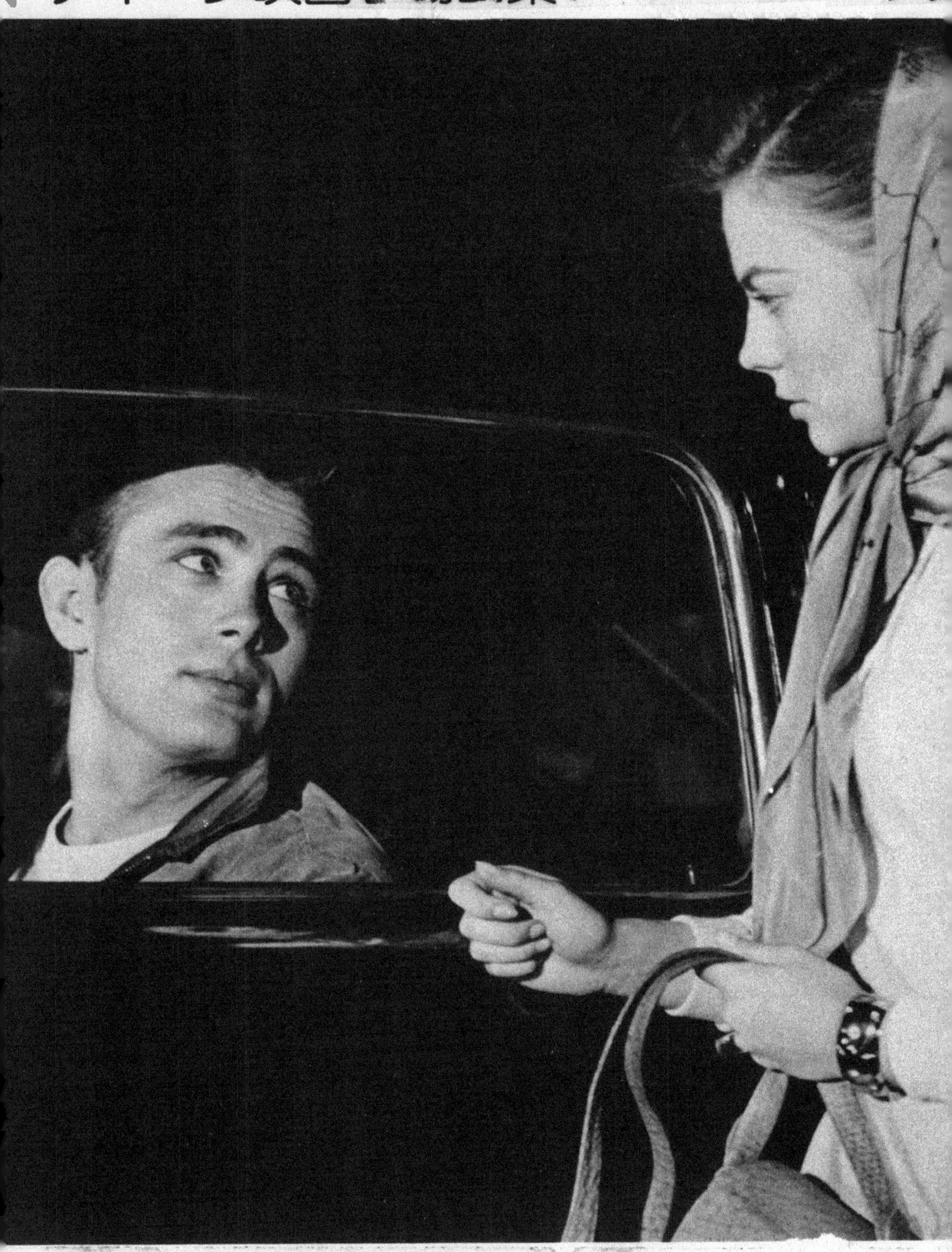

「理由なき反抗」

GIANT

ELIZABETH TAYLOR
and
ROCK HUDSON
in
GIANT

with
JIMMY DEAN
in his last and greatest film

● There was so much that was new to Leslie. Her name was Benedict now; she was Jordan "Bick" Benedict's bride. And they had just arrived at Bick's huge ranch in the sprawling state of Texas— so different from the green Maryland country where she'd grown up. She was determined to love it, though, as much as she'd loved its tall and powerful owner from the first day she'd seen him. He'd come to Maryland to buy her father's beautiful stallion, War Winds —the spirited horse that was her favorite. When he'd gone home, some weeks later, to the 595,000-acre ranch known as Reata, he'd taken two prizes—War Winds and Leslie.

Yes, it was all new to her—new in the land's vastness, its openness, new in its people's thinking and attitudes, new even in the language she'd have to learn in order to deal with the servants. Of Mexican origin, they mostly spoke Spanish. Wet-backs, they were called. Curiously, Leslie found, Texans considered them less than human. Even her own Bick had frowned in annoyance when she'd thanked the two Mexican girls who took their baggage on their arrival.

"Don't overdo it," he'd said. "We don't behave like that—making a fuss over those people. You're a Texan now. You're my wife."

continued →

3. They always seemed to fight—if not about Mexicans' rights ... then about how the children were going to be brought up.

To Bick, Leslie looked as fragile as antique china...

1. Leslie paused in her tea-pouring. "I read about Texas until five this morning," she announced. Eyes flashing, she turned to Bick. "You married?"
2. Bick was married now—to Leslie. He'd just brought her home to Reata when Jett Rink (Jimmy Dean) pulled up. Jett looked Leslie over real well.

...but at heart she was strong and stubborn as steel...

Jett was like Leslie. Nothing could stop either from getting what each

GIANT
continued

JIMMY DEAN IN HIS LAST AND GREATEST FILM!

"I'm still myself," she'd told him, with dignity. "Elsewhere, being gracious is acceptable."

"We're gracious. You've been reading too many books. That's your trouble."

She was hurt, but then amused by a thought. "Fine thing, standing here quarrelling—with the rice still in our hair!"

So they'd kissed, and overriding all else was the strong, intense feeling that drew them together. But lovemaking could take only part of the time; during the rest Bick was cowman, rancher, boss, doing work he exulted in. It was hard for Leslie, in the beginning, to get used to her own role. Luz, Bick's older sister, ran the huge house and wanted to keep on running it. The hands had a tremendous respect for Luz—even the one named Jett Rink, who clashed with Bick like a hammer against an anvil. Luz was Jett's friend, his only friend, and the one reason why he remained on Reata against Bick's will. Luz was a strong woman.

Not that she and Leslie didn't get along. The older *(continued on page 28)*

4. Jett drove Leslie through the filthy Mexican village. "Part of beautiful Reata," he observed sarcastically. Leslie was disgusted at the squalor.

wanted...

THE CAST

Leslie Benedict ...... **Elizabeth Taylor**
Bick Benedict .... **Rock Hudson**
Jett Rink .... **James Dean**
Vashti Snythe .... **Jane Withers**
Uncle Bawley .... **Chill Wills**
Luz .... **Mercedes McCambridge**
Luz Benedict II .... **Carroll Baker**
Jordan Benedict III ... **Dennis Hopper**
Mrs. Horace Lynnton .... **Judith Evelyn**
Dr. Horace Lynnton .... **Paul Fix**
Sir David Karfrey ..... **Rodney Taylor**
Bob Dace .... **Earl Holliman**
Pinky Snythe .... **Robert Nichols**
Angel Obregon III .... **Sal Mineo**

(credits on page 87)

5. Jett inherited a piece of land—and suddenly he had the proud look of a man who owns something. He was sure the land held oil, would make his fortune.

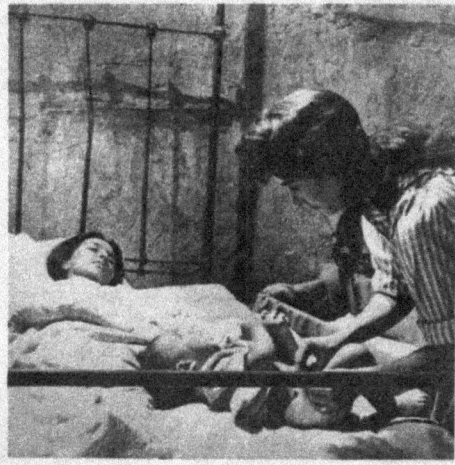

6. Leslie felt compassion for the Mexicans. She aided Mrs. Obregon and baby Angel.

7. Jett hit it. His hunch paid off; his gusher came in. He was rich now—soon he'd be richer even than Bick Benedict. He wanted Leslie to be first to hear the news.

8. Bick saw Jett come up to Leslie, devotion in his eyes. Jealously, he hauled off.

27

...Leslie won her

9. Rick, upset that his grandson looked so Mexican, tried not to show it. Until...

10. A diner owner called the boy wet-back. Bick got mad!

11. Leslie screamed when Bick got the worst of it—but she was really terribly proud.

GIANT continued

woman, however, tended to treat her brother's wife like a fragile ornament, someone Bick had wanted and rightfully got, but not one to perform any useful function on a ranch like Reata. Quietly, Leslie determined to change this attitude.

Then came a party—an old-fashioned *barbacoa*. Luz had arranged it so that Leslie could meet the neighbors. She met friendly people with odd names, such as Eula Jakes and Jo Ella Beezer, Aurie Hildebrand, Fernie Kling. Vashti Hake was there—the girl Bick might have married if he hadn't met Leslie—with an announcement that she and Pinky Snythe, head man on her ranch, had just been wed. Leslie enjoyed herself thoroughly until Luz, supervising the refreshments, called out, "Come and get it or I'll throw it in the creek!"

There were whoops of enthusiasm. Turning toward the outdoor table, Leslie stopped, stunned by what she saw. "What's that?" she asked Bick.

"The best you ever ate, honey—real Mexican *barbacoa*." He brought her closer. "We take the calf's head and skin it, wrap it in canvas, and put it in a pit on mesquite coals."

A line *(continued on page 84)*

fight—but Jett's triumph was clouded by spite and booze!

 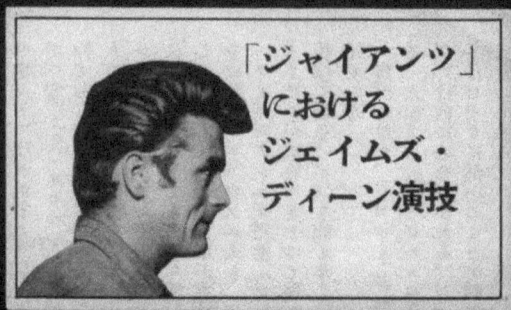

「ジャイアンツ」におけるジェイムズ・ディーン演技

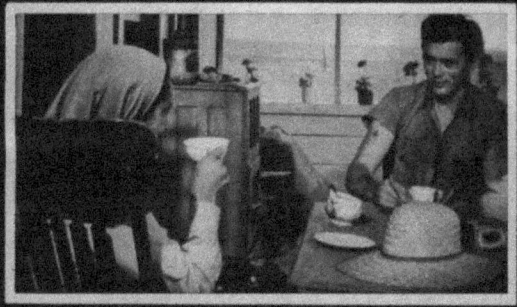 

81

特別読物「ジャイアンツ」

"GIANT"

二百五十萬エーカーのテキサス大牧場に營なまれる「巨人(ジャイアント)」的な人間の生活をえがいた西部小説の傑作

解説

山本恭子
Kyoko Yamamoto

原作者エドナ・ファーバア女史は、現代アメリカの大衆人氣作家のうちでは、我々日本人のあいだにも最も親しまれている作家の一人であろう。彼女の長篇小説は『ジャイアンツ』を含めて十一作品あるが、そのほとんどがベスト・セラーになり、そのうちの大半が映画化されている。わが國に紹介されたものは、まず『ソウ・ビグ』『シマロン』『サラトガ本線』などがある。『ソウ・ビグ』は戰前『母』という題名で日本で封切された。主演はバーバラ・スタンウィック、監督はウィリアム・ウェルマンであったが、この原作はサイレント映画でも既に映画化されており、戰後、ジェーン・ワイマン主演でも映画になっている。『ショウ・ボート』も戰前戰後を通じて映画化されること、確か三回に及んでいる。それだけでも、女史が如何にポピュラリティ（大衆性）を持つた作

その忘れ得ぬ思い出の中にジェー

ジミーと知合った仲だつた。同い年の二人は、よく仕事が終ってからスタジオ附近のスタンド・バーなどで一杯のビールに人生を語り合ったのだった。ジミーは「エデン」によつて再度のハリウッド入りをするまでで、いかにハリウッドの一部の人たちによつて痛めつけられたかを繰返して語った。そして彼は、ハリウッドに根強くはびこる悪習に對して實といつたあらゆる惡襲に對してくまでも反抗し、それを打破しようと意氣ごんでいた。

「しかしジミーは決してハリウッドそのものを憎んでいたのではない。彼は心からハリウッドを愛していたのだ。だが彼の心に刻まれた苦い經驗は、しばしば彼を孤獨の中に閉じこめた。そして彼はその解放感を仕事のポケットに、インギン無禮な給仕との口論に求め、メニュを見るような、家に吹わず(?)コップ

の水を注ぎこんだり、ニックがそこへはまったお砂糖をこぼし入れたりしてその家での生活の多くの夢と共に沒入することに最上の慰めを感じていたらしい。この家を訪れる者はごくわずかに限られていたようだが、そこではみな親切に奢しあつて、人のよい、いつかてなしをしている連中がいると、ジミーは手當り次第テーブルにある野菜を自分の鼻につっこんだり、耳にはさんだりしてその連中の目をそばだたせ、彼等のお喋りを中斷した。またジミーに酷似しているといわれるワーナーの新進スティヴ・ロウランドは、ジミーへの多くの記憶の中から特に印象深い思い出をこう語っている。

「僕がテストを受ける日、スタジオはジミーの"ジャイアンツ"のクライマックス・シーンの撮影準備で賑つていた。二人は一流料理店な

名演技

映画の仕事にたずさわるタフな人たちまでが、慘もなく、ただすすり泣きしたといわれる「ジャイアンツ」の名場面。ジミー・ディーンの生命を永久に傳える名演技

ヴ、いい役者になろうと思ったらまずその役柄に集中することだ、あらゆる場合にその人物に對する想像力を擧げてその人物の生活の中で自分も生活する事だ」と、いった。そしてその時の彼自身はそのジェット・リンクのテキサス訛のニ一擧手一投足までジェット・リンクになりきっていた。

「こうしてジミーの訓えのおかげだ磨きながら僕を手招きした。そしてら、ジミーとのこの訓えを身につけ僕の一生の努力によって永久に亡れた彼は、片隅に坐ると悠々靴をの一生の努力によって永久に亡

かしい個性と才能によって永久にびることはない。」

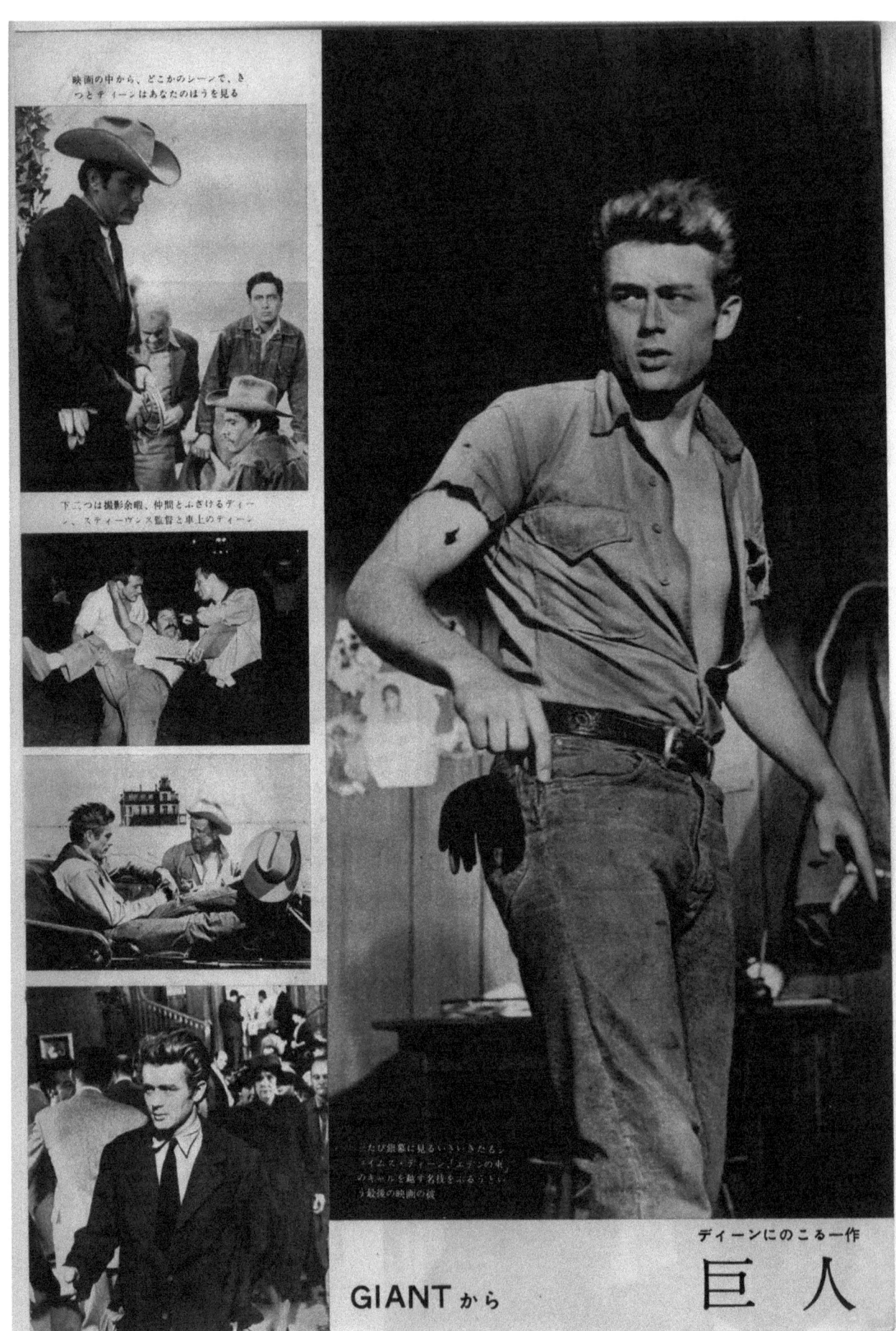

映画の中から、どこかのシーンで、きっとディーンはあなたのほうを見る

下二つは撮影余暇、仲間とふざけるディーン、スティーヴンス監督と車上のディーン

GIANTから

ディーンにのこる一作

巨人

育ちではあるが、彼の若さと、そこからくる柔軟性は、いずこをも彼の自由な天地とさせた。

しかし彼は、多くの俳優志望者と同様その世界で名を成そうとはまったく思われない人間であった。

例えばこの映画に共演したエリザベス・テイラーは申し分なき美女であり、ロック・ハドスンは美男でガッシリした體格と同様思慮深い青年であったが、ジミーは彼等と一緒に仕事をするに何の感激をももっていなかったことには驚いた。彼は自分の仕事と生活になぜか非常に性急であったため、いつも闘志なき美女であるはずの彼女にさえ鬪志を吹き込む演技やあらゆる傳統に新風をもたらす結果になったと、わたしには信じられる。だがその一面、彼自身の「行っている」にもかかわらず、他の人たちからは非現實な突拍子もない人間に見られた。しかしながらその彼獨得のものであり、情があり、それはいわゆるハリウッド的感覚からはずれて自我の強い向きには理解し得ぬ天與の贈物ともいうべきを何ものかにつねに覚られてしまっている青二才に過ぎない、と見る向きのあったことも否めない。

わたしの感ずるジミーは、正しい事を正しくなそうとする青年であり、善美なるものを夢見るような面持でいるに充分であった。

そうしたジミーには、彼をよく知る友人や肉親でさえ驚くほどの結婚式典次第が貼られてあり、その傍には結婚の宣誓文が彼の手によって書かれてあるかと思うと、ある頁にはラヴス・オールド・スウィート・ソング〟の歌詞があり、他の頁にはラング〟の歌詞があり、他の頁には赤ん坊の顔だけがやたらと貼られた中に、

「見よ、おさなごの目、そこにはかぎりなき望みと光を見出さん」といった彼の創作が飛び出していたかと思えば、他の頁には、彼の有名な句や、エドガー・アラン・ポウの「アナベル・リー」の一節が書かれているといったぐあいである。

また今もわたしの目によくうかぶのは、何かしくじりをしたのに気付いた彼が、良心の苛責をごまかそうと、一度の強い近眼鏡をかけ

☆

そうした時、わたしは彼が幼くして母親を亡し、母親に甘えたり知ギマギさせられると同時に可愛てはまた彼獨得のヒューモラスに堪らなくさせられてしまう。わたしはこの撮影中しばしばこのかぎりない失われた歳月に對してのかぎりない郷愁を求めあえいでいる彼を感じずにはいられなかった。

だが次の瞬間、眼鏡をはずすヤニッコリする彼の急變ぶりには、ドてのかぎりない失われた歳月に對いる彼を感じずにはいられなかった。

またジミーには、彼をよく知る友人や肉親でさえ驚くほどの懐古趣味な一面があった。彼が大事にしているスクラップ・ブックを見たわたしの友人の話によると、それには珍らしくもない劇場の切符や、誰がどこで演じたのかわからないハムレットの批評の一部や他の映画のせりふ、自分の映画のせりふなどがいつも抜き書きされているある頁には、色彩の結婚式典次第が貼られてあり、その傍には結婚の宣誓文が彼の手によって書かれてあるかと思うと、ある頁にはラヴス・オールド・スウィート・ソングの歌詞があり、他の頁には赤ん坊の顔だけがやたらと貼られていた。

彼のその直感力、特に自分の役柄に對するそれ、しばしばわたしも一步をゆずらせられたものだが、結果はいつも彼の正しさが證明された。また彼の演技というものの質價を、彼ほどに高く評價していた人間も私は他に知らない。だから一たん彼が何かをやろうとする競技に私も全力を傾ける。そして、もし自分が負けと知ると、いさぎよくカブトをぬいで相手に敬意を表した。

ある日セットでジミーはチャプリンの物まねをした。それに続いて彼の友人のニック・アダムス（ピクニック）が今度はマーロン・ブランドをまねた。するとジミーはその二ックに腹をかかえて笑いころげると、自分のチャプリンをいさぎよくひっこめて、ニックにアンコールをせがみ心からの

拍手を送った。

☆

また、これはジミーが映画入りする前の話だが……ある日ハリウッドの街を歩いていた彼が、懷中には五十仙しかなく、お晝をだべるかというより、それはその生活の総てではなかったろうか。それほど演技は彼の心身に喰い入り、彼自身の人間として生きる喜びにも、いや生きることの事自體にもなっていたのではあるまいか。

これはおそらく彼自身にも答えられぬ疑問であったろう、しかしジミーをよく知る者にとって、彼がその魂の悩みまで演技につくしている人間という印象に魅了され、また忘れ得ぬところである。そしてその印象は、わたしも同様に感じ、また彼と同様の人間として訪れた、ジョン・フォード監督の名作「男の敵」を再上映している映画館へ飛び込んでしまったのも忘れて、ふとところ具合もあいにくに雷を落すそうとしていた彼の手にあい、何もいえなくさせられたのを告白せざるを得ない。なせなら、それは彼がそれを得特の魅力と心得て悪用しているのではなく、彼が持って生れた正しい演技への強い正義感からきているのがわたしにはわかるからだ。彼はその成長期に大切な母を失ったが、ものの善悪に對する鋭い直感と、演技に對する正しい判斷力を、演技の中に身につけた。

他人を見るのでさえ彼には肉体的な肌などとはかけがえなき精神的な満足なのである。いや満足がその魂の悩みまで演技につくしている人間という印象に魅了され、また忘れ得ぬところである。そしてその印象は、わたしも同様に感じ、また彼と同様の人間として訪れたジェット・リンクについて語り合ったのも、最後に私が彼を見た時も戀らなかった。

ジミーはわたしたち一行が彼よりおくれてロケ先から歸ったと知ると、わたしをセットへ訪ねてきた。そしてへ入ってきて話しかけ無言でわたしを手招きした。わたしが「ここかしら」というと、彼はただかしらを横に振って、「こっちへこい」と彼は強くわたしに向っていた。そこでわたしが先に立って步き出すと、銀灰色に光るポルシェの前にくるといかにも愛美を見せる少年のような誇らしさで、

「僕のスパイダーにも美時しをさせてやらないくちゃねえ、じゃ、さようならよ」

と、未だにジェット・リンクを想わす例の笑い顔をみせていったのだった。

ああジミー、きみは今も、わたしがあれほどレース・カーに乗ってはいけないよ、といつたことをうらんでいるだろうか……

Mr. George Stevens's View on Jimmy

ジョージ・スティーヴンスの語る
"ジミーはわたしの心に生きている"

死後に発表された ジェームス・ディーン物語 10

「ジャイアンツ」のスナップ、左よりスティーヴンス監督、ジミー、リズ

なくり合いを現代化した趣きがあり、またなぐり倒されはしても彼の男らしさに、レズリーが眞底憧れているのを、形の上にあらわれているのを、スチーヴンス演出に、一糸亂れずそれぞれの登場々面に全力をしている。

さて巨人とは、ジャイアントとアメリカ合衆國最大の州テキサスも、"巨人"だが、彼の場合はレズリーとジョーダン、それにジェット・リンク、また夫婦と子供たちの心理の安渉をいろいろと拘泥した策にちがいない。アメリカ合衆國も"巨人"にちがいない。ジョーダン・ベネディクトも巨人であろう。また彼が言う、百年後にレスリーも、小

さい弱い女性だが"巨人"であろう。しかしリンクは大富豪郎も、巨人だと云える筈だ、と。そのジョーダン・ベネディクトは、レズリーの内助の功によって理想のアメリカ人の"祖先"となる。平凡な、誠實な人間なのだ。そのような人間の一人一人こそが巨人なのである。

去り落ちたが三十年の時代経過は衣裳や自動車はもちろんだが、ベネディクト邸の室内装飾を変え、ることによって示され、その効果の見事さは賞讚するに値するともう

附記しておきたい。成人した子供たちを演じる多勢の新人俳優たちも、スチーヴンス演出に、一糸亂れずそれぞれの登場々面に全力をしている。

スチーヴンスは、前述したレズリーとジョーダン、それにジェット・リンク、また夫婦と子供たち等の心理の安渉をいろいろと弄せず、適當な、それも短いセリフで映画的に處理するという演出をしていることを、あらためて附記しておきたい。成人した子供たちを演じる多勢の新人俳優たちも、スチーヴンス演出に、一糸亂れずそれぞれの登場々面に全力をしている。

"巨人"にしたレズリーも、小

人間にはひどく稀に、いかなる場所にいかなる場合におかれてもピタリとその環境に自分を適應させ、しかも人々の興味や注視の的にされる人間がある。ジミーはそうしたく少數の人間の一人であった。

"ジャイアンツ"のテキサス・ロケ中、彼は最も興味ある目的物として寫眞家たちの注視の的にされていた。ジミーはそれをわざわらしくて、氣の向かぬ時にはわざとカメラにソッポを向いたり、逃げまわったりしたが、それで彼はいつかジミーが思いがけぬ時には素晴しい自然なポーズを見せ、やんと知っていたのである。例えば彼が美しい夕燒雲を背に、獨り馬の鞍などにもたれてめい想にふけっていたり、或は馬上で投縄を戲れたり、時にはそれをあざやかに投げるところなどを辛抱強く待ちかまえたものである。

ジミーはテキサス人ではなく、インディアナ生れでインディア

今でもわたしには、どこからかジミーがふいに顔を出してくるのではないかと考えるには、彼はあまりにも鮮やかな印象をわたしに刻みつけているから…

☆

その日も彼はスタジオのラッシュ・ルーム（できあがったばかりのフィルムの試寫室）で、例の通りわたしの目の前の席に陣取り、画面を深く埋めて彼のシーンがうつる頭をガゼンモクモクと頭をもちあげてわたしの方を振向くや彼はガゼンモクモクと頭をもちあげてわたしの方を振向く

と、
「どうです？ どうせお氣に召さんでしょ」
とでもいいたげな顔つ

きをして二タリと笑う。小憎らしいヤツなどと、もしわたしがいらだちでもしたらそれは彼の思うツボなのである。ところがほんとのところ、わたしは画面の中の彼が大氣に入りであるばかりか、目の前にいるきしたくさをする彼も堪らなく好きなのだ。わたしに對することにはいつのころからかわたしをすっかりとりこにしてしまった。

それは彼の、隣に誰がいようとも頬杖をついたり、その指の間からのぞき見してクスクス笑いころげたりする動作かもしれない。また時には自分の感情が思うように相手に通じないと子供みたいにむずかしって、カンシャク玉をハレツさせるような彼も、いかなる場合にもその魅力を失することはあり得ないのだ。そしてこれらの総てを、彼の最後作となる「ジャイアンツ」に盛り込んだと信じるわたしにとって、彼の死

は現實であり得ない。現實のジミーは、わたしの知るジミーであり、わたしと共に生きているジミーである。

☆

「ヘイ、ミスター・スティーヴンス いいことをおしえましょうか？」
彼がそうおしかけてきた聲は、今もわたしの耳元にまざまざときこえる。

「ねえ、あの〝ジャイアンツ〟中のジェット・リンク、あれこそ僕の役ですよ！」

それはもう一年近くも前のことである。「ジャイアンツ」の脚本をわたしに告げるべく方々探しまわって、わたしのところへやってきたのだった。

そして今、そのジェット・リンクから笑いかけている彼は試寫室のスクリーンからわたしの方を横目で見ながら、
「ホラね、スティーヴンスさん、やっぱり僕がいったとおりでしょ。僕にははじめっからちゃんとわかっていたんだ」

STAFF:
Produced by .... George Stevens and Henry Ginsberg
Directed by .... George Stevens
From the novel by .... Edna Ferber
Screenplay by .... Fred Guiol and Ivan Moffat
Music Composed and Conducted by .... Dimitri Tiomkin
Director of Photography .... William C. Mellor

CAST:
Leslie Benedict .... Elizabeth Taylor
Bick Benedict .... Rock Hudson
Jet Rink .... James Dean
Vashti Snythe .... Jane Withers
Uncle Bawley .... Chill Wills
Luz Benedict II .... Carroll Baker
Luz Benedict .... Mercedes McCambridge
Jordan Benedict III .... Dennis Hopper
Mrs. Horace Lynnton .... Judith Evelyn
Dr. Horace Lynnton .... Paul Fix
Sir David Karfrey .... Rodney Taylor
Bob Dace .... Earl Holliman
Pinky Snythe .... Robert Nichols
Old Polo .... Alexander Scourby
Angel Obregon III .... Sal Mineo

ジェイムズ・ディーンは、百万長者（ロック・ハドソン）と、東部うまれの美しい妻（エリザベス・テイラア）、きびしい労働とこの映画の最後の出演シーンがすんで二週間ののちに、死んだ。文字通りの遺作である。しかしこの遺作は、まさに天才俳優の霊前に贈るにふさわしい、まれにみる秀作となったといわれている。ディーンにとってこのことは、何よりものはなむけではないか。彼は今地下で、傑作をもって彼の最後を飾ってくれたジョージ・スティーヴンス監督に、あの優しい笑顔で感謝を呟いていることだろう。

原作は、一九五二年に発表された、エドナ・ファーバアの西部小説。一九二〇年代から現代に至る三十年のテキサス地主一家の物語である。主人公は二百五十万エーカーの牧場をもつ

三十年前の牧畜業者がもっていた荒々しい行動派の牧場召使にすぎなかったが、やがて運命は彼に土地をあたえ、土地は石油を生んで、三十年の歳月は彼に石油王の名声をほしいままにさせる。テキサスの王冠は、いま彼らの手にゆずり渡されたのである。

プロデューサアとしてのジョージ・スティーヴンスは、この原作に目をつけて以来、巧妙にファーバアを口説いて彼女をパートナア

として映画化に参劃させた。鮮やかな製作者ぶりと伝えられるが、むろんこの映画における"監督としての"彼に帰せられなければならないだろう。製作費は五百万ドル。たいした額にはちがいない。

封建的ともおもえるテキサスの社会組織の中で、若かった二人には三十の年輪のシワがきざみこまれて若い彼らは、親の心から遠く離れて彼ら自身の道を進んで行く。子供たちが生れ、育ち、そして若い彼らは、大きな歴史の流れの中で徐々にその姿をかえて行くのだ。ジェイムズ・ディーンの演ずるジェット・リンクもその一人。若い頃の彼は、

テキサスは、そしてそこに生きる人々にその姿をかえて行くの

STAFF★CAST
製作ジョージ・スティーヴンス、ヘンリー・ギンズバアグ、監督ジョージ・スティーヴンス、原作エドナ・ファーバア、脚色フレッド・ギュイオル、アイヴァン・モファット、撮影ウィリアム・メラア、作曲ディミトリ・ティオムキン
★レスリー（エリザベス・テイラア）、ジェット（ジェイムズ・ディーン）、ビック（ロック・ハドスン）、ヴァシュティ（ジェイン・ウィザアス）、ラズ（マアセデス・マッケンブリッジ）ラズ・ベネディクト二世（キャロル・ベイカア）

　それ以上に立派なのは、「ショウ・ボート」の作者のきらびやかなベストセラア小説を、"社会的リアリズムのムードに生きた秘密は、そこにあるのであった。外誌の批評によると、エリザベス・テイラアとロック・ハドスンの演技は、彼らの最上に属するという。ハドスンの姉になるマアセデス・マッケンブリッジもたみごとな西部の人間像を創った。そして、それらを更に抜いてディーンのジェットは、その天才をみせる。三時間十八分、彼のファンを襲う恍惚と苦痛は、どれほどのものであろうか。〈一九五六年度作品・三時間一八分・色彩〉

　彼はこのテキサスの現代叙事詩を、「ママの想い出」や「シェーン」のあの悠容せまらぬスロウ・ベースで描ききる。彼はたいへんなパーフェクショニスト（完全主義者）だといわれており、全シーンをあらゆる角度から撮りあげて、全製作期間の四分の一は、その無数のショットの編集に費したとい

がそれ以上に立派なのは、「ショウ・ボート」の作者のきらびやかなベストセラア小説を、"社会的リアリズムのモニュメンタルな傑作"（タイム）にまで仕上げた、スティーヴンスの映画魂なのであった。

ジョオジ・スティーヴンス監督作『巨人』開始

エリザベス・テイラア映画にジェイムズ・ディーンが抜擢

The Giant

西部劇「シェーン」によつて高き名を一段と高からしめた正統派監督の雄ジョオジ・スティーヴンスが、大方の期待のうちに再び西部を舞台にして作る新作がこの『巨人』である。しかしこの西部劇ではアクションよりも、彼の本道である生活描写が主眼である。その意味でエドナ・ファーバアの原作は絶好のものである。ファーバアは戦後のファンには「ショウ・ボート」や「サラトガ本線」の原作者として知られるが、戦前に西部生活劇として映画史上の貴重な一石と目される「おゝ母よ」（原作「シマロン」という映画化の例を有する地方主義作家である。この映画も舞

台はテキサス、一九二〇年代から今日に及ぶ三十年間に亘り一万エイカアの大領土を開拓して行く坊やタイプの善良な青年実業者（ロック・ハドスン演）をめぐる地方生活を描くものである。彼がヴァージニアへ行き、エリザベス・テイラア扮する南部良家の子女と結びつくのだが、月日と共に豪放な緑の開拓地に同化されて行くところが西部生活劇たる映画『巨人』の、大きなポイントの一つであると思われる。出演顔触れで何よりも評判高きものは、以上の二人に加えて、「エデンの東」の余りにも評判高き新人ジェイムズ・ディーンが、俄か成金の開拓者の一人に扮して活躍することである。尚、この映画の題名『ジャイアント』はこの大開拓地に挑む人間を指すと同時にテキサス州を指している。

Giant

Reviewed by PAUL ROTHA

Directed by George Stevens. Produced by George Stevens and Henry Ginsberg. Screenplay by Fred Guiol and Ivan Moffat. Based on the novel by Edna Ferber. Director of photography, William C. Mellor. Music composed and conducted by Dimitri Tiomkin. Production designed by Boris Leven. Editor, William Hornbeck. Associate editors, Fred Bohanan and Phil Anderson. Assistant director, Joe Rickards. Set decorator, Ralph Hurst. 2nd Unit director, Fred Guiol. 2nd Unit assistant director, Russ Llewellyn. 2nd Unit photography, Edwin DuPar. Costumes designed by Marjorie Best and Moss Mabry. American. Warner Brothers. Warnercolor. Cert. A. 200 mins.
Leslie Benedict, ELIZABETH TAYLOR; *Bick Benedict*, ROCK HUDSON; *Jett Rink*, JAMES DEAN; *Vashti Snythe*, JANE WITHERS; *Uncle Bawley*, CHILL WILLS; *Luz Benedict*, MERCEDES McCAMBRIDGE; *Luz Benedict II*, CARROLL BAKER; *Jordan Benedict III*, DENNIS HOPPER; *Mrs. Horace Lynnton*, JUDITH EVELYN; *Dr. Horace Lynnton*, PAUL FIX; *Sir David Karfrey*, RODNEY TAYLOR; *Bob Dace*, EARL HOLLIMAN; *Pinky Snythe*, ROBERT NICHOLS; *Old Polo*, ALEXANDER SCOURBY; *Angel Obregon III*, SAL MINEO; *Judy Benedict*, FRAN BENNETT; *Whiteside*, CHARLES WATTS; *Juana*, ELSA CARDENAS; *Lacey Lynnton*, CAROLYN CRAIG; *Bale Clinch*, MONTE HALO; *Adarene Clinch*, MARY ANN EDWARDS; *Gabe Targot*, SHEB WOOLEY; *Angel Obregon I*, VICTOR MILLAN; *Sarge*, MICKEY SIMPSON; *Mrs. Obregon*, PILAR DEL REY; *Dr. Guerra*, MAURICE JARA; *Lona Lano*, NOREEN NASH; *Swazey*, NAPOLEON WHITING; *Lupe*, TIM MENARD; and *Watts*, RAY WHITING.

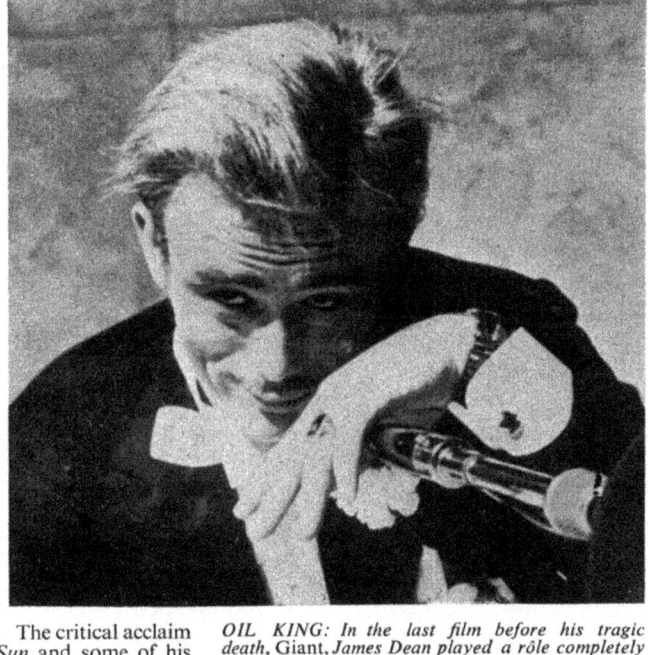

OIL KING: In the last film before his tragic death, Giant, James Dean played a rôle completely different to his previous screen work. He is seen as Jett Rink, of Edna Ferber's novel, the poor boy who strikes oil. Photo: Warner

UNLIKE its title, this is not a film of tall stature. It sprawls its mammoth length recumbent for nearly three and a half hours. Whether this inordinate footage is genuinely needed to screen Edna Ferber's best-selling novel, or whether it is aimed at giving the audience more for its money in these competitive days—is your guess or mine. (One remembers back to the late silent-film days when some cinemas billed three feature films plus variety acts in one programme in an effort to lure back reluctant filmgoers.) No matter the reason, to sit through *Giant* is a tough test of endurance and I can take my celluloid.

Reminiscent of the same author's *Cimarron*, the story spans three generations of a Texas cattle family from 1923 till today. It attempts, if not to explain then to show the brash, one-track mindedness of those who have made their millions "in oil" or "in beef," or in both, who have reached a stage where their wealth has brought power without responsibility and who, like their fathers, still fundamentally believe that settlement by physical force is surer and faster than settlement by reason.

Shocking Conditions

This is the "philosophy" that dictates Bick Benedict's (Rock Hudson) life and which he cannot reconcile with the "humanism" of his wife Leslie (Elizabeth Taylor), the girl he brings from Maryland to Texas along with a champion stallion. Leslie's efforts to alleviate the shocking conditions of the Mexicans (called wetbacks presumably to placate national feelings), who work on the vast Reata Ranch, her refusal to accept the traditional rôle of subservient wife and her support for their son, Jordy (Dennis Hopper) when he stubbornly picks on a medical career rather than follow in his father's footsteps as a rancher—these represent the "liberalizing" influences which are ultimately supposed to "convert" Bick Benedict to a more humane outlook on life.

When, at the story's climax, Bick fights and loses against a roadside "diner" owner over an incident of colour segregation, Leslie disregards the principle for which we imagine Bick had fought. She appears delighted only by the fact that a Benedict has, for once, not had his way. This, to me, was no surprise. I was never convinced of Bick's conversion anyway. An ingrained outlook on life is not changed that fast—except in fiction and films.

I have not been a particular admirer of George Stevens's work in the past. The critical acclaim given to *A Place in the Sun* and some of his other films puzzled me, though parts of *Shane* I liked. Here he does catch the great emptiness of the Texan landscape and the dramatic impact of oil discovery. He is at his best out-of-doors, when action lets him get ahead with his story; at his dullest when bogged down in long static sequences of slowly-spoken dialogue. Thus the film progresses in a series of jolts brought to a stop by wadges of studio dialogue. It lacks that deep and inevitable surge forward which a theme of this bigness must have if it is to hold progressively. There are great gobs of gooey sentimentality (especially over children) which I personally found revolting, but which, I must confess, are true of many American ways of life.

Thick Music

Stevens is not helped by the "mood" music of Dimitri Tiomkin, who belongs to the concert-orchestra class of film composer and who overlays almost every sequence with thick swathes of "symphony" music. Stevens has, let me say, a nice eye for an occasional shot and his use of the camera is seldom pedestrian; but he seems to lack confidence in his style. The picture meanders and jolts alternately through its 18 reels, one-third of which could have been dexterously cut.

Out of a huge speaking cast, many small parts are nicely played. Of the principals Elizabeth Taylor carries off the honours with a rounded, subtly built up performance. Of those asked to span thirty odd years, she does it the most convincingly, growing old in mind as well as in appearance. Rock Hudson and James Dean age largely by make-up and wardrobe. Hudson acquits himself with restraint, but somehow lacks the stature of the part.

And Dean?

Drunken Tycoon

What can one say in face of The Myth? It is a contrived, studied and mostly artificial performance as the young farm-hand who strikes oil and becomes a dollar-crazy tycoon. While still the foxy, hesitant, cunning youngster he has moments of impact. His scene of the discovery of oil on his plot and his announcement of the news to the Benedict family are his high-spots. As the wealthy drunken tycoon owning a fabulous luxury hotel and dominating civic life in the city, wooing with whisky the teen-age daughter of his former employer, I found Dean so mannered and exhibitionistic as to be repellent in a way not, perhaps, intended by the rôle. It is a calculated, erratic and unsubtle performance lacking the depth of his promising work in *East of Eden* under Kazan.

Among the many lesser parts, Benedict's sister is capably played by the always-excellent Mercedes McCambridge (she is killed off too soon!), and the Mexican actress, Elsa Cardenas, gives a sensitive and lovely handling to Juana, who marries Benedict's doctor son.

Set design and photography are commendable.

Yet none of it adds up to the epic qualities such a theme demands. True Texans will probably like it slightly more than they are said to have liked the book. Its shirking of the real issue at the end will satisfy their ego.

A full-page Still of the Month of James Dean in Giant *appeared in the August 1956 issue of* FILMS AND FILMING.

BABY DOLL

Produced and directed by Elia Kazan. Screenplay by Tennessee Williams, from his play *Twenty-seven Wagon-loads of Cotton*. Director of photography, Boris Kaufman. Art director, Richard Sylbert. Music by Kendall Hopkins. A Newtown Production. American. Warner Bros. Cert. X. 114 mins.
Baby Doll Meighan, CARROLL BAKER; *Archie Lee Meighan*, KARL MALDEN; *Silva Vacarro*, ELI WALLACH; *Aunt Rose*, MILDRED DUNNOCK; *Rock*, LONNY CHAPMAN; *Mayor*, JIMMY WILLIAMS; *Doctor*, JOHN DUDLEY; *Nurse*, MADELLAINE SHERWOOD; *Sheriff*, WILL LESTER; and various inhabitants of Benoit, Mississippi.

ST. VITUS'S dance has been the over-riding disorder in a sad number of Hollywood directors for over a year now. The more talented the film-maker, the more convulsive has become the camera and the cast. Preminger, Robson, Wise, Ray—all their best films seem way behind them. Where are they going, and when will it end? Where, above all, is Elia Kazan going? He is the most talented of them all, and *Baby Doll* is undoubtedly his most "difficult" film to date. It is time to breathe, and take stock, and (if only *he* would too) relax.

Talent is the malady, of course: too much of it. You just cannot find the wood for the

to page 22

IT HAPPENED TO ME:

A MEMENTO FROM JIMMY DEAN

■ When I met Jimmy Dean here in Texas, I didn't know who he was. The next day a friend took me to the set of *Giant* and there I saw Jimmy and recognized him—from the night before.

The night before, I was driving alone into Marifa when my car started missing as if it was about out of gas. It got so bad that I had to pull off the highway and stop. Naturally, I was frightened and I couldn't imagine what I could possibly do to find out what the trouble was. I knew I wasn't out of gas.

Dreading what was about to happen, I got out of the car. No sooner had I done this, when a white vehicle stopped behind me. The driver left his headlights on and got out of the car. He looked just like any other Texan—wearing a wide brimmed hat, jeans, and a dangling white shirt. He spoke so friendly and pleasant like, that I became grateful rather than scared.

He asked for a flashlight and I found one in my glove compartment. He raised the hood and after a quick examination, he laughed and pointed out the trouble to me. It was just a loose cable running from the battery. He fixed it for me.

"The motor is steaming," he said. "I bet you haven't checked the water lately."

"Nope," I answered. "I just go."

"Well, if you want the car to go when you say go, you had better have it checked at the next station." He laughed again and slammed the hood down.

"You drive fast, huh?" he asked.

I must have looked puzzled because he went on to explain that he had noticed me at a roadside restaurant only a few minutes before.

He then went around to my car window. Taking a card out of his pocket, he flipped it on the front seat.

"A little Texas memento. Read it! It could save the blond head! You go first," he continued, "and I'll follow you into the metropolis." We both laughed.

On Main Street in Marifa, I waved goodbye to Jimmy Dean. It was the first and last goodbye I would say to him.

The card that he gave me is a joke postcard. I shall keep it always, although I now find it very sad to read. And to remember. It goes like this:

> *At sixty miles an hour sing*
> *This world is not my home anymore*
> *At seventy miles an hour sing*
> *Nearer to my Lord am I*
> *At eighty miles an hour sing,*
> *Lord, I'm Comin' Home.*

● Name Withheld

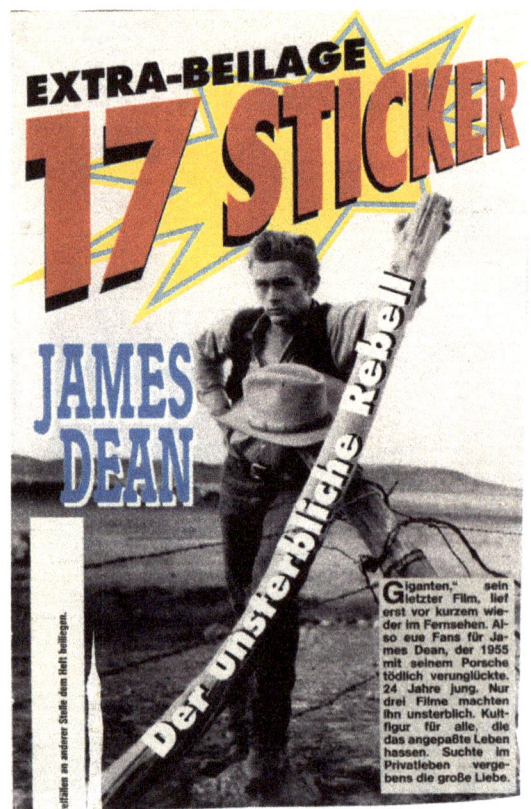

JAMES DEAN WAR IMMER EIN REBELL – VOR UND DAHINTER

Giganten

Jett war hoffnungslos in Leslie

Kurze Begegnungen – Jett hat eine Öl

Es war nicht nur die letzte Szene, die James Dean für „Giganten" zu drehen hatte, es sollte seine letzte Film-Szene generell sein. Dean, als alter Mann zurechtgeschminkt, schläft betrunken an seinem Schreibtisch ein. Jimmy spielte den Arbeiter Jett Rink, der es bis zum Öl-Millionär brachte. Aber sein Traum, den gehaßten Bick Benedict zu vernichten und mit der schönen Leslie zusammenzuleben, erfüllte sich nicht.

Der letzte Drehtag war der 22. September 1955. Am 30. September 1955 verunglückte James Dean mit seinem silbergrauen Porsche Spider tödlich.

Er wurde nur 24 Jahre alt. Den Wagen hatte sich Jimmy erst wenige Tage zuvor gekauft. Er war für seine Raserei bekannt gewesen.

Die meisten von Euch zeigten sich von „Giganten" (lief gerade im Fernsehen) und vor allem von der schauspielerischen Leistung Deans beeindruckt.

Hinter den Kulissen brodelte es bei den Dreharbeiten zu diesem Mammutfilm gewaltig. Zunächst waren Schauspieler wie Richard Burton und Alan Ladd (zwei grobschlächtige Typen) für die Rolle des Jett Rink im Gespräch. Regisseur George Stevens wollte aber mehr eine Charakterstudie dieses Außenseiters zeigen und kam auf James Dean, der mit seinen Filmen „Jenseits von Eden" und „Denn sie wissen nicht, was sie tun" für Furore gesorgt hatte.

Zwischen dem Regisseur und Jimmy kam es bald zu Streitigkeiten. Jimmy haßte es, den ganzen Tag am Drehort zu sein, auch wenn er nur eine kurze Rolle zu spielen hatte. Als er an einem Tag nicht mehr eingesetzt wurde, erschien er am nächsten Morgen nicht am Drehort. Jimmy wütend: „Ich bin keine Maschine. Wenn ich mich gewissenhaft auf eine Szene vorbereite, dann erwarte ich auch, daß sie sofort gedreht wird."

Am besten verstand sich Jimmy mit Elizabeth Taylor, die damals 23 Jahre alt und von umwerfender Schönheit war. Den beiden wurde sogar ein Verhältnis angedichtet. Elizabeth klärt auf: „Wir waren wie Bruder und Schwester. Jimmy kam mit Problemen zu mir, er steckte voller Probleme, war unsicher, nervös, rauchte pausenlos. Wenn ich ihn berührte, zuckte er zusammen".

Als Elizabeth Taylor die Nachricht von Jimmys Tod erfuhr, brach sie zusammen und mußte in ein Krankenhaus eingeliefert werden.

Rock Hudson, der Darsteller des Bick Benedict, dagegen lachte über Jimmy: „Der Kerl machte sich immer warm wie ein Sportler. Kurz vor Drehbeginn sprang er in die Luft, hatte dabei die Knie fast am Kinn. Oder er lief wie ein Irrer umher und stieß schrille Schreie aus wie ein Vogel, der verfolgt wird".

Trotz aller Streitereien wurde „Giganten" nicht nur ein großer Kassen-Erfolg, sondern auch einer der bemerkenswertesten Filme aller Zeiten.

Wie in seinen Filmen war der stark kurzsichtige James Dean auch im wirklichen Leben ein Außenseiter. Er hing sehr an seiner Mutter, hatte Probleme mit Mädchen, ließ niemanden so richtig an sich heran, war leicht aufbrausend. Ein Rebell, der unvergessen bleiben wird.

Peter Raschner

NEUER Starschnitt: JAMES DEAN

in Lebensgröße – sein ergreifendstes Bild. Das müßt Ihr sammeln...

3. PROGRAMM

In Frankfurt III sind die Dean-Fans bestens bedient: Sie können um 20.15 Uhr den Kinofilm „Giganten" (Foto: Liz Taylor & James Dean) sehen

Große „James Dean"-Aktion
Jacken, Kassetten und Poster zu gewinnen!

Scharf hinsehen: In welchem Film spielten Liz Taylor (damals noch zart und süß) und James Dean zusammen?

James-Dean-Fans können sich ab Januar die besten Filme ihres Idols kaufen. Die Firma Warner Home Video bringt nämlich zu Beginn des neuen Jahres die Dean-Klassiker „Giganten", „Jenseits von Eden" und „...denn sie wissen nicht, was sie tun" als Kaufkassetten auf den Markt. Jeder Film kostet 39,30 Mark, alle drei zusammen als sogenannter „Set" 99,95 Mark. Jeweils drei dieser Sets und zwanzig James-Dean-Poster können Sie bei dieser Aktion gewinnen, die cinema gemeinsam mit Warner Home Video durchführt. Der Hauptpreis jedoch wird Sie, wenn Sie zu den glücklichen Gewinnern gehören, in die Lage versetzen, ein bißchen wie der schöne Rebell auszusehen. Denn zehn rote Jacken im James-Dean-Stil sind ebenfalls bei dieser Aktion zu gewinnen. Sie müssen nur noch unsere Quizfrage richtig beantworten:
In welchem der drei obengenannten Filme mit James Dean hat Liz Taylor mitgespielt?
Schreiben Sie den Titel auf eine Postkarte und senden Sie diese bis zum 18. 1. 1989 an cinema, Stichwort: „Dean", Postfach 13 21 74, 2000 Hamburg 13. Der Rechtsweg ist ausgeschlossen. Viel Glück!

PICTUREGOER December 29 1956

1957 will see the British showing of "Giant"—epitaph to a brief but brilliant film career. Here its photographic director recalls...

The JAMES DEAN I knew

In Giant, James Dean ages throughout the story. He starts as a young farmhand

by WILLIAM C. MELLOR

who was director of photography on the Crosby - Hope "Road" films, "A Place In The Sun" (for which he won an Oscar), "Giant," and currently "Love In The Afternoon," shot in Paris

THERE were just a few of us at the Warner studio preview theatre — director George Stevens, Liz Taylor, Rock Hudson, one or two others. We were watching some of the final rushes of *Giant*. One figure was absent. He was not in the theatre, not in that day's rushes.

As we were talking over the scenes—all of us pretty happy with things—a message came in. A little Porsche sports car had crashed on State Highway 41, not many miles from the studio. The driver, James Dean, had been killed.

This was a moment I shall not forget. Elizabeth Taylor, highly strung, emotional, broke down and sobbed—she remained in a state of near-collapse for three days. George Stevens was stunned. Rock Hudson was silent. All I remember George saying was: "It can't be true. It just can't."

While we were making *Giant*, I think we all knew that young Jimmy Dean was giving a performance that not even the extreme adjectives of Hollywood could adequately sum up. It's not often a unit gets a feeling like that in the disjointed, sometimes confusing hurly-burly of making a film.

We had the feeling with Jimmy Dean on *Giant*. We have a similar feeling now on *Love In The Afternoon*, which has been shot under Billy Wilder's direction in Paris. Audrey Hepburn is as different from Jimmy as chalk from cheese—except for one thing. And that is a first-rate instinctive talent.

When, in the preview theatre that day, we heard Dean was dead, we knew Hollywood—and picturegoers—had lost a talent that might never be replaced. We DIDN'T know how grotesque would be the aftermath.

There has been so much written about James Dean since then — so much trash, morbid sensationalism, phoney sentiment, so much vulgar rubbish—that I'm almost scared to add anything.

You must have read, or read about, the Dean-Isn't-Dead stories, the pulp magazines that were rushed out, the so-called James Dean disc albums, the girl who claimed to have been Jimmy's secret bride.

I want to write simply as an ordinary guy who knew Jimmy Dean as a workmate. No gimmicks from me; no psychological probing. All this crazy mixed-up stuff since his death makes me sick. And I think it would have sickened him as well.

He wasn't a headline-seeker. He once said: "An artist should be judged on his performance only. All the rest is unimportant." If the youngsters who rave so crazily over him now are really his admirers, I wonder why they don't respect his words?

When Jimmy took his little Porsche Spyder out for the last time, he thought his work on *Giant* was over. In fact, George Stevens intended to take a couple of extra-close-ups to cut into some longer shots of Jimmy. Fortunately, the film isn't harmed by the omission.

What's my lasting memory of James Dean? Simple. A picture of a small-town boy, rocketed to success without warning, without preparation — an average young American still confused by a new life, not yet adjusted to fame, fortune and fan mania.

Crazy-mixed-up, as many writers have said? No more so than many other youngsters who happen to be a step or two off the path they've been brought up to walk.

He'd say some odd things sometimes. One day I wanted

Continued on page 24

Then Dean, who has inherited some property, drives co-star Elizabeth Taylor over his land

Oil tycoon Dean—much older now—is greeted by a screen newcomer, Carroll Baker

Picturegoer (UK), 29 Dec 1956

to talk over a scene with him. We were walking over to the parking lot. Suddenly Dean said: "Take a good look at me. You may not get the chance again."

An odd thing to say? You're right. It had me puzzled. But kids often say funny things, maybe just for laughs.

His manner was never exactly formal, or conventionally polite to anyone.

I remember Dean once explained this side of himself to a visiting journalist, quite simply. "I came to Hollywood," he said, " to act, not to charm society."

Dean had the same outdoor interests as thousands of other youngsters. He was, as you know, crazy over sports cars and motor-cycles.

We filmed a lot of *Giant* out on location. Often at night he'd go out rabbit-shooting with a local boy who helped him with the Texan accent.

Between takes, he often sat alone—a frail-looking boy with glasses that made him appear kind of brooding. But he'd talk with the unit and was pretty quick with the banter.

In front of the camera he had an instinct that was nearly uncanny. I don't recall ever working with anyone who has such a gift. I recall one scene where he was in shadow and had to lift his head to the light.

We explained how it should go and he played it exactly right to the half inch first time. He just seemed to *know* how it should be, without rehearsal or anything.

Don't think, though, that he was the sort of actor who's just left to play a rôle as he likes. He and director Stevens worked very closely together — each, fortunately, admired the other, respected the other's judgment.

Dean tended to be slow in his scenes and George Stevens had to hurry him up a bit. But remember that he had made only three pictures.

Yes . . . a very remarkable young man. I'm glad I worked with him, got to know him. I'm sorry that since his death so much pseudo-psychological mystery has been built up around him.

But I shall always remember James Dean WITHOUT all the complications that have been added. I'll remember him as a pretty average American boy—a rebel, like so many more, but with the healthy, normal, outdoor interests.

With this difference, as George Stevens says: " He had an individualized approach that is opening up a new tradition of acting in Hollywood."

THAT SEEMS TO ME A HANDSOME ENOUGH MEMORIAL FOR ANY YOUNG ACTOR.

GIGANTEN
Wahnsinns-Drama mit James Dean, Elizabeth Taylor und Rock Hudson

SAT1
23.8.
22.05 Uhr

Der letzte Film des unvergessenen James Dean. Ein Streifen (dauert 183 Minuten) mit einer wahren Star-Besetzung. Der reiche texanische Viehzüchter Bick Benedict (Rock Hudson) will in Maryland einen wertvollen Hengst kaufen. Dort lernt er die blutjunge Leslie (Elizabeth Taylor) kennen. Für beide ist es Liebe auf den ersten Blick. Leslie kehrt als Mrs. Benedict mit Bick auf seine Ranch „Reata" zurück. Bicks Schwester Luz kann Leslie nicht leiden. Ihre mütterliche Zuneigung gilt dem Ranch-Gehilfen Jett Rink (James Dean), den wiederum Bick nicht mag. Bei einem Ausritt verunglückt Luz tödlich. In ihrem Testament vermacht sie Jett zum Ärger ihres Bruders ein Stück Land. Das Land

Kommen nicht zusammen: Jett (James Dean) und Leslie (Elizabeth Taylor)

scheint jedoch nur ein kümmerlicher Brachboden zu sein. Doch eines Tages schießt Öl aus einem Bohrloch. Jett wird im Laufe der Jahre immer reicher. Reicher als der ihm verhaßte Bick. Aber die gesellschaftliche Anerkennung bleibt Jett versagt. Er ist seit Jahrzehnten auch unglücklich verliebt: in Leslie. Als „älterer Herr" verliebt er sich dann in Luz (Carroll Baker), die ein Ebenbild ihrer Mutter Leslie ist. Vater Bick verbietet seiner Tochter den Umgang mit Jett. Doch Luz trifft sich weiterhin mit ihm. Zwischen Jett und Bick kommt es zum Krach.

DER KNÜLLER

THE FOOTPRINTS OF A GIANT

HIS TRUE GREATNESS

From the producer of *Giant*, a salute to genius.

■ James Dean impressed me as a young man eager to accomplish much as quickly as possible. He certainly was successful in motion pictures. In 16 months of film acting he left a more lasting impression on the public than many stars do in 30 years.

After working with him on *Giant* I can understand why the impact of his personality was so great. Though he was not an easy person to know, it was worth breaking through his reserve. He was naturally shy and did not like to make small talk. Once Jimmy felt he could trust a person he opened up. He was an exciting and stimulating person to be with. I believe he could be described as a genius.

He was well informed on many subjects. Jimmy believed an actor must do more than portray himself on the screen. His performance should be a bit of life. He reasoned that to be able to give realistic portrayals an actor should learn as much and do as many different things as possible. He was always studying.

Jimmy was a perfectionist in everything he attempted. His manner of approach to the role of Jett Rink, the Texas ranch hand who becomes an oil millionaire in *Giant*, was an example.

Any good actor would have spent many hours learning a Texas accent as Jimmy did. But the average actor wouldn't have done the many little extra things Jimmy did to make his portrayal as nearly perfect as possible. He rode horseback daily, he learned to rope cattle and to play a guitar. He didn't have to do any of these in the picture. Yet Jimmy felt he would obtain a deeper understanding for the character if away from the set he did what was natural for Jett.

Jimmy's skill with the rope paid off concretely in one sequence. It was inside the big mansion of Jett's employers, played by Elizabeth Taylor and Rock Hudson. Jimmy nonchalantly did a rope trick as he delivered his lines. Needless to say, he stole the scene.

My admiration for Jimmy grew during the months I was privileged to know him. He was one of the rare people about whom one can truly say, "He is not dead." James Dean and the magic quality he had on the screen will never be forgotten.

By **HENRY GINSBERG**

(Top) Working intimately with Jimmy on his last film were director and co-producer George Stevens, author Edna Ferber and producer Henry Ginsberg who wrote the tribute above. They knew his serious side at work (center), the carefree boyishness with which he could relax (below). Jimmy loved children, would always find time for them when they came to the set, never turned them away from his door at home. His dream was for kids of his own.

ジェイムス・ディーン最後の映画
「ジャイアンツ」
いよいよ公開決定

ジェームス・ディーン
エリザベス・テーラー
ロック・ハドソン

巨匠ジョージ・スチーブンス製作・監督
原作■エドナ・ファーバー
脚本■フレッド・ギュイオル
　　　アイバン・モファット
音楽■ディミトリー・ティオムキン

ワーナーカラー
ワーナー・ブラザース映画

原作■早川書房刊
サントラ盤■キャピトル・レコード

新春第2弾ロードショウ　丸の内松竹(201)3720　■団体鑑賞券450円

ジャイアンツ

GEORGE STEVENS
GIANT

広大なテキサスに誇りと情熱を賭けた激動の人間像！
雄大なスケールで美しく描く愛の大ロマン！

IN MEMORIAM

EAST OF EDEN, U.S.A., 1954

Certificate: A. *Distributors:* Warner Bros. *Production Company:* Warner Bros. *Producer/Director:* Elia Kazan. *Script:* Paul Osborn, from the novel by John Steinbeck. *Photography:* Ted McCord. Filmed in CinemaScope. *Colour Process:* Warnercolor, print by Technicolor. *Editor:* Owen Marks. *Art Directors:* James Basevi, Malcolm Bert. *Music:* Leonard Rosenman. *Sound:* Stanley Jones. *Leading Players:* James Dean (*Caleb Trask*), Julie Harris (*Abra*), Raymond Massey (*Adam Trask*), Jo Van Fleet (*Kate Trask*), Burl Ives (*Sheriff*), Richard Davalos (*Aron Trask*), Albert Dekker (*Will*), Lois Smith (*Ann*), Harold Gordon (*Albrecht*). 10,272 ft. 114 mins.

1913, in Salinas Valley, California. Cal, younger son of a lettuce farmer, is a wild adolescent, believing himself unloved and misunderstood by his austere father, and obscurely jealous of Aron, his elder brother. When he learns that his mother, long believed by himself and Aron to be dead, is running a shady establishment at Monterey, he decides he has discovered why he is " no good ". He goes secretly to see his mother, who, drunken and embittered, takes a fancy to him. War comes, and Adam Trask's farm falls on bad days. Cal, jealous now of the happiness of Aron and his sweetheart Abra, decides to help his father. He gets his mother to advance him 5,000 dollars, and triumphantly presents it to his father on his birthday. But the gift is misunderstood and repudiated, and Cal, in desperation, relieves his anger by telling Aron about their mother. Aron at once enlists for the front, and Adam has a stroke. It is Abra who reconciles tormented son and stricken father.

Elia Kazan's new film, awarded the *Prix Dramatique* at the 1955 Cannes Festival, is handsomely, impressively mounted, loaded with detail and effect; but the impression it makes is dull and pretentious. The Steinbeck novel, on episodes from which the story is based, makes great play with Biblical parallels—Cal and Aron compared to Cain and Abel—while failing to justify them. Relationships are explored with a good deal of superficial emphasis, but few of them seem real. Cal's jealousy of Aron, indeed, is almost completely unmotivated; in the first half of the film there is apparently no tension between them, in the second they are suddenly bitter antagonists. And when Aron enlists for the front, everyone assumes at once that he will be killed, in order to justify calling Cal Cain.

This hollowness at the centre is emphasised by Kazan's treatment, even more obsessed with camera " style " and acting " business " than his previous films. Minor characters are overladen with distracting mannerisms of voice and gesture, sentences of dialogue are perversely broken up for spurious " naturalism ". James Dean, a newcomer from the stage of evident talent, is encouraged to imitate Marlon Brando and sacrifice his individuality, which only occasionally breaks through, in doing so. Julie Harris as Abra brings a rather hard, calculated quality to her part, and Lois Smith as a maid, Harold Gordon as a German doctor are allowed fussily to overplay. The most impressive and consistent performance comes from Jo Van Fleet as Kate Trask, and the scene of the first encounter between her and Cal is by far the best in the film. Here Kazan gets down to the essence of the situation, and reminds one of what a talented director he can be. For the rest, the attempts at " significance " and meaning induce a sense of strain and inflation.

Suitability: A, B.   July 1955   G.L.

REBEL WITHOUT A CAUSE, U.S.A., 1955

Cert: X. *dist:* Warner Bros. *p.c.:* Warner Bros. *p:* David Weisbart. *d:* Nicholas Ray. *sc:* Stewart Stern. *adapt:* Irving Shulman, from a story by Nicholas Ray. *ph:* Ernest Haller. CinemaScope. *col:* WarnerColor. *ed:* William Ziegler. *a.d.:* Malcolm Bert. *m:* Leonard Rosenman. *sd:* Stanley Jones. *l.p.:* James Dean (*Jim*), Jim Backus (*Father*), Ann Doran (*Mother*), Virginia Brissac (*Grandmother*), Natalie Wood (*Judy*), William Hopper (*Judy's father*), Rochelle Hudson (*Judy's mother*), Corey Allen (*Buzz*), Sal Mineo (*Plato*), Dennis Hopper (*Goon*), Edward Blatt (*Psychiatrist*). 9,973 ft. 110 mins.

Jim is the adolescent son of well-to-do parents: weak father, dominating mother. His inner conflicts express themselves in acts of violence and trouble with the police, the implications of which his parents refuse to face. At school, Plato—child of divorced parents—is drawn to him, as Jim is drawn to Judy, a girl unbalanced by her father's sudden withdrawal of affection from her in favour of her younger brother. Jim and Buzz, Judy's rowdy boy-friend, quarrel; and after an inconclusive knife-fight, they agree to meet later for a " chicken run "—an endurance test which involves driving a stolen car as near as possible to the edge of a cliff, the winner being the last to leap free. There is an accident, and Buzz goes over with his car. Jim feels he must go to the police, but his parents object; Buzz's gang also threaten to beat him up. Jim and Judy flee to a deserted house in the hills, where they are joined by Plato. Buzz's gang follows, and Plato shoots one of them; he in turn is shot as the police arrive. As a result of these events, the parents of Jim and Judy acquire new insight, and are prepared to view their love sympathetically.

The central triumph of *Rebel Without a Cause* is the character study of Jim; Nicholas Ray and the late James Dean have created a powerful and moving portrait of a tormented adolescent, and the analysis of the tensions which beset him has an insight, an understanding, rare in this kind of film. By setting him on the right side of the tracks, the facile explanations of poverty, etc., are out of the question; instead, some brilliantly written and directed scenes probe the relationship of his father and mother and, in doing so, provide the sharpest, angriest comment on some patterns in American family life that has been seen in the cinema. Particularly striking is the scene when Jim tries to explain his feeling after the " chicken run " accident, and in his parents' reaction the whole gulf between them is exposed. Equally intuitive is the handling of Judy's strong emotional attachment to her father, and her rage at his sudden, nervous rejection of it. The rhythm, the tone, of disturbed youth is remarkably conveyed in all these scenes, and the ironic, tender sequence in the deserted house, when the three youngsters suddenly express all their feelings of uncertainty and isolation in a wild night game, is another triumph. It is only the resolution that seems a little hurried. But as a whole this is a film of outstanding talent, the first that has allowed its director's scope full play since *They Live by Night*.

The knife-fight scene, incidentally, has been drastically curtailed by the British censor, and becomes momentarily incomprehensible.
Suitability: A.   February 1956   G.L.

A downside to having one's film journals bound is that they're then difficult to scan. These are from the British Film Institute's Monthly Film Bulletin. *Eden* and *Rebel* are reviewed by Gavin Lambert, a friend of *if....* director, Lindsay Anderson, On Anderson's death, Lambert wrote a scurrilous biography outing him. *Giant* is reviewed by Derek Prouse.

GIANT, U.S.A., 1956

Cert: A. *dist*: Warner Bros. *p.c.*: Warner Bros. *p*: George Stevens, Henry Ginsberg. *d*: George Stevens. *sc*: Fred Guiol, Ivan Moffatt, from the novel by Edna Ferber. *ph*: William C. Mellor. *col*: WarnerColor. *ed*: William Hornbeck. *a.d.*: Boris Leven. *m*: Dimitri Tiomkin. *songs*: "There's Never Been Anyone Else But You" and "Giant", Paul Francis Webster and Dimitri Tiomkin. *sd*: Earl Crain, Sr. *l.p.*: Elizabeth Taylor (*Leslie Benedict*), Rock Hudson (*Bick Benedict*), James Dean (*Jett Rink*), Jane Withers (*Vashti Snythe*), Chill Wills (*Uncle Bawley*), Mercedes McCambridge (*Luz Benedict*), Carroll Baker (*Luz Benedict II*), Dennis Hopper (*Jordan Benedict III*), Judith Evelyn (*Mrs. Horace Lynnton*), Paul Fix (*Dr. Horace Lynnton*), Rodney Taylor (*Sir David Karfrey*), Earl Holliman (*Bob Dace*), Robert Nichols (*Pinky Snythe*), Alexander Scourby (*Old Polo*), Sal Mineo (*Angel Obregon III*), Fran Bennett (*Judy Benedict*), Charles Watts (*Whiteside*), Elsa Cardenas (*Juana*). 17,731 ft. ? mins.

Bick Benedict, a rich cattle rancher, takes his Maryland bride, Leslie Lynnton, home to his Texas estate. Leslie finds the great household ruled by Bick's overbearing sister Luz, who suffers a fatal fall when she ill-treats Leslie's favourite stallion. In her will, Luz leaves a small part of the ranch to Jett Rink, a moody but deeply ambitious ranch-hand. Rink's dreams of wealth come true when he strikes oil.

Meanwhile Leslie and Bick have three children, all of whom frustrate their parents' plans for their future. The son, Jordy, marries Juana, a Mexican, in the face of Bick's deep-seated feelings of racial superiority. Luz, their youngest daughter, infuriates Bick by riding in Jett Rink's rodeo parade at the opening of his luxurious hotel and airport. When Juana is refused admission to the hotel's beauty salon on racial grounds, Jordy brawls with Jett and is thrown out by the latter's henchmen. Bick, out of loyalty to his family, challenges Jett to a fight, but leaves him in disgust when he discovers he is drunk. Jett attempts to address the distinguished assembly gathered for the opening, but slumps over the table in a drunken stupor. Young Luz, who has been fascinated by Jett, is completely disillusioned, and the family return home. On the way they stop at a roadside restaurant, whose owner insults some poor Mexican customers. Bick defends them, and is beaten in a fight. Back home he abjectly confesses to Leslie his sense of defeat. She assures him that, for the first time, she considers him a truly successful man, having at last fought for a worth-while cause.

The novel on which the film is based is clearly a massive, sprawling work. Usually such novels, when they are concerned with rich life and traditional loyalties, are kept going by a rough gusto and vigour. *Giant*, however, is not a vigorous work: it is extremely leisurely, sometimes to the point of tedium. Its concern is not with unusual depths of character; its people remain for the most part on the level we have come to expect from the American family saga. On the other hand, the romantic pair—the dyed-in-the-wool rancher and the Maryland belle—do convincingly broaden and mellow with the advancing years and their marital ups-and-downs.

In the beginning there are some brilliant satiric scenes in the high-toned Maryland household where the rough-hewn Texan first meets his love. Later, in Texas, events lose their edge. Luz is rather a conventional figure; and the most entertaining moments are the glimpses of the unpolished neighbours (Jane Withers, the lucy thirties child-star, is perhaps the best of these). The least satisfactory aspect of the film is the performance of James Dean. In the early stages of the film, where he is still the problem child of the ranch, he is convincing enough; but when, later, he is called upon to portray the middle-aged successful prospector, he is out of his depth; and his failure weakens the last part of the film. Many scenes are distinguished by Stevens' personal qualities; in the quiet scenes of the married couple together, he shows himself as one of the cinema's leading creators of a truly intimate mood, which Rock Hudson and Elizabeth Taylor admirably interpret. When, half-way through, the film becomes mainly concerned with the theme of racial intolerance, its sentiments are irreproachable, but its exposition naive. One is sceptical that the dear son of the prejudiced Texan should fall in love at sight with a Mexican girl mainly, it seems, because she studies medicine. It is somehow too late in the day by then for such contrived circumstances to grip one—particularly since by the time this stage in the film is reached nothing can hide the truth that *Giant* would be both more entertaining and compelling if it were an hour shorter.

Suitability: A, B.

February 1957   D.P.

THE JAMES DEAN STORY

OF all the strange phenomena to which the mass idolatry of the cinema has given rise, few equal the James Dean legend. Dean was killed when only one of his three films had been released; and it was not until several months after his death that the cult began to grow to the strange proportions it eventually reached. The excesses are not entirely explained by the purely romantic interest of the actor—his indefinite sexiness, his violent and youthful death—nor by his undeniable talent. It was more that Dean found a striking sympathy between his own temperament and background and the parts he was called upon to play; and through them he was able to strike, very accurately, some characteristics of his whole generation.

The James Dean Story (Warners), directed by George W. George and Robert Altman, and scripted by Stewart Stern (who wrote the screenplay for *Rebel Without a Cause*) is a contribution and a stimulus to the legend. The film breaks new ground by its purely documentary approach; the way with show-business life-stories has always previously been to avoid using the least fragment of authentic material (for *The Buster Keaton Story* even some of the comedian's classic slapstick was, disastrously, re-staged). Apart from a few staged details (most of them unsuccessful) all the material in this film is documentary—stills of Dean at various stages of his life, shots of the places in which he lived, interviews with the people who knew him and worked with him, a tape recording he made of a conversation with his family, a screen-test for *East of Eden*. The weakness of the film arises from the attempt to spin out this material—enough for a good thirty-minute short—to feature-length. In its repetitive analysis of Dean's personality and problems, its overlong interviews and excessive use of stills, the film becomes from time to time tedious, and is forced into pretentious over-writing.

At the same time, it makes surprisingly few concessions to the fan-following. Apart from a rather embarrassing sequence dealing, apparently, with the Pier Angeli affair, and interviews with two young actresses who were somewhat fruitlessly 'dated' by Dean, there is no attempt to manufacture a 'love-interest'. Even the presentation of the rather morbid details of Dean's dreadful death is done with reasonable tact.

The film really convinces you that it is a serious attempt to probe the character of this extraordinary, talented and undoubtedly tormented young man, with his self-confessed longing for someone to love and for flamboyant success, his sense of isolation and of parental deprivation. If it rarely gets further than a lot of words, it is probably because Dean's real problems, socially and psychologically were at once too involved and too familiar for this sort of discussion.

DAVID ROBINSON

Sight & Sound (UK) Autumn 1957

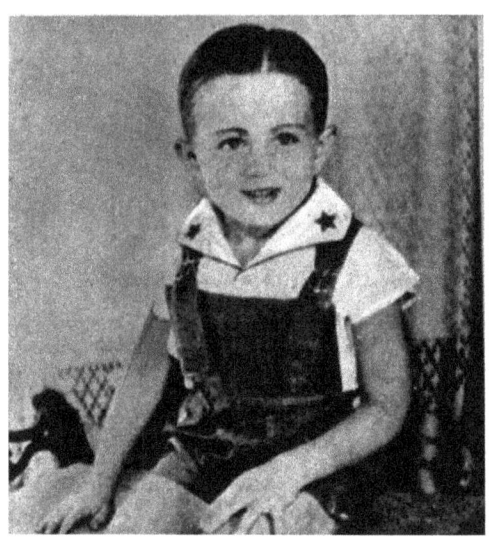

James Dean with his father on leave
from World War Two

Childhood

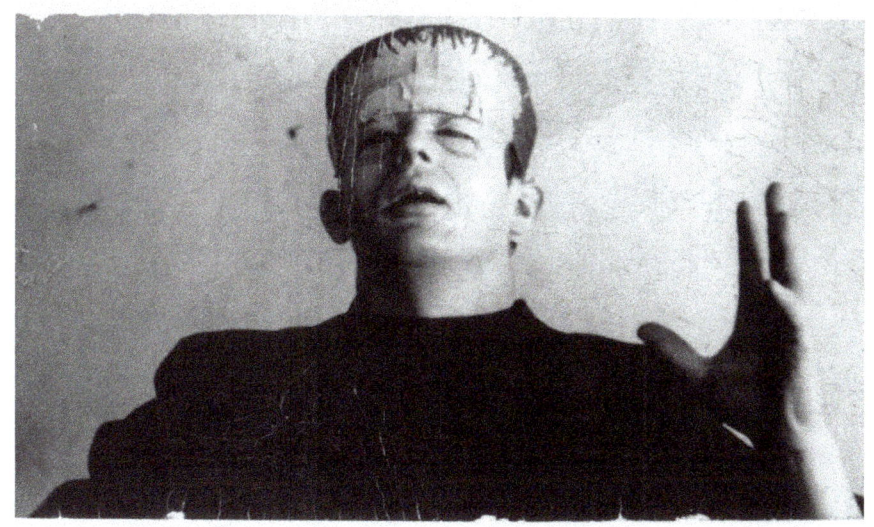

"Nature kindly warps our judgment about children, especially when they are young, when it would be a fatal thing for them if we did not love them. This fond blindness is itself a slavery, a hard slavery, when you think of it, to feel a compulsory and sleepless affection . . ."

Many of Jimmy's scrapbook pages consist of paintings and photographs which he clipped out of magazines and newspapers with poetry or significant text pasted on them. They express his love of children and his sympathy for the lost and lonely. In a way, Jim thought of himself as a lonely child searching for life's meaning in the only way he knew, through love, beauty and art. Whether or not he had found it at the time of his death is not important. What IS significant is that Jimmy never stopped looking.

We know what's important to a man by the things he keeps. Jimmy Dean kept many things . . . . scraps of paper, sketches, newspaper articles. When we looked them over we learned a lot of things about Jimmy . . . we think you will too.

This painting was one of Jimmy's first attempts to create immortality. The orchid, painted for a teacher in high school, was withering, so he painted it to last forever.

"The peace and hope and faith that babies have brought since the world began recompense for any hardship and peril and heartache." / "Sleep and rest, sleep and rest, / father will come to thee soon; / Rest, rest on mother's breast, / father will come to thee soon; / Father will come to his babe in the nest. . . ."

"The guess is nearly the get— well, a half or a quarter; the former's the "yes, but not yet" of the latter. So take the nibble—though need be satisfied barely— of what shall finally feed you entirely."

"When he passes thru the gate of adolescence into maturity, from the shelter of your home into the unknown, he'll be strong, confident, and fearless. He'll be kind and generous because he himself is rooted in love and in gentle ways. In short, he'll be the kind of lad you'd like him to be!"

Jimmy's own scrap- books

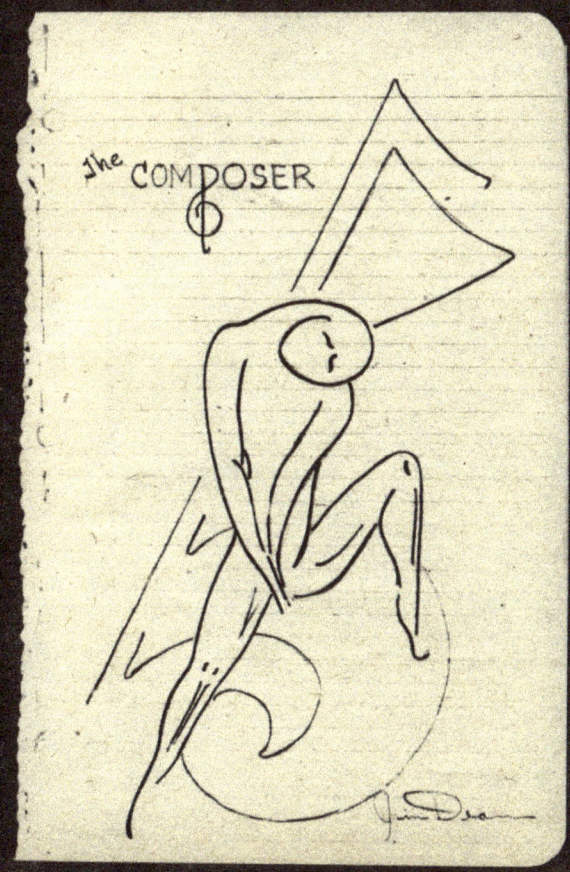

James Dean Anniversary Book 1956 (Dell)

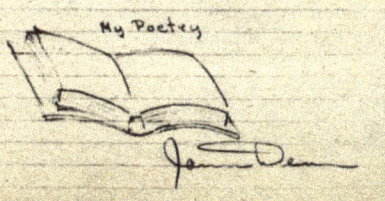

These two sketches are from Jimmy's notebooks. He signed them both, so he must have felt they expressed something important. So do we.

JAMES DEAN — THE BOY I LOVED

By Jimmy's Grandmother
EMMA WOOLEN DEAN

*When you voted him
one of your favorites
for a Photoplay Gold Medal Award,
I knew you loved him, too.
And I knew you would want
to know him the way I did*

● None of us will ever forget that last family reunion we had with Jimmy in the spring of 1955. He had finished "East of Eden." He'd got his wish: he knew he was a good actor.

Jimmy had been to New York, then came here to Fairmount before returning to California. Everybody here was excited —not that Jimmy had to be an actor to be welcomed in Fairmount; he didn't. People here always liked him. But this was different. When "East of Eden" was at the drive-in, so many people went it made a traffic jam.

But, in spite of all the fanfare, Jimmy only wanted to be with his family. We all gathered out at my daughter Hortense's farm. Hortense and Marcus Winslow raised Jimmy after his mother died. Jimmy and Charlie—that's my husband—had just come back from the cemetery, where Jimmy had taken pictures of his great grandfather's and great-great grandfather's graves. When they came in, Jimmy turned to Charlie and said, "Grampa, do you think you could do some auctioneering?"

Now my husband Charlie has always claimed his father was the best auctioneer living. So with us, what Jimmy said was kind of a little joke. When Jimmy was little, Charlie would hold him on his knee and auction him off to me, and I'd buy him and Jimmy would laugh.

Well, it ended up this time that Jimmy talked Charlie into auctioneering little Markie Winslow's dog right back to Markie. (Markie is Hortense's and Marcus' little boy.) We laughed, but didn't think anything about this little joke until the next day when Jimmy opened this "satchel" he'd had standing around. It turned out the satchel was a tape recorder. You should have seen my husband's face when Jimmy played it back! Charlie said, "Hey, you shouldn't have done that without telling me. I used some words there that maybe don't belong in polite society."

Well, Jimmy wouldn't give in. He said, "That's how I'm going to take you back to California *(Continued on page 84)*

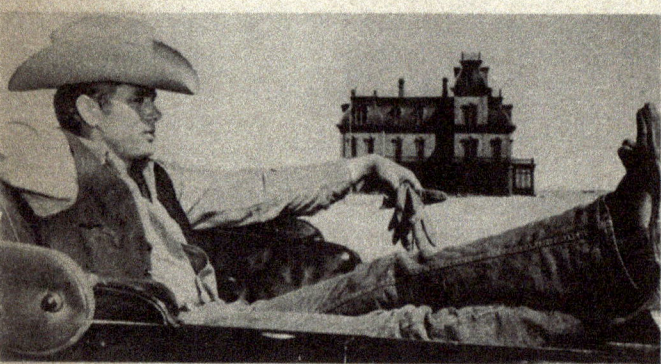

On location for "Giant," Jimmy's last picture. Far right, with Natalie Wood in "Rebel Without a Cause." At right, in "East of Eden," with Julie Harris

James Dean—The Boy I Loved

(Continued from page 57)

with me—for now. But someday I'm going to have a nice house and I want you and Grandma to live with me."

That was our Jimmy. His family meant a lot to him and he meant even more to us. While we're not the ones to do much lollygagging around, kissing and hugging each other, it does seem that whenever we're going to be separated and have to see someone off, we all have tears running down our faces.

You might say we're a close-knit family. That's what comes from living in one place for so long. The first Deans came from around Lexington, Kentucky, and settled in Grant County, Indiana, about 1815. My family, the Woolens, and Jimmy's mother's family, the Wilsons, got here about the same time.

Mostly, we've been around Fairmount or Marion—sixty, seventy miles from Indianapolis—ever since. Charlie and I live on Washington Street, in Fairmount, but he still farms, as he has always done. Charlie's a great hand at having two or three things going at once. At various times he's been a stock buyer, run a livery stable, sold automobiles and raced a string of horses. We're not rich, but we're not poor, either. So long as I live, I'll always have a porch to sit on, a rocking chair to rock in and a clock that strikes.

We have three children, Hortense, Winton and Charles Nolan. I don't want to get a lot of "begats" into this, as in the Bible, but so as you can keep all of us straight, I'd like to say that you couldn't ask for a nicer bunch of grandchildren and great grandchildren.

Hortense married Marcus Winslow and they have Joan and young Marcus. Winton married Mildred Wilson and Jimmy was born February 8, 1931. Charles Nolan married Mildred Miller and they have Joseph, David and Betsy Jane. Joan, who is now Mrs. Mayron Reece Peacock, gave us our first great-grandchildren, Gerrell Reece and Jane Ann.

They're all dear to us, but Jimmy was almost like a son in each of the families. We all tried to make it up to him for losing his mother.

I'll never forget the day Winton's letter came telling us that Mildred couldn't get well. They lived in Santa Monica where Winton was supervisor of the dental laboratory at the Veterans' Hospital. Jimmy was just nine then. Winton asked if I could come out. Mildred, who was so young and lovely, had cancer. I took the letter to our doctor and he judged I'd be there six to eight weeks. I was gone seven, and when I brought Mildred's body back, Jimmy was with me, for after the services out there, I gave Winton the Winslows' message.

I said, I recall, "Now Winton, I want you to think this over carefully. If you see fit to let Jimmy come back to Fairmount, Hortense and Marcus would like to take him. They'll raise him for you, if you want." Having a boy on the farm would be nice. Joan was then their only child. Markie wasn't yet born.

Well, poor Winton just sat there and stared. At last he said, "It never occurred to me I might be separated from Jimmy."

But Winton knew what he faced. He had a living to earn and didn't have a single relative in California. At last he said, "You can't find a finer man than Marcus Winslow, and so far as choosing between the way my sister would mother Jimmy and how some housekeeper might take care of him, there's just no question."

Hard as it was, I've always felt Winton made the right choice, particularly since it turned out that he was drafted about eighteen months later.

It helped that the Winslow farm already was home to Jimmy. For a while, when Winton had worked in Marion, they had lived in the little cottage up beyond the Friends' Back Creek meeting house, on the corner of the farm.

And just to show you how Marcus and Hortense welcomed Jimmy, they even gave him their own room and moved across the hall. Hortense said, "He liked our bedroom set better. It was maple and that seemed right for a boy."

I don't mean to brag, but Hortense and Marcus are a daughter and son-in-law any woman would be proud to own. They do their share in the community, and besides their organizations, Hortense plays piano for the Friends' Sunday school and Marcus is interested in Earlham College, a Quaker school near here. Both are wise and gentle and have a great gift for loving. Theirs is like a Quaker home should be. You never hear a harsh word. Best of all, they are happy as well as good—and that's what Jimmy needed most after the shock of losing his mother.

Joan, too, made a great fuss over Jimmy, and so did her friends. Always, there were lots of young people around, for they all loved to come to the Winslow farm.

It's just two miles north of town and it's a beautiful place. Several farm magazines have used pictures of it on their covers and camera clubs come there for

---

Be sure to watch the

**PHOTOPLAY
GOLD MEDAL AWARD
PRESENTATIONS**

on Lux Video Theatre—NBC-TV

10 p.m. EST, Thursday, February 9

---

their outings. Every Winslow for generations has done something to improve it. The big square white "new" house, built in 1904, stands on a hill and the land rolls down to the farmyard with its white barns and sheds. A stand of timber along the creek sets off the buildings. In the near pasture, there's a big pond. Marcus ran an electric line out and strung lights so the kids could skate on winter nights. Summers there was always a picnic going.

Maybe the best way to tell you how Marcus and Jimmy got along would be to repeat what one of Jimmy's classmates said to me. "Ma Dean," he said, "I always envied Jimmy. My dad never took time to play with me, but Marcus was forever out there shooting baskets with Jimmy or passing a football or taking him hunting or showing him how to do stunts."

For Jimmy, it soon added up to health, happiness and that charge of energy which later was sort of able to break right through a movie screen. Seems like he could do anything. A professional figure-skating teacher who happened into our town gave him a few lessons, then said Jimmy was as good a skater as he was. Jimmy also wanted to play basketball and, although he wasn't big and rangy like most boys that make the team, he was quick and sure of himself and turned out to be a good player.

One reason Jimmy could do so well was that he was a born mimic. Charlie and I used to laugh about it when he was a little shaver. Charlie and Jimmy always were awfully fond of each other. If Charlie sat with his knees crossed, Jimmy crossed his; if Charlie stretched out his legs, Jimmy did, too. It was more than just mocking Charlie's gestures. Even then, Jimmy seemed able to *be* another person.

He did right well with his 4-H projects. The first year he had baby chicks, the second a garden and then it was cattle. Eventually, his Guernsey bull won grand champion at the county fair.

But the funniest was Jimmy's pig. As a farm boy usually does, Jimmy got the runt of a litter. He bottle-fed it and it became his pet. There would be Jimmy and his dog, crossing the yard and that pig, running along behind, squealing and oinking and trying to keep up with them.

Marcus and Hortense saw that Jimmy had every advantage. He could draw and paint and work with clay. When Joan took dancing lessons, Jimmy got them, too. Hortense tried to teach him piano, but there was too much playing to be done outdoors for him to ever want to practice. Violin was no better, but when they got him a bass horn, Jimmy took to it. That and drums. Before he finished high school, he could play almost any instrument in the band.

He sure took after Charlie when it came to cars. Charlie bought his first car in 1911 and horrified the town by scorching along at 35 miles an hour. Jimmy learned to drive a tractor first, and then his bikes. He had a little boy's bicycle first, then his whizzer—a bike with a motor. A real noisy motor. You could hear Jimmy coming three miles away. Then he got to trading. Start an Indiana boy with a jackknife and he'll end up with a house and lot. Jimmy swapped his whizzer for a little foreign cycle and after that his motorcycles got larger and larger.

Clearest proof that Jimmy could do whatever he set his mind to was his marks in school. In grammar school, they called him Quiz Kid. It helped that he went to visit his father nearly every vacation, for then he'd stand up in class and tell about places he'd seen. In high school, it was a different story. Jimmy got the notion it was what he called "square" to study. Well, his senior year, Marcus had a talk with him. "You'll never get into college with such grades," Marcus told him. Well, sir, Jimmy got down to business. He stayed on the honor roll all year.

He had a hard time making up his mind whether he wanted to be an actor or a lawyer. Winton favored law, but he hadn't seen Jimmy in as many plays as the rest of us. Marcus, who always encouraged Jimmy in all he wanted to do, helped him decide on his school. First Jimmy wanted to go to Earlham, where Marcus went, but Marcus pointed out that if he wanted to act, he'd better go to California.

It was becoming plain to all of us that acting was the thing Jimmy was best at. He won declamatory contests, even a state one, but the thing that convinced us he was an actor was his appearance in a church play, called "To Them That Sleep in Darkness." Jimmy played the blind boy. Well, I'll tell you, I wished he wasn't quite so good at it. I cried all the way through.

Jimmy was in his glory when Joan got married to Reece Peacock. Markie was still a toddler, so it was Jimmy who was in the mischievous little brother position. It was during the war and rice was hard to get, but Jimmy found some. He went to store after store and saved it up for weeks. Then he tied stuff to their car. He sure fixed it up so they went clanking down the road.

I like to remember, too, the understanding Marcus and Jimmy reached before he left Fairmount. Jimmy wanted to earn his way, do it all himself, but Marcus knew that would be difficult. So Marcus said, "Now Jimmy, I don't want you running up a board bill. Stay out of debt. If you get short, let me know." Winton, I understand, said the same.

It was nice that Jimmy could spend a year with his father. Winton had been five years a widower when he married Ethel Case in 1945. Jimmy lived with them that first year when he attended Santa Monica Junior College. Later he went to UCLA and then to New York to study at the Actors Studio.

Thanks to television, we felt we shared those New York days with Jimmy. We had to buy television sets as soon as he began getting parts in programs. Marcus and Hortense had one of the first sets around here, and then Charlie and I got one. The old grapevine got going every time Jimmy was on *Lux* or *Studio One* or some program like that. They'd announce it in school and the neighbors would come streaming in to watch.

It's hard for us to understand why Jimmy's life had to end so soon. Seemed like he was just beginning to give other people the same kind of pleasure he had always given his family.

One thing I'll always be glad of is that Jimmy did get that house he wanted and that he had a chance to show it to some of those closest to him. Last fall, both Marcus and Hortense and Charles Nolan and his Mildred went out to see Winton and Jimmy. Marcus and Hortense had ended their visit and were driving back. They didn't know about Jimmy's accident until they got back to Fairmount.

Jimmy had wanted his father and Charles Nolan to see him race that day, but at the last minute, Charles Nolan decided he couldn't make it down to the racetrack and still start for Indiana the next morning. Jimmy had their tickets in his pocket when he was killed on the highway.

We never saw such a crowd as came to Jimmy's funeral. The ministers tried to comfort us. Rev. James DeWeerd, who was on the school board when Jimmy was in school came from Cincinnati. He's the one who said that Jimmy, in his few years, had lived as much as some people do by 90. Our own pastor, Xen Harvey, said this was only part of Jimmy's own great drama. The first act was life, the second death, and the third, which Jimmy was just entering, was the Hereafter.

We have found comfort, too, in all that our close neighbors have done for us and in the wonderful letters people we don't even know have written. Friends continue to send flowers. On his grave at Christmas, we counted fourteen wreaths, a cross, a vase of fresh flowers, a vase of bittersweet and a big basket of red roses. We are touched that Jimmy earned such devotion.

But the greatest comfort comes from our children's children. Whenever little Markie or Reecy draw me a picture, or when small Joe mimics a television star, or when the others give us their bright smiles, Charlie and I know that the spark which Jimmy had has not died. It's the little ones we must think of now.

When I stand on the hill by Jimmy's grave, I sometimes feel I can look one way and see the work done by all the Deans who have been here. Then I can look ahead and see the promise of those still to come. Sometimes it is comforting just to have lived so long in Indiana. THE END

© Dennis Stock

待望の公開近いディーンの伝記記録映画

ジェイムズ・ディーン物語

ワーナー配給

不世出の天才俳優ジェームス・ディーンは一九五五年九月三十日に死去するまで、出演映画はわずか三本（エデンの東、理由なき反抗、ジャイアンツ）という少ない数でしたが、彼の人気はいやが上に増大し、それに附ずいして、伝説めいた記事であらわれるにいたりました。そして、ついにそれらの決定版として「ジェイムズ・ディーン物語」という彼の短い一生を描いた記録映画が完成しました。

CONTACTS

JAMES DEAN IN TIMES SQUARE >>

PHOTOGRAPHER DENNIS STOCK
YEAR 1955
LOCATION TIMES SQUARE, NEW YORK

It was on a rainy afternoon in February 1955 that James Dean walked along in Times Square, shoulders hunched and head lowered, towards the photographer Dennis Stock. On the third frame Stock knew he had his shot, but he took one more just to make sure. "Times Square was the key image in this whole series of photographs, which I took as a kind of visual biography for *Life* magazine. We'd left Hollywood and gone back to Dean's home in Fairmont, Indiana, and then to New York. It was a kind of re-enactment of his growing up. He'd been part of the Actors Studio, which was in the vicinity of Times Square; he'd performed in a play in the vicinity of Times Square, and he was surrounded by movie theatres full of stars, which he aspired to be. Times Square was one of the platforms from which he was launched, and that's the reason the picture remains memorable."

The iconic image, which has appeared in magazines world-wide and which was hung as a four-storey banner in Times Square a few years ago, is unusual for a movie-star portrait because the figure of Dean sits very small in the frame. "This shot was the most atmospheric. Times Square has as much significance as Dean does. In fact, he wasn't very famous at the time. *East of Eden* was about to come out when I shot this feature. Of course, neither of us knew he was going to die seven months later."

JOANNA PITMAN

The Times (UK) 29/11/2003

Was there more to James Dean than being a rebel? Yes, says **Dennis Hopper** who remembers an astounding acting talent while **Tom Shone** reveals new film finds that show a different Dean

'Biggest star I ever knew'

The Guardian (UK) 6.12.90

IN this second edited extract from his Guardian Conversation with Derek Malcolm Dennis Hopper recalls a ride with the Rebel

'I THOUGHT I was the best young actor in the world when I was 18-years-old, I had played Shakespeare, and I didn't know any actor that could touch me. My first film is Rebel Without A Cause, and I see an actor that's acting so far over my head I don't know where I am.

I'm really confused. I grab him and throw James Dean into a car and say, 'What the hell are you doing? I thought I was the best actor I had ever seen until I saw you work, and now here you are doing things that I can't even comprehend.' I would read the script, I was a very good technical actor, I gave line-readings, I could interpret almost anything, I could play characters but it was all preconceived. He was doing everything differently every time. He was doing things that weren't written on the page.

He was being searched in the jail sequence — he was drunk and suddenly he's playing with the little monkey with cymbals, I don't know where that came in, I didn't read anything about a monkey with cymbals. He's all curled up in a foetal position playing with this monkey, then suddenly he's being searched in a police station with his arms up and it's tickling him and he's laughing, or he's making siren sounds, or he's saying that they are all like a zoo and it was just amazing to me. Not just improvising but taking the words of the page and making them live.'

So anyway I threw him into this car and I said 'I thought I was the best actor that I knew until I saw you.' And then we talked about motivation, he asked me if I had problems with my parents and if there was an anger there and I said 'Yeah, I hate my parents.' He said 'Was that one of the reasons you wanted to go into the theatre?' I said 'Yeah, I felt that I could get my anger out there and communicate with an audience.'

He said, 'We have similar drives, mine comes out of hate too, my mother died when I was nine-years-old. My mother died and I used to go to her grave and I used to cry and say mother, why have you left me and that turned into mother, I hate you, I'm going to show you, I'm going to be somebody. So that's the drive but what you have to do now is to get rid of all your preconceived ideas and start doing things and not showing them. The simplest of things, like drinking a drink . . . you just drink the drink, you don't act it, smoking a cigarette you just do it, you don't act it.'

When he died my whole sense of destiny, the things that I believed in, went. Dean told me the reason he knew he was going to be remembered was that he has Brando on one hand saying 'Go fuck yourself', and he had Montgomery Clift on the other saying 'Please forgive me for what I've done,' and somewhere in the middle was James Dean.

But to do three films and be remembered! He wanted to direct movies, we had dreams. This was not a great friendship, he was older than I was — he was 24, I was 18 — but we had a working teacher relationship that was unique. So we had dreams as far as work was concerned. We were going to work together.

When I come to Europe — he always talked about it but he never came to Europe — he's everywhere, here at the NFT, on a T-shirt in Moscow, a discotheque in the South of Spain, a restaurant in Sweden, or on the Champs Elysees out of a window. There's Humphrey Bogart, Marilyn Monroe and James Dean and yet he only made three movies. He was unquestionably the most talented and the biggest star that I ever knew. He never knew his stardom, because he never had a success while he was alive. Only in Hollywood was anyone aware of him. The most money he ever made was $17,000 for Giant and he spent all of that on the car that he died in.

DM: What do you think would have happened to him if He hadn't died? Would he have become a great superstar. Would he have directed movies?

DH: The world is very fickle. He would have been a compulsive creator and a great one. I would assume it would all be fine, but I find in this business you are only as good as your last movie. Don't buy a house because who knows whether you'll be working next week.

The greatest actors that I had ever seen were Marlon Brando, Montgomery Clift and Dean. Dean was stranger and different, more introspective and interesting than the others. There are only three males that I have ever encountered who have that kind of quality that when they enter a room half the room follows them when they go into another room. One was Marlon Brando, Bob Dylan when he was young — and James Dean.'

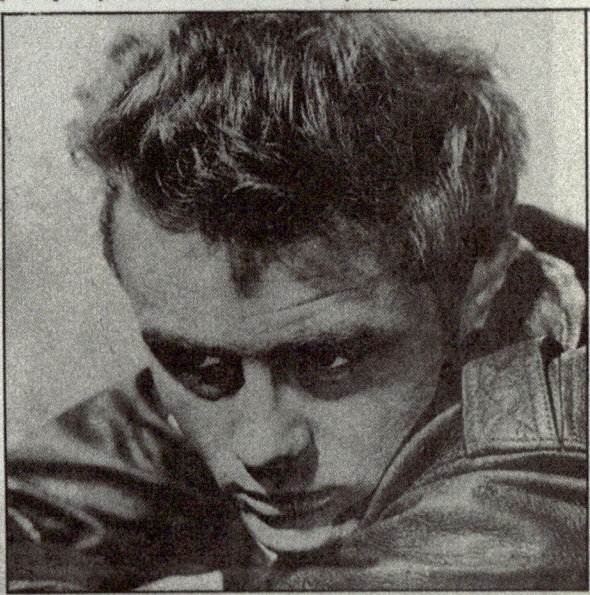

James Dean: 'He wanted to direct movies, we had dreams'

Television

Nineteen of James Dean's complete television appearances, two commercials and two clips are contained in this 3-disc DVD released in 2018 in the USA. Extras include photo galleries by Roy Schatt, Frank Worth and Sanford Roth. Highly recommended

James Dean's TV times

JUST weeks before he killed himself on the road James Dean made a road safety advert. With an irony that beats even Yul Brynner's anti-smoking ads, it starts by showing the drag race in Rebel Without A Cause and ends with the star, just off the set of Giant, complete with stetson, explaining: "I used to fly around a bit, I took a lot of unnecessary chances, but now I drive on the highway extra cautious. . . . Take it easy on the highway." Two weeks later — at the age of 24 — he wrote himself off in his new Porsche, thus preserving forever his youthful, rebellious image.

Dean's acting reputation has since perched rather precariously on his relatively small cinematic output. James Dean made only three movies, right? Wrong. It is a little known fact that between his arrival in New York in 1951 and his first screen role in 1954, he also appeared in more than 25 TV dramas and several adverts.

"He simply didn't just burst on to the scene with those three films. He had a significant body of TV work as well," says Robert Batscha, president of the New York Museum of Broadcasting, which has scoured archives and private collections to piece together some of these gems which London's National Film Theatre will be showing throughout December.

"I think the work particularly significant because you see how James Dean evolved. The first thing we have is him playing Francis of Assisi. Then a Pepsi commercial where he was chosen simply because he looked like an all-American boy. Then you see him developing and testing the character that later made him famous."

Dean arrived in New York to study acting. Attending Lee Strasberg's method acting classes intermittently, one of his first roles was chalking up the score on the game show Hallmark Hall of Fame. He did it with extra-rebellious vigour; on the first night breaking the chalk, on the next producing a teeth-grating screech. But between 1951 and 1954 he also chalked up more than 25 made-for-TV dramas. Almost from the start he was cast as the rebellious but vulnerable hepcat, misunderstood and persecuted. The season at the NFT kicks off with two, The Unlighted Road and A Long Time Till Dawn: "Hello I'm James Dean, welcome to the playhouse. . . ."

In the first he plays a drifter caught up in racketeering amd murder and in the latter, a rebellious teenager.

But the tapes also answer the often-asked question of whether Dean could play roles other than that of the rebel. In The Bells Of Cockaigne Dean actually plays a parent, trying desperately to pay his child's medical bills, and in The Evil Within he plays a lab assistant to Rod Steiger's mad scientist.

"They show he could play other roles than that of the rebel," says Batscha, "you realise he actually had a broad range."

Sheila Whitacker, who obtained tapes for the NFT, says, "It is the biggest unanswered question why they haven't been shown before." The trouble was that few survived because the TV companies would often wipe the tapes once they were broadcast. Says Bascha, "We had to scour the country: our own archives, the James Dean museum in Ohio, private collections. A complete list doesn't exist even now."

Two other rarities to be shown are the two commercials made by Dean, the one for road safety, and the one for Pepsi-Cola. It is an adman's dream. "Wanna have more fun? Then come on along and join the Pepsi crowd," lilts a voiceover. Cue the Pepsi crowd, larking around in a Fifties' retro bar. At the centre of the crowd, fooling over the piano: James Dean. Cut to Jimmy backslapping with his male buddies and downing the Pepsi. Forget Tina Turner and Michael Jackson, this beats the lot.

The ad takes on an added piquancy given the subsequent appropriation of Dean's image by the advertising industry. Since his death it has been used to sell everything from beer to the NatWest bank, and last year this — along with spin-off merchandise — posthumously earned more than $100 million for the James Dean foundation, owned by his surviving family who have the license to produce anything from T-shirts to stetsons. **TS.**

● *James Dean — The Television Work, runs at the NFT from Saturday to December 31. Free tickets are available from the box office (071-928-3535).*

6.12.90

Hill Number One, first broadcast 25 March 1951

T.K.O. (The Bigelow Theatre) 29 October 1951

The Trouble with Father, Season 2 Episode 8, *Jackie Knows All*. 7 December 1951

Into the Valley (CBS) 27 January 1952

Sleeping Dogs (The Web) 20 February 1952

Ten Thousand Horses Singing (Studio One, CBS) 3 March 1952. Dean apppears in a two or three shots as a hotel bellboy. He improvises a couple of words, "Yes" and "Ten", and breathes and sighs deeply to draw attention to himself in what was meant to be a completely silent role. John Forsyth stars.

The Foggy, Foggy Dew (Lux Video Theatre, CBS) 17 March 1952. Lost apart from silent clips.

Prologue to Glory (Kraft Television Theatre, NBC) 21 May 1952

Abraham Lincoln (Studio One, CBS) 26 May 1952

The Forgotten Children (Hallmark Hall of Fame, NBC) 22 June 1952

The Hound of Heaven (The Kate Smith Hour, NBC) 15 January 1953

The Case of the Watchful Dog (Treasury Men of Action, NBC) 29 January 1953

The Capture of Jesse James (You are There, CBS) 2 August 1953

No Room (Danger, CBS) 14 April 1953

The Case Of The Sawed-off Shotgun (Treasury Men of Action, NBC) 16 April 1953

The Evil Within (Tales of Tomorrow, ABC) 1 May 1953. With Rod Steiger.

Something for an Empty Briefcase (Campbell Summer Soundstage, NBC) 17 July 1953

Sentence of Death (Studio One, CBS) 17 August 1953

Death Is My Neighbor (Danger, CBS) 25 August 1953

Rex Newman (The Big Story, NBC) as Rex Newman, 11 September 1953 re-creation crime show.

Glory in the Flower (Omnibus, CBS) 4 October 1953

Keep Our Honor Bright (Kraft Television Theatre) 14 October 1953

Life Sentence (Campbell Summer Soundstage, NBC) 16 October 1953

A Long Time Till Dawn (Kraft Television Theatre, NBC) 11 November 1953

The Bells of Cockaigne (Armstrong Circle Theatre) 17 November 1953

Harvest (Robert Montgomery Presents, NBC) 23 November 1953

The Little Woman (Danger, CBS) 30 March 1954 & **Padlocks** (Danger, CBS) 9 November 1954

Run Like A Thief (The Philco-Goodyear Playhouse, NBC) 5 September 1954

I'm a Fool (General Electric Theatre, CBS) 14 November 1954. Ronald Regan introduced the post-Death repeat: "It was a performance that helped to attract nationwide attention to his talent.. And we present it as one the landmarks in his progress towards the great roles in his brief career. Those of who worked with Jimmy Dean carry an image of his intense struggle for a goal beyond himself. Curiously enough, that's the story of the boy he portrays tonight." It's impressive filmed theatre, with sets that suggest both naturalism and expressionism.

The Dark, Dark Hours (General Electric Theatre, CBS) 12 December 1954. With Ronald Reagan.

The Thief (The U.S. Steel Hour, ABC) 4 January 1955. With Mary Astor.

The Unlighted Road (Schlitz Playhouse of the Stars, CBS) 6 May 1955

© General Electric Theatre

television's memories of jimmy dean
continued

■ He was on the threshold of greatness in 1953—the slim blond boy of brooding sensitivity. He was one of so many youngsters who'd come to New York from Ohio or Maine or—like Jimmy himself—from Indiana. In all the talented, hopeful crowd Jimmy stood alone. Though he was still a student (at Actor's Studio), already the spark of genius glowed in him. Elia Kazan, the movie director who discovered Marlon Brando, saw it and predicted future stardom. But it was television that gave Jimmy his first roles. In 1953 he played a few bit parts, and casting directors buzzed, "Did you see that fellow Dean? Something electric about him!" Late that year *Kraft Theatre* was the first TV show to star the unknown James Dean. Now, on the heartbreaking anniversary of his death last September 30, here on these five pages are rare pictures of the teleplays where Jimmy won his first fans.

continued on following pages

VIDEO FAREWELL. Four months before his death Jimmy returned to TV for tender portrayal of boy accused of murder, cleared by sweetheart Pat Hardy (Schlitz Playhouse, *Unlighted Road*). Play was rerun last June.

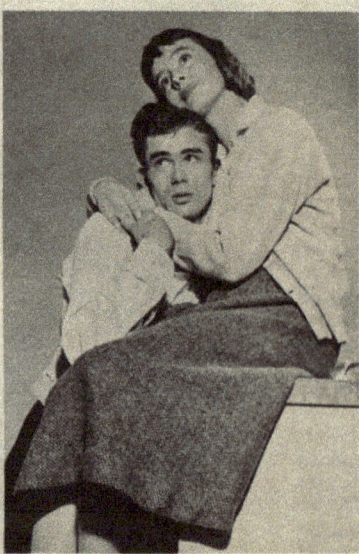

FIRST STARRING ROLE. Jimmy played a tormented murderer waiting with his girl, Naomi Riordan, for police to close in, on Kraft Theatre's stark *A Long Time Till Dawn* (Nov. 11, 1953).

REHEARSAL. Jimmy showed up in black suit, camel's-hair cap and vest (left), early showing individuality that rocked Hollywood.

The Foggy, Foggy Dew

TV STAR PARADE 29

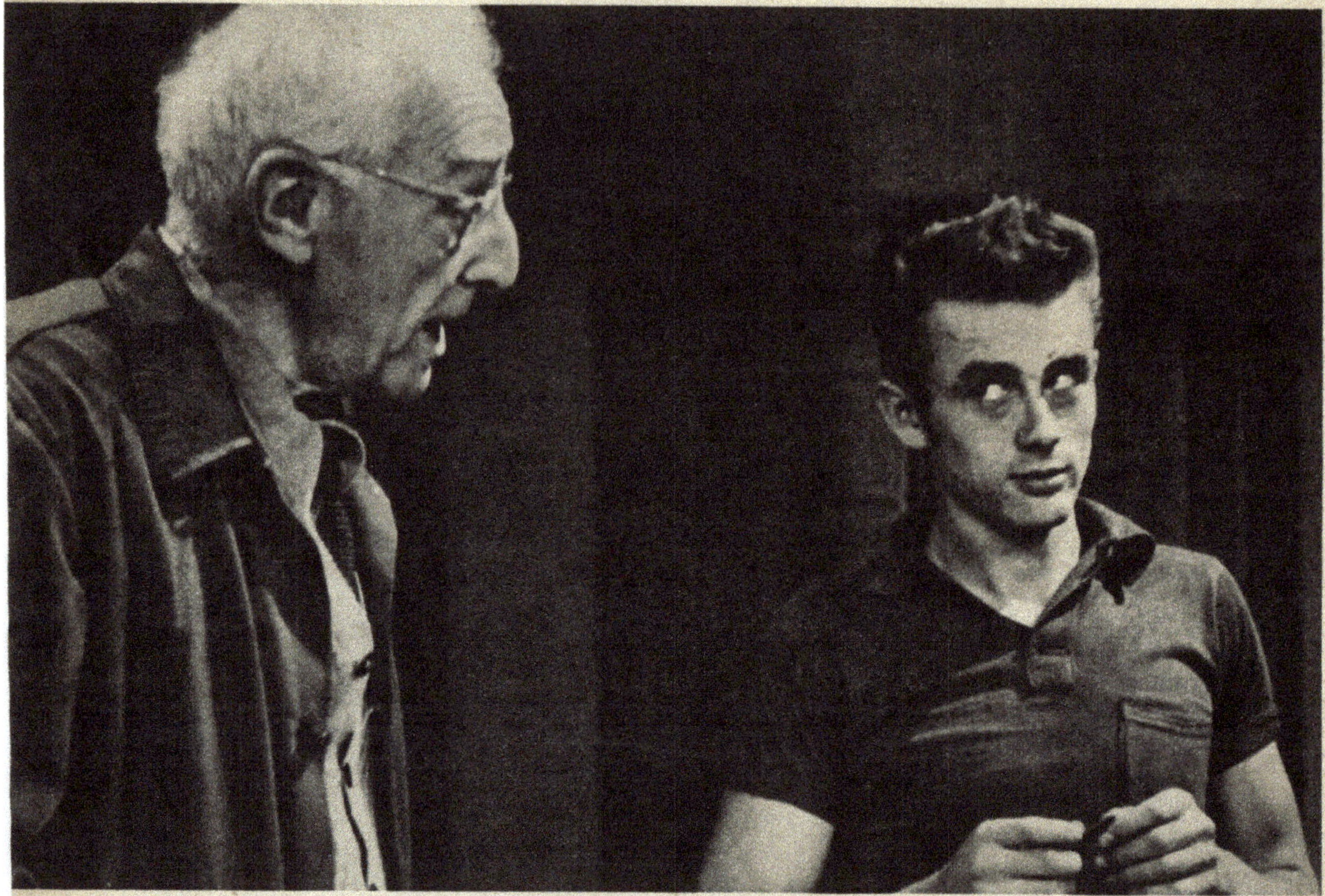

UNSTABLE. Led on by Betsy Palmer (now on ABC's *Masquerade Party*), Dean tries to kill her when she mocks him, in *Death Sentence* (Danger, Aug. '53) with the late Walter Hampden. Jimmy and Betsy, both from Indiana, were friends offstage. "Sometimes Jimmy got

television's memories of jimmy dean *continued*

It was the paradox of Jimmy Dean—in his personal life, and as an actor—that gave his video performances such impact. Hardly out of boyhood, he was still searching, still confused—like the troubled, often violent heroes he portrayed. But there was also the tenderness in Jimmy, the capacity to experience emotion deeply and therefore project it to an audience. An actor who could make you cry, who could twinkle with mischievous humor, who could *live* scenes of explosive drama, then follow with believable moments of repentance . . . television gave Jimmy a different role every few weeks. He, who was to have so little time, had time enough for this one thing at least—to perfect his art and broaden his range through constant practice. If Jimmy's talent was a gift to us, his audience, we can thank television for its part in his development.

TYPICAL ROLE. A cynical Jimmy and fellow bellhops discuss the loss of jewels by hotel guest. He hides secret loneliness from pals.

MENACE. As police fugitive, Jimmy terrorizes Mildred Dunnock, then comes to pity her spinster existence, in *Padlocks* (Danger, Nov. '54). A show staffer recalls: "Jimmy, like the hero, was sensitive but running from life."

homesick in New York, and he liked to talk to me," Betsy remembers. "We got along very well. He was so wonderful."

RUN LIKE A THIEF—Philco Playhouse, Sept. 5, 1954

TOUGH GUY. Jimmy confronts waiter Kurt Kasznar (a father image to him), who found and concealed gems.

TOUCHING GOOD-BY. When disillusioned Jimmy leaves, Kasznar and his wife (Gusti Huber) decide to return gems, and haltingly Jimmy reveals yearning to belong to someone.

Sometimes the going was very tough—and he was glad to get jobs as an extra—even jobs that involved having custard pies thrown at him! Here he is in one TV role

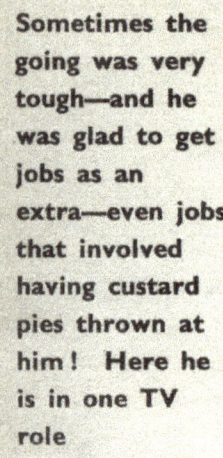

Success at last—Jim in Broadway play, THE IMMORALIST, in which he played the part of an Arab. He received an award for this role as Most Promising Newcomer

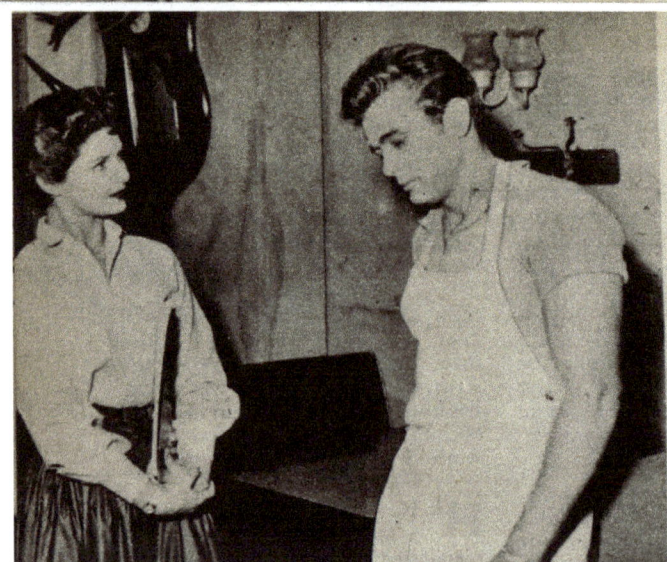

This picture shows him in a TV play with Pat Hardy. He played the part of a waiter in a cafe

Hill Number One

A Family Theater 'Triumphant Hour sponsored by The Family Rosary Crusade, directed in Hollywood by Arthur Pierson. Thirteen players are listed in the opening credits, including Ruth Hussey and Roddy McDowall, but Dean is only listed in the closing credits. A heavy artillery unit shells an unseen enemy on Hill 46 in Korea. In the waiting for promised coffee to arrive the men strike up a pleasant conversation. 'Professor' Roddy McDowall tells them it's Easter Sunday. The Padre brings the coffee in a jeep and eases the gripes of the men by telling them about Hill Number One: "It was taken by on man, alone." The Padre's words take us back in time. An earnest well-written film. Dean appears on screen after 32-minutes playing the disciple John: "Surely we did not spend three years following the Master to turn again to our nets.?"

I'm a Fool (1953)

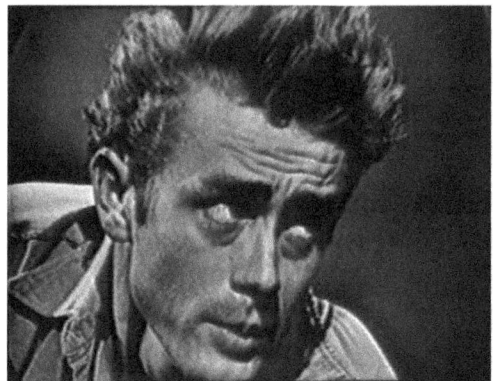

Death is My Neighbor from *Danger* (1953)

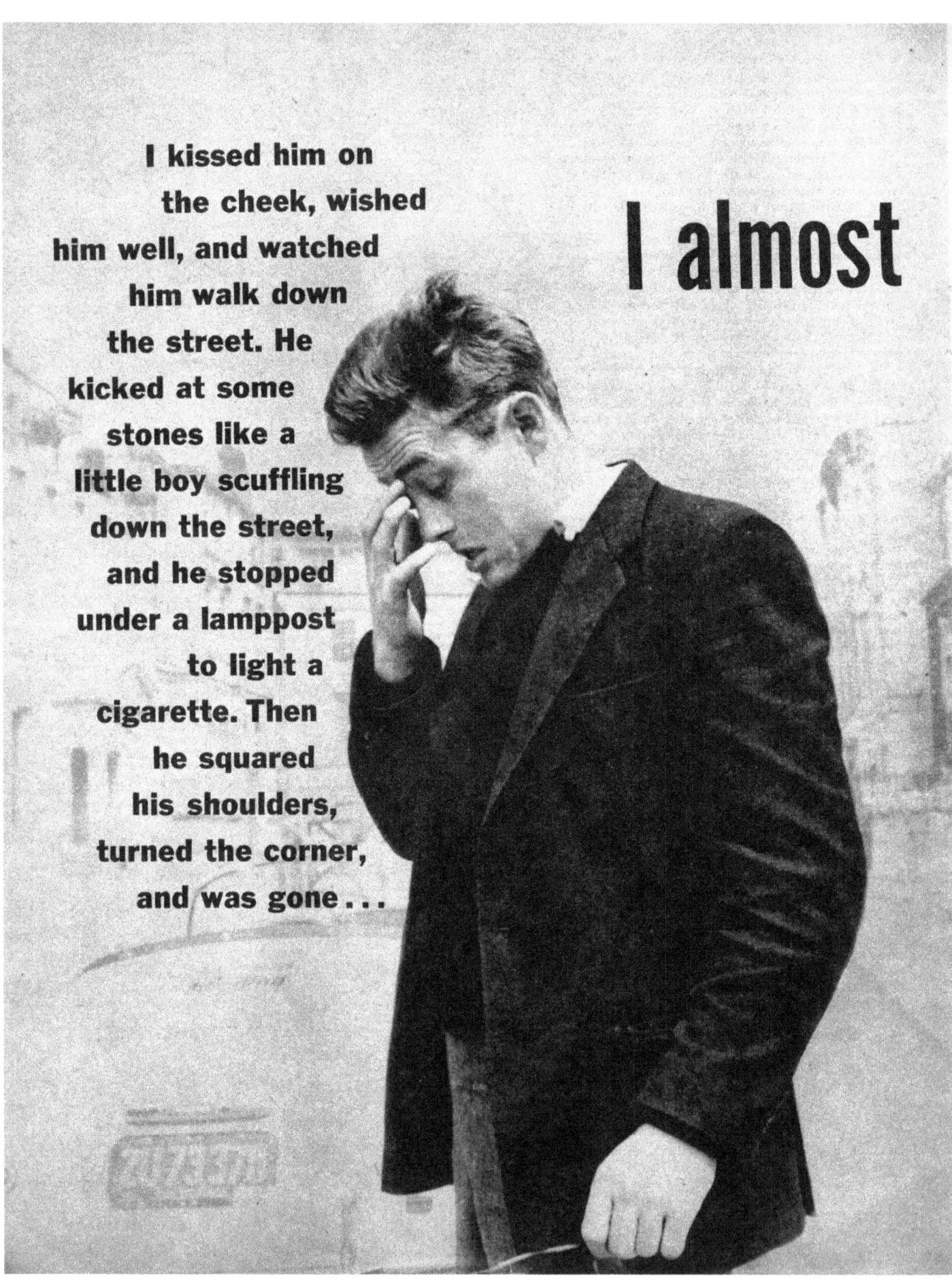

I kissed him on the cheek, wished him well, and watched him walk down the street. He kicked at some stones like a little boy scuffling down the street, and he stopped under a lamppost to light a cigarette. Then he squared his shoulders, turned the corner, and was gone...

I almost

married Jimmy Dean

by Beverly Wills *as told to Helen Weller*

I was Jimmy Dean's girl friend. We went
steady for seven months, and at one time we talked about
getting married. I loved Jimmy at that time and I
understood him as few people did.

We met on a blind date about five years ago. He was
a bashful boy behind big horn-rimmed glasses and his hair
looked as though it hadn't been combed in weeks.
When we were introduced he merely said, "Hi,"
and stared at the floor.

Finally we got into his car and drove to a shore picnic—and
he hardly said a word. He was a little self-conscious about
his car, not because it was beat-up looking, but because
he couldn't whip any speed out of it. "Good old
Elsie," he said with a wry kind of smile,
stroking the wheel. "I call her Elsie because she's slow
as a cow. I hate anything slow. I wish I could trade
this in for a fast job." After that little speech, he
clammed up and didn't say another word.

I thought he was pretty much of a creep until
we got to the picnic, and then all of a sudden he came
to life. We began to talk about acting and
Jimmy lit up. He told me how interested he was in the
Stanislavsky method, where you not only act out people,
but things too.

"Look," said Jimmy, "I'm a palm tree in a
storm." He held his arms out and waved wildly. To feel
more free, he impatiently tossed off his cheap, tight
blue jacket. He looked better as soon as he did, because
you could see his broad shoulders and powerful build.
Then he got wilder and pretended he was a monkey.
He climbed a big tree and swung from a high branch.
Dropping from the branch he landed on his hands
like a little kid who was suddenly turned loose. He
even laughed like a little boy, chuckling uproariously
at every little thing. Once in the spotlight, he ate it up
and had us all in stitches all afternoon. The 'creep'
turned into the hit of the picnic.

I learned that it was nothing for Jimmy to run
through a whole alphabet of emotions in one evening,
alternating sharply from low to high and back again,
and no one could ever tell what mood would hit him.
A couple of nights later, we went to a movie and during the
picture Jimmy sat hunched forward, his chin cupped in his
hands, looking something like that statue of the thinker.
When I tried to whisper something to him, he shushed
me up. He was so completely absorbed in the performance
on the screen! *(Continued on page 82)*

ENJOY A PERMANENT, BIG PAY CAREER as a PRACTICAL NURSE

EARN AT HOME WHILE LEARNING

FREE SAMPLE LESSON shows how easily you can become a professionally trained practical nurse by home study in a short time. NO HIGH SCHOOL NEEDED. No age limit.

FOR FREE LESSON and FULL INFORMATION MAIL COUPON NOW!

```
Post Graduate Hospital
School of Nursing
5D37 Auditorium Bldg.
Chicago 5, Illinois

Name..........
Address.......
City..........State..........
```

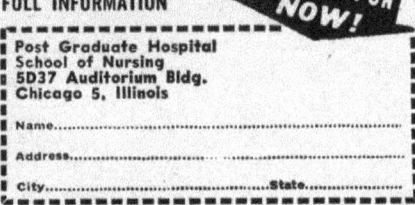

FREE ENLARGEMENT of your Favorite Photo

FROM FAMOUS HOLLYWOOD FILM STUDIOS
Just to get acquainted, we will make you a beautiful studio quality 5 x 7 enlargement of any snapshot, photo or negative. Be sure to include color of hair, eyes and clothing, and get our Bargain Offer for having your enlargement beautifully hand-colored in oil and mounted in a handsome frame. Limit 2 to a customer. Please enclose 10¢ to cover cost of handling and mailing each enlargement. Original returned. *We will pay $100.00 for children's or adults pictures used in our advertising.* Act NOW!
HOLLYWOOD FILM STUDIOS, Dept. F-337
7021 Santa Monica Blvd., Hollywood 38, Calif.

WHY DON'T YOU WRITE?

Writing short stories, articles on fashions, homemaking, business, hobbies, travel, local, club and church activities, etc., will enable you to earn extra money. In your own home, on your own time, the New York Copy Desk Method teaches you how to write the way newspaper men and women learn—by writing. Our unique "Writing Aptitude Test" tells whether you possess the fundamental qualities essential to successful writing. You'll enjoy this test. Write for it, without cost or obligation.
NEWSPAPER INSTITUTE OF AMERICA
Suite 5717-C, One Park Ave., New York 16, N. Y.

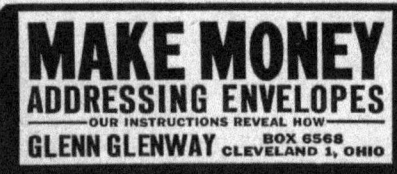

MAKE MONEY ADDRESSING ENVELOPES

OUR INSTRUCTIONS REVEAL HOW
GLENN GLENWAY BOX 6568 CLEVELAND 1, OHIO

Shrinks Hemorrhoids New Way Without Surgery

Science Finds Healing Substance That Relieves Pain—Shrinks Hemorrhoids

For the first time science has found a new healing substance with the astonishing ability to shrink hemorrhoids and to relieve pain — without surgery.

In case after case, while gently relieving pain, actual reduction (shrinkage) took place.

Most amazing of all — results were so thorough that sufferers made astonishing statements like "Piles have ceased to be a problem!"

The secret is a new healing substance (Bio-Dyne*)—discovery of a world-famous research institute.

This substance is now available in *suppository* or *ointment form* under the name *Preparation H.** Ask for it at all drug counters—money back guarantee. *Reg. U.S. Pat. Off.

I almost married jimmy dean

(*Continued from page 53*) Jimmy was still in this somber mood when we left, and when we got into his car he didn't say a word. Suddenly he said, "I feel like some music." He started to sing "Roll, Roll, Roll Your Boat."

I was beginning to see Jimmy every day now and I noticed that he always wore the same clothes, a blue jacket and gray slacks. Either that or a pair of jeans. That was all he owned.

Once he spilled coffee on himself and it left a stain on the slacks. He jumped up and was so mad at himself. I couldn't understand it, because Jimmy didn't seem to give a hoot about clothes.

"It's only a pair of pants," I said, "send it to the cleaners."

"That's just it," he said. "I can't even pay the cleaners, and I wanted to go to the studio tomorrow and see about a job."

Jimmy wanted more than anything else in the world to become an actor. But he couldn't get a job. It would almost kill him when he'd go out to see the casting directors and return with nothing. He never lost confidence in himself, but he was angry because no one else shared that confidence. He would come by and see me after a fruitless interview, and he'd be in a black mood. "The director said I was too short," he once mumbled savagely. "How can you measure acting in inches? They're crazy!"

They also told him he wasn't good-looking enough, and always that he wasn't the type. Usually, when the casting heads told him this, Jimmy would get so mad he'd insult the men right back!

A charmer as well

I was doing a part in the radio version of *Junior Miss*, and Jimmy would sit in on the rehearsals and watch. One day, they needed a young man for one of the roles and Hank Garson, the director, asked me if my boy friend could handle it. "Of course," I said happily.

I introduced Jimmy to Mr. Garson. "Have you ever done anything in radio?" asked the director. Any other actor, faced with such an opportunity, would have said *yes*, but not Jimmy. I think he was a little angry at the director for having let him sit around for so many weeks before offering him a job, and he wanted to show off. Anyway, Jimmy looked defiantly at Mr. Garson and said, "No." "Sorry," said the director, and walked away.

I ran after Jimmy. "Why did you say that?" I asked. "Why didn't you tell him you could do it? If you'd only been nice he'd have given you a chance."

Jimmy was still stubborn. "I don't have to lie to get a job in radio. Either he can give me a chance because he thinks I can act, or he can take his old job."

But although he used to rub many people—unfortunately, important people—the wrong way because of his hurts and resentment, he could charm the birds off the trees when he wanted to.

My mother didn't share my enthusiasm for Jimmy, nor was my mother to blame. Jimmy had the knack of putting his worst foot forward when he was in the mood.

Morose and moody

I think it was the rebel in him. My mother—she's Joan Davis—was a success; he wasn't. Inside, Jimmy felt a little antagonistic toward many of the people who had achieved success in a profession where he couldn't stick his foot in the door.

He'd walk into our living room and promptly slump down in my mother's favorite arm chair, his foot dangling over the side, and sit like that for hours without saying a word. The only action we'd see out of him was when he'd reach out for the fruit bowl and eat one piece of fruit after another until the bowl was empty. When my mother would walk in, Jimmy never stood up, never said *hello*. He just remained slouched in the chair, munching on the fruit and staring moodily into space.

At the dinner table, his behavior was usually the same. Jimmy was always hungry. He loved pot roast, so I tried to have it for him whenever he was over. He'd wolf down two helpings of the meat with that same morose expression on his face, and mother would squirm.

It was more than his manners that disturbed my mother. She was afraid we were becoming serious. By this time I was wearing Jimmy's gold football on a chain around my neck. We were going steady and my mother couldn't think of any boy who had a more uncertain future than Jimmy! She thought he was too wild and would never settle down.

"Mom was flabbergasted"

My high school senior prom was coming up and, of course, I was going to take Jimmy. He was working as an usher at the time, and although he was in debt, he managed to put aside a few dollars every week so that he could rent a tuxedo. He asked me to go with him to the place where you rent these things, and when he saw all the dinner suits on racks he acted like a little boy in a candy store. He tried on one after another, and finally settled on a white jacket, black pants, dress shirt and bow tie. The rental on the whole works amounted to five dollars, and I don't think I ever saw Jimmy look happier.

"Imagine me in one of these things," he crowed, posing in front of a long mirror.

Although we sat out most of the dances —Jimmy didn't rhumba or jitterbug—he was in wonderful spirits the night of the prom. Some of the kids at school joined us and he laughed a lot and told funny stories. My mother stopped by with some friends for a few minutes, and even she was fascinated by Jimmy's personality that night. He jumped out of his chair when she came to our table and even helped her off with her stole. "Good heavens, I've never seen him like this before," said mother, flabbergasted but charmed.

The only other times I saw Jimmy that happy was when he was racing his motorcycle furiously. No matter how depressed he was, if Jimmy had a chance to get behind something that had terrific speed, he would laugh and come alive again.

When Jimmy learned that I had a little boat with an outboard motor, he was eager to try it out. Jimmy drove it around the cove, the salt spray making his face and his glasses glisten. I thought he enjoyed it, but he was disappointed because he couldn't get my little boat with its ten horsepower motor to whip up any great amount of speed. After that little ride, which I thought would turn out to be such fun, Jimmy was in the dumps again.

We wanted to get married

I soon discovered that his moods of happiness were now far outweighed by his moods of deep despair. He was almost constantly in a blue funk. He still couldn't get an acting job and he was growing increasingly bitter. I hated to see Jimmy become so blue. When he was happy, there was no one more lovable. When he was depressed, he wanted to die.

These low moods became so violent that he began to tell me that he was having strange nightmares in which he dreamed he was dying. The nightmares began to give him a certain phobia about death.

"If only I could accomplish something before I die," he once said despairingly.

Like a lot of kids who go steady, we began to talk about getting married. I was not yet eighteen and we both knew my parents would never give their consent, so we planned to wait until my eighteenth birthday, which was a couple of months off, and elope. I had saved some money from my radio work, and we thought we would go to New York where we hoped Jimmy could get a break in the theatre.

But the dream didn't last long. A couple of months later, I had moved to Paradise Cove, a beautiful spot way out at the beach, where I was to spend six months with my father—my parents are divorced. The first week Jimmy drove out the long distance he began to gripe. "It's such a long drive, I'm running out of gasoline. Why can't you meet me in Hollywood?"

But I felt at home at the beach. I was with a lot of happy kids whom I'd grown up with every summer, and we were having lots of fun. Somehow, in this happy-go-lucky atmosphere, surrounded by boys and girls who didn't seem to have a care in the world, Jimmy stuck out like a sore thumb. He wore the same blue jacket and gray pants, only they seemed even shabbier next to the tailored slacks and sports shirts the other fellows wore. The whole crowd was very cliquey, and when Jimmy came by they looked at him as though he didn't belong.

Deeper into the shell

Jimmy was very sensitive and it hurt him very much to be looked down on. He sensed their patronizing attitude and withdrew deeper and deeper into a shell. I think he wanted to hurt them back, too. I've often wondered if he recalled this period in his life when he portrayed the sensitive feelings of the rejected youth in *Rebel Without A Cause*.

One afternoon, the fellows were playing football on the beach. Jimmy joined them. Jimmy used to be very intense about everything he did, particularly if he wanted to show off. The other fellows were playing casually, since they weren't wearing protective football gear, but Jimmy plunged into the game like a tiger. He was out for blood. He was very strong, anyway, and he tackled one of the fellows with such ferocity that the boy yelled out in pain and the rest of the fellows ran over to pull Jimmy off him. After that, the fellows labelled Jimmy a bum sport and wouldn't talk to him.

Jimmy was miserable. He felt like an outsider in his work; he felt like an outsider with this crowd. The resentment made him sink all the more into rebellious moods that even I couldn't understand.

At a dance at the Cove one night, Jimmy remained in this strange mood. When one of the boys cut in and tried to dance off with me, Jimmy saw red. He grabbed the fellow by the collar and threatened to blacken both his eyes. I should have realized that this was his way of paying back a member of the crowd who had hurt him. But I was embarrassed. I ran out to the beach, and Jimmy walked after me, scuffing angrily at the sand, complete misery on his face. We had an argument and I pulled his gold football off the chain.

An air of bravado

A few days later, Jimmy called and told me that a friend was driving to New York and would give him a free ride. I was glad he called. I had been thinking of Jimmy ever since we broke off, and I realized more and more that this was a hurt and misunderstood boy. I wanted to remain his friend. I wished him luck.

A few months later my mother took me on a trip to New York. I had Jimmy's address. He was staying at the Y and I called him up. We met in Central Park and my heart went out when I saw Jimmy walk up in the same blue jacket and gray slacks. That meant that he still hadn't gotten a job.

There was an air of bravado about Jimmy which soon crumpled when he told me that he hadn't been able to land a part in a show. He was depressed, and he was hungry, too. I insisted that I buy us both a spaghetti dinner and he took me up on it. I think it was the first square meal he had had since he left Hollywood to come to New York.

I told him I was engaged to be married, and he told me about a girl he had met in New York who was a lady bullfighter. I could see that he was fascinated by this colorful girl. He showed me a tiny matador sword which he wore in his lapel, and he had gone overboard on the subject of bullfighting.

Later, he walked me back to my hotel. Just before he left he said, "I'm trying out for a part in a play tomorrow. It's a good, gutsy part. If I get it, I think this will be the break I've been waiting for. Maybe even Hollywood will sit up and take notice. I'll show them. If I don't get it," he paused, fingered the little sword in his lapel, and the familiar little smile played over his lips, "well, then I'll go to Mexico and become a bullfighter."

I kissed him on the cheek and wished him well, and then watched him walk down the street. He kicked at some stones like a little boy scuffing down the street, and he stopped under a lamp-post to light a cigarette.

Then he squared his shoulders, turned the corner and was gone.

He never did go to Mexico. **END**

Jimmy Dean can currently be seen in George Stevens' production of Giant, *a Warner Bros. release.*

Wool·n·Wash
makes your woolens purr-r-r

Soft warm woolens are yours in the twitch of a kitten's tail with this pale golden liquid. WOOL-N-WASH dissolves instantly in the coldest water, whips up a froth of eager suds that harms nothing but dirt. Absolutely safe for your finest woolens, your sheerest lingerie, and there's no residue ever. WOOL-N-WASH'S own antistatic agent draws the cling from synthetics, while its brightening agent does dazzling whites, makes all colors brighter. And, best of all, WOOL-N-WASH is kind to your hands. Try a bottle today! At better stores everywhere.

SINCE 1876, MAKERS OF FAMOUS PUTNAM FADELESS DYES

MONROE CHEMICAL COMPANY   QUINCY 5, ILLINOIS

In memory of Jimmy

To mark that day, two years ago, when James Dean died, Photoplay pays tribute with the stories of two girls who knew him—one unknown, the other a star

She was a struggling dancer. He was a lonely actor. Together in the cold, hard city of New York they loved, and laughed and dreamed. This is Elizabeth Sheridan's own story:

The first time I ever knew that Jimmy Dean existed was one afternoon at the Rehearsal Club in New York. It was raining. He was sitting in the living room, and I heard him ask a lot of other girls if he could borrow an umbrella, and nobody seemed particularly interested in whether he got wet or not. So I loaned him mine and he was overly grateful. A couple of days later, he came back and returned it. One of the biggest interests that he had at the time was bullfighting. He caught my interest because I was also interested in bullfighting. That, I think, was the important reason we got together at the very beginning.

Then, I was dancing in a trio, two boys and me, and we were rehearsing about two or three blocks away, and one night these two guys came to the Rehearsal Club for a rehearsal that we were going to have, and Jimmy asked if he could come along and watch. So he did, and he was very much impressed by the whole thing. We had a habit of stopping in this place—a little neighborhood joint—to have something to eat before we went home, and Jimmy came along with us.

I remember it was a very funny incident. We liked a certain kind of beer that was out at the time called Champale. It seemed it was somebody's birthday, but I can't remember whose it was, and Jimmy was, more or less, my date. The waiter, when I ordered Champale, thought I said *champagne,* and he came back and he brought a bottle of champagne and Jimmy's eyes almost popped out, because at that time he was living at the "Y" and he didn't have a cent, and he was borrowing from everyone in town and, instead of saying, "You made a mistake of some kind," he said, "Oh no, I can pay for it." He made a big thing about that. It was funny. *(Continued on page 102)*

"When I first met Jimmy, he looked like a straggly, hungry kid who needed a friend. Later, I found he always looked that way."

IN MEMORY OF JIMMY

Continued from page 70

My two dancing partners and So Height were there, too, I think. Everybody used to meet at this place. Jimmy didn't impress me one bit when I first met him. I thought he was a little straggly kid that somebody had brought in—actually that's more or less what happened. One of the girls took a liking to him at a TV rehearsal and brought him there to give him a good meal because he looked hungry, he looked lonely, he looked like he needed a friend. Actually, years later, I found out that he always looked that way. And up until the rehearsal night, he didn't one way or the other impress me.

A couple of nights later, I remember, I was sitting in the living room of the Rehearsal Club and Jimmy was there, too. Boys were allowed to visit the girls up until 11:00 or 12:00 P.M. I forget what time it was and there were two couches, one facing the other. I was sitting in one and Jimmy was sitting in the other. And I was reading a magazine and he was reading a magazine, too. I quoted something out of the one I was reading and his answer was a quote out of the magazine that he was reading and we carried on a conversation like this for about fifteen minutes—you know, real fun—and we both got a kick out of it. Suddenly, he said, "I have an idea. Would you like to go up to Tony's, the place that they have this Champale?" And I said, "All right. What the heck!"

So we went around there and we sat down in a booth and a couple of kids that both of us knew were in the next booth and we got into a conversation and his ideas and my ideas sort of jelled and he became interested and so did I.

Then we started drawing pictures on a napkin, I remember, and I was very much impressed about the way he could draw. Jimmy was sort of self-taught in almost everything he did. He was a very good artist, so I started to draw the only thing I knew how to draw—a tree. And he remarked how good it was and we just seemed to be getting to know one another closer and closer all the time. I think he was more impressed than I was at first.

A couple of nights later I had a costume-fitting somewhere up in the Bronx, and Jimmy said he would meet me at a little place around the corner. He was just sitting around the Rehearsal Club and I didn't take him too seriously. When I finished this costume-fitting and I was going by this place—Tony's—instead of going straight home, I went in just to see if Jimmy was there. And he was and it turned out to be his birthday and he started saying all sorts of things about that was the best birthday he had had in years.

When I first met him he drank beer, but after I got to know him very well, he really didn't take to drinking much.

Then we started going around together quite steadily. He used to call me at night or in the daytime—any time he happened to feel like it. He'd play records for me over the telephone. We would sit and talk for hours and hours and it was a desperate kind of feeling he had towards seeing me any time that he had a spare moment and talking to me any time he had a spare moment, almost like he didn't have anybody else, either. He just sort of hung on and, I guess, I must have been particularly lonely at the time, too, because we got to be inseparable.

One thing that was quite remarkable about him was that he never for one instant thought that he really couldn't make it. I mean he always knew that he would one day be a star, and there was no question in his mind about it at all. He was interested in the stage. Well, actually he was just interested in acting.

He got a couple of television parts during the first year that we were together in New York. In one of the first ones he played a soldier that was up for court martial and, I think, hanging or something like that. He was supposed to die and he was called in to see the President and it was a very dramatic scene. He didn't have too big a part, though. He always insisted that I come to his rehearsals, and he always wanted me to come to his performance and sit in the back and wait for him until he got finished, and then he would always want to hear my criticism on how he did. He seemed so sort of insecure in his acting and yet he must have thought he was good because he had no doubts about getting to the top.

Well, after this went on for a month he would call me and I would see him almost every night. We would either go around the corner for a beer, or just sit in the Rehearsal Club and talk, or meet on the street, or I would go and watch one of his shows, or we would sit in an automat until late at night talking about scripts or trees or grass or bugs or anything.

He told me he did a lot of sketches and stuff and put them up on the wall at his place. He spent a lot of time teaching me how to draw. He got about one or two television shows and I, in the meantime, was working on Mitch Miller to do something about my singing which was lousy. Jimmy was very firm about my singing. He never really thought that it was too good. He wanted me to continue dancing, although the auditions didn't turn out very well.

Then we went through a period where he couldn't get work and I couldn't get work, so I went to American Photograph Corporation and started working there as a retoucher. We used to eat together. We ate Shredded Wheat. We bought a lot of sugar and a lot of milk and we ate Shredded Wheat, sugar, and milk for dinner at my place lots of times. I had this little card table that we would set up with candlelight and make a big thing about our dinner of Shredded Wheat, sugar and milk.

We both lived right near Central Park so we used to walk there in the evenings a lot and sit on the rocks in the park and talk and during the day, if he had it free and if I had it free, we used to practice bullfighting. I would be the bull and he had a cape which was given to him by Sidney Franklin. It still had some blood on it. I remember him talking about it.

Then I made a record for Columbia with Mitch and I remember the day Jimmy and I went all over town looking for a place where we could play it. We found this record store and we went in and we listened to my record a couple of times and we criticized it to the end and he said, "I think you should dance."

Then we really got in pretty bad condition because neither one of us had any money and I remember I quit American Photograph and he came over that night and we had fights about that and I said well all my time was going to American Photograph and I didn't have any time to spend on following any sort of a career. He got mad and walked out.

Fifteen minutes later the telephone rang and I went downstairs and it was Jimmy and he said couldn't we please go around together again. He was so unhappy and I was, too, and we made a date to meet in Columbus Circle under the pigeons and we were going to go to a movie. I went up to meet him and he was sitting there. He looked as if he'd been there for hours waiting and it seemed like our first date. We were both so miserable about being poor and not getting anywhere that it was most exciting and one of the best dates that I had with Jimmy.

We went to a movie on Forty-second Street and held hands the entire time and then instead of going back to the "Y" he came over for a while. I lived in a tiny little place off Eighth Avenue and if there were two people in it it was crowded. And Jimmy and I figured out how we were going to give a party together. We wanted to give a big party, inviting all sorts of commentators and theater critics and stars.

Then I got a job with my girl friend Sue's boyfriend to start as assistant choreographer and it was in New Jersey (Ocean City), so I went down there. Jimmy was living in the Iroquois Hotel with his friend Bill Bast, and I was down there about a month, I guess, and he came down. I went up to New York for a visit to see him and talked him into coming back down with me for two or three days. He came down and he seemed pretty unhappy.

He was around a lot of stock people. He was around the theater and everything, but he wasn't doing anything and I think he was kind of depressed and in a hurry to get back to work. He went back to the city and after that I heard that he was going to go on a cruise with his producer, who was doing the play "See the Jaguar."

With the end of the summer, I went back to New York and I didn't have any place to stay. Jimmy had made arrangements for me to stay with this friend of mine, Anne Chisholm. In the meantime, he was out sailing somewhere off the Cape. For some strange reason or other I was on a bus one night. I didn't know when he was due back in the city, and I was just passing on the bus the place that we first had a couple of drinks, the place that was right around the corner from the Rehearsal Club. All of a sudden I saw him walking down the street going towards Tony's Bar. I leaped off the bus and I saw him turn into this bar and I went in after him. When I got there he was in a telephone booth trying to locate me, and I rapped on the door of the telephone booth, and I had never seen him more shocked. We had a great big mad love scene right in the middle of the floor.

Then I got a job working in the Paris Theater as an usherette. That was when we decided to take this trip to Indiana. We were going to hitchhike all the way. To me it seemed like a wonderful escapade, so we induced Bill Bast to come with us and we started out of the city. I remember we went to New Jersey by bus through the tunnel, got off at the other side, and started thumbing on the highway there.

We got a ride through half a state, I think, and we made Indiana in three rides. The last ride we got was with a very, very famous baseball player. He was catcher for the Pittsburgh Pirates, but since then he has been sold, and I don't remember what club he has been sold to. He was very worried about the three of us. He didn't know exactly what we were doing on the road hitchhiking, and he knew we didn't have much money.

I remember he had a Nash Rambler. It was very comfortable and most of the time Bill sat in the front seat and Jimmy and I huddled in the back because it was freezing cold. We would sing songs and then we would ask him all about baseball players and what they were like, and Jimmy didn't say too much all the way out. We all seemed to be having very much fun.

He left us in Indiana at a crossroads where we could telephone Mark, who was Jimmy's uncle. And just before we left, this baseball player took Bill aside (we found out later) and offered him some money for us, to take care of the three of us, and Bill refused and he said if ever we were all in New York some time we could get together. I think it was the next season we were supposed to meet him at the Roosevelt Hotel, where the ball players stayed, and he was going to take us out on the town and treat us to a time.

And then we called Jimmy's family and Uncle Mark came and called for us, and we spent a perfectly glorious week on his farm in Indiana. We were up about seven or eight o'clock in the morning. We were out shooting things. We would throw tin cans up in the air and practice shooting, and we went horseback riding and we visited Jimmy's school, his old teachers, and we sat in on the rehearsal of a high-school play and Jimmy coached

We visited Jim's grandmother and grandfather. We met his father, who came all the way from California. He is a wonderful man, a dental technician and while he was out there, he gave Jimmy two new front teeth—they were coming loose because he had his teeth knocked out in football when he was a kid.

Then just about the end of the week Jimmy got a telephone call from New York saying that he got the part in "See the Jaguar," so we had to hurry back. We started out on the highway again going back to New York and we got a ride all the way back to New York with this man who owns oil in Texas. A very rich guy. He had ulcers. He said he couldn't eat anything and every time we would stop and get something to eat, he would go out and get violently ill by the car and then we would start off again.

On the ride back into New York, all of us were very, very depressed, as I remember, especially going into New York through the tunnel, because we didn't want to get back into the city. Even Jimmy didn't want to get back into the city, because we were having so much fun in Indiana and it was the freshest air the three of us had smelled in a long time.

Then it all started. He got swept up in the theater. He went out on the road, I think to Boston with "See the Jaguar." I didn't hear from him for about a month. Then one night he called and said he was back in the city, and that they were opening in two nights and he came down to see me at the Paris Theater where I got my old job back as an usherette.

One night I was working at the Paris Theater and he came with his friend Bill Bast and Bill's friend Tony. We all went out and celebrated because he got the part in "See the Jaguar." That was one of the last fun times that I ever had with Jimmy because after he got into the play, I didn't see much of him. As a matter of fact, he sort of disappeared after opening night. He seemed completely different once he got involved with "See the Jaguar" and Arthur Kennedy.

We sat in a neighborhood joint the night that he came back, after I had finished work, and he seemed to have something really bothering him, and I asked him what it was. The way he talked it was so hard and his gestures and everything were hard and sort of I-don't-give-a-damn kind of thing. He wasn't warm at all the way he used to be when we first went around.

But he wasn't always this way. I remember one time he went out for groceries or something and while in the grocery store he called me on the telephone. I don't know what had happened from the time he left until the time he got to the grocery store, but when he called he said he didn't have anything really to call about except that he wanted to get married, and he said, "we must get married before we get caught up in all this."

I remember him saying that, and he came back and that was one night when he seemed like he was afraid. There were lots of times when I felt that he was afraid. The way he hung on to me at the very beginning. After he got established, then I was afraid and I started to hang on to him, and he didn't seem to want the responsibility of having anybody hang on to him because he was going up too fast. That was just extra added weight.

What happened to Jimmy after that I don't know. In the first period of work in New York when he started getting up there he started getting television shows maybe once a month, which was a lot for him at the time. He had a lousy attitude about working. It seemed like he didn't care about rehearsals. He didn't care about the way he dressed. Sometimes he didn't even care about whether he was decent to people or not, as long as he was acting. He felt the *business* of show business was degrading.

The change. I wish everybody could have been with us in Indiana. The way he treated the animals. The way he treated even the dirt around the farm. Sort of the love he had for nature and everything showed me how completely simple he was. Simple in his ideals. Whether he was sure of what they were or not I am not sure, but he had them. They were growing But it made him pretty bitter, and he seemed to relax much more when we were out in Indiana.

One of the biggest things about him that I can remember is his love for animals The way he could get so close to them, and animals get close to him. This, to me, is quite a key to somebody's character

After "See the Jaguar," he disappeared I found out he moved back into the Iroquois Hotel after Boston, and it took me about two months to find him. When I did, I called him one night and I went over to see him. He was living in this little hotel room, and he seemed in even a worse condition than he was when he was so hard and bitter about New York business, and the guff that you have to take with the theater in trying to get somewhere. He was studying Greek philosophy and reading Roman history and was studying music.

Howard Wilder was an interesting person and so he took up with Howard Wilder. He would hang on to anybody Anybody that he felt he could get something out of—not money-wise or material-wise He felt that any knowledge he could gain from anybody was valuable. As a matter of fact his time was valuable. He seemed to be in a hurry about something. I don't know what. Maybe a feeling that he wasn't going to live very long. I don't know.

Even though many of the articles that I have read about him say that Jimmy was well educated, I don't think so. He didn't have as much schooling as he had wanted and he tried to catch up with it all the time. He taught himself how to paint. He taught himself many things.

One thing he always kept telling me all the time even in his letters to me when I was in stock is that a person must know the field that he is going into. You have to know your art. This is something that he stressed all the time.

He liked steaks. He liked good steaks. He was always talking about steaks but in the early part of our friendship we didn't do much eating, and he didn't take too much notice of what he was eating when he ordered. He made up real crazy dishes when he was living in the hotel, and I used to come and eat with him because neither of us had much money and we had to concoct things other than Shredded Wheat. That was when we really ran out of money. Before that first part we used to buy canned meats and make hashes and stuff. Clothes Jimmy never cared about. He didn't take care of his clothes very well, either. He would send them to the cleaners and maybe sometimes he would forget about them and I would have to get them out for him. He liked blue jeans. He lived in blue jeans most of the time, as everybody knows, and T-shirts. He had an old lousy camel-hair coat that some girl had given him when I first met him and felt sorry for him. And he had a raincoat which I always had my eye on. I just adored that raincoat. It was three-quarter length. I made a deal with him that he could have my blue jeans if I could have his raincoat. And he finally gave it to me and I still have it. That and a picture are about the only two things that I can remember keeping.

Lots of times we used to walk along Fifth Avenue and look in the store windows. Mostly it was cars. He was fascinated by cars. He always wanted a Jaguar and I always wanted a Jaguar and there was a place on Broadway up around the Sixties, a great big store window that had all sorts of cars in it. We used to hang around and look in the window and dream about the Jaguar we were some day going to get. It turned out he got a Porsche or it got him.

My roommate and I had a great Dane, a beautiful dog. I used to take him for walks in Central Park. I remember I called Jimmy one afternoon and told him that maybe he would like to see our dog that we had just acquired, and I would be in Central Park at such and such a time and at such and such a place. So I remember I was playing with the dog in this great big field and I saw Jimmy and we must have spent a good hour there just running with the dog and throwing things for him, and having him run and bring it back to us and this is one of the few times that I saw him laugh during the last days that I ever saw him.

Two years ago, after I lived in St. Thomas, Virgin Islands, I came back to New York and my first dancing partner, Fobiel, heard I was home and called me. He said he met Jimmy on the street and had a conversation with him, and told him that I was in New York and where I was. Within an hour Jimmy called me. I was over at a friend's house and we were going to have a party, and on the phone, it was the strangest feeling I got. I could almost visualize Jimmy doing flips and stuff while he was talking to me, because it seemed like I didn't know he had such a wonderful life out in Hollywood and so many things had happened to him. I thought he would be so terribly happy but he didn't seem to like it at all.

He seemed like he would rather be around his old friends, and he seemed like he was glad to hear from me and went on and on about how he missed me and how much he was thinking about me, and one of the first things he said was he got a horse. He always knew that I loved horses. And this gave him a large charge. Every time he would see a horse he would go blocks out of his way to point it out to me, or pet one down around Fifth and Fifty-ninth Street, where they all park.

He wanted to know immediately where I was and if he could come up, and I said we were having a party and he said he was with Jane Dacey, his agent, and Leonard Rossman, who had written the score for "East of Eden." They were going out to get some dinner and could they come up so I said sure. So about an hour later he called from Sardi's and said that they were eating dinner and he had forgotten the address. What was it again?

They came up and it was a wonderful homecoming, and he was happy to the point of almost hysteria. He was leaping and jumping all around like a clown, which he did very often when he was happy and I remember wherever I went at that party —if I would go into the kitchen to get food—he would follow me out there and stand and talk. Never anything about Hollywood or what he was doing but what *I* was doing, or how was the old gang. It seemed that he had just been away from home, and all of a sudden he found it again and he seemed jovial on top—but very unhappy underneath, somehow.

We left together. I remember he asked me what I was going to do. If I was going to go home. I said I didn't quite know, and he acted like he wanted to at least have a drink or talk a little bit more before I took the train for Larchmont, but Leonard Rossman talked him out of it and talked him into going to another party. So the three of us took a cab together and I got off at Grand Central. I remember, just before I left, he squeezed my hand in the cab and asked me if I were happy. I told him that I would be as soon as I could get back to the islands and he said, "I know what you mean," as if more or less he wished that he had found a place to go to where he could be happy. Then he said, "Now that I am more or less established and can help you, I wish you would come out to Hollywood, and I'll see if I can get you some dancing." He was the greatest enthusiast that I had about my dancing. He thought I was the living end. And that's the last I saw of Jimmy.

When I heard about Jimmy's death, I was sitting in a movie house in Puerto Rico, where I live now, and I heard a newsboy shout out in the streets that James Dean had been killed in a sports car accident. A lot of thoughts raced through my mind, mostly what I've been telling you about. About the desperate feeling he always had in wanting to see me any time, anywhere . . . about his fascination for cars and how he always wanted a Jaguar. But how he didn't like to drive and always made me do it.

I may forget a lot of other people, but no matter what happens, I'll never forget Jimmy Dean.

THE END

■ Several weeks ago Warner Brothers tossed a press party to announce the production start of *Giant,* starring Elizabeth Taylor, Rock Hudson and James Dean.

The shindig was held at the studio, and unlike any of the other principals, Jimmy Dean arrived late. He wore blue jeans and an old red flannel shirt. When the producer introduced him to the audience, Jim refused to rise or smile, or even acknowledge the applause. Moodily he sat in his seat, stared at his boots. When a photographer came close to photograph him, he quickly put on his dark sun glasses.

"Would you be kind enough to remove your glasses, Mr. Dean?" the photographer asked.

Jimmy made out as if he didn't hear.

"Why don't you give the guy a break?" a reporter asked the twenty-four-year-old acting genius from Fairmount, Indiana. "After all, he's got a job to do."

Dean shook his head. "I didn't mean to be rude. It's just that I've got bags under my eyes, and I need a shave."

In another corner of the room, a studio representative, watching the entire scene, muttered under his breath. "That's typical of the guy. I hope the Army drafts him and teaches him a little cooperation."

Jimmy is not particularly well-liked by some of his studio colleagues these days, because he refuses to show up for interviews, declines to be photographed, breaks appointments with reckless abandon and insists upon keeping his private life private.

"Maybe publicity *is* important," he admits. "But I just can't make it, can't get with it. I've been told by a lot of guys the way it works. The newspapers give you a big build-up. Something happens, they tear you down. Who needs it? What counts to the artist is performance not publicity. Guys who don't know me, already they've typed me as an odd ball."

So, too, as a matter of fact, have a lot of Hollywood girls who've met Jimmy at various private parties.

One young actress, who prefers to be nameless, tells about the recent time Dean came to a bongo-drum "kick" with his girl friend Lilli Kardell.

"After we were introduced," she recalls, "I said, just by way of starting a polite conversation, 'You're getting a lot of good publicity these days, all about your wonderful performance in *East Of Eden.*' His answer to that was, 'Most of it is a bunch of ———.' Only he didn't put it that delicately.

"I don't know," this actress continues, "whether he was trying to compensate for his shyness or what. He certainly is not typical of Hollywood actors. He will come into a room and for twenty or thirty minutes he'll say nothing. He won't even open his mouth. Then, mention something about drums or acting or bull fighting, and you can't stop him. He talks on and on with great power and intelligence. He's a strange one, all right."

Lilli Kardell, the nineteen-year-old Swedish actress, once under contract to Universal-International, has dated Dean more than any other girl in movieland. Although she declines to use the word love, she admits she's "gone" on the little guy.

"Jimmy," she explains in her (Cont'd on pages 70-74)

Daredevil Dean is hell on wheels. Racing his Porsche in local meets, he wins handily at 120 mph plus, earns the respect of racing pros but the word around the studio is "that crazy kid is going to kill himself."

James Byron Dean is a free-wheeling individualist who breaks all the

Modern Screen (USA) August 1955

LONE WOLF

rules except one—he travels fastest who travels alone / by Richard Moore

LONE WOLF

Scandinavian accent, "is a nice man. Some of those things he does, it is because he is youthful, and it takes time to handle fame. One must first learn how. But he is really very polite, very kind. They tell me he does not smile enough. Not true. He smiles much. He has a good sense of humor."

In other film quarters, however, the Dean sense of humor is generously described as "slightly perverse."

Jimmy himself, for example, likes to tell how he scared the wits out of a supposedly sophisticated and worldly photographer.

"A couple of months ago," Dean narrates, "this fellow, you know Dennis—well, Dennis went back to Indiana with me. Wanted to shoot me on the farm. Hometown stuff.

"One day we walked into town, and I stopped by Wilbur Hunt's. Wilbur runs a kind of general store in Fairmount. He's also the town mortician, and in the back he's got a selection of caskets. 'Mind if we shoot some stuff in here?' I asked Wilbur.

"He's a wonderful guy. 'Help yourself,' he said. So we went into the back. There were these caskets. I got into one of them and lay down. 'Go ahead,' I said to Dennis. 'Start shooting.' He thought I was kidding, but I always wanted to see how I'd look in a casket. Besides you should've seen the expression on Dennis' face.

"Anyway, he shot the pictures. Great stuff. Sent them into *Life*. Know what? The editors wouldn't publish a single one. Printed some stuff of me around the farm. Country boy—that routine."

Country boy—those two words—offer the key to Jimmy Dean's seemingly strange behavior. He acts awkward and this awkwardness is interpreted as rudeness. Actually, it seems that Jimmy retreats into his shell when he can't handle a new social situation, such as a studio shindig, or a top-level interview or a swank Hollywood get-together. He appears sullen and non-cooperative, but largely because he feels out of place and doesn't know what to do. Also, he is by nature fiercely independent and resents doing anything that rubs against his grain.

Let him like something, however, and he goes the whole hog.

Not too long ago he was at a party with Eartha Kitt and a bunch of other talented entertainers. Eartha started to sing. Jimmy sat down on the floor and grabbed a bongo drum. Two friends joined him. Eartha singing and Jimmy on the bongos. You should've dug it. Simply crazy, wild, out of this world.

Later that night they began to use the tape recorders. Jimmy has three or four which he uses all the time. "Great," he says. "Help me in my work. Like this part of Jett Rink I play in *Giant*. I had tape recordings of fellows with Texas accents. The thing to do is not to exaggerate the drawl. Get it just right."

Jimmy and Eartha sang and played the whole night with about ten other Hollywood characters. Dean recorded the festivities, and next day in the sanctity of his one-room garage apartment, played the tape recordings over and over again.

He has a great collection of African chants and knows a lot about tribal customs and *mores*. He is also a bull-fighting *afficionado* and one of the crack stock-car racing drivers in the country. This love of racing is currently giving the Warner moguls a fit.

During the filming of *Rebel Without A Cause*, for instance, Jim Dean raced his Porsche in the Palm Springs and Bakersfield Meets. As soon as he was finished with his Saturday scenes, he'd take off for the racing grounds. He was a winner in both races, hitting over 120 mph.

According to a veteran California driver, "This Dean kid is fearless. He drives as if he had some secret agreement with Death to lay off him. He's relatively new to speed-racing out here. Matter of fact we never heard of him until he showed up down at the Springs. We thought maybe he was one of those Hollywood characters looking for kicks or publicity. Hell, no. This kid really knows the business. He's one helluva fine rider. Knows what he's doing every minute."

In addition to his Porsche, Jim recently bought himself a hopped-up British Triumph motorcycle. Frequently he tears into the studio astride his mount to give one executive heart failure. The executive watches Jim zoom down the road, then sadly shakes his head and mutters, "That crazy kid is gonna kill himself."

At this point in his life James Byron Dean is living strictly for himself. He has no one to support, no one to please, no one in the world to cater to except James Byron Dean.

Although his father and step-mother live only eight or ten miles away from his Hollywood hideaway in the hills, he rarely visits them. Just why he isn't there more often is hard to tell.

Winton Dean, Jim's father, has what he thinks might be an adequate explanation for his son's behavior.

"I'll tell you this," he says. "My Jim is a tough boy to understand. At least, he is for me. But maybe that's because I don't understand actors, and he's always wanted to become one.

"Another reason is that we were separated for a long period of time, from when he was nine until he was eighteen. Those are the important, formative years when a boy and his father usually become close friends.

"Jim and I—well, we've never had that closeness. It's nobody's fault, really. Just circumstances. I came out to California in 1936 with Jim and his mother. Came right out here to Santa Monica. Worked in the Veterans' Hospital, dental technician. Did the same thing back in Indiana. Back there I worked for the Veterans' Hospital in Marion.

"A few years later, Jim's mother came down with cancer. She was only twenty-nine. The doctors told me it was hopeless. I didn't know what to do. How do you tell an eight-year-old boy his mother's going to die? I tried. In my own stumbling way I tried to prepare Jim for it. Tried to tell him about the sorrow that was coming. Many times I tried to tell the boy what was coming. I just couldn't make it.

"Jim's mother passed away before she was thirty. I was broken up. So was the boy. I couldn't look after him and work, too, so I sent him back to Indiana to live with my sister and her husband. They raised Jim on their farm. And what a fine job they did. In high school, you know, he was a standout athlete, specializing in track and basketball. Absolutely tops.

"When Jim came out here," Mr. Dean continues, "to go to Santa Monica College, he stayed with us—I was remarried by then—and we got along just fine. He was always crazy about acting, and I remember saying to him a couple of times, 'Jim, acting is a good hobby but why don't you study something substantial? Why don't you become a lawyer?' But no, it was acting with him all the way.

"Nowadays, he lives in a world we don't understand too well—the actors' world. We don't see too much of him. But he's a good boy, my Jim. A good boy, and I'm very proud of him. Not easy to understand. No, sir. He's not easy to understand. But he's all man, and he'll make his mark. Mind you, my boy will make his mark."

On the basis of only one film, *East of Eden*, Jimmy Dean has already made his mark. After *Rebel Without A Cause* is released and *Giant* is completed, the studio expects that the boy will become "the hottest actor in the business."

By then, however, Jim may not be in the business. He may be enrolled as a private in the Army of the United States. Only a few weeks ago he was called down to the Los Angeles induction station for his Army physical. Although he's extremely near-sighted and can't see very well without glasses, he is otherwise in good physical condition.

A stint in the service doesn't faze Jim one bit. Other actors bemoan the loss of revenue that military service entails, but Dean has never built his life around money. "Never had much," he says, "and don't need much. If the Army wants me I'm ready."

When that particular remark was relayed to a Hollywood beauty whom Dean had been seeing frequently before he took off for *Giant* location work, she pursed her lips and wrinkled her brow.

"Sure, he's ready to go," she repeated. "Jimmy Dean is ready to go anywhere, any place, any time. He's a free soul. Only," she pouted, "I don't want him to go. With all his crazy ways he's the cutest little guy we've had around Hollywood in a long, long time. Problems or no, he's a boy we'd all like to hang on to. A regular little tiger, that one." END

As heartbreaking as the passing of this great young actor are the real reasons why he sought escape from this world in speeding cars. This is the truth about the accident that killed James Dean.

■ *The sleek, low-slung Porsche Spyder bolted along Highway 466 near Paso Robles, California, like a streak of greased lightning. It was a beautiful car. It cost $7,000. "This baby'll do 150 miles an hour," cried the young man at the wheel to his companion, over the powerful throb of the motor. Then he smiled. An exultant smile. A smile of triumph. Here, at one with the elements of motion and space, a man could be free. . . .*

A grinding screech of brakes, as another car appeared suddenly at an intersection. A horrifying crash of tearing, crumbling metal. And then, the awful stillness that always descends upon the scene of a serious accident, until it was rent by the screaming sirens of patrol cars and an ambulance rushing from a hospital in Cholame.

Dazed and shaken, Donald Turnupseed, a young college student, emerged from the wreckage with only minor injuries. He'd been driving alone, and was making a left turn at the intersection when the collision came.

The two occupants of the other car couldn't get out. Gravely injured, they were taken from what, just a few moments before, had been the shiny, new Porsche —now a pile of smoldering junk. It had been hit in the center, virtually sliced in two. Would either be alive when the ambulance reached the hospital? One of them, identified as Rolf Weutherich, 28, a mechanic and friend of the driver, made it. The driver didn't make it. Suffering from multiple fractures of both arms and internal injuries, James Dean, 24, Hollywood's most brilliant young actor, died.

In all the grief-stricken hearts the inevitable question welled up: Why? What was it that compelled Jimmy Dean to pursue this dangerous, deadly hobby of racing sports cars? For it was this, indirectly, that led to his death; he was on his way to the road races at Salinas when the accident occurred.

To understand it, you have to delve into the complexities of Jimmy's intense, moody character—and into the events of the days just before the fatal crash.

Just a few weeks before, Jimmy had seemed to be happier, more at peace with his world than he had since he came to Hollywood. He had made the discovery that, in spite of the many phonies that feed upon an actor's fame, he had many real friends in the cinema city. It seemed that, at last, Jimmy really felt he "belonged." He talked enthusiastically about a plan to bring a branch of the famed New York Actors' Studio, where he got his training, to Hollywood for the benefit of the young players there. He was just as enthusiastic about his own future, confided that he was going to save his money and invest it wisely, with a view to producing and directing his own films. He constantly carried about the set what he called his "director's notebook," jotting down all the information he could get.

He'd found a new romance, too, with pretty starlet Ursula Andress. Dressed in a tux—very rare for him— he took her to the benefit of the Thalians, a group of young people with charitable aims.

Then, he and Ursula quarreled, and she broke off the romance. "Oh, I wish I hadn't," she cried hysterically between sobs, when she heard the news.

In her grief, the poor girl tried to blame herself, though in fact she'd done everything she could to help Jimmy. He was, Ursula reveals, a soul-searcher, always examining himself, trying to improve, and constantly asking for advice. "He needed desperately someone to understand him," says 19-year-old Ursula. "I tried to help and to love him, but it didn't work."

That Jimmy had a high regard for Ursula, nevertheless, is evident in the fact that she was the person to whom he came with his new Porsche, to share with her the thrill that he got from it.

But friends close to him say that, though he didn't show it, Jim was haunted by his old love for Pier Angeli, a love from which he never quite recovered.

Yet there was something else, something Jim gave away in one short sentence he uttered shortly before he died: "My fun days are over." This statement, which few took note of, holds the key to the story.

Those who recklessly condemn Jimmy for his love of speed racing should stop and think what it's like to be only 24 years old, and saddled with tremendous responsibility. Jim Dean was looked upon as a great actor, with a fabulous future. Millions of dollars, the jobs of countless studio people, were being staked on that future, and he knew it. And he had every intention of fulfilling that enormous obligation, of abandoning all the thrilling sports, the fun times.

The road race at Salinas was Jimmy's last fling. In his speeding car, with the wind rushing past and the hum of the motor like a song in his ears, he could say goodbye, if only for a few moments, to the heavy cares that burdened his shoulders, the fears, the loneliness of being misunderstood and unloved. And goodbye to youth. Goodbye . . . Goodbye. . . .

James Dean is free forever, now. Free from a life that brought him fame, but little happiness.

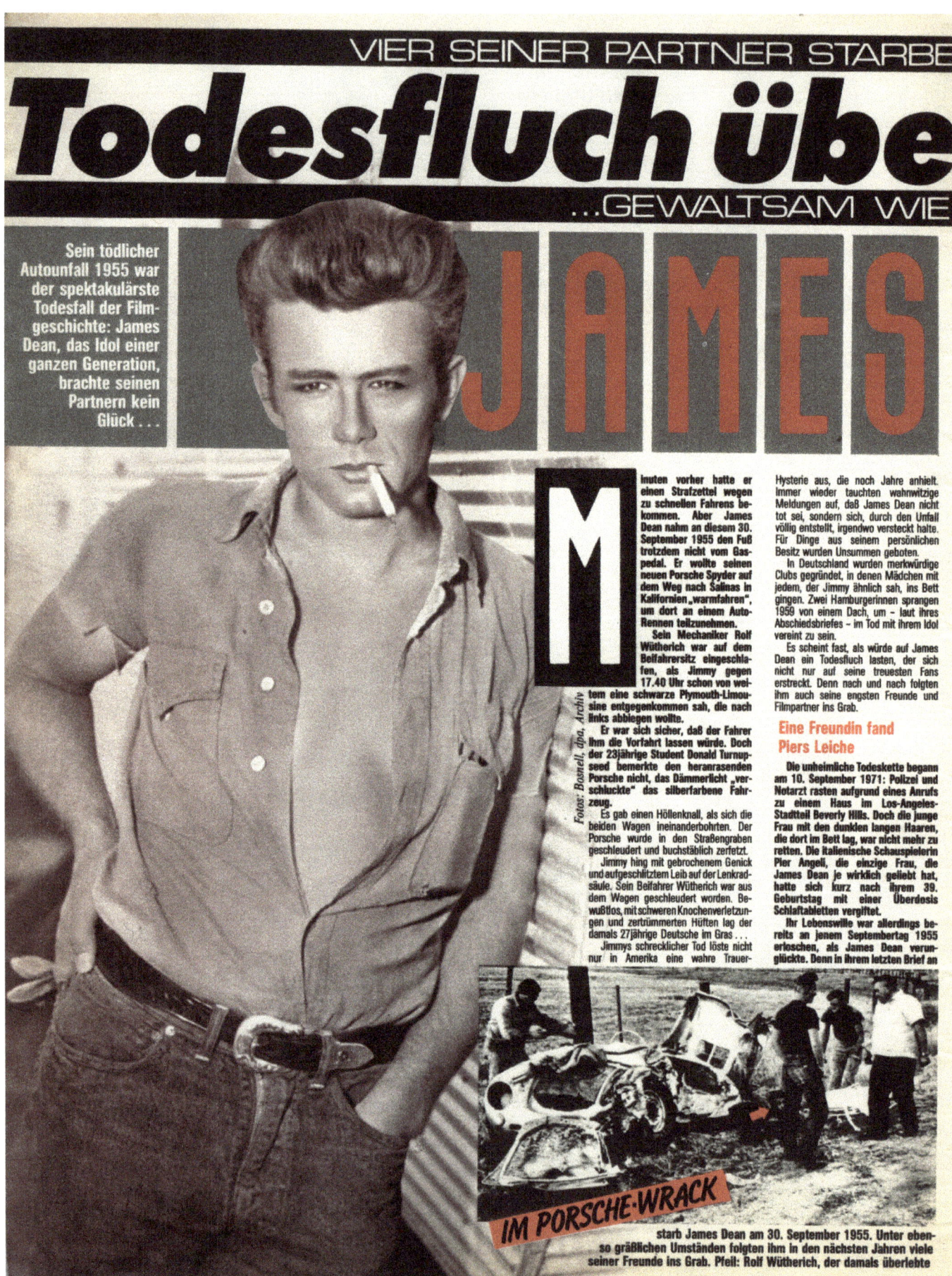

VIER SEINER PARTNER STARBE
Todesfluch übe
...GEWALTSAM WIE
JAMES

Sein tödlicher Autounfall 1955 war der spektakulärste Todesfall der Filmgeschichte: James Dean, das Idol einer ganzen Generation, brachte seinen Partnern kein Glück...

Minuten vorher hatte er einen Strafzettel wegen zu schnellen Fahrens bekommen. Aber James Dean nahm an diesem 30. September 1955 den Fuß trotzdem nicht vom Gaspedal. Er wollte seinen neuen Porsche Spyder auf dem Weg nach Salinas in Kalifornien „warmfahren", um dort an einem Auto-Rennen teilzunehmen.

Sein Mechaniker Rolf Wütherich war auf dem Beifahrersitz eingeschlafen, als Jimmy gegen 17.40 Uhr schon von weitem eine schwarze Plymouth-Limousine entgegenkommen sah, die nach links abbiegen wollte.

Er war sich sicher, daß der Fahrer ihm die Vorfahrt lassen würde. Doch der 23jährige Student Donald Turnupseed bemerkte den heranrasenden Porsche nicht, das Dämmerlicht „verschluckte" das silberfarbene Fahrzeug.

Es gab einen Höllenknall, als sich die beiden Wagen ineinanderbohrten. Der Porsche wurde in den Straßengraben geschleudert und buchstäblich zerfetzt.

Jimmy hing mit gebrochenem Genick und aufgeschlitztem Leib auf der Lenkradsäule. Sein Beifahrer Wütherich war aus dem Wagen geschleudert worden. Bewußtlos, mit schweren Knochenverletzungen und zertrümmerten Hüften lag der damals 27jährige Deutsche im Gras...

Jimmys schrecklicher Tod löste nicht nur in Amerika eine wahre Trauer-Hysterie aus, die noch Jahre anhielt. Immer wieder tauchten wahnwitzige Meldungen auf, daß James Dean nicht tot sei, sondern sich, durch den Unfall völlig entstellt, irgendwo versteckt halte. Für Dinge aus seinem persönlichen Besitz wurden Unsummen geboten.

In Deutschland wurden merkwürdige Clubs gegründet, in denen Mädchen mit jedem, der Jimmy ähnlich sah, ins Bett gingen. Zwei Hamburgerinnen sprangen 1959 von einem Dach, um – laut ihres Abschiedsbriefes – im Tod mit ihrem Idol vereint zu sein.

Es scheint fast, als würde auf James Dean ein Todesfluch lasten, der sich nicht nur auf seine treuesten Fans erstreckt. Denn nach und nach folgten ihm auch seine engsten Freunde und Filmpartner ins Grab.

Eine Freundin fand Piers Leiche

Die unheimliche Todeskette begann am 10. September 1971: Polizei und Notarzt rasten aufgrund eines Anrufs zu einem Haus im Los-Angeles-Stadtteil Beverly Hills. Doch die junge Frau mit den dunklen langen Haaren, die dort im Bett lag, war nicht mehr zu retten. Die italienische Schauspielerin Pier Angeli, die einzige Frau, die James Dean je wirklich geliebt hat, hatte sich kurz nach ihrem 39. Geburtstag mit einer Überdosis Schlaftabletten vergiftet.

Ihr Lebenswille war allerdings bereits an jenem Septembertag 1955 erloschen, als James Dean verunglückte. Denn in ihrem letzten Brief an

IM PORSCHE-WRACK starb James Dean am 30. September 1955. Unter ebenso gräßlichen Umständen folgten ihm in den nächsten Jahren viele seiner Freunde ins Grab. Pfeil: Rolf Wütherich, der damals überlebte

'The Death Curse Over James Dean - his colleagues died violently'

DEAN?

ZERSCHMETTERT lag Jimmys Mechaniker in seinem Honda Civic (u.), mit dem er 1981 gegen eine Hausmauer gerast war. 26 Jahre vorher hatte er auf dem Beifahrersitz des Porsche Jimmys Todesfahrt (Foto links) überlebt

ERTRUNKEN im Pazifik ist Natalie Wood, Jimmys Partnerin aus „Denn sie wissen nicht...". Ihre Leiche wurde neben diesem Schlauchboot (o.) aus dem Wasser gefischt

ERSTOCHEN wurde Sal Mineo 1976 von Nachbarn an der Auffahrt zu seiner Hollywood-Villa aufgefunden (o.). Auch als Jimmys Freund in dem Film „Denn sie wissen nicht..." starb Sal Mineo eines gewaltsamen Todes

VERGIFTET mit einer Überdosis Schlaftabletten hat sich die italienische Schauspielerin Pier Angeli. Sie konnte ihre große Liebe James Dean (l.) nie vergessen

einen Freund schrieb sie: „... die Liebe liegt weit hinter mir. Sie starb an dem Steuer eines Porsche. Seit 16 Jahren bin ich allein."

Mit 17 war sie bereits eine erfolgreiche Schauspielerin. James Dean hatte Anna Maria Pierangeli – wie sie richtig hieß – in den Filmstudios von Hollywood kennengelernt. Drei Jahre galten die „kleine Garbo" und der „Rebell" als Traumpaar. Doch Piers ehrgeizige Mutter hintertrieb die Freundschaft mit dem „amerikanischen Beatnik und Habenichts" – wie sie Jimmy bezeichnete. Sie fädelte die Hochzeit mit dem italo-amerikanischen Sänger Vic Damone ein. Pier beugte sich als folgsame italienische Tochter dem Willen ihrer Mutter.

Ihre große Liebe James Dean konnte sie allerdings nie vergessen. Ihre erste wie auch ihre zweite Ehe mit einem italienischen Komponisten, zerbrach. Ihre Karriere vernichteten der Alkohol und ihre Tablettensucht. Freunden gestand Pier: „Nachts wache ich oft auf und wünsche mir immer, nicht mein Mann, sondern Jimmy solle neben mir liegen."

Sal Mineo starb gewaltsam wie im Film

Fünf Jahre später, im März 1976, gellten gegen 21 Uhr laute Schreie durch das Villenviertel West-Hollywoods. Drei Nachbarn, die sofort zu Hilfe eilten, fanden nur einen toten Mann mit tiefen Messerstichen in der Brust in einer riesigen Blutlache an der Auffahrt zu seinem Haus liegen.

Es war der 37jährige Schauspieler Sal Mineo, Jimmys Partner in „Denn sie wissen nicht, was sie tun". Der gewaltsame Tod, den er damals vor den Filmkameras durch die Kugel eines Polizisten starb, wurde 21 Jahre später brutale Wirklichkeit. Nur, daß die Polizei jahrelang im Dunkeln tappte. Der 22jährige Pizza-Austräger Lionel Williams, damals bereits wegen anderer Delikte im Gefängnis, gab sich dann selbst als Täter zu erkennen. Vor seinen Mithäftlingen prahlte er mit seinem Mord an Sal Mineo.

Am 21. Juli 1981 erfüllte sich das tödliche Schicksal von Rolf Wütherich, dem er bei dem Unfall mit James Dean nur um Haaresbreite entronnen war. Der ehemalige Porsche-Mechaniker und Rallye-Profi (53) raste in seinem Honda Civic nach einem feucht-fröhlichen Kegelabend mit überhöhter Geschwindigkeit und nicht angeschnallt gegen eine Hausmauer in der schwäbischen Ortschaft Kupferzell.

Wütherich hatte den Tod seines Freundes Dean nie verwinden können. Zwar hatten ihn die Ärzte nach dem schrecklichen Unfall während eines zwölfmonatigen Klinikaufenthalts wieder zusammengeflickt, doch sein Inneres blieb zerbrochen. Er quälte sich mit Selbstvorwürfen, daß er Dean ans Steuer des nagelneuen 160-PS-Renners gelassen hatte.

Wütherich begann Tabletten zu schlucken, verlor seinen Job beim Porsche-Kundendienst in Kalifornien und kehrte nach Deutschland zurück. Doch das Bild vom toten Jimmy ließ ihn nie los. Zehnmal wechselte er seinen Arbeitsplatz, viermal die Ehefrau. Nach einem Kegelabend mit viel Alkohol starb er in den Trümmern seines Pkws – wie einst sein Freund James Dean.

Natalie nahm ihr Geheimnis mit ins Grab

Noch im selben Jahr starb der letzte überlebende Star aus dem zweiten James-Dean-Film „Denn sie wissen nicht, was sie tun". Natalie Woods Leiche trieb am 29. November 1981 vor der Küste der Insel Santa Catalina/Kalifornien im Pazifik. Es war das Ende eines Wochenendes, das die 43jährige Schauspielerin mit ihrem Mann Robert Wagner auf ihrer Jacht „Splendour" verbracht hatte.

Die Todesumstände werden sich wohl nie genau klären lassen. Es ist von Alkohol, von Eifersuchtsszenen und einer nächtlichen Auseinandersetzung mit Robert Wagner die Rede. Jedenfalls muß sich Natalie kurz vor Mitternacht mit dem Beiboot von der Jacht entfernt haben. Denn am nächsten Morgen trieb ihr lebloser vollbekleideter Körper 182 Meter vom Strand entfernt in einer abgelegenen Bucht neben diesem Schlauchboot.

Wer wird wohl der nächste sein, den Jimmys schrecklicher Todesfluch ereilt? *M. Rüdiger*

Übrigens: Am 12. März gibt's mit Jimmy ein Wiedersehen auf der Mattscheibe in „Jenseits von Eden"

Jimmy's eccentricities—sloppy clothes, slurry speech, mixed-up manner—were only surface signs of his rebellion. Today's teen-agers, recognizing this, have made him a symbol of their own inner conflicts. Though parents think this sometimes fanatic devotion is morbid and unhealthy, within bounds the Dean Cult has done much good.

It's being channeled, for instance, by the Dean Foundation—a nationwide organization headed by Fairmount businessmen and set up to help struggling artists in all fields. Specifically, this devotion has inspired talented young people who might have otherwise given up in despair and defeat to keep on with theater work.

The memory of Jimmy Dean has provided a cultural contribution, too, in prodding the reading habits of teens. For example, kids learning that Dean's greatest ambition was to play Hamlet, read the Shakespeare opus for themselves to see why.

The present teen-age generation is rebelling against the mess their parents left them; they need an emotional outlet. If these kids have found an idol who embodies their frustrations and dreams, if this is their way of preparation for adulthood, why should mothers and fathers try to stop them? Parents should, instead, try to understand this devotion. In time they may even learn to love, not fear, the memory of James Dean.

Like his loyal fans, Jimmy'd put his mind to something—chess, a girl he liked—and nothing could distract him.

...and yet he lives again

With TV and movie re-runs, Dean's not forgotten. Also available is Ken Kendall's remarkable life mask.

James Dean Anniversary Book 1956 (Dell)

Text reproduced through the courtesy of Collier's

Sanford Roth was caught off guard when Jimmy snapped this one.

Jimmy relaxes after completing his greatest performance, the banquet scene in Giant.

Elizabeth Taylor did many scenes like this—some tense, some tender—with Jimmy.

THE ACTOR AT WORK...

the photographs of
SANFORD ROTH

■ "Jimmy's professional life was coming sharply into focus," says Roth, who photographed Dean during *Giant* and was driving behind him on the day of his fatal accident. "Offstage he was still an enigma—or a trial—to more prosaic folk. But a photographer is sometimes allowed a certain insight. Dean has been described as a meteor, a great Dane puppy, a crazy-mixed-up kid, a poet. He was all of these things and—at the same time—none of them. His laugh was a half-silent chuckle, as though he were embarrassed by exuberance. Yet his enthusiasms were huge: they ran through the whole spectrum of human interests from motorcycles to classical music, to jazz, to bullfighting (he practiced with a cape in his home), to cats. He had the austere good sense of an Indiana Quaker (which he was), and the defense mechanism of a turtle. In his case, the shell was his own private world: the music of Bartok and Schönberg, the polished steel innards of his new racing car, the writers he'd recently discovered—Jean Genêt, Curzio Malaparte and Gerald Heard. He had no time for reporters. But at least one, columnist Hedda Hopper,

MORE

Without any warning, Jimmy laughingly hurled the rope at Roth. Fortunately, the camera was strapped around his neck

...AND AT PLAY

Edna Ferber, author of Giant, tried her hand at roping.

really loved Jimmy, and says, 'He was like quicksilver. He had a sure instinct for drama. Yet, what I remember most is the little-boy quality shining from behind those thick glasses of his.'

"The project of the moment absorbed Dean completely. And he held skill in high esteem. I was talking to him one day about a sculptor I know in Italy—one of the great ones—about his way of working and his philosophy of life. This prompted Jimmy to tell me he, too, was a sculptor, of a very minor grade. He'd had no formal study, but worked with clay, using old toothbrush handles and spoons for tools. He wanted professional advice and criticism; and I suggested he see Pegot Waring, a friend of mine and a fine sculptor. She took him on as a student and was astonished at the ease and agility with which he worked.

"He wanted to walk down the Boulevard Montparnasse in Paris, to study sculpture there, to buy crazy sweaters in Capri and to meet Cocteau and Miro. He knew the world was round, but he never stopped trying to prove it to himself."

Liz didn't seem displeased when Jimmy "hog-tied" her in some off-the-set shenanigans.

Jimmy had made the most of his work in Texas. He learned to rope, ride and break calves.

The old West watched the new when Gary Cooper met Jimmy on the set. Coop had been a Dean fan since _Eden_.

"When Jimmy studied photography, nobody escaped his camera, not even me," Schatt says. This was at Museum of Modern Art.

PORTRAIT OF THE ACTOR IN A BIG TOWN

the photographs of
Roy Schatt

■ When young Jimmy Dean left UCLA and went East in 1953, there were only a few people who recognized in him the seeds of future greatness. One of these was Roy Schatt, the New York photographer who has shown a knack for discovering young talent long before the studios sit up and take notice. Dean spent many hours at Schatt's midtown studio, and naturally became interested in photography. Within a few months, Schatt had another full-time student on his hands. (His others have included Elia Kazan and Susan Strasberg.) "Nothing Jimmy ever did was just a sideline," Roy told us. "He put everything he was into everything he did. In his photography, he was constantly searching for the new, even the odd. Sometimes the results were bizarre. But it was always Jimmy." Roy Schatt, too, was snapping shutters as fast as he could load his cameras. Some of the candid shots he took during parties at the studio with Jimmy at the bongos, and his quiet portraits of a young man heading for stardom, form an important part of the photographic record of a brief but blazing career.

James Dean Anniversary Book 1956 (Dell)

"Even in those days, you could sense he was troubled."

"Times like this in my studio, only the music mattered."

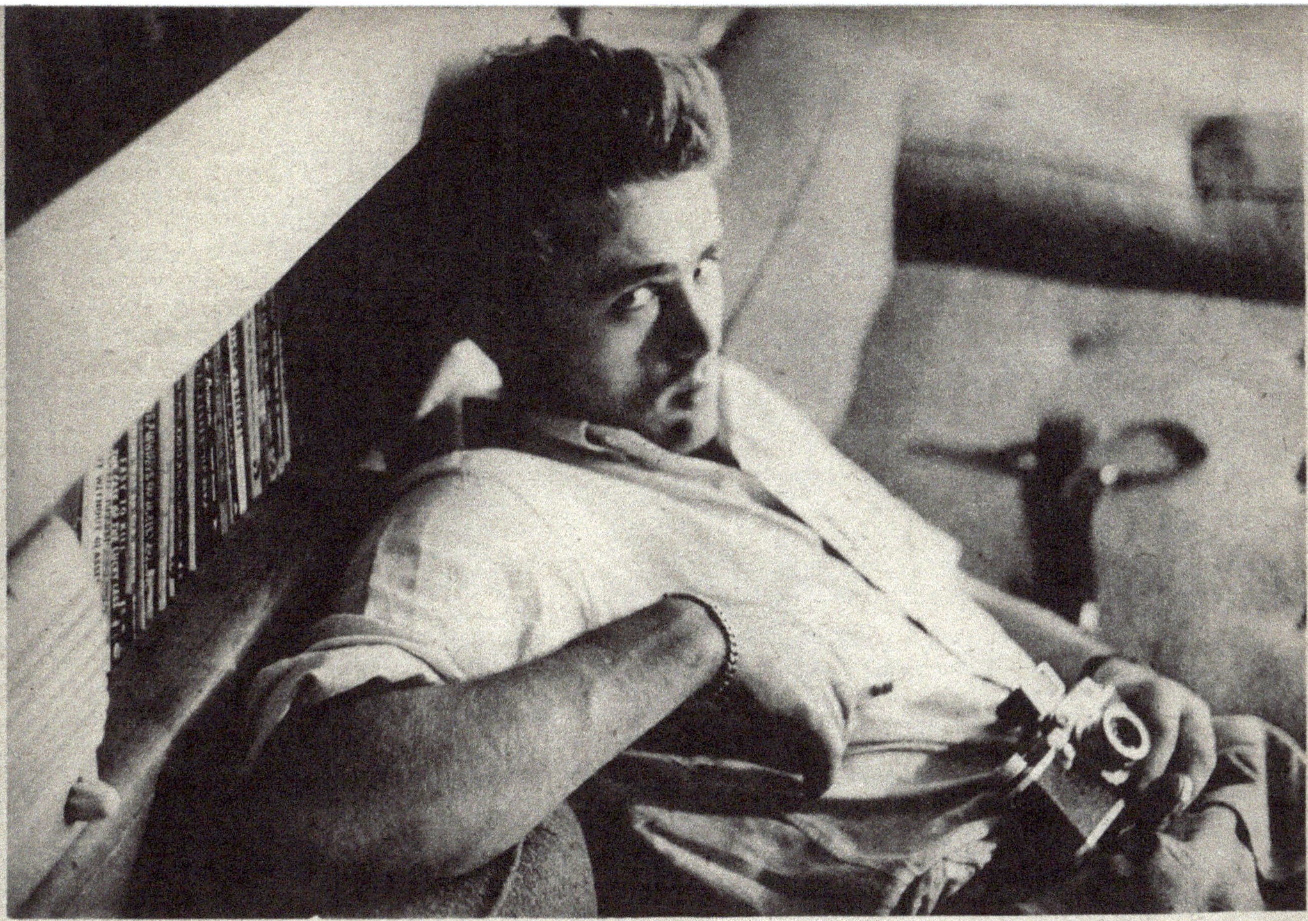

"And when resting, there was a part of him that never relaxed. He seemed to be listening to something none of us could hear."
"Sometimes he would just stare into space, as if he knew his future. He looked like he was astonished by it, but never afraid."

The James Dean Story

直木久蓉・画

ヴァレンティノ以後、かくも映画史上にその死を惜しまれたスタアがあつただろうか。しかも死後にあつて生前をしのぐこの人氣の理由は、彼のどこに秘められているのか。彼の歩んだ道を、彼の生涯を、最も廣い調査の下に、こゝにディーンの全貌として紹介……

ジェームス・ディーン物語

神様にでも "氣まぐれ" なときがあるのでしょうか。あまりにも多くのギフト（恵まれた天分）を一身にあつめ、この世に生を享けたがゆえに、あまりにもかけがえらようなき思慕の情を人々の胸にうえつけながら、はかなくうち去っていったジェームス・ディーン。

だが今となつては、それをしも神の "みこころ" として、ただ在りし日の彼をしのびましょう。それが彼の魂を安らげ、彼を愛する私たちの心の渇きをいささかなりにもいやすのではないでしょうか。

"ジミー星" の誕生

インディアナ州マリオンにきらかな雪の降る一九三一年二月八日の朝、イースト・第四番街にあるグリーン・ゲイブルス・アパートメントという簡素なコテージの一室に玉のような男の子が生まれました。そこから近い集會所の一隅に職場をもつ歯科醫ウィントン・ディーンと妻ミルドレッドの間にできたその子は、ジェームス・バイロン・ディーンと名付けられ、生れた数日後からフェアモントのソシントン街八〇二番地にあるディーン家代々の家で育ちました。

ディーン家は、一八一五年頃にケンタッキー州のレキシントンからこのインディアナ州へ移住してきた舊家で、その赤ん坊の祖母エムマの生家ウーレン家も、ママのミルドレッドの出たウィルスン家もほぼ同じ頃にこゝへ移り住んだ舊家でした。代々農牧を業とするディーン家の當主チャールス・D・ディーンとエムマの間には、ウィントンとチャールス・ノーランという二人の息子と、ホーテンスという娘があり、その長男ウィントンが同じフェアモントの農牧業者ウィルスン家の美しい娘ミルドレッドと結婚して、できた息子がその玉のような赤ん坊でした。

"ジミー" と呼ばれ、やわらかい金髪に、輝くばかり碧く澄む瞳をもつその子は、家族の者みなから愛され、日増しに美しく育ちました。彼が五つになった時、パパのウィントンはロサンゼルスのヴェテランス病院に勤めることとなり、ジミーも両親と共にそこへ移つてゆきました。

やがてブレントウッドの小學校へ通いだしたジミーには、メリー・ルーというガールフレンドもできましたが、その頃から機械いじりが好きだった彼が、何よりスリルを感じるのはパパが買っていだいた水ポンプで遊ぶことでした。またパパゆずりか手先も器用な彼にママはヴァイオリンを習わせましたが、このおけいことはあまり徹迎しなかった彼も、七つのお誕生日に両親から贈られたポニイは大歓迎。ママお手製のカウボ

仲良しのナタリー・ウッドのスウェードのジャケットに共演記念のサインをするジミー

「理由なき反抗」のロサンゼルス・ロケでファンの肩の上でサインしているジミー

ピア・アンジェリと「スタア誕生」の試写會に出席した頃のジミー。

イ服を着た彼は、ヒエロの衣裳を着た級友たちをお招きしたパーティでは、サッソウとボニィに打乗って豆カウボーイぶりを發揮するなど、樂しい日々を送りました。

だが彼が九つになったある日、ママのミルドレッドは、忽然とこの世を去ってしまったのです。彼女はだいぶ前から癌を患っていましたが、餘命いくばくもないとわかってからも、パパは幼い息子にそれというに忍びず、まだ二十九歳の若さで美しくやさしいママに突如いなくなられたジミーのおどろきと悲しみはたとえようもな

く、ウィントンは召集され、十八ヵ月間も軍隊生活をせねばなりませんでしたから。

月日以來陽氣だった彼も無口な子になり、あどけない中にもどこかやるせないかげをやどすようになりました。

嫁の死ぬ七週間前から看護にきていた祖母のエムマは、ウィントンに、一人息子の幼いジミーを殘して勤めに出るむずかしさを説き、妹ホーテンスのウィンスロウ夫妻が彼等の愛娘ジョーンと同様にジミーを育て度いとの意向を傳えて、ジミーを故郷のフェアモントへ連れ帰ることにしたのです。この祖母さんの提案はたしかに正しいことでした。それから間もな

く彼がまず仲良しになったのは家で、生れたての小豚を自分の部屋へつれてきて牛乳で育てた彼は、小豚たちからもすっかりなつかれ、彼が愛犬や愛馬と野原に散歩にゆく時などは、いつも小豚たちが彼のあとを追って妙な鳴き聲を立てながら走ってゆくという

微笑ましい風景が見られました。人々からやさしくされれば されるほど、彼の心は亡き母の面影を追い求めたのでしょうか。そうした彼にはかえって無心の動物たちの方が氣やすい慰め手であったようです。

しかし暇さえあれば彼を連れて大きなショックをうけたジミーの傷心をやわらかく包むかに見えました。

・J○エーカーもある農場へ帰り、やさしいウィンスロウ叔父叔母夫妻の一家に加えられ、日曜には敬虔な村人たちとクェーカー教Quakerの教會へゆくといったこの平和な生活は、母の死という大きなショックをうけたジミーの傷心をやわらかく包むかに見えました。

彼は次第に親しみを見せるようになり、特に彼が繪や木彫りなどに興味をもつと知るやすぐに道具を買い與えて、「好きなことは何でもやってごらん」というこの叔父には、彼の親しみは急激に増してゆきました。こうしてやがて家族のみんなにこの叔父が、まず人々を驚かせるのがならわしでした。それをきいながらジミーはいつかそのおとぎ話を、自分の想像の世界で演じるようになったのです。そして翌日になると、それを人々の前で演じて見せたり、時には祖父さんの口まねやしぐさまでして見せるのですが、これがまた祖父さんそっくりなのです。そうした彼の特殊な天分は人々を驚かせ家中を陽氣にして笑わせる中心で、ますます一家のペットになりました。見よう見まねでピアノを弾くようになった彼に、ホーテンス叔母さんは熱心にピアノを教え、また從姉のジョーンがダンスをするのをまねる

ついていたジミーが、まず人々を驚かせたのは、その物まね上手なことでした。彼は毎晩チャス祖父さんと一緒に寝るのですが、彼の親しみは急激に増してゆきました。

「ねえ、グランパ、今夜もなにかお話して」

と淋しそうにいうジミーに、祖父さんはいつもお伽話をしてきかせるのがならわしでした。それをきいながらジミーはいつかそのおとぎ話を、自分の想像の世界で演じるようになったのです。そして翌日になると、それを人々の前で演じて見せたり、時には祖父さんの口まねやしぐさまでして見せるのですが、これがまた祖父さんそっくりなのです。

THE JAMES

by DAVID GRIFFITHS

DEAN—he yearned for a love which he never found...

WHEN a racing car speeding at 70 mph along a California highway on the afternoon of September 30, 1955, slammed head-on into another car, a legend was born. James Dean, 24-year-old actor was dead, and the James Dean cult had begun.

Next Friday (November 1) Associated-Rediffusion presents *The Legend of James Dean*—a macabre story of the hysterical fan-worship accorded the late actor by "Deanagers," adolescents who have adopted the actor as a symbol of their own worries and fears.

Often it is probably no more than youthful perversity that gives them a bizarre pleasure in idolising a dead man. Sometimes the cult seems to go far beyond this.

Dan Farson, interviewing a "Deanager" for *This Week*, was told: "The older generation have God. We have James Dean."

Two Brighton girls (who will be seen on Friday's programme) have built a candle-lit shrine to Dean. In London, a fan club formed only a few weeks ago has a booming membership which includes a man of 68 and a girl of 11.

But mostly the Dean appeal is to teenagers. His lost manner, inarticulate mumbling and social awkwardness (essentially the same in the three films in which he starred) struck an ecstatically responsive chord in many a mixed-up kid.

The Dean frenzy reached its peak in the United States about a year ago, when Warner Brothers were receiving about 8,000 letters a month addressed to Dean, and almost everybody who had had the slightest connection with him was badgered for information and souvenirs.

Movie-fan magazines found him at the top of readers' lists of favourite stars, and special Dean magazines became big business. Around 2,000,000 copies have been sold. At least one journal contained spirit messages: "Read his own words from the beyond."

The British Dean craze seems to have been growing steadily, and is probably about to reach its peak with the release of Warner Brothers' biography, *The James Dean Story*, a documentary written by Stewart Stern, who wrote the screenplay of *Rebel Without A Cause*.

A large part of Dean's story is told with still photographs, and the makers certainly had no shortage of material to choose from. I doubt if any actor has ever been more frequently photographed than Dean.

Some of these pictures, extracts from his films, and interviews with people who knew him or who worship his memory, will be seen in next Friday's examination of the legend.

The subject of this legend was born James Byron Dean in 1931, in Fairmount, Indiana. When he was eight, the family moved to California. A few months later, his mother died of cancer.

She had obviously lavished a great deal of affection on her only son—the choice of the middle name, Byron, indicates the extent of her romanticism—and had been ambitious on his behalf, always encouraging signs of artistic talent, and providing him with dancing and violin lessons. When she died, Jimmy's father sent him back to Indiana to be brought up on a farm by his uncle and aunt.

For his college education he returned to his father and stepmother in Santa Monica, California, and went to the University of California to study law and theatre arts.

A scene from his last film *Giant*, co-starring Elizabeth Taylor. He died before it was finished

DEAN LEGEND

A tense moment in *East of Eden*, the film which made him a star overnight—and the idol of teenagers

The legend lives on in *The James Dean Story*, a film biography of a young man of talent who symbolised the "mixed-up" kids of his generation

Although an indifferent performer at that time, he became interested in amateur dramatics. In his spare time he began hanging round TV and film studios in Hollywood. One of his first jobs was playing John the Baptist in a religious film, *Hill Number One*.

Even in that role his unusual sex-appeal must have come across, for the girls of the Immaculate Heart High School in Los Angeles formed the first of many James Dean fan clubs.

Hollywood was in no hurry to discover him, so he went to New York for training at the Actors' Studio, home of "Method" acting.

Here he met Marlon Brando, who became an influence on his life and acting that Jimmy never shook off. Like Brando, he slouched around in leather jackets, and, later, defied Hollywood conventions.

The film and theatre director Elia Kazan, who directed several of Brando's films, also discovered Jimmy at the Studio.

After a few parts, and some good critical notices, on Broadway, Dean was hired by Kazan to star in the screen version of Steinbeck's *East Of Eden*. And when the film was released, James Dean *was* a star. Shortly afterwards he made *Rebel Without A Cause*, and immediately following its completion he began work on *Giant*. Before the cameras had finally stopped rolling on *Giant*, Dean was dead.

Success brought riches but not happiness to James Dean. People who knew him slightly tell me he was often inexcusably boorish. It was hard to like him and hard to get to know him. But a few people who knew him well had great sympathy and affection for him.

He yearned for a love to replace his mother's, but apparently never found it. Instead, he got involved in terrible quarrels, drank heavily, and drove too fast.

While I was discussing *The Legend Of James Dean* with producer Ray Dicks, he said how difficult it was to find anybody in England who knew Dean. I remembered a young man who had known quite a few Actors' Studio people in New York. Ray rang his agent, who said the man was abroad. So I rang the man's brother. He told me that a man who knew Dean well was in London probably doing some work for Granada Television.

As I repeated the name, Dicks jumped up excitedly, went to the bookcase and came back waving a paper-back. It read: *"James Dean. A biography by William Bast. The brilliant young actor's art and life—told by the man who knew him best."*

Bast was quickly traced, and Ray invited him round to Television House. He turned out to be a charming and intelligent young writer who came to Britain to help write Alan Young's *Personal Appearance* show.

He has agreed to talk about his late and legendary friend next Friday night.

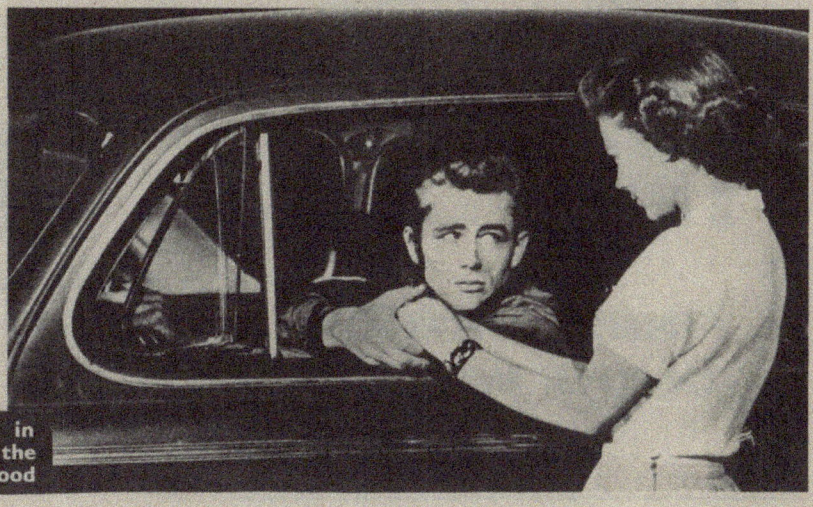

Remember the daredevil car race in *Rebel Without a Cause*? The girl in the drama of youth was Natalie Wood

LONDON FILM FESTIVAL

● 'Come Back To The Five And Dime, Jimmy Dean, Jimmy Dean' (Nov 14)

'Jimmy' points the way ahead

ROBERT ALTMAN has always occupied a unique position among contemporary American directors. A film-maker with independent sensibilities who has worked consistently for the Hollywood majors, he has produced a series of quirky, unconventional films such as "Brewster McCloud", "McCabe And Mrs Miller", "The Long Goodbye', "Nashville", "Three Women", and "Quintet".

But although he was tolerated by Hollywood after the enormous success of "MASH" in 1970, the uneven box office performance of Altman's subsequent films did little to endear him to the new breed of studio executives who came to the fore in the late '70s.

Altman himself was far from happy with the way the situation was going, and the virtual shelving of his last film for Fox, "Health", and the uncertain handling of "Popeye" by Paramount and Disney were the final straws as far as he was concerned.

So it is not surprising to discover that his latest film, "Come Back To The Five And Dime, Jimmy Dean, Jimmy Dean", is a totally independent production.

"I can't make the films the majors want to do, and they can't make the films I want to do," he says. "I really want to do small independent films like 'Jimmy Dean' from now on."

"Jimmy Dean" began life as a stage play. Written by Ed Graczyk, it centres on the 20th anniversary reunion of a James Dean fan club in a small Texas town close to where "Giant" was filmed. The women who make up the fan club reminisce about the past, and for one of them in particular, the effect the filming of "Giant" had on her life.

More painful

As the play progresses, the reminiscences — and the relationship between the characters — become more painful.

The play had been performed in regional theatres when it came to Altman's attention. However, it was staged with different casts for the sequences in the past and the present.

Altman's initial major decisions were to use the same cast for both past and present, and to cast, in addition to established actresses such as Sandy Dennis, Marta Heflin and Karen Black, the singer Cher in a key role.

Altman had been attracted to the play "by its trashy, soap opera quality. It's like a downmarket Greek tragedy, where these women tell us their personal dramas.

"And I thought it said some interesting things about what happens when the circus comes to town — in this case what effect a film being made has on a town, and how people remember it for years after. It's about the way people transfer fantasy into their lives, because they've allowed them to be empty. And it's an off-centre love story."

However, Altman's liking for the play was not shared by the critics when it opened on Broadway.

"But the play didn't close, because we were in the black all the time. People heard about it, and came to see it. The critics couldn't understand it, and wouldn't leave us alone.

"So when we decided to make a film of it, we kept it very quiet. Everyone said 'Oh, Altman's making his failure on video'. But we ignored it, and carried on making the film."

Altman and his cast shot "Jimmy Dean" in 17 days on Super 16mm on a budget of 800,000 dollars. "I guess we could have gone to a major and got a big advance, but they destroy this type of film. So we raised the money independently — half through Viacom, although it's not made for cable TV, it'll be released theatrically, and half through an independent producer, Mark Goodson."

Altman clearly is happy with "Jimmy Dean" and the reception it has had so far at festivals such as Venice and Deauville. And he intends to pursue the "small is beautiful" policy with his next projects, which he wants to make independently on reasonably low budgets.

His next film will be "Streamers", again based on a stage play, which he plans to shoot in Montreal with some of the same technical team from "Jimmy Dean".

And in England next year he wants to make "Easter Egg Hunt", a "story of sexual frustration" set in 1915, in which he hopes to star Geraldine Chaplin and David Bowie.

His other plans include a Broadway musical, and a full release for "Health", if he can buy the film back from Fox. The picture was shelved more or less unseen after Alan Ladd left the company, and although it was made at the time of the presidential elections, Altman is confident it could do well in the US and Europe if carefully handled by a small distributor.

He is certainly confident about the future of his new company, Sandcastle 5, which he formed after selling the larger Lion's Gate last year.

"The major film companies are destroying themselves looking for the golden egg. I'm sure smaller companies such as mine will flourish."

By Colin Vaines

● On the set of "Come Back To The Five And Dime, Jimmy Dean, Jimmy Dean"; Cher and director Robert Altman.

Screen International (UK), 13.11.82

Films & Filming
November 1971

From an interview with Robert Altman who made his debut as the director of *The James Dean Story* in 1957. Altman's films of the 1970s form a body of work unmatched in excellence in the American cinema of the era.

How did all this start for you?

I was stationed in California during the war, and I came back afterwards with the idea of becoming a writer. I had a partner then, a man called George George, and between us we wrote some treatments—one of which, something called *Bodyguard*, we eventually sold to RKO. Lawrence Tierney was in it. Another thing we sold was an idea for an episodic movie to George's uncle, an old time director called Eddie Marin. It was called *Christmas Eve*, and Eddie made it with Benedict Bogeaus. George Brent and Randolph Scott were the stars. Those two things apart, it was a pretty frustrating time.

You weren't involved in the making of either of those?

Hell, I couldn't even get on the sets. I even remember saying I'd work for nothing! But when you're that eager they don't want you around, so in the end I decided to go to New York—hoping to get into the business from that end. What happened, though, was this—I stopped off in Kansas City to see my parents, who told me that a film group, a documentary outfit, had opened up offices there. So I went down to see them, lied about everything, spinning lots of Hollywood tales, and got a job! The Calvin Company was the name of the group, and I stayed with them for about six years. It was a great training period. I wrote, directed, produced and edited, there wasn't anything I wasn't into. We made films on assignment from Gulf Oil and Caterpillar Tractors, that sort of thing.

Do any of these movies exist today?

Somewhere.

Had you given up on your ambition to work in Hollywood during all this?

Not for one moment! I even quit The Calvin Company to come back to Hollywood, thinking that the studios might be impressed with my documentary experience. I spent a year knocking on doors, but no one wanted to know. The only thing I managed to do was a series of tv spots for The Catholic Bishop's Fund. Frustration reigned supreme. So I went back to Kansas City again, this time with the idea of starting my own documentary outfit. The first thing we shot was a short about baseball for some bread company. Then, with some independent money coming from a man whose father had a cinema chain, I wrote, produced and directed a feature called *The Delinquents*. It cost about 63,000 dollars to make and was later sold to UA for about 150,000 dollars.

It was while I was back in Hollywood cutting the movie, that George George asked me to work with him on a notion he had of doing a documentary based on the life of James Dean. Now at that point in time I was very much anti-Dean, having just worked with an actor to whom Dean was a god, someone who really was nothing more than a walking collection of Dean mannerisms; the most impossible actor I've ever worked with. So I said to George, 'The Jimmy Dean Story, now that's one picture I'd love to do providing we can really attack it from a no nonsense viewpoint with none of that horseshit hero worship.' Each of us then put 2,500 dollars into the pot and we formed a little company to go back to Dean's home town, Fairmount, Indiana, for some on the spot interviews and things. Incidentally, Lou Lombardo, who later turned editor to cut *The Wild Bunch* and *Brewster McCloud*, was the cameraman on that. Later, on bringing the footage back to Hollywood, Stewart Stern, who wrote *Rebel Without a Cause*, became involved in writing the narration for us.

Making that picture was like doing a jigsaw puzzle, the money came in bit by bit. I must have spent a year on it all told. Finally, we had a picture of sorts, enough of one for NBC to get interested for tv—they offered us 300,000 dollars for a single showing. But we were oh-so-cocky. We felt we were sitting on a goldmine. We all believed we were going to be millionaires! We finally made a deal with Warners for some footage on Dean, including a screen-test he made for *East Of Eden*, which included their right to handle the picture. The film died, of course; one of the biggest bombs of all time. Maybe our timing was off. It's a pretty good little picture today I feel. Funny, I started with the idea of taking Dean to bits, but in the end I guess we all got caught up in the mystique of the man. The material tends to woo you, I find; something that happens to me on every film. Even in *Brewster McCloud*, where my original thought had been to crucify those people in Houston, I changed my attitude once I got to know those people.

I can remember some fuss about the film not being nominated for an Academy Award . . .

What it was was this—we thought we would get nominated for entry in the Best Documentary class; but the committee that make the selections voted us down. The picture which finally won was a rather bad movie about Albert Schweitzer. The reason they gave for their decision ran along the lines that our film was obviously made for profit, whereas the general idea of documentaries is to encourage people to make worthwhile films regardless of their money value (if only they had looked into our bank accounts). So, really, Albert Schweitzer won the Oscar rather than James Dean.

Did you get any vibrations from the Dean-cult while making the film?

They were all over us. We had so many Dean look-alikes come to us for jobs, that we figured out a scheme of hiring them all as ushers for the premiere! We had people come to us with secret things to sell—an old shoe or a dirty shirt. You never saw so many freaks. As for that rumour about Dean not being dead, just too scarred to continue his career—well, he banged himself up so badly he died, that's all. That boy is well and truly dead.

Natalie Wood reviews "The James Dean Story"

Photoplay (USA)

I love movies. If I didn't, I'd be in some other business. Just the same, I dreaded going to the screening of "The James Dean Story." I was invited to the first Hollywood showing, put on by the Screen Directors Guild. As you must know, this picture had a personal meaning for me. And it must have had the same hypnotic appeal for a lot of other people in the industry, because the theater was packed. I noticed several of Jimmy Dean's friends there —people like Dennis Hopper, Marlon Brando.

I'm sure they felt just as I did: Can we last through the picture? Will we still be here when the title "The End" comes on and the projectionists shut off the machine? I didn't think I would be there.

But I was. The picture held me from start to finish. I'll tell you why we were all worried. We weren't afraid of being overcome by emotion. We were afraid that the picture would distort and change the Jimmy that we knew. Sure, he wore a leather jacket and motorcycle boots; sure, he raced his cars. But the violence that accompanies too many of the kids who follow him was not part of his makeup. And we were afraid that this stranger Jimmy Dean would be the boy in the picture.

We all knew that this film was designed for one purpose, like most movies: to make money. But this money-making venture was based on the death of a friend of ours. I thought that Jimmy Dean's death on September 30, 1955, would be just the basis for somebody's financial gain. So I was ready to get up and run out of the theater. I didn't, because I found myself looking at a picture beautifully done, in the best of taste.

The makers of "The James Dean Story" were as honest as they could be in making this film. And it could have so easily been what I feared. We've heard too much of the legend about Jimmy Dean. This legend would have been the practical reason for making a profitable picture about Jimmy. Instead, the picture destroys that reason. It separates the legend from the real Jimmy Dean. And, at the same time, it shows us both.

More important, it establishes—and it does this definitely—*that he is dead.* The pictorial reenactment and later evidence shown should stop, once and for all, the ghoulish tales that try to contradict the death certificate. These weird stories have only disgusted and saddened people who really loved him, because we know he would have accepted the fact of death just as he accepted and welcomed life. It's something that happens to all of us.

Watching this full-length feature, running eighty minutes, I was fascinated by the amazing quality of the black and white photography. The biography-documentary is told in a most unusual fashion, combining film clips of Jimmy, his family, his friends, his acquaintances who might have become friends if there had been more time. Clips from his three movies are included, so moviegoers can compare the Jimmy they knew with the Jimmy his close friends knew.

Some of the real-life footage is truly great. And some of it looks pretty corny and amateurish. But that only makes it seem more real, because it's like the home movies you might take in your own backyard—of people you know as well as we knew Jimmy.

The movie often uses still pictures of Jimmy and his friends. And the "Camera Eye" technique brings all these to life. On the sound track, you hear Jimmy's voice or the voices of people who knew him or the voice of Martin Gabel, a fine actor who does the narrating. The whole story is tied together so well that it seems like any of the wonderful feature-film biographies made about famous personalities, in or out of show business.

"No matter how long I live," you hear the voice saying at the beginning, "it won't be long enough." Then come the terrible noises of the crash *(Continued on page* 102)

NATALIE WOOD REVIEWS JAMES DEAN STORY

Continued from page 72

on the road to Salinas. And the narrator says: "James Dean died today. He lived with a great hunger."

Quickly, the scene shifts to a year later. "Giant," Jimmy's last movie, is being premiered at Grauman's Chinese Theater in Hollywood. And the crowds present aren't all there for the picture's living stars. Why has Jimmy Dean become such a great star so quickly? Why is he still loved, followed with such unparalleled enthusiasm?

The picture tells us why. It takes us back to Fairmount, Indiana, where Jimmy went to live on the farm of his aunt and uncle, after his mother's death. We meet the aunt, uncle, grandparents, high-school teacher, basketball coach, motorcycle-shop owner—all interviewed before the watching and listening cameras and microphones. Their recollections of Jimmy seem completely honest. No professional actors or actresses could possibly copy the way they talk. I *know*. I'm an actress, and I know only two kinds of people could talk like this: the greatest actors in the world; or real people, just saying simply what they really think.

Then the camera shifts to the Sigma Nu house on the UCLA campus, where a couple of Jimmy's former fraternity brothers tell us about the experiences they shared with him. After this, New York City: excitement, hunger, frustrations that accompanied his struggle to get ahead in the theater world.

Now we come to the Hollywood part of Jimmy's life, and I can tell you that the movie's producers have made the right choices again. We hear from Patsy D'Amore and Billy Karen of the Villa Capri restaurant, who affectionately remember the many evenings he spent at their place. And, as an actress, I can assure you that the fanciest Oscar-style acting couldn't measure up to sincere talk like this. The same is true of Lilli Kardell, a Hollywood girlfriend of Jimmy's, and pals Glenn Kramer and Lew Bracker.

The ending really stopped me. I heard a tape recording of Jimmy's voice, talking to his family and trying honestly to discover what made him tick. I kept thinking that the ticking was going to end so soon afterwards—too soon.

All of us—Jimmy's friends—want to thank the producers of the picture for showing him this way, as he really was. We were so afraid of the unhealthy legend that made a hero or a young god out of him. He was just one of us, an eager young person who desperately wanted to accomplish something. Was he trying when he destroyed himself? We don't know.

Ironically, this movie shows how much he could have accomplished in his work if he had had more time. Jimmy Dean could have handled any type of role, beyond the single-themed parts he played in "East of Eden," "Rebel Without a Cause" and "Giant." One thing is certain: "The James Dean Story" will encourage more re-issues of those films. And that's good news. Here, of course, I'm prejudiced. Yes, I was a friend of Jimmy Dean's. And I love fine movies, no matter who's in them.

Maybe I'm prejudiced in another way, because of my age. "The James Dean Story" is the story of a unique young man —but he was like the rest of us in a good many ways. Looking at him so closely, we may understand ourselves better.

Stewart Stern, who wrote the screenplays for "Rebel Without a Cause" and "The James Dean Story," says aptly of Jimmy: "He believed that the cry of the world is for tenderness between human beings—all human beings—and he felt that to be tender requires more courage of a man than to be violent. Men are brave enough for war, but not yet brave enough for love. That's what Jimmy thought."

I feel this very strongly, because it's what we were all trying to say in "Rebel." In that picture, Jimmy wasn't misunderstanding—people were misunderstanding him. He was not the rebel; he was hungering for sympathy and guidance.

"The James Dean Story" will please Jimmy Dean fans, of course. As for people who can't understand why there *still* are Dean fans—now they'll know. THE END

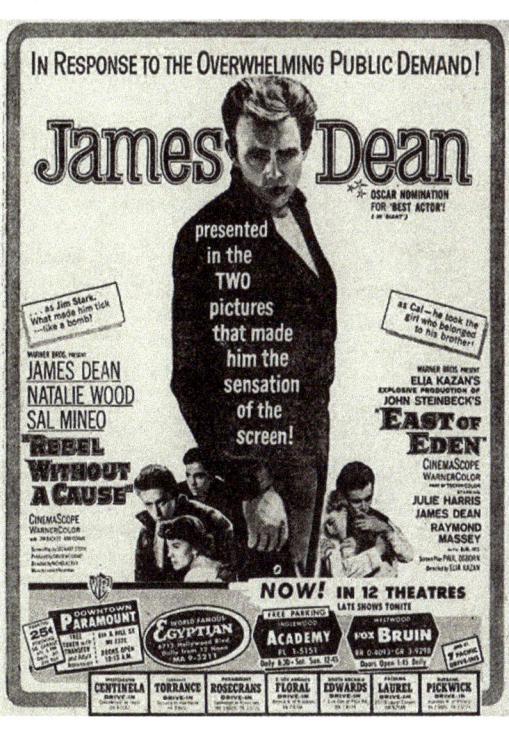

JIMMY DEAN: *two memories*

● *Bob Middleton* (Jimmy's friend at Fairmount High School) remembers:

"Jim wanted to be perfect. I don't think he liked anything better in the world than accomplishing something that was a challenge.

"The evening before he left for California, he drifted over to my house. After a while my dad got up and brought back a .38 revolver. He handed it to Jim. My dad is an excellent marksman. Jim was a good shot with a rifle but he had never fired a revolver. 'Want to try?' my dad asked. Jim nodded.

"They went outside and my dad started shooting. For a few minutes Jim just stood there and watched. Then he took the gun and duplicated nearly every shot my father had made. It was an almost impossible thing for anybody to do the first time he picked up a revolver, and neither my dad nor I will ever forget it."

● *Nicco Romanos* (Jimmy's landlord during the last few months of his life):

"He liked always to laugh and make jokes. I had a key to the house. Sometimes, in the mornings, I would come in and wash the dirty dishes and make coffee for him. Never were there any glasses with liquor in them, only glasses with milk and Coke and occasionally beer. When the coffee was ready he would come down and look around the kitchen and say—because many years ago I was in the ballet—'From the Imperial Russian Ballet, I have got myself a good maid.' Then he would laugh.

"Once he did not come into the kitchen. I found him in the living room looking up the big stone fireplace. 'What's wrong, Jimmy?' I asked.

"He laughed. 'This is fine, now,' he said. 'But where the devil am I going to get the wood to fill it in the winter?'

" 'So?' I said, joking him. I pointed to two twelve-year-old pine trees in the yard. 'There's your wood, Jimmy. All you have to do is chop it down.'

"The next day I found the two trees chopped into logs and stacked in the middle of the yard. To make a joke with me he had had a company come in the night to chop them. I will never forget how he laughed when he saw his joke was a success."

THE SUNDAY TIMES, NOVEMBER 10, 1957

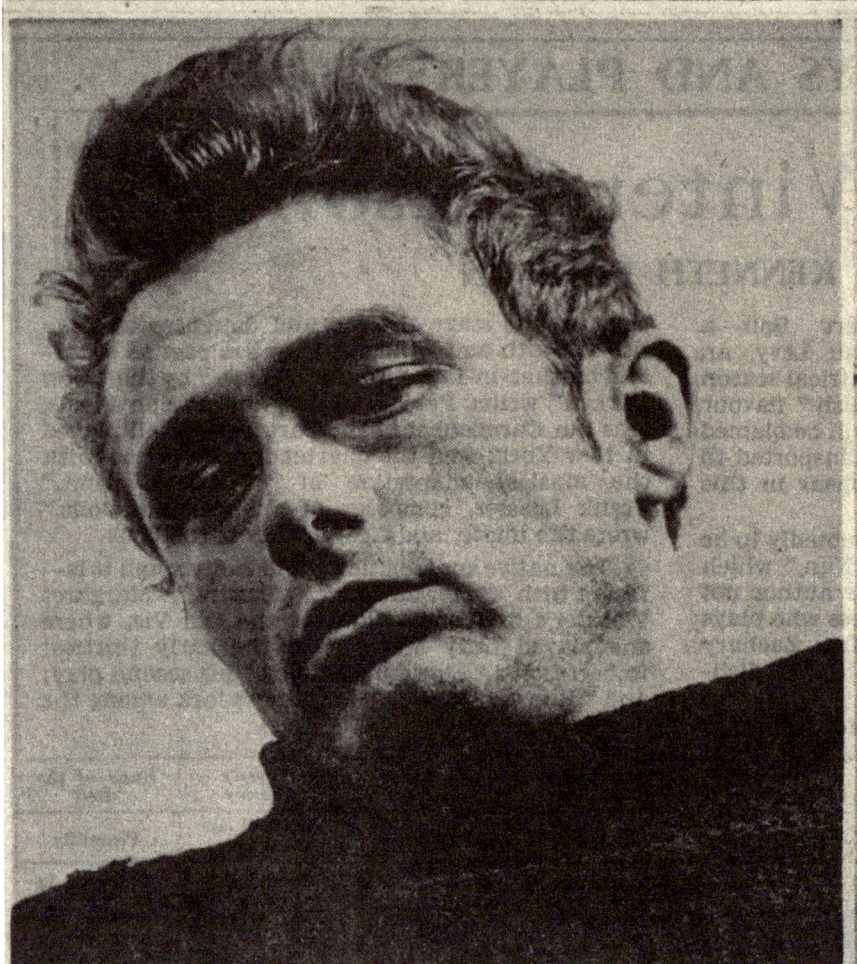

JAMES DEAN, seen in these two photographs from the film reviewed by Dilys Powell, has become a cult in this country as well as in the United States. He was killed in a sports car crash in September, 1955, at the age of 24. "Now that Dean's gone," asked a young idolater on the B.B.C., "who's going to express our frustration?"

Martin Sheen as Kit, copying a familiar stance

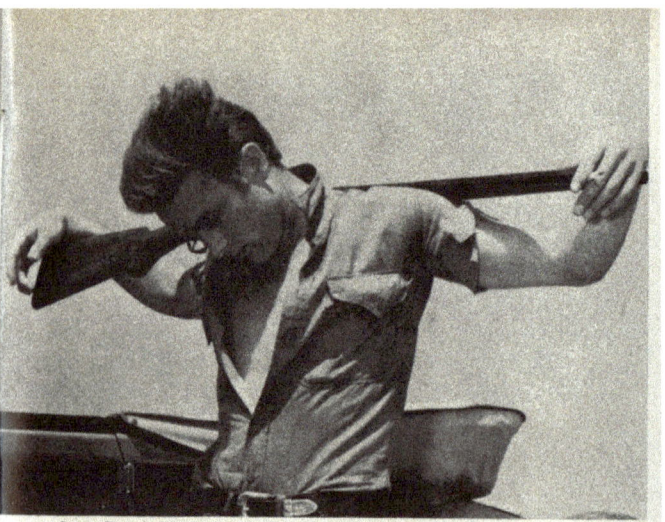

James Dean in 'Giant', who becomes the idol of a young killer in 1959

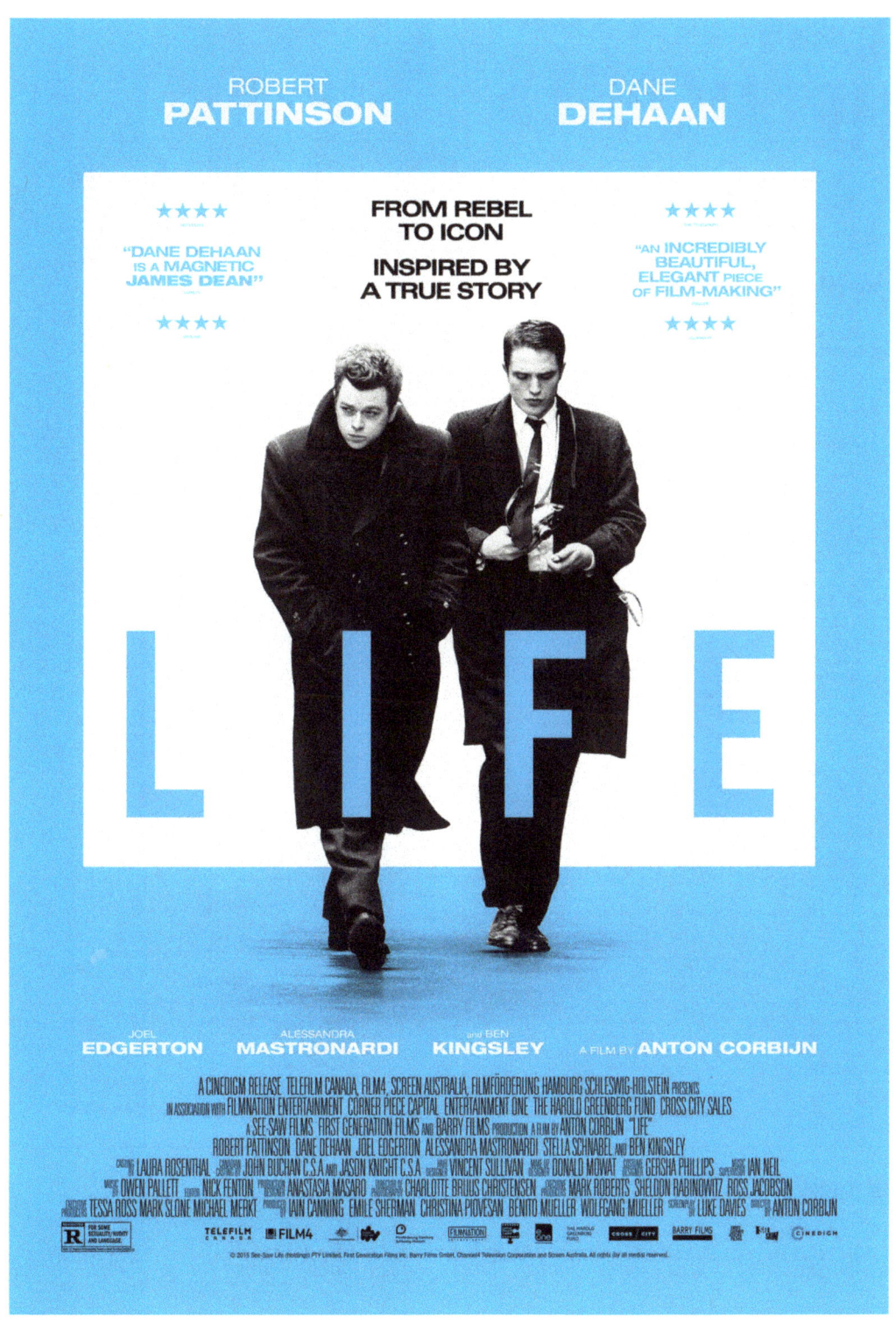

American poster for the feature film by the great Dutch photographer, Anton Corbijn

PICTUREGOER November 30 1957

DEAN HATED THE MOVIES

—says the man who was his closest friend

THIS is one of the most incredible truths yet revealed about James Dean. The man whom many picturegoers and critics regarded as the best young screen actor of his day hated acting for the screen.

"Jimmy often said it was just a drag." My informant was twenty-six year old William Bast, Dean's closest friend who shared lodgings, confidences, arguments and plans with Jimmy during the five turbulent years before his death. Bast's honest and revealing biography, "James Dean," is a best seller both here and in America.

Could we take it then, I asked, that had he lived he might very well have given up filming? "I doubt it," said Bast. Reason? Just like you and me, Dean liked the lolly! "Would you give up a hundred thousand dollars a picture?" Bast asked.

Yet none of his films really satisfied Dean. "He only went to Hollywood to work with Elia Kazan in *East Of Eden*." And a Warner contract went with it. "Jimmy," said Bast, "would always go into a film believing it was the one thing in the world he wanted to do and that the director was perfect. And always he'd be disillusioned, because no one's perfect."

Certainly, *East Of Eden* was the film that came closest to his ideal. But was it true, I asked, that on *Rebel Without A Cause* he took over the direction from Nicholas Ray? "Yes, I'm afraid it is. Jimmy liked Ray. But, when Ray saw how things were turning out, he sensibly let Jimmy have his head."

And "*Giant*"? I hadn't anticipated the explosion that followed. I'd assumed—mistakenly—that even so individual a character as James Dean would appreciate working with a director like George Stevens.

I was wrong. "It was fine at first. But then again disillusionment set in. You could call it a clash of personalities. When Jimmy realized that Stevens wasn't on his side, that was the finish." Certainly, according to Bast, Stevens behaved insensitively toward Dean, making small issues the excuse for big arguments, bawling Dean out on set in front of everyone and so on.

"A lot of Jimmy's best scenes were edited out of the film. And a great deal of the banquet episode at the end was cut. The rushes I saw of him were terrific."

That wasn't the way it turned out in the final edited version of the film. Which probably explains why Dean's last screen performance was such a disappointment to us.

Was he really a problem child, from Hollywood's point of view? "Sure he was. He refused to have anything to do with the publicity people. But later he realized that by refusing to co-operate with publicity he was getting more publicity that if he had co-operated. I guess he hated Hollywood as much as anyone can hate it."

Bast vigorously denounces the legend that has been built up around Dean: this idea that he's the personification of rebellious lonely youth. "If Jimmy had had this kind of adulation before he died—he'd have died. People confuse him with the kind of parts he played.

"Sure, he was lonely. Not physically, he had plenty of friends. But like many young people he'd been hurt and consequently he was always on the defensive. But he was growing out of it. He began to realize, before he died, that he could trust people.

"And he laughed a lot. Mention that, will you? People seem to get the idea that he seldom laughed."

Yet, in condemning the macabre legend of James Dean, I wonder whether Bast isn't perpetuating another kind of legend. The legend that Dean was some kind of acting genius who, at twenty-four, was perfectly justified in questioning the direction of an experienced film-maker like Stevens; a privileged being who, while accepting the fruits of Hollywood stardom, was somehow exempted from putting up with the discomforts of that stardom.

After some time spent discussing James Dean, I can't help thanking Hollywood for Tony Curtis. But the fact remains, legend or not, Dean was and still is the most controversial figure in the film world.

RONALD MORRIS

James Dean was lonely . . . and Hollywood called him moody. But he also knew how to laugh

---

24H LE MANS 08/07/2018 08:01

James Dean's Porsche, a "giant" at the Le Mans Classic

In addition to a screening of "Rebel Without a Cause" at the 9th edition of the Le Mans Classic, the memory of actor James Dean (1931-1955) was alive and well on the track thanks to a Porsche (grid 2) he once drove.

To get a feel for what Porsche meant to James Dean, let's go back to 1955. On 26 and 27 March, James Dean took the wheel of a Porsche 356 Super Speedster for a race at the circuit in Palm Springs in southern California. The actor won the qualifying race and reached the third step on the podium the next day...then moved up to second after Ken Miles was disqualified (10 years later, he would become a favorite driver in Ford's offensive at Le Mans)!

The day after that, James Dean was on the set with director Nicholas Ray for the first day of filming "Rebel Without a Cause." He entered another race on 1 May in Bakersfield, finishing second on the heels of scoring pole position in his class. After being forced to retire in Santa Barbara at the end of the same month, he was expected to take the wheel again after wrapping the movie "Giant" in the summer. On 30 September, he hit the road in his new Porsche 550 RS Spyder, nicknamed "Little Bastard," for a race in Salinas. But he never made it.

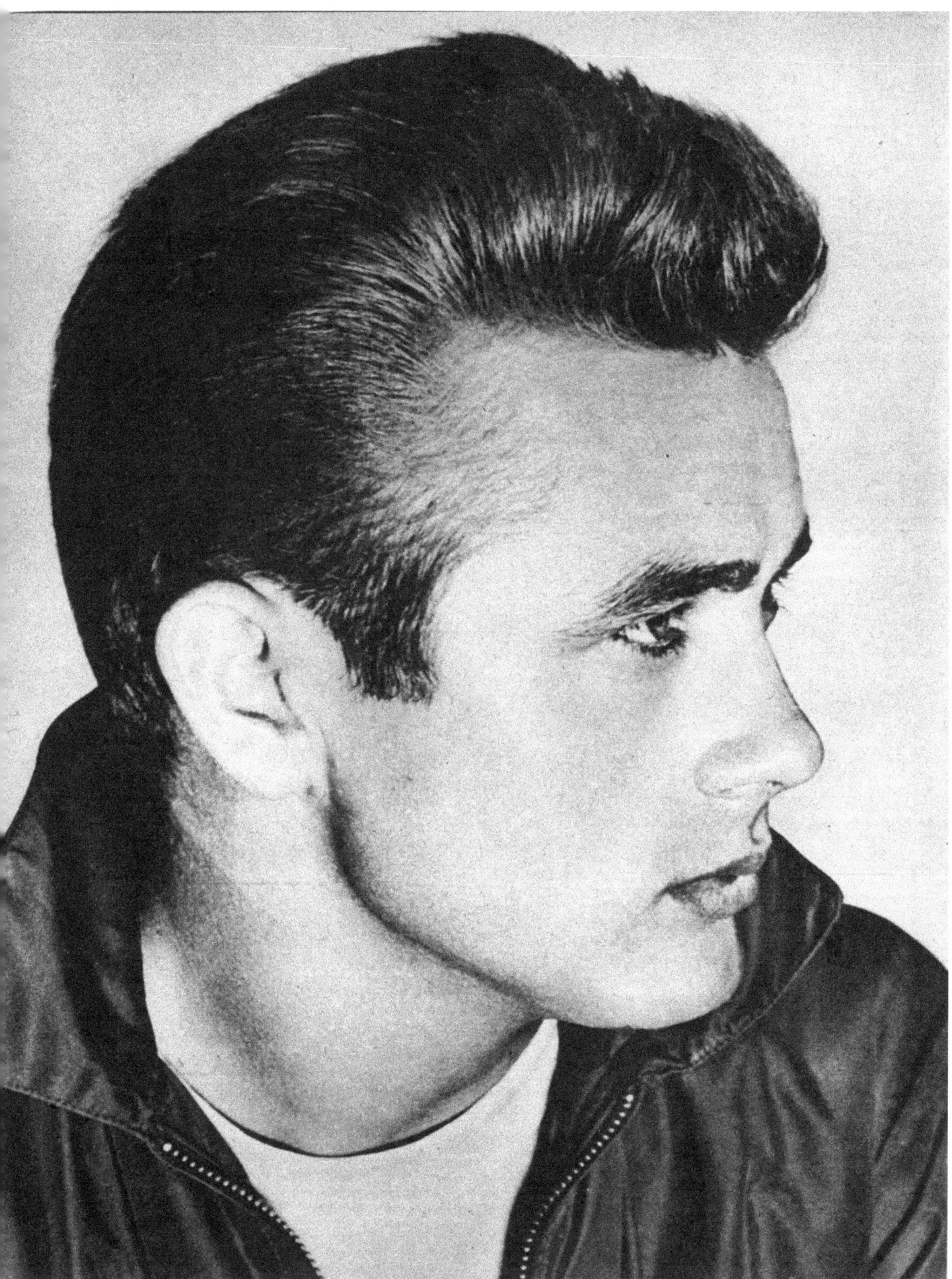

JAMES DEAN:

before and behind the camera...

Shown here as he looked to a photographer on the
East of Eden set, Jimmy liked to take pictures of
his friends as they looked to him. For a gallery
of these exclusive portraits, turn the page ▶

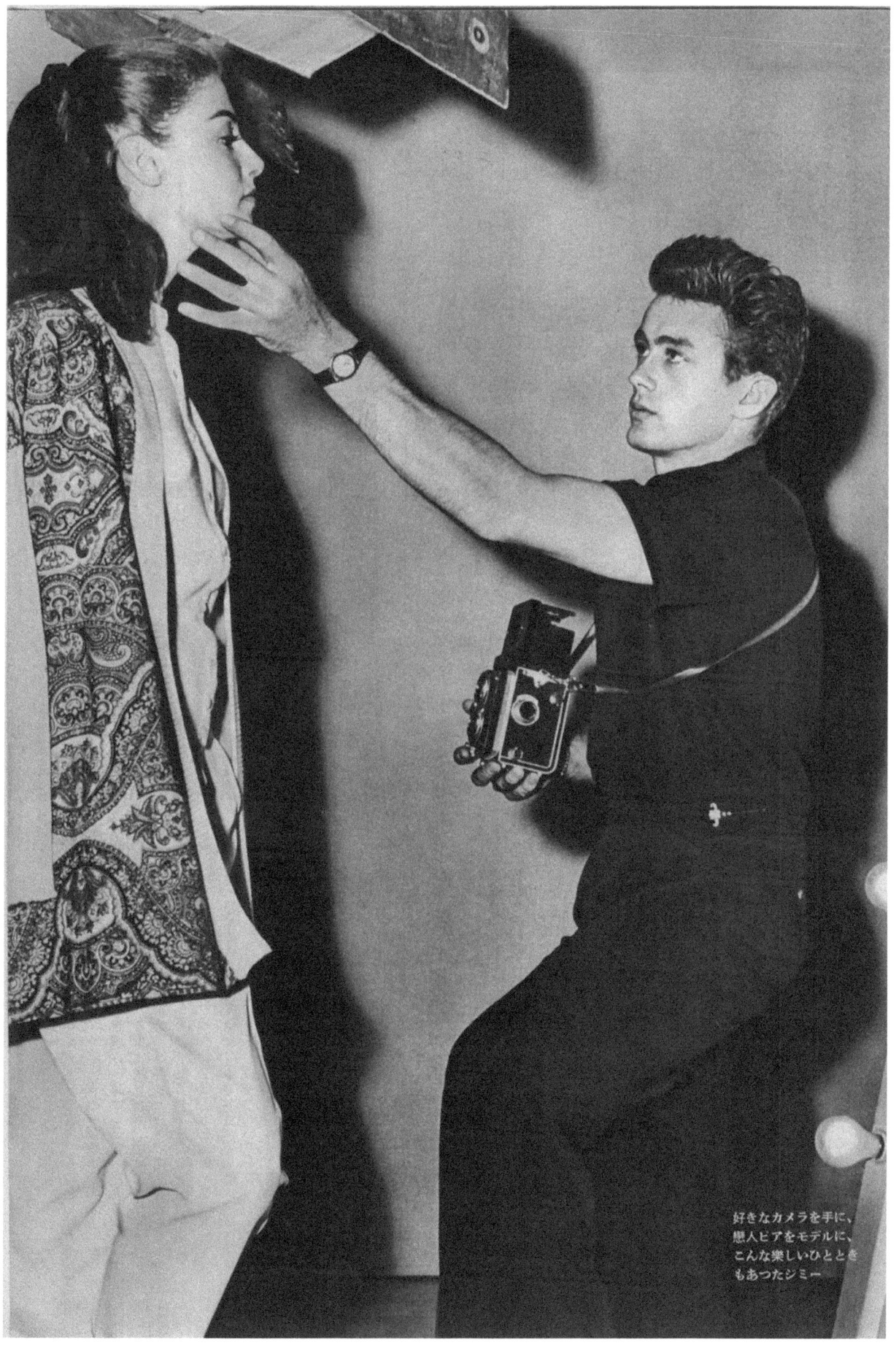

好きなカメラを手に、
恋人ピアをモデルに、
こんな楽しいひととき
もあつたジミー

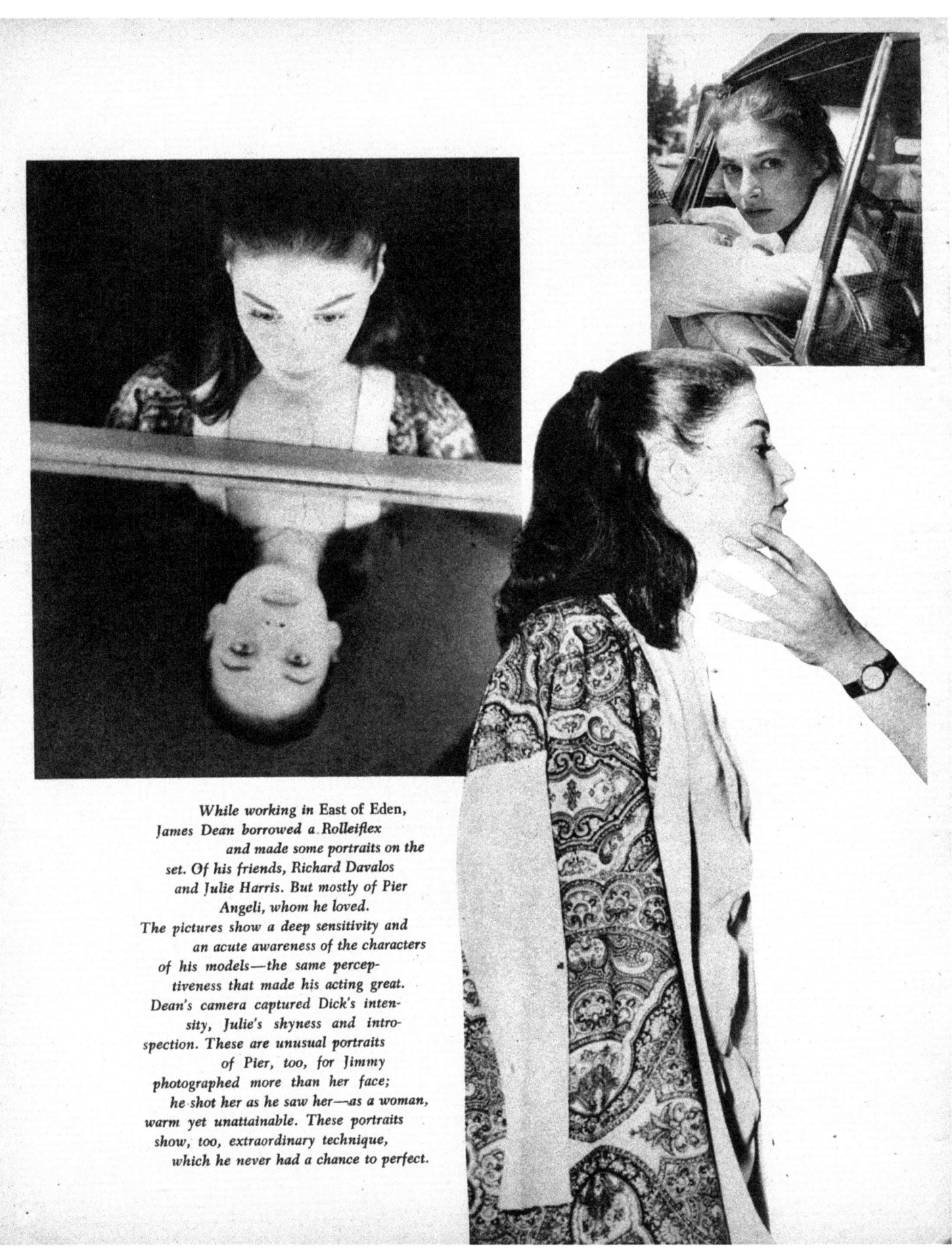

While working in East of Eden, James Dean borrowed a Rolleiflex and made some portraits on the set. Of his friends, Richard Davalos and Julie Harris. But mostly of Pier Angeli, whom he loved. The pictures show a deep sensitivity and an acute awareness of the characters of his models—the same perceptiveness that made his acting great. Dean's camera captured Dick's intensity, Julie's shyness and introspection. These are unusual portraits of Pier, too, for Jimmy photographed more than her face; he shot her as he saw her—as a woman, warm yet unattainable. These portraits show, too, extraordinary technique, which he never had a chance to perfect.

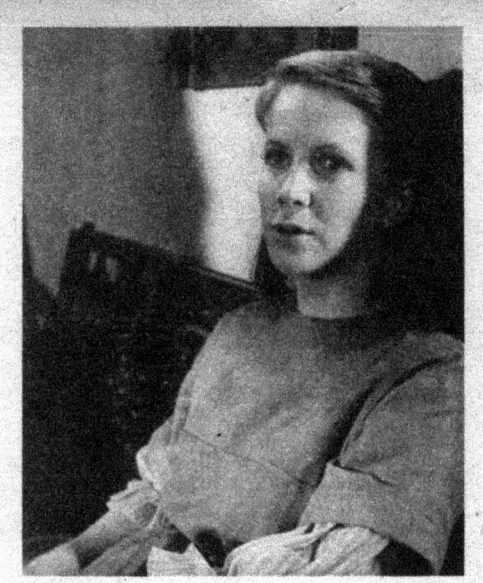

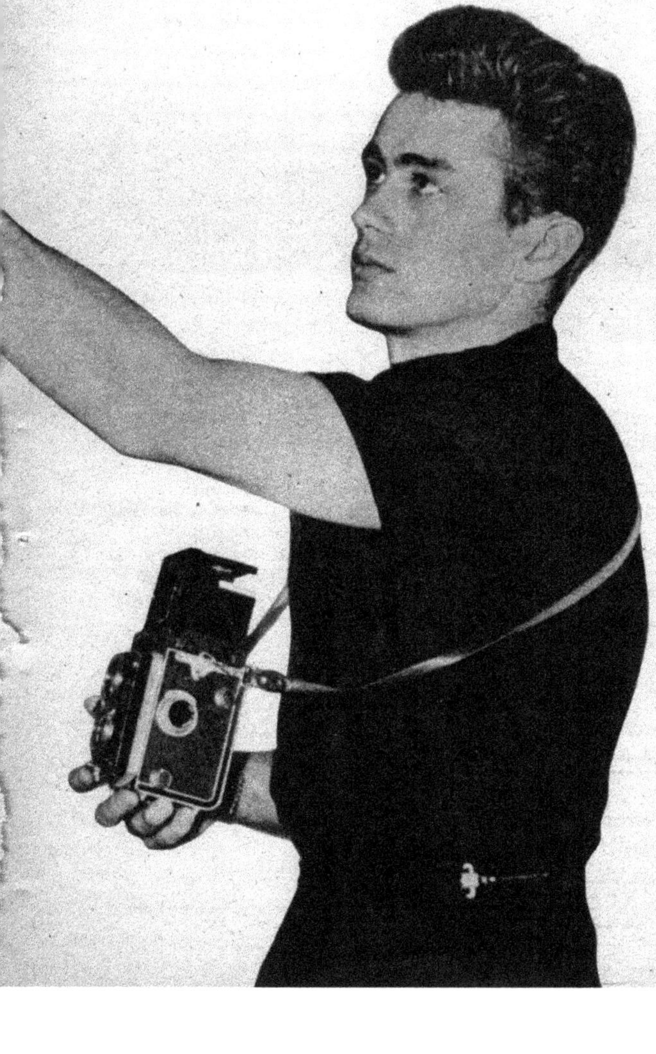

**the same sensitivity
Dean showed as an actor,
he brought to his
work with a camera**

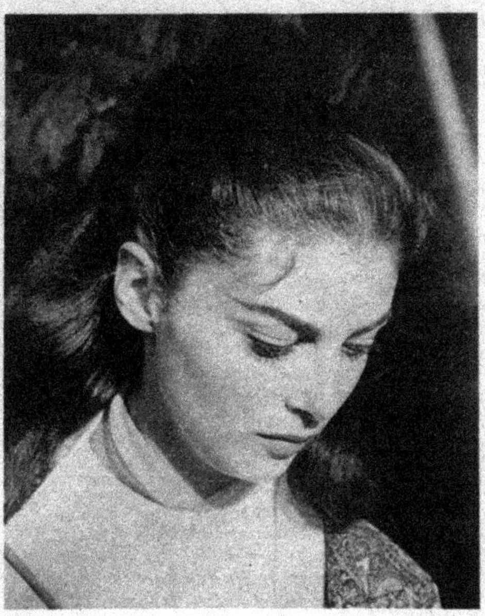

上はピア・エンジェリ、下はジュリー・ハリス、いずれもムードを狙つた大胆な習作

ジミーの"わが恋せし乙女"ピア・エンジェリ連作の一つ、ジミーの写真は彼の性格を反映してこうしたロー・キー・トーンが多いようだ

ジェイムズ・ディーンが撮した写真

DID YOU KNOW HE WAS HOLLYWOOD GREATEST AMATEUR PHOTOGRAPHER?

ディーンはハリウッドで最も素晴しいアマチュア・キャメラマンだつた

「エデンの東」の兄役に扮したディック・ダヴァロスを撮つた傑作

映画やサンフォード・ロスのスチルとかデニス・ストックの組写真に見る通り、ジェイムズ・ディーンは被写体としても優れていただけでなく、自ら写真を撮る事にも優れていた。綺腕ごとの作品でなくムードや性格の描写を狙う本格的人物写真で、愛用機もニコンという玄人筋の最高級キャメラであつた。彼が身に蔵していた多くの天才的素質の一つと言つてよいだろう。ここに掲げた貴重なるジェイムズ・ディーン撮影作品が何よりの証明と思う。

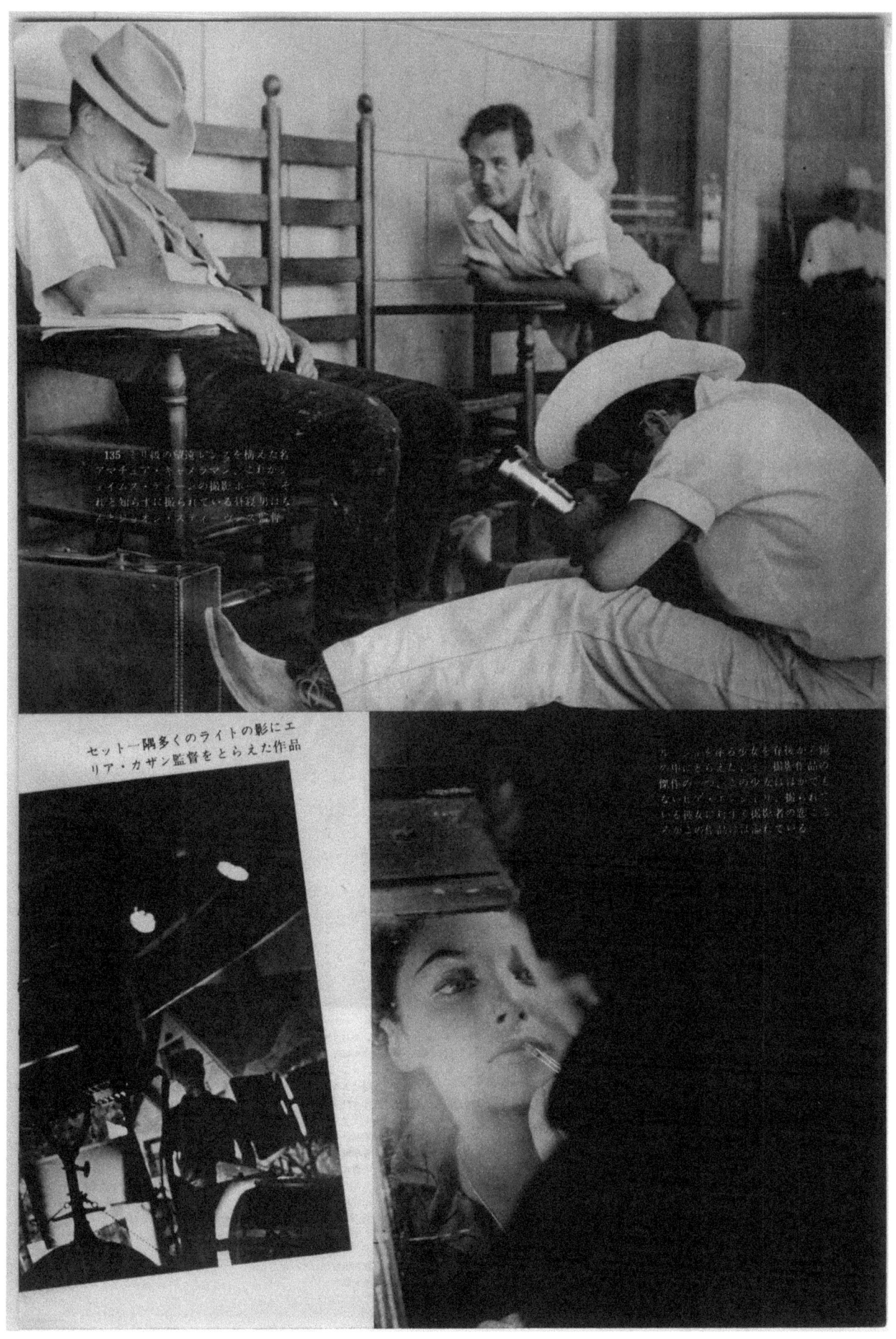

James Dean und seine Triumph

© Roy Schatt

25 RIESEN-POSTER *50 x 70 cm*

James Dean, fotografiert von D. Stock

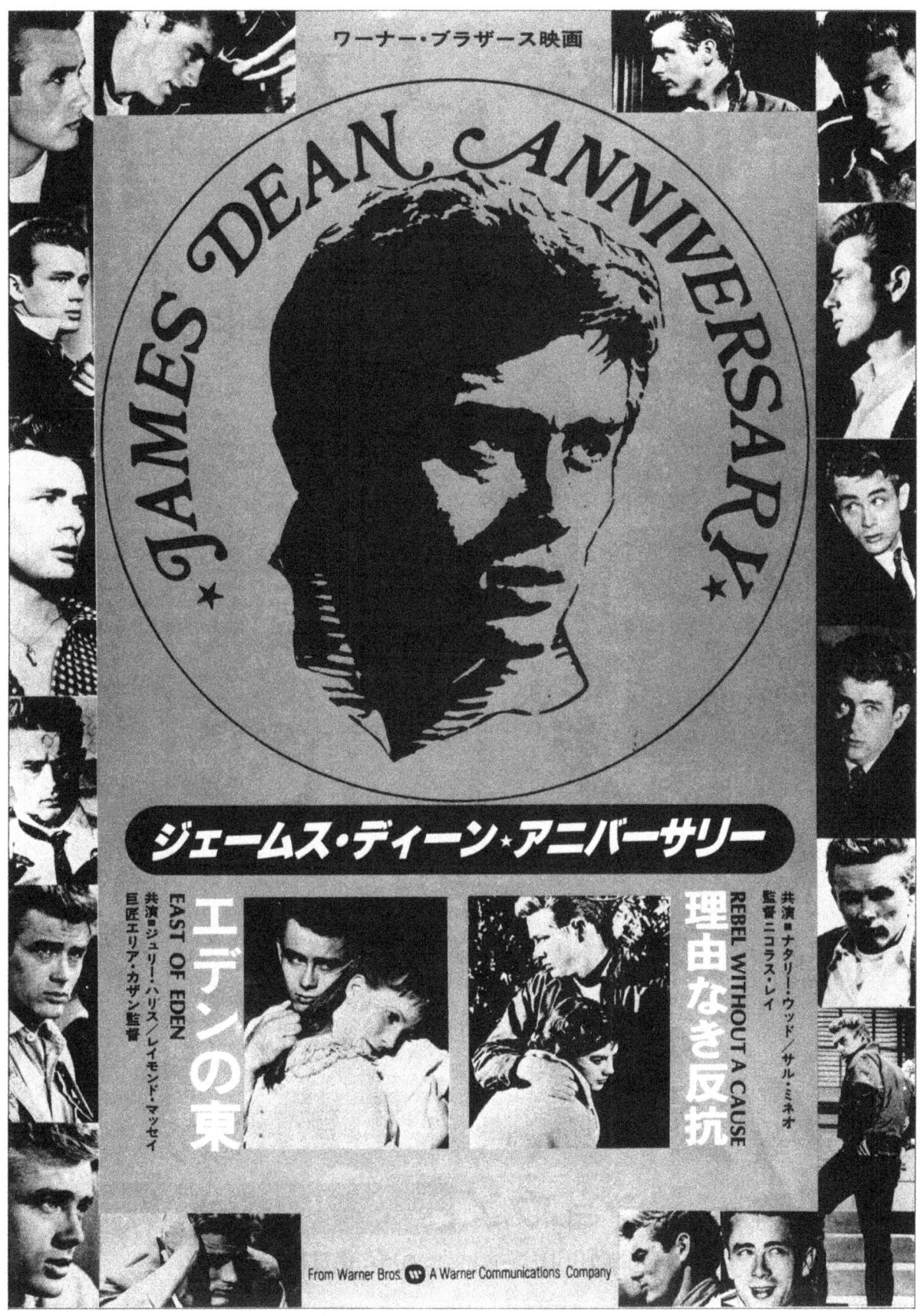

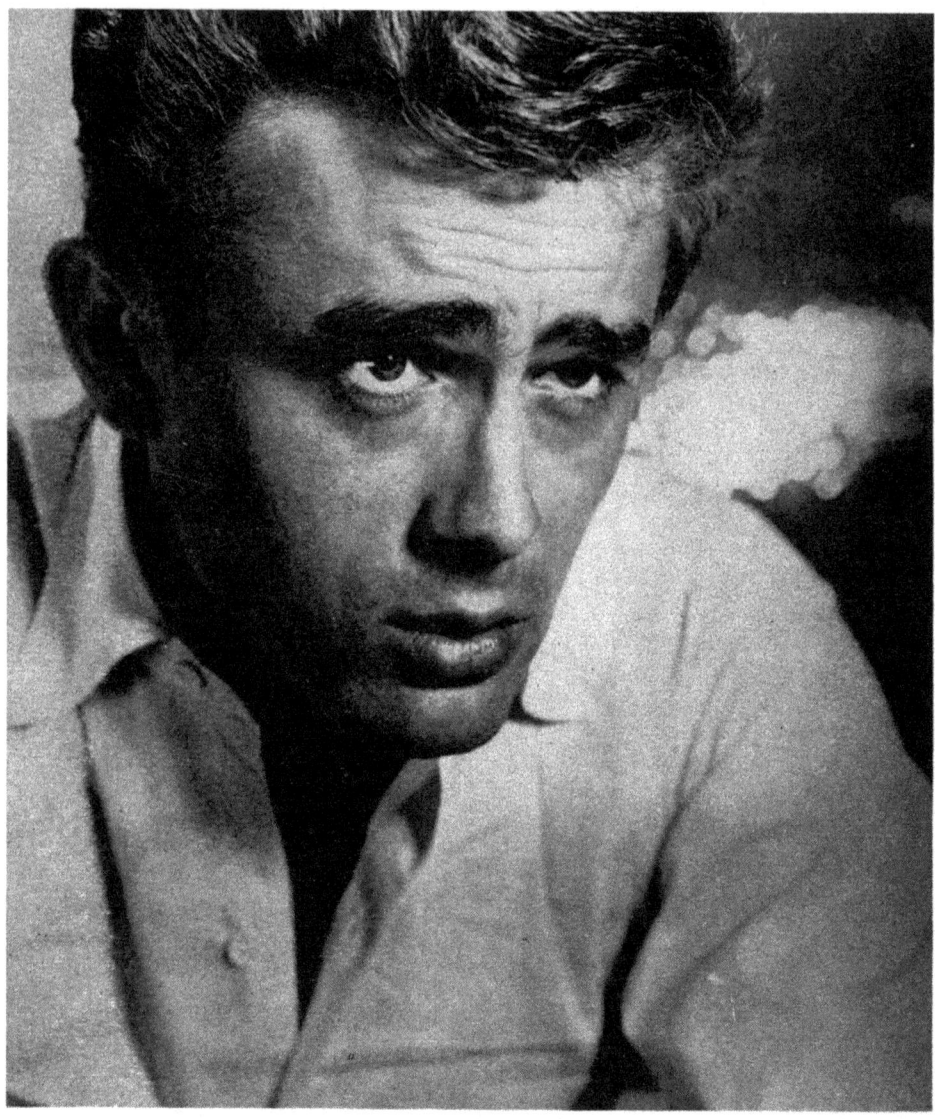

DEAN
— Ten years after

by ROBIN BEAN

Films & Filming

'*In James Dean, today's youth discovers itself. Less for the reasons usually advanced: violence, sadism, hysteria, pessimism, cruelty, and filth, than for others infinitely more simple and commonplace: modesty of feeling, continual fantasy life, moral purity without relation to everyday morality but all the more rigorous, eternal adolescent love of tests and trials, intoxication, pride, and regret at feeling oneself "outside" society, refusal and desire to become integrated and, finally, acceptance—or refusal—of the world as it is*'.
Francois Truffaut in *Arts* (26.9.56)

On September 30, 1955, James Dean died in a car crash just after completing *Giant*. The image that Dean created on screen has survived more strongly than that of any other actor up to that time, and both *East of Eden* and *Giant* have been continually re-issued in practically every country since they first appeared. *Rebel Without a Cause* was withdrawn from circulation some while ago, which, from the point of view of understanding Dean's appeal to youngsters in the mid 'fifties, is the key film. *Eden*, in Britain at least, was more successful after the release of *Rebel* than before it; although *Eden* was the best of the three films Dean made, it was *Rebel* (plus a reverent, rather than morbid, sympathy for the character because of his death) that created the idol; the one to emulate.

Neither Dean nor *Rebel Without a Cause* were completely 'original' — both were progressions on feelings and themes that had been developing in the American cinema since the early 'fifties. *Rebel* came out of the main stream of the 'social conscience' themes that had earlier attracted Kramer, Robson, Wise, Zinnemann and Kazan, which hit its most explosive proportions in *The Wild One, On the Waterfront,* and *Blackboard Jungle*. But *Rebel* came out as the more effective and disturbing film. It showed compassion and human warmth towards its younger characters; with the blame for their nonconformist (or if you prefer it rebellious) activities being dumped squarely on society and on parents in particular. The middle class was becoming the dominating force; dominating through its new economic affluence rather than through its positive thought. The thought seemed anything but positive: there was the postwar apathy to being involved in social issues, the complete lack of faith in political leaders, the breakaway from religion.

James Dean and Natalie Wood in Nicholas Ray's 'Rebel Without a Cause' (1955) youths seek out 'thrills', and the parents take the full blame . . .

. . . Elia Kazan's 'Splendour in the Grass' (1961) rebelled against the psychological neurosis of the films about youth. Said Kazan 'If your parents raised you wrong you should realise this as soon as possible and go your own way'. With Warren Beatty and Natalie Wood

The husband was popularly thought of as well meaning but weak-willed, dominated by a sharp-voiced ogre of a wife whose main pursuit in life was that of living better than the woman next door. Through this the teenagers were being forced into finding their own independence as early as possible, helped by generous allowances from soft father and driven to it by nagging mother. *Rebel Without a Cause* was written by Stewart Stern, based on records from juvenile courts, in an attempt to find out just where the blame lay for the alarming increase in the number of arrests of minors. To the teenagers satisfaction, it was placed on the parents.

The opening sequence had Dean being arrested for drunkenness, having found him curled up in a street with a toy monkey. He greets the sight of his irate mother and weak-willed, but concerned, father with a dazed 'Happy Easter, Happy Easter'. The parents start bickering at each other, which builds until Jim screams 'You're tearing me apart! You say one thing, he says another, and everybody changes back again'. Juvenile officer to the rescue, and he takes Jim into his office for a quiet chat; though this doesn't start until Jim has had a futile swing at the law in protest for being talked at as though he is a 'delinquent'. 'It's like a zoo', he explains. 'He always wants to be my pal, you know, but how can I give him anything? I mean I love him, and all that type of stuff, an' I don't want to hurt him, but I don't know what to do, except maybe die. Now, if he had the guts to knock mum cold, then maybe she'd be happy, and she'd stop picking on him. Because they make mush out of him, you know . . . just . . . mush: I'll tell you one thing, I don't ever want to be like him' . . . 'How can a guy grow up in a circus like that?' . . . 'Boy, if . . . if I had one day when . . . when I didn't have to be all confused and different, and feel ashamed, you know, and felt that I belonged some place . . .' So it has established that the 'rebel' does have a cause, that he really would like to fit into a happy family, that the parents are one step away from the divorce court, and that the law is sympathetic but powerless.

The whole social attitude has changed a lot since 1955. Teenage independence is accepted: most do not have to depend on grants from their family, they can go straight into a job and earn almost as much as their father. Responsibility for their actions is considered to be their own. Psychology has become as tired as its theories. Psychologists still busy themselves with deciding why there were teddyboys, beatniks and mods and rockers; why there is group hysteria for pop groups. But no one really seems to care, apart from seaside shop owners, because teenagers are spending their own money and it is their own responsibility what they do with their lives. Their idol, if they have one, is their own personal satisfaction; not a screen image or a pop singer . . . sounds have become more important than personal images, hence the fast mortality rate on singers. Those that survive have their image mellowed by 'respectability', no longer the property of a movement or an age group, with a much more flexible identity, like Presley, Sinatra and the Beatles; Marlon Brando and Paul Newman.

There is no contemporary feeling in youth that can be expressed in one individual characterisation; no one seems to concern themselves so intently with their own relationship with other people. The real social problems of today are either impersonal or out of the control of the individual: nuclear menace, warfare in border states, space research, science and racial equality—they cannot provide the hero figure that would involve an audience to a point where they could feel they could do anything about it. The subjects have become clinical and unemotional, the immediacy of their importance has been lost in argument and counter-argument, a series of half measures and bungling. The teenage identity is also obscure, they feel independent enough to handle their own problems without looking for an epitomy of them. But this is not to say that they have fixed ideas on what they want to achieve in life, quite the reverse. It is more a playing for time, an acute awareness that they are young and that they 'have plenty of time' before they worry about the future. Love, like money, has become a relative thing; there are adequate superficial alternatives. You have the occassional anti-hero, like Hud or Berry-Berry, but their appeal is not because the old man was a drunk or their mother a tyrant, but in their complete disregard for others. Knock a few broads about, as that is what they're for, make fun of the old boy for he's a comic anyway. The appeal of Bond is the same—unbelievable fantasy in which he is anti-romantic, women are just wrestling partners, and part of an extravagent mechanical computor, the link between the gimmicks.

In films the youth image is as elusive as that of the British cinema—it no longer has an 'identity'. You can still get away with the 'sensitive' youngster in a film, providing it has sincerity. But it doesn't represent anything more than that one individual character.

For this reason one cannot claim that James Dean has had any lasting effect on other actors. Actors have had to change with the mood, to adapt to being as versatile as possible, to shy away from an image. Dean would have been 34 this year, and it is unlikely that the image he crea-

The most sensitive penetration of the world of youth was in Frankenheimer's 'The Young Stranger' (1956), sincerely honest and unsensational. With Kim Stanley and James MacArthur

ted in his three main roles would have lasted as long as it has because of his death. After *Giant* he was to have played the part that Paul Newman took in *Somebody Up There Likes Me*, which might seem like odd casting. Newman's view is that 'Jimmy could have played that part, by God yes. I think had he lived he would probably have surpassed anybody that we have in the motion picture industry today'.

When Dean first appeared, he was classed as another Brando, as subsequently most young actors were classed as another James Dean. Clift, Brando, Dean and Newman all came from the same acting school, which led to the comparisons between them. Newman suffered a lot from these: 'I was pigeon-holed as a Brando, which really bugs me, not because of the comparison which I rather enjoy, but that's what I refer to as lazy journalism — "He's a Brando type . . ." So when they would say that to me I would say "Well, what do you think is Marlon's basic quality, what do you think he carries around with him as an actor?" And I would see a lot of blank faces, and a lot of blinking eyes. And they'd say "What do you mean?" "If there is a comparison, then how can we be compared, on what level?" There'd be a lot of blank stares and flittering eyelids. "That's kind of lazy, unless you know what Marlon's basic quality is, even things fragmented, what they are, then it's ridiculous to make comparisons with him". Marlon's quality that he carried with him in the early days was just the extraordinary threat of eruptibility, and that certainly was not the quality I carried in my first movies, it was anything but that'. The Actors School didn't just produce a series of actors in one image: the actor had only his own personality and talent.

Film makers did try to find, strongly aided by fan magazines with limited imagination, a second James Dean without ever understanding why he had evoked such a tremendous response to himself, or realising that Dean basically was a very talented actor. Imitations of *Rebel* came along under titles like *Rock, Pretty Baby!* Sal Mineo, who was in *Rebel*, went into teenage violence films like *Crime in the Streets* (with John Cassavetes) and *Killer Dino*. The only film to have a success comparable to *Rebel* was *Die Halbstarken* (equivalent to teddy boys) which labelled Horst Buchholz as the German James Dean and had him in competition on the popularity charts there with a dead star. (*East of Eden* has just been re-issued in Germany, only two years after its last release). The only films worth noting in this period to come out of America were: John Frankenheimer's first film *The Young Stranger*, with James MacArthur as the son of a film executive whose relationship with him is as impersonal as that with his employees, the nearest the cinema has come to Salinger's treatment of youth in *Catcher in the Rye*—never trying to be sensational, played with sensitivity and sincerity but not lacking in humour, the only incident of 'violence' is when youth floors a cinema manager who went out of his way to ask for it anyway; Philip Dunne's *Blue Denim* with Brando de Wilde as the youth who gets his girl friend (Carol Lynley) pregnant, a little contrived in its solution, but otherwise very intelligently handled; and Arthur Hiller's *The Careless Years* (made by Kirk Douglas' company) with Dean Stockwell and Natalie Trundy, which at least had an original approach of its own—a little too sensitive for the distributor for it had a very limited release. Mark Robson's *Peyton Place*, now regarded with some scepticism as the forerunner of another weepie cycle, was very perceptive in its treatment of youth which Robson took a great deal of care over. The Sanders Brothers *Crime and Punishment USA* attempted to transpose Dostoievski's classic on the criminal and his conscience to modern day Los Angeles with surprising success, the high point being in the cat-and-mouse relationship between Frank Silvera and George Hamilton. Hamilton went into Minnelli's *Home from the Hills* after that, gave another good performance as the son who has to struggle against prejudice and tradition; but since then his performances have been too casual, almost lazy.

After this the search for new actors became a little hysterical: studios tried to start their own schools without much success. Young actors were put into B picture subjects without success, hack scripts and mediocre directors were partly to blame, but some of the actors were just... untalented. Young singers were tried as actors — Frankie Avalon, Paul Anka,

One of the most successful of the European teenage problem films was Tressler's 'Die Halbstarken', with Horst Buchholz and Christian Doermer

Tommy Sands (who did one good teenage comedy, but with a title like *Love in a Goldfish Bowl* it seemed fated to die) and Fabian. Presley turned in a good performance as the half breed of *Flaming Star*, but the film (which had only two songs, both of which were dispensed with in the first five minutes) was not as successful as the others he made, and Presley has subsequently settled down to a more compromised screen image. 20th-Fox provided Richard Beymer with several good roles, without much success, his only notable performance wasn't until Franklin Schaffner directed him in *A Woman of Summer*. Albert Zugsmith brought back the old formula crime film, now transposed to high school or similar settings, so you had Russ Tamblyn as some sort of agent trying to clear up drug peddling amongst America's teenagers in *High School Confidential*; and kidnapping, violence and near gangsterism in a military academy in *Rich, Young and Deadly*.

The turnover of young talent by now was tremendous: to list all the people who appeared in films for the first time in the last ten years in America alone would fill two pages of this magazine. Acting schools, the theatre and television couldn't keep pace with the demand, and there came the period of the non-actor, the youth discovered by some 'talent scout' waiting for an elevator. Only one of these discoveries survived.

There was the move to develop new 'personalities' (ie someone who plays virtually the same role in each film) like Steve McQueen and Troy Donahue, the colour scheme of the latter being rather intriguing — blue eyes, jeans and a red jacket in the most outlandish of the Delmer Daves films he made, *Parrish*, in which the most sensitive thing turned out to be the tobacco crop.

The 'New American Cinema' came up with some interesting subjects, but generally uninteresting individuals, with the exception of Frank Perry's *David and Lisa*.

While the studios persisted with some young people on the basis of the more films they were put in, the more chance they had of catching on with audiences, there were other young actors who seemed to disappear after one or two films but who appeared to have more talent than most, like Lee Kinsolving and Don Dorrell. Others like Michael Landon disappeared into television series.

The James Dean tag still seems to stay with the publicists, only recently a biography of Rod Lauren compared him to Dean which on the basis of the films he has made like *Strike Me Deadly*, *The Black Zoo* and *Terrified* seems to show

Left: the new generation of 'stars', actors rather than idols—Paul Newman in 'The Hustler'; Albert Finney in 'Night Must Fall'; and Marlon Brando in 'Bedtime Story'

an extraordinary lack of insight.

There was also the wave of the 'second generation' actors: Peter Fonda, Patrick Wayne, Robert Walker Jr. and Jim Mitchum.

In Britain, the young actors have at least been their own prototypes; Albert Finney in *Saturday Night and Sunday Morning*; Tom Courtenay in *Loneliness of the Long Distance Runner*; Terence Stamp, who switched from angelic innocence in *Billy Budd* to the hoodlum of *Term of Trial*. In Britain, the theatre forms a more solid and interesting basis for the actor than the cinema, so while you find Peter McEnery doing Disney epics like *The Moonspinners* and *Prince of Donegal*, in the theatre he has been doing far better things like *The Seagull*.

In France, *Cinemonde* was continually comparing every new actor with Dean (for a while the magazine each September had an anniversary feature on Dean). Alain Delon was the first (recently the magazine changed its line and now compares new actors to Delon) yet it was through *Faibles Femmes*, a light comedy with him as a sort of Don Juan who almost gets assassinated by three young females, rather than a *Rebel* type film that he became popular. Belmondo borrowed a few mannerisms from Bogart for *A bout de Souffle*, which proved more successful for him than teenage dramas like *Les Tricheurs*. Gerard Blain, Charles Belmont, and Christian Perez were the ones who took over the 'sensitive adolescent' roles without making any real impact, Jacques Perrin was an exception.

In the past few years, the finest film in its treatment of two young individual's is Chukhrai's *Ballad of a Soldier*; tender, emotional, sentimental, yet very observant, the smallest detail or reaction conveyed beautifully. This is the film one has the most pleasure in recalling.

To return to America, the director who has had the most influence on young actors is undoubtedly Kazan (who direc-

Alain Delon in Clement's 'Plein Soleil'—twisted moral values and sympathies, with his playing of the 'angelic' killer

ted Brando, Dean and Beatty in their first important rôles). That these actors have been compared in terms of character reactions, 'mannerisms' and so forth is due more to Kazan than to the actors. He has a very strong image of his young hero which one suspects comes more from himself than the writer—and this is so apparent in *America, America* in his handling of Stathis Giallelis. He, more than Brando, was responsible for the 'new' style of acting. In *Eden* he created the image which Dean developed in more contemporary terms in *Rebel*, one that he drew as much from his knowledge of Dean as from Steinbeck's character. He didn't like Dean becoming an idol 'He's not an idol of mine, and I didn't particularly like what he was. I think I told the truth about a character like that in *East of Eden*, but I didn't like the result which was to blame your parents for everything'. But to the youth of the 'fifties this proved very acceptable.

Wrote Edgar Morin in 'The Stars': 'James Dean is indeed a perfect star: god, hero, model. But this perfection, if it has only been able to fulfill itself by means of the star system, derives from the life and death of the real James Dean and from the exigence which is his own as well as that of a generation which sees itself in him, reflected and transfigured in twin mirrors: screen and death'.

15

JAMES DEAN
the first American teenager

Directed by Ray Connelly (who wrote the screenplay for That'll Be the Day and Stardust), the film pieces together the fragments of the short life of the first real American youth idol through excerpts from his three major films, clips from television plays and contributions from Dennis Hopper, Nicholas Ray, Natalie Wood, Leonard Rosenman, Sal Mineo and Sammy Davis Jr. Produced by Sandy Lieberson and David Puttnam

James Dean, who tried to reject the Hollywood publicity machine, yet enjoyed posing for non-Hollywood young photographers

An actor who drew his strength from American aggressiveness

'He had a sense of aloneness'—Elia Kazan, who brilliantly manipulated a raw talent into the embodiment of vulnerability in 'East of Eden'

in camera

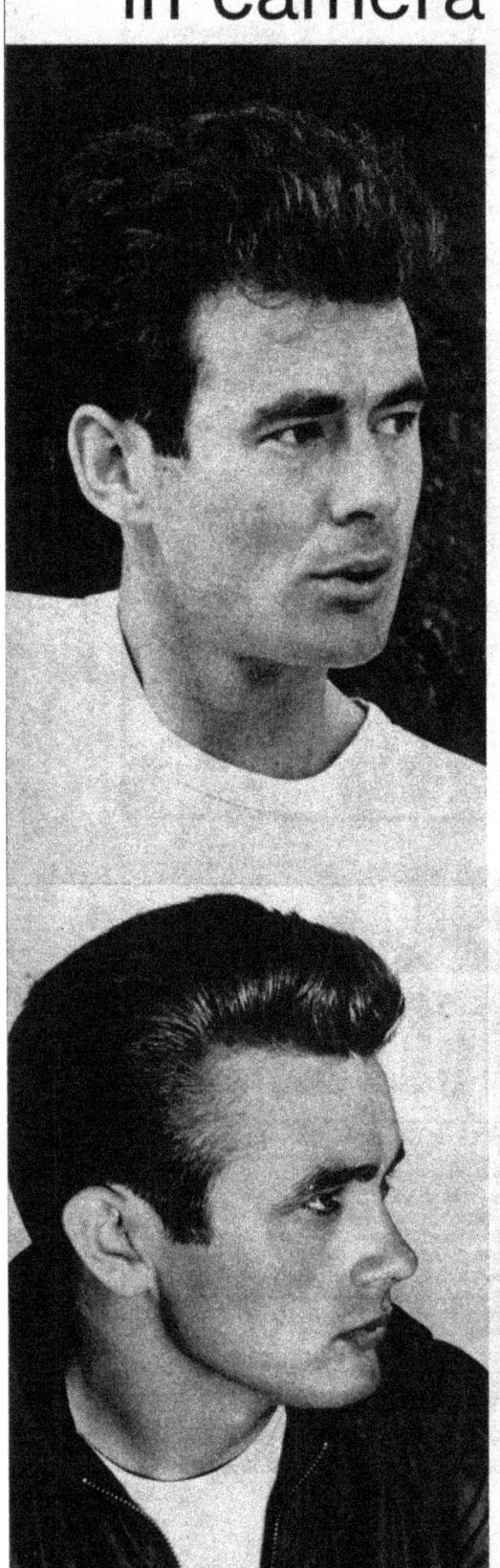

Tryin' to be like him

DURING THE LAST THREE years Hollywood has produced a number of 'biopics' based on various legendary idols of 'the silver screen'—among them *Gable and Lombard, W C Fields and Me, Won Ton Ton the Dog who Saved Hollywood* (the most satisfactory of the group in that Gus conveyed the feelings of how a contract star really did live a dog's life) as well as fictionalised impressions of the 'good old days' such as *Hearts of the West* and *Nickelodeon*. Generally none were that successful at the box-office, and favourable reviews were rare. We await, with mixed feelings, Ken Russell's view of *Valentino* with Rudolf Nureyev (who's not exactly a 'look-a-like').

For a number of years there have been various projects mooted on the life of James Dean, but there was always the problem of who would play him. So far he has had two documentaries made about him—Robert Altman's 1957 exploitation piece and more recently the Sandy Lieberson/David Puttnam *The First American Teenager* which at least was an honest, if not entirely satisfactory, attempt to evaluate his power as a performer and the complex, illusory reality of the person. His portrait dominates the stage of *Grease*, which has been playing to capacity houses in New York for five years (and is currently being filmed), while one's memory of all the young actors in the late 'fifties who were labelled 'the new James Dean' conjures up a long list from which there are no doubt many omissions: Dean Stockwell (*The Careless Years* was his comeback film after a brief retirement following his child star status), Brandon de Wilde, John Saxon, Horst Buchholz, Alain Delon, Troy Donahue, James MacArthur, Rod Lauren, James Darren and so on.

It was, therefore, somewhat of a shock a few months ago to learn that there was going to be an attempt to stage a British musical based on his life, and the subsequent dramas of auditioning over 500 would-be Deans which ended in the hiring of a California rock singer, who was then fired from the show, as was the original director, while a choreographer departed, as well as one of the main supporting actors. Only a short while before the show was due to open a final choice was made —it sounded like desperation time and, given the fact that British musicals have had a pretty poor reputation of late, it gave it all the earmarks of a potential fiasco.

The result of this extraordinary venture is an interesting, if far from satisfactory, attempt to portray the life of James Dean in relation to the three films in which he starred: the major character developments come out of his associations on and off set with Elia Kazan, Nicholas Ray and George Stevens as well as the 'doomed' relationship with Pier Angeli. Various other characters crop up such as Natalie Wood, Elizabeth Taylor, Hedda Hopper and Vic Damone, which all give the appearance of a random flick through a pile of newspaper clippings. In fact, the main weakness of the show is that it is scripted by John Howlett, the author of the least satisfactory of the Dean 'biographies' which in itself was a compilation of secondhand source material. This, combined with a sub-*Grease* score, puts *Dean* very much into the minor musical league (though substantially above other British musical attempts of late, which doesn't say too much in its favour), which hardly makes it suitable for one of London's largest theatres (seating 1559). The lyrics and score are unmemorable and the sup-

The biggest mistake was the casting of one actor to play the roles of Elia Kazan (above, in a reconstruction of the making of 'East of Eden'), Nicholas Ray and George Stevens—directors who had little in common either in terms of their work or as individuals

Glenn Conway (above left) gives a remarkably eerie portrayal of James Dean (left) in the British musical 'Dean'—on stage his resemblance to Dean is far more convincing than the photographs suggest. More than that, he captures the complexities of the actor very well, rising way above mere impersonation

Films & Filming (UK), October 1977

One of the most successful scenes: Anna Nicholas as Elizabeth Taylor (she also plays Pier Angeli and Natalie Wood) with Glen Conway during the making of 'Giant', combining Dean's bull-fighting fantasies

porting cast is poor. A particularly bad device is having a number of actors playing two or three roles each—particularly puzzling is why the youth who plays Dean as a boy (for the scenes when his mother died and he was nine years old) and also the Sal Mineo character from *Rebel*. And why one actor was cast to play the roles of Elia Kazan, Nicholas Ray and George Stevens is beyond comprehension—they were all so completely different both in their styles of films and in the way they handled actors, yet as portrayed here by Murray Kash they ultimately merge into one (the good, the bad and the indifferent). More successful is Anna Nicholas who has to play Pier Angeli, Natalie Wood and Elizabeth Taylor, which she manages commendably. Particularly good is her interpretation of Pier Angeli, and she has a neat on-stage transition from Natalie Wood to Miss Angeli. She is aided by an excellent singing voice (which the rest of the cast seem to lack) and has a very effective number 'Play That Song Again'.

Yet with all its faults and the limitations of its material (there are so many facets of Dean's character that are not dealt with—the script reeks of fan-magazine style writing with its references to newspaper items and incidents) *Dean* has one strong factor in its favour, and that is Glenn Conway who is extraordinarily effective in capturing the mood of a character as reflected through his screen performances. Conway's performance rises above mere imitation—and one must say that aided by some imaginative lighting there are often moments when he looks extraordinarily like Dean almost to the point of a cold shudder running down your spine—and he is spectacularly effective within the limitations of the script. By his final moment before the car crash when he addresses the audience, after everyone on stage has left him, with 'Is nobody coming?', in that hurt, hesitant, pleading fashion that was Dean's main appeal, Conway comes so desperately close to pulling off a seemingly impossible task—that of bringing a character back to life to the point of us being able to say 'Remember what you said? "If I live to be a hundred years old I'll never be able to do all the things I want to".'

RB

Take One (Canada, 15.7.1979

One more bullet?

David Thomson's encore on *Rebel Without A Cause* (Mar., 1979) reminded me of something about the closing sequence that has always puzzled me. The disturbed—and armed—Plato hides in the planetarium; Jim goes in, talks to him, calms him, manages to borrow the gun, and, unknown to Plato, removes the clip. When Plato comes out of the planetarium he panics, brandishes the pistol and is killed by a policeman. Cut to Jim, waving the clip and shouting that he has the bullets. Then we go on to other things, and the implications of the scene are dropped. Was it supposed to show the disregard the adults have for the teens? Or to show that Jim is not so hot himself—it hardly helps to grab the bullets and not tell anyone. Or—and I've seen nothing about this in any review I've read—did someone point out to Nicholas Ray that Jim didn't get *all* the bullets? There's still one in the chamber. Some semi-auto pistols won't fire with the clip removed, but some will. With no more information than the movie provides, it's possible that Plato could have killed someone with the last round.

You never know what the audience will spot—the revolver that James Mason (as Gentleman Brown) casually tosses in the water in *Lord Jim* is a model that won't be available for more than fifty years after the period of the film. While the six-shooter that never runs dry may not be an important flaw in the Gene Autry type of movie, films with more significant pretensions can't afford such boners, especially when, as in *Rebel Without A Cause*, they weaken the hero's efforts.

Frank W. Oglesbee
Ames, Iowa

James Dean – unausgelebte Sehnsüchte einer ganzen Generation

John Howlett
James Dean.
Eine Biographie

Von Klaus Humann

Der erste Film mit James Dean, den ich gesehen habe, war „Denn sie wissen nicht, was sie tun". Damals war ich achtzehn und wohlerzogen. Er hat mich nicht verändert. Ich hab auf den Mythos gewartet und James Dean gar nicht gesehen.

Als ich John Howletts Buch bekam, hatte ich Angst vorm Lesen. Wie kann man diesen Giganten beschreiben, ohne ihm zu Füßen zu liegen? John Howletts Biographie ist keine Hymne an den Star und Rebellen, keine Heldenverehrung, keine aufgeregte Fanschreibe mit Silberflimmer. Eigentlich eher das Gegenteil. Howlett versucht uns einen ziemlich durchschnittlichen Jungen zu beschreiben – verkorkste Jugend, verständnisvolle Großeltern, der gütige Pfaffe des Ortes, harte Theaterjahre in New York – der es dann irgendwann packt und mit seiner fast unheimlich anmutenden Energie und Zielstrebigkeit all die Widerstände und unausgelebten Sehnsüchte zu visualisieren verstand, die mit ihm eine ganze Generation von Heranwachsenden bedrängten. Seine Stärke war die Nähe, die er einem gab und die zugleich die Nähe war, die er zu seiner Rolle lebte. Er stand in der Zelluloideinsamkeit, wie man selber dastand, wenn man alle gegen sich hatte. Und man fühlte sich nicht mehr so allein.

Howlett zeigt uns viel von dieser Nähe, viel von der Wut und den Träumen, und er bleibt dabei der distanzierte Beobachter. Großartig die Stellen, in denen er mit Worten das zu beschreiben versucht, was mir oft in der Hast des Films verlorenging: Deans unnachahmliche Art, seinen Körper das sagen zu lassen, wo die Worte stumm blieben. Howlett erklärt, warum James Dean ein großer Schauspieler war und nicht nur der Rebell und Outcast, der Typ.

Bleibt mir noch anzumerken, daß Jörg Fauser das Buch gut übersetzt hat – so, daß es wichtig ist, es zu erwähnen – und daß es trotz der Bilder kein Bilderbuch ist. Die Bilder zeigen nur das, was Worte nicht können.

Verlag Monica Nüchtern, München 1977, 199 Seiten, 22,80 Mark.

Noch'n Dean

John Howletts ausgezeichnete Dean-Biographie (in der Übersetzung von Jörg Fauser) besprachen wir in Heft 8/77. Jetzt gibt's noch eine, *James Dean*, von Horst Königstein. Erschienen ist der Band in der Reihe „Menschen" des Dressler-Verlags, in der auch die Lebensgeschichten von John F. Kennedy und Olga Korbut herauskamen.

Dressler macht Jugendbücher, und wenn Du eine jüngere Schwester hast, kannst Du ihr ja Königsteins nett und durchaus kenntnisreich erzähltes Werk schenken. Schenk ihr gleich noch eine Postkarte dazu, denn sie wird dem Verlag schreiben wollen. *(„Wessen Biographie möchtest Du lesen? Mach uns Vorschläge! Begründe sie! Unter den besten Vorschlägen von allen Einsendungen werden Beatles-LPs verlost!").* Für Dich selbst aber leg besser noch genau 'nen Zehner auf die 12,80 Mark, die dieser *James Dean* kosten soll, und kauf Dir den Dean von Howlett.

Still Dean - John Howlett's excellent Dean biography (in the translation by Jörg Fauser) we discussed in Issue 8/7. Now there's one more, *James Dean*, by Horst Königstein. The volume appears in the series, *People,* published by Dressler-Verlag alongside new biographies of John F. Kennedy and Olga Korbut.

John Howlett looms large in James Dean studies, with his fine book and his London play. His other big contribution to Rebellion art is co-scripting with David Sherwin the first drafts of *if....* (1968)., the masterpiece that gave us Malcolm McDowell as an anarchist schoolboy.

アクターズ・スチュディオの本読み風景

ボンゴ・ドラムのリズムはジミーを原始と野性の世界へ呼び戻す

名声と栄誉と税金の町ニューヨークでジミーは何時も孤独だった

Torero – das war Jimmys Traumberuf

Jimmy in „Denn sie wissen nicht, was sie tun"

„Heiße Öfen" waren seine Leidenschaft

Als Student spielte er (vorn Mitte) Baseball

The Dean Myth

James Dean is dead; but he continues to receive more fan mail than any living Hollywood star. Mass hysteria, morbid curiosity, necromancy—what is it that has made the Dean myth? FILMS AND FILMING Hollywood correspondent, CLAYTON COLE, here analyses the causes and results of the influence this boy, who made only three films, has had on millions of filmgoers.

JAMES DEAN, aged 24, with one picture on release, one completed, and one currently in production, died in a car crash. That was September 1955. Since his death, the phenomenon of a posthumous interest unequalled in Hollywood history—which includes the hysteria over the death of Rudolph Valentino—has swept the world. No other star has so touched the public imagination. There have been eulogies to him in such diverse publications as the intellectual review *Poetry*, and such typical fan publications as *Photoplay*. No strata of society has wholly escaped the unique spell of the boy who left *Rebel* and *Giant* behind him as monuments to he who was both. All those who were associated with Dean have been ruthlessly thrust into the spotlight. No one more so than Kenneth Kendall, the sculptor of the Dean head which has been mentioned or reproduced in almost all of the recent Dean material.

Something of the lonely, misunderstood quality that is in the heart of every human being seemed to manifest itself in his characterisation of Cal Trask in *East of Eden*. In him they perhaps found a mirror of themselves. Who was he? What was he? Suddenly everyone had to know. An increase of magazines and albums have attempted to fill this need; piecing together a tapestry of fact and fiction, laying bare a family life for all to inspect, and furthering their own interpretations of Jimmy Dean.

Fan Letters

Although he is dead, eight thousand fan letters a month are addressed to Dean. Few Hollywood stars can equal that. The writers ask for souvenirs—hair, piece of clothing, a particle of the smashed car; but the majority of fan letters is addressed to him as though he were still alive.

One mass circulation movie-magazine summed up this fever thus: "Dean is a great star. We use the word 'is' because it is not proper to refer to immortal beings in the past tense—and James Dean is immortal."

The Dean Myth started with the funeral in his hometown, Fairmont, Indiana. It was attended by more people than the town's total population of 2,700 and the Rev. Xen Harcey, who delivered a eulogy, concluded: "The career of James Dean has not ended. It has just begun; and remember, God Himself is directing the production."

Since the showing of *Rebel Without a Cause* the fan craze for more news about Dean has grown. The fan magazines in the States are desperate for new Dean material. They have interviewed almost everyone from his mother to the waiter who served his meals in the Villa Capri, his favourite restaurant.

Thousands of people have been to Griffith Park where *Rebel* was made. They have gone stone by stone over the ground where Dean was standing when Sal Mineo (Plato in the film) was shot by the police.

From The Beyond

There is a fortune for the man who has a genuine unpublished photograph of Jimmy Dean. Photographer Sanford Roth has two shots of the dead actor taken a few minutes after the crash. He refuses to release them.

Four magazines devoted exclusively to Dean have recently appeared. One has a front cover title reading: *JIMMY DEAN RETURNS! Read His own Words from the Beyond.* His father has written a book. So has Nicholas Ray, who directed *Rebel*. There are Jimmy Dean recordings. For five dollars fans can buy a life-size replica of the Dean head, finished in plastic that looks and feels like human flesh.

There are rumours that his studio, Warner Brothers, plans to film his life story.

The Hollywood shop where he bought the jacket he wore in *Rebel* has been inundated with orders for similar jackets (about £8 a time).

Julie Harris, who starred with him in *East of Eden*, has fan letters almost every day asking: "What was it like when Jimmy kissed you?"

George Stevens, director of *Giant*, Dean's last film, has received threatening letters because of false statements that he had cut scenes in which Dean appeared.

Nick Adams, who acted in *Rebel*, and who has several of Dean's personal belongings, has had his home burgled by souvenir-hunting fans.

The reissue of *Rebel* and *East of Eden* in the States as a double-feature programme, has played to standing room only business everywhere they have been shown.

Artist Kenneth Kendall, who knew Dean well, told me:

"Diamond bright, and with as many facets, Dean was many things to many people; for he reflected their own interests. To an artist he was one thing, to a musician another, and to a racing enthusiast yet another. To me, he was the eternal spectator—occasionally participating, but even then aware of the reactions of others. Perhaps this was how he increased his actor's store of pantomime, for theatre was his motivating art.

Unreality of Death

"That he is not yet dead to many an admirer, that his grave has been visited by thousands, is now being held up as a morbid phenomenon. Dean's tragic end was many a youngster's first experience with the unreality of death. To these youngsters it was a hero's death, and one which could be mourned openly without the embarrassing restraint which attends family bereavement. To beat the world at 24 is an adolescent's dream. James Dean made that dream a reality: young people want not to forget it. Can we really call them morbid? Is the reaction more unusual than the situation itself?"

The sleepy community that gave birth to James Dean has now galvanised itself into action to channel some of this enthusiasm into the coffers of a James Dean Memorial Fund. The fund will enable talented youngsters to prepare themselves, through dramatic training, for an encounter with the beasts who roam the jungles of Hollywood and New York.

"James Dean came to me and commissioned a sculptured likeness—a likeness that was to become his own memorial," said artist Kendall. "Since that time I have found myself tied, not altogether unwillingly, to his legend. I have watched as the blinding incandescence of his posthumous fame has illumined many an insignificant participant in his story to world prominence. Players have skyrocketed to fame through their association with him. My own work has been seen in leading publications, on television and in motion pictures; not for its own merits, but because it is faithful to an ideal."

The Dean myth reflects an era—as tense, as neurotic, as uncertain, as vital as the boy it made its symbol.

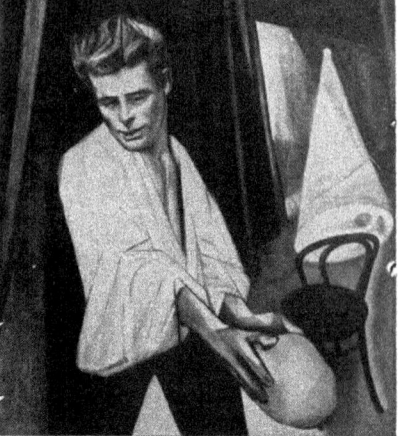

HAMLET: Portrait of James Dean as Hamlet, by artist Kenneth Kendall. Dean wanted to play Shakespeare before his tragic death in 1955. Now the portrait is displayed near Hollywood's Sunset Boulevard.
Photo: Los Angeles Museum of Fine Arts

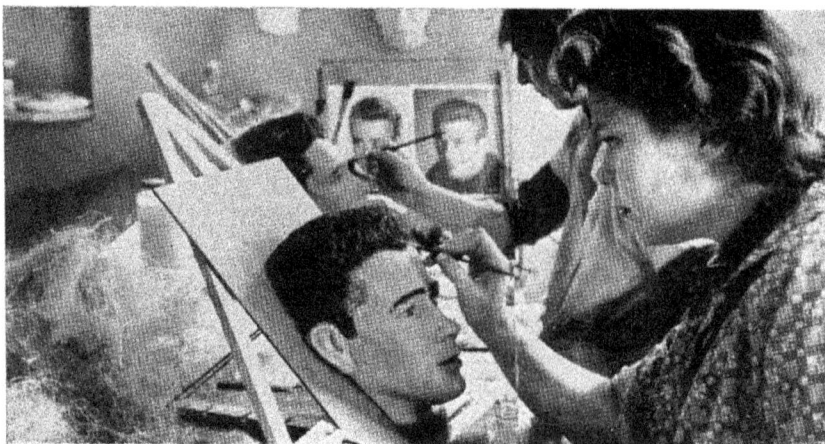

FANTASTIC: Thousands of flesh-like masks are being made in Hollywood for sale to Dean fans. *Photo: Life*

Trying to buy love: James Dean as the sensitive if strong-willed son, who tries to earn recognition from his stuffy, religious father (Raymond Massey), in Elia Kazan's 'East of Eden' (1955)

James Dean. Dean's important films can be counted on one hand, but his influence —later carried on by his ever-present sidekick and admirer, Sal Mineo—is still being felt today. The Kazan film which brought stardom to James Dean was *East of Eden*, the story of frustrated love existing between a father and his two sons. In what has been described as a modern Cain and Abel story, Dean plays a teenager who is envious of his younger brother, the favoured son. The father (Raymond Massey) is a stuffy, overly-religious farmer who doesn't understand the boy's moodiness. To make matters worse, the boy learns early in the story that his mother, who was thought to be dead, is really a madam in a nearby town. This leads to a series of explosive encounters both with his younger brother (Richard Davalos) and his insensitive father.

Yet another film, the classic *Rebel Without A Cause*, appeared in 1955 and set the sociological community on its ear. It was basically a story of a boy's reaction to his parents' unwillingness to face their own problems; James Dean's portrayal of the boy continually having to prove his masculinity has become his most famous role. Not wanting to be labelled a 'chicken' he accepts a dare to race in a jalopy. In the race, a driver is killed and the boy is held responsible for the death, so he runs away with his girlfriend (Natalie Wood) and a young admirer (Sal Mineo). Never were emotions between father and son (not to mention other members of the family and community) at such a fever pitch, and many similar films followed this same pessimistic trend.

After the death of James Dean in 1956, the tradition of the disaffected youngster at odds with society was carried on by Sal Mineo, who was Dean's friend and admirer in *Rebel* . . . and also appeared with him in *Giant* (1956). In Mineo's first film, *Six Bridges To Cross* (1955), he played a delinquent who later grew up to become Jerry Florea, the gangster. (The adult Florea was played by Tony Curtis.) *The Private War of Major Benson* (1956) was the story of an Army major (Charlton Heston) who becomes the commandant of a Catholic military boarding school. The film was basically a comedy, but the major's lack of sensitivity and stern authoritarian rule was sometimes not so funny. It certainly was *not* a good example of a healthy man-boy relationship to see Sal Mineo going out of his way to concoct mischief and Charlton Heston going out of his way to suppress it. In *Dino* (1957), Mineo plays another delinquent who this time is returned to his home after three years in a reformatory. He immediately begins to fight with his hated, stupid father (Joe DeSantis) and he is barely rescued from lifelong delinquency through the interest of a social worker (Brian Keith) and his girlfriend down the block.

While fathers were generally becoming weaker, at least some of the films, like *Dino*, gave the youngsters somewhere to turn when their fathers turned them off. A little-known, but beautiful British film is a perfect example of the outsider taking the place of the ineffectual father, and represents somewhat of a reprieve from the tragic alienation of youngsters in other stories (and often in real life). The film was *The Spanish Gardener* (1957), the story of a British consular official (Michael Hordern stationed in Spain, who is embittered toward life and has an overly possessivenes love for his son. Finding his father too restrictive, the boy (Jon Whiteley) finds a beautiful relationship with the peasant gardener (Dirk Bogarde), who understands the boy's need for robust play and the companionship of other children. Unfortunately, the father becomes an unsympathetic figure, a man trying desperately in all the wrong ways to win the affections of his child.

From the article *Where have all the fathers gone?* by Gerald Jones in *Films & Filming*, July 1974

リイ11月号目次

特集 ジェームスディーン

表紙──エリザベス・テイラー
色刷口絵──マリリン・モンロー
　　　　　　ソフィア・ローレン
口絵──オードリイ・ヘップバーン
目次──ジェームス・ディーン

三周忌を迎えて

ディーンの記録映画「ジェームス・ディーン物語」を中心にここに最後のディーンの特集を読者に贈る‼

折込口絵　ジェームス・ディーンカレンダー （一一）
口絵　ジェームス・ディーン大判ポートレイト （一四）
アート口絵　ジェームス・ディーンのおもかげ （一五）

写真物語「ジェームス・ディーン物語」 （一九）

この記録映画には、ディーン生前のフォートが一〇〇枚近く使用されている。そのうち五〇枚を九頁のグラビアに満載し、ディーンの生前の面影をここに偲ぼうとする‼

希望対談　風がふけばロマンスが生れる
　　　　　　　　ピア・アンジェリイ（四二）

ドロシイ・マローンの危い曲芸　ダニイ・ケイ（三四）

裏街とテレビと大砲と　荻　昌弘（三三）

パット・ブーンとシャーリイ・ジョーンズの
新しいイギリス映画「イタリアの想い出」（四〇）

裸身のマルティヌ・キャロル（三七）

ジュリエッタ・マシーナ
（イタリーの生んだ最高の女優）植草甚一（五〇）

一流プロデューサーのジェリイ・ウォルド氏マジメに語る
トニイ・カーティス（栄光の陰に涙あり）（六六）

パット・ブーン（歌でつづったラブレター）（六四）

ハリウッド便り（一七六）

Rätselhafter Mord in Hollywood:

James Deans Partner wurde erstochen!

'James Dean's partner was stabbed to death!'

Opfer der Bluttat ist Sal Mineo (37), der als Twen (Foto unten) in den 50er Jahren zwei unvergessene Filme mit „Jimmy" drehte. BRAVO schildert, wie es zu dem Verbrechen kam . . .

Der Tatort: Hier fand man den blutenden Sal Mineo in der Tiefgarage seines Hauses am Sunset Strip. Oben: Der Schauspieler kurz vor seinem Tod

Zwei von Sal Mineos größten Filmerfolgen: Links mit Eva Marie Saint in „Exodus", oben als jugendlicher Psychopath mit James Dean in „... denn sie wissen nicht, was sie tun"

Ein Schrei voller Todesangst ließ gegen zehn Uhr abends die Bewohner eines Apartment-Hauses am Sunset Strip in Hollywood hochschrecken. Ein Mann schrie: „O mein Gott, nein! Helft mir! Hilfe!" Dann war es still. Nur das Geräusch von sich hastig entfernenden Schritten war zu vernehmen.

Ein Hausbewohner lief sofort in die Tiefgarage, aus der die Schreie gekommen waren. Er erkannte sogleich, wer dort blutend vor ihm auf dem Boden lag: Es war der 37jährige Schauspieler Sal Mineo, der in dem Haus eine Wohnung hatte. Der Wagen des Schauspielers stand eingeparkt in einer Box. Der Nachbar versuchte sofort, mit Mund-zu-Mund-Beatmung zu helfen. Es war umsonst. Ein Messerstich mitten ins Herz hatte Sal Mineos Leben ein Ende gesetzt. Er verblutete am Tatort.

Der Mord bleibt ein Rätsel: Weder die Brieftasche noch Uhr oder Ring des Schauspielers sind gestohlen worden. Andere Hausbewohner haben einen blonden, mittelgroßen Mann im Alter zwischen 20 und 30 davonlaufen sehen. Bis Redaktionsschluß tappte die Polizei in puncto Täter und Motiv noch völlig im dunkeln.

Sal Mineo war an diesem Abend von den Proben zu seinem neuen Theaterstück gekommen, das in Kürze Premiere haben sollte. Der Schauspieler hatte sich, nachdem es im Film ruhiger um ihn geworden war, mehr auf die Bühne konzentriert. Dabei galt er in den fünfziger Jahren einmal als der Nachfolger von James Dean. Zweimal hatte er neben dem Unvergessenen vor der Kamera gestanden. Für „... denn sie wissen nicht, was sie tun" und für „Giganten". Mit diesen beiden Rollen schaffte er den Durchbruch. Es folgten u. a. die Filme „Entfesselte Jugend", „Dino, der Bandit", „Die Gene-Krupa-Story". Sein größter Erfolg war die Rolle eines israelischen Terroristen in dem Film „Exodus".

Jürgen Tiedt

The boy who refuses to DIE

James Dean Lives On . . .

Unforgotten . . . Unforgettable

■ In the months since the life of 24-year-old James Dean was so suddenly snuffed out, an uncanny thing has happened. In the history of Hollywood tragedies, there has never been anything like it. It is almost as if from somewhere in the Great Beyond, with the same intense fire that always burned bright in him, James Dean is defying the fates that took his life before it had really begun, defying them to make him die.

We see it very clearly, now: James Dean is not dead. He is not going to die. We know, because we have the evidence—in many ways. Most poignantly, in the letters and phone calls that are pouring into our office every day. Of course, a certain amount of such interest was to be expected. But, after an interval of mourning, it would normally stop. *It hasn't stopped.* And, much more significantly, *the people do not speak of Jimmy as if he were dead.*

He is with us, too, when we talk to those who knew him closely, as a friend—and still speak of him as a friend. He is with us in a darkened theater, making the silent place come alive with his vivid brilliance in *East Of Eden*, or *Rebel Without A Cause*. No matter *(Continued on next page)*

"Dead? Not Jimmy Dean. He still lives and he still acts, not in movies but in our memories. Was he passed over in the voting on this year's Academy Awards? We have given him our own award—our love. And yet much as we love him, we now know there was Someone who loved him even more." L. B., Spokane, Washington

"Jimmy Dean lives on in the hearts of those who loved and admired him as an actor of unequaled talent and a young man of sensitivity and personal greatness. Dearest Jimmy, you will never be forgotten. Your star will always shine." F. F., New York, New York

"Many, true, have come and gone,
Great men doing their part in life and passing;
The world has lost its princes before
But never one like you"
Name Withheld By Request

"I sit day after day and ask myself why. Why was our beloved James Dean taken from the world when he had so much to offer? I only hope that somehow, some way, he can see how much we still love him." J. B., Salt Lake City, Utah

THE BOY WHO REFUSES TO DIE

(Continued)

how often we see these films, so vital was Jimmy's performance that they are ever new, ever exciting.

Mr. Henry Ginsberg, producer of *Giant,* recently spoke of this strange powerful vitality that was peculiarly Jimmy's—how it touched and inspired everyone who worked on the picture. Said Mr. Ginsberg, "He lived with such burning intensity that, in retrospect, it almost seems that he knew he wouldn't be with us long, and his work was truly remarkable. I believe his was one of the finest acting jobs ever seen on the screen."

In talking with others with whom Jimmy was closely associated in his last days, we get the same feeling—that on them, he still exerts a tremendous effect.

But most significant of all is the strange and awe-inspiring public reaction to Jimmy Dean—an overwhelming demonstration that this extraordinary young man has won a lasting living place in the hearts of people everywhere. "I suppose you think I'm silly to feel like this," said a girl who called us the other day to relate her lasting admiration and love for this great star. We assured her that we didn't think her silly at all; we have found those same sentiments shared by countless other folks who have called and written in exactly the same way.

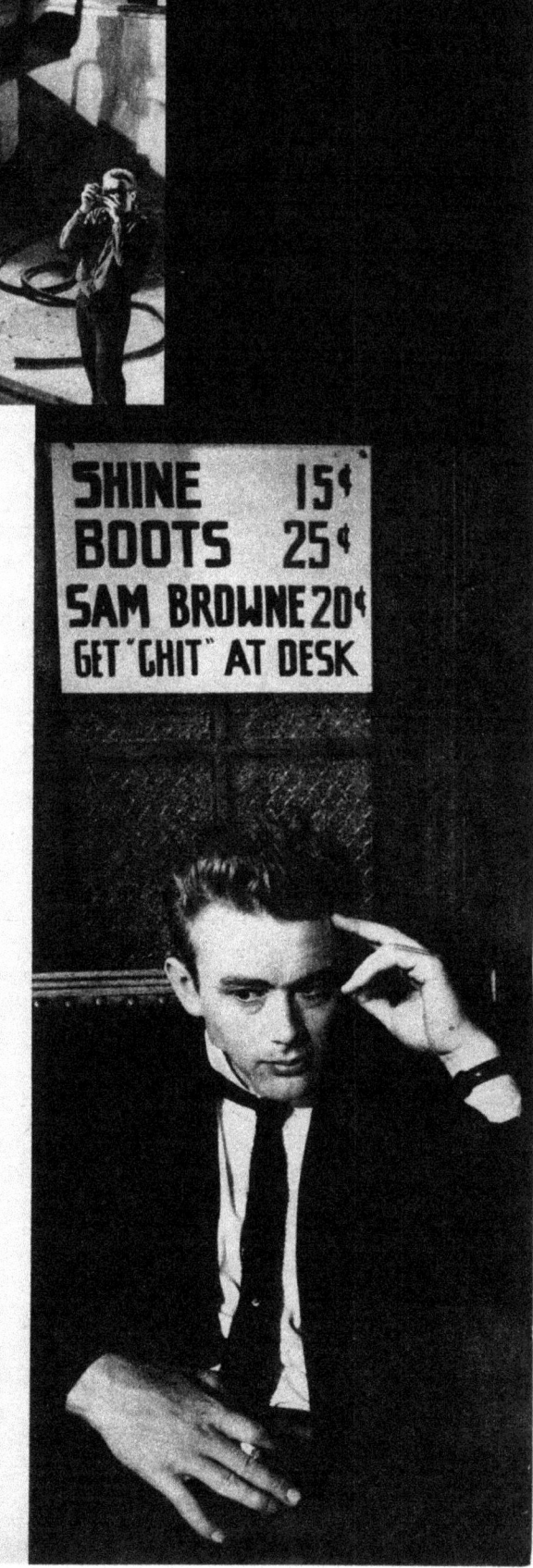

"Jimmy was a combination of many things—a skyrocket, an idealist, a cynic and a dreamer, a thunderbolt, an uninhibited extrovert and a little lost boy. Through the almost unbearable beauty of his acting, he reached out to us all, and I don't believe that anyone who ever saw James Dean act could remain unmoved by him; no one could forget him afterwards." M. M., Bristol, Connecticut

天才の顔 ★ この顔は永遠に消えて行くか

ジェイムズ・ディーン死して早や二年、彼を恋い慕う人の心は永遠に変らないであろうが、この顔が年毎に我々から遠ざかり行く淋しさを誰が否定し得よう。歳月はかくも冷酷である。いま彼の生前のありとあらゆる記録、写真、ゆかりの品々などをフィルムに納めた一本の映画「ジェイムズ・ディーン物語」が公開されるということは、我々がこの淋しさを克服すべき最後のチャンスである。ディーン・ファンよ、今度こそ彼の顔に向かつて、最後のそして最大の別れの挨拶を、祈りの声を捧げられよ……

Im Alter von neun Jahren hatte Dean seine Mutter sterben sehen. Er war mit dem Tod vertraut; für ihn war er eine Realität des körperlichen Verfalls und des persönlichen Verlusts. Und was immer Reverend De Weerd ihm an Theorien über die Natur der Sterblichkeit eingeprägt haben mag, Dean blieb vom Tod besessen. Er versuchte mit Clownereien in offenen Särgen ihn durch Gelächter zu vertreiben, und er idealisierte ihn, um ihm den Schrecken oder die Geheimnisse zu nehmen.

Kaum verwunderlich deshalb, daß Dean auch Vorahnungen seines eigenen frühen Todes hatte. Aber es war nicht so sehr ein Todeswunsch, sondern ein übermächtiges Bewußtsein von der Nähe und Unvermeidbarkeit des Todes.

Doch in jener schicksalhaften letzten Septemberwoche 1955 schien Deans Zukunft vielversprechend und rosig. Er hatte bereits einige gute Rollen-Angebote in der Tasche. Und seine Agentin Jane Deacy war auch in Hollywood angekommen, um mit Warner einen 900 000-Dollar-Vertrag auszuhandeln. Es ging dabei um neun Filme in sechs Jahren und einem freien Jahr dazwischen.

Dean hatte sehr unterschiedliche Vorstellungen, was er in diesen zwölf freien Monaten tun wollte, und erzählte jedem eine andere Version. Jane Deacy erzählte er von seiner Absicht, den Hamlet zu spielen. Der Bildhauerin Pagot Waring erklärte er, er würde in diesem Jahr riesige Skulpturen im Grand Canyon hauen. Die Roths erfuhren, daß er einen langen Urlaub machen und Europa bereisen würde. Und seinem Porsche-Mechaniker Rolf Wütherich vertraute er den Plan an, sich zwölf Monate ganz dem Rennfahren zu widmen.

Im Schaufenster sah Jimmy den Spyder...

Dean bestellte auch sofort einen Lotus-Sportwagen aus England – diesmal kein Straßenmodell, sondern einen richtigen Rennwagen. Es war klar, daß sein erstes Interesse in diese Richtung ging, nachdem er wegen des „Giganten"-Vertrags seine Renn-Aktivitäten vier Monate hatte einstellen müssen.

Ende des Monats war eine Renn-Veranstaltung in Salinas anberaumt. Als Dean im Ausstellungsraum seines Autohändlers einen 6000-Dollar-Wettbewerbs-Porsche sah, ging er sofort hinein und kaufte ihn. Der „Spyder 550" war ein seltenes Stück, und Dean wußte, daß er Monate auf den Lotus warten mußte.

In den paar Tagen vor dem Rennen fuhr er mit dem neuen Wagen in Hollywood herum, um den Motor einzufahren. Aber am Donnerstag zeigte der Kilometerstand erst rund hundertsechzig Kilometer. Dean sagte deshalb zu Wütherich, wenn das Wetter am nächsten Tag gut wäre, könnten sie genausogut mit dem Porsche nach Salinas fahren, anstatt ihn auf den Anhänger zu laden.

Dean war in Hochstimmung. Er fand, daß das Rennen eine Gelegenheit zum Feiern war, und er wollte, daß seine Freunde dabei wären. Er rief sie alle am Donnerstag oder Freitagmorgen ohne viel Erfolg an – auch Lew Bracker, einen Versicherungs-Vertreter und Rennfanatiker, der in den letzten Monaten enge Freundschaft mit Dean geschlossen hatte.

Bracker führte für Dean Verhandlungen wegen einer Lebensversicherung. Donnerstag oder Freitagfrüh besuchte er Dean in San Fernando, um sich von ihm eine Liste der Leute geben zu lassen, die als Nutznießer der Versicherung eingesetzt werden sollten. Dean bat

'Three years after his death, James Dean got more fan letters than any living Hollywood star'

Fortsetzung von Seite 47: Noch drei Jahre nach seinem Tod bekam James Dean mehr Fan-Briefe als jeder lebende Hollywood-Star

richtiges Testament aufzusetzen und darin auch die Versicherung aufzunehmen. Dean rief deshalb seinen Anwalt an und machte für die folgende Woche einen Termin aus. So kam es, daß zur Zeit des Unfalls kein Testament vorlag und alles an den Vater ging, den einzigen Verwandten, der, beabsichtigt oder nicht, in der Liste der Nutznießer nicht auftauchte.

Strafzettel wegen zu hohen Tempos

Außer dem Mechaniker Rolf Wütherich waren die einzigen Freunde, die nach Norden mitkamen, Sandy Roth und ein anderer Rennfanatiker namens Bill Hackman. Dean gab ihnen den Ford-Kombi mit dem Anhänger, während er und Wütherich den Porsche nahmen. Der silberne Flitzer trug schon an der Seite in schwarzer Farbe Deans Startnummer, 130, zusammen mit dem Kosenamen, den Dean ihm gegeben hatte: „Der kleine Bastard".

Freitag, den 30. September 1955, machten sie sich gegen zwei Uhr nachmittags auf den Weg. Sie verließen Los Angeles im Norden über die Ridge Route, hielten unterwegs an einer Raststätte, um einen Happen zu essen. Und in Bakersfield wurden sie von einer Verkehrsstreife angehalten und bekamen einen Strafzettel, weil sie in einer Siebzig-Kilometer-Zone hundert Kilometer drauf hatten.

Es geschah dann zwischen 17 Uhr 40 und 17 Uhr 50 auf der Kreuzung der Highways 466 und 41 auf einer leeren, flachen Strecke, als das Licht zu schwinden begann. Eine schwarze Plymouth-Limousine, gefahren von dem 23-jährigen Studenten Donald Turnupseed, der auf der 466 Richtung Südost fuhr, verließ ihre Bahn, um nach Nordosten abzubiegen. „Der muß halten", schrie Dean. „Der muß uns doch sehen!"

Der leichte Sportwagen krachte in den Plymouth und wurde wie Papier zerknüllt. Rolf Wütherich wurde schwer verletzt ins Freie geschleudert. Dean war auf dem Fahrersitz eingeklemmt, vom Lenkrad aufgespießt.

Der Kombi mit Roth und Hackman kam fünf oder vielleicht zehn Minuten später. Ein Krankenwagen war schon alarmiert. Donald Turnupseed lief im Schock herum, aber so gut wie unverletzt. Er wiederholte ständig: „Ich hab' ihn nicht gesehen!" Rolf Wütherich lag bewußtlos am Grasstreifen. Er hatte schwere Kopfverletzungen und ein gebrochenes Bein.

Sandy Roth machte Aufnahmen von den zwei Wagen, für den Fall, daß sie als Beweismittel gebraucht würden. Die Fotos, die er von Dean machte, der bewußtlos in dem zerknüllten Porsche festsaß, während des Wartens auf den Krankenwagen, hat er keinem Menschen je gezeigt. Kopf und Gesicht wiesen anscheinend keine Verletzungen auf; aber Deans Genick war gebrochen, und sein Körper hing aufgeschlitzt auf dem Lenkrad.

Der Kult um Jimmy nahm verrückte Formen an: Diesen „James-Dean-Altar" richtete sich ein Fan mit Jimmy-Bildern, Platten und Blumenschmuck ein

Jimmy starb im Krankenwagen
'Jimmy died in the ambulance'

Nach dem medizinischen Gutachten starb James Dean im Krankenwagen, auf dem Weg zum Krankenhaus, ohne das Bewußtsein wiedererlangt zu haben.

Einige Minuten, nachdem der Krankenwagen den Schauplatz verlassen hatte, kamen zwei Streifenwagen der Polizei, um den Unfall aufzunehmen: Captain Tripke und Polizeibeamter Nelson. Sie hatten die Nachricht von dem Unfall um 17 Uhr 59 per Polizeifunk erhalten.

Am Unfallort fanden sie eine verstörte Menschenmenge vor; etliche Leute hatten den Porsche schon identifiziert. Der Plymouth stand noch an der Kreuzung, der Porsche weiter oben, an der nördlichen Biegung der 466. Bis zum Punkt des Zusammenpralls wies die Fahrbahn des Porsches eine Bremsspur von zehn bis dreizehn Metern auf.

Abgesehen davon, daß Dean zweifellos sehr schnell gefahren war, wurde der Unfall entweder dadurch verursacht, daß Turnupseed den schnellen, niedrigen und silberfarbenen Porsche in der Dämmerung nicht erkannte. Eine spätere Darstellung legt nahe, daß Turnupseed mitten auf der Kreuzung hielt, bevor er abbog, und daß er das Manöver fortsetzte, weil er dachte, daß der Porsche wegen ihm mit dem Tempo heruntergehen würde. Es könnte aber auch sein, daß dabei der Fuß des Fahrers vom Kupplungspedal rutschte. Deans Bremsspuren würden die Theorie ebenfalls unterstützen. Das später gefällte Gerichtsurteil ließ alles offen: Fahrlässigkeit auf beiden Seiten.

Noch in der Nacht des Geschehens wurde James Deans Leichnam offiziell von seinem Vater im Leichenschauhaus von Paso Robles identifiziert. Am 8. Oktober 1955, nach der gerichtlich angeordneten Leichenschau zur Feststellung der Todesursache, wurde Dean in Fairmount beigesetzt. Der Trauergottesdienst fand in der Friends' Back Church statt. Die Trauergemeinde war bei weitem größer als die Einwohnerschaft der kleinen Stadt.

Der Gottesdienst wurde von Pastor Xen Harvey und Deans altem Freund Reverend De Weerd abgehalten. Die Grabrede schloß mit den Worten: „Die Karriere von James Dean ist nicht zu Ende. Sie hat gerade begonnen. Und Gott selbst führt dabei Regie."

Aber kein Gott könnte das makabre Nachspiel zu Deans Tod geplant haben.

Noch drei Jahre nach seinem Tod bekam James Dean mehr Fan-Briefe als jeder lebende Hollywood-Star, obwohl Warner außer der routinemäßigen Reklame für seine Filme kaum etwas tat, um die Legende am Leben zu erhalten. Warner weigerte sich sogar, einen offiziellen Fan-Club zu unterstützen oder ihn auch nur anzuerkennen. Das einzige Zugeständnis bestand darin, ein Büro mit einem festen Sekretärinnen-Stab einzurichten, um die Post zu beantworten und Fotos zu verschicken.

Gerücht: Sein Grab sei leer

Wo Warner sich weigerte, auszubeuten, griffen sofort Dutzende von Verlegern und Plattenfirmen zu. Aus Deans Tonbändern wurden Raubplatten gepreßt, Schlager erschienen mit seinem Bild auf dem Cover, und Songs wurden ihm gewidmet oder über ihn verfaßt. Zeitschriften brachten Sensations-Storys oder Klatschberichte über den toten Schauspieler. Kurzlebige Fan-Magazine, oft nur mit einer Ausgabe, jagten sich gegenseitig an den Kiosken. Ein New Yorker Ladenmädchen, das behauptete, in überirdischer Verbindung mit Dean zu stehen, verkaufte eine halbe Million Exemplare von ihrer Publikation „Jimmy kommt wieder!".

Die Weigerung, an seinen Tod zu glauben, führte zu wilden Gerüchten, denen zufolge Dean noch lebte, aber so entstellt war, daß er versteckt werden mußte. Fans belagerten Sanatorien, in denen sie ihn vermuteten. Andere wollten wissen, daß Dean, um der verhaßten Publicity zu entkommen, die Identität des Mechanikers Wütherich angenommen habe. Und wenn ein Mädchen seine Adresse samt Foto in einem Schließfach einer Zeitung hinterlegte, würde er in einer Vollmond-Nacht sich über ihre heiße Stirn beugen . . .

Es gibt immer noch Leute, die behaupten, das Grab in Fairmount sei leer, weil Dean nie beerdigt worden sei; oder, falls man ihn doch beerdigt hätte, sei sein Leichnam bei Nacht, als die Erde noch frisch war, aus dem Grab entwendet worden. Von dieser Absicht freilich waren die Behörden in Fairmount unterrichtet gewesen, und noch Wochen nach der Beerdigung stellte die Ortspolizei Tag und Nacht einen Wachtposten am Friedhof auf.

Aber der Totenkult trieb Blüten, die noch makaberer waren: Ein gewisser Dr. William Eschrich kaufte den zertrümmerten Porsche, und der relativ unbeschädigte Motor und das Getriebe wurden regelrecht ausgeweidet. Man behauptete später sogar, daß jeder Wagen, in den irgendein Teil des Dean-Porsches eingebaut worden war, verunglückte.

Gegen „Eintritt" auf den Todessitz

Ein geschäftstüchtiges Pärchen kaufte dann Dr. Eschrich die Karosserie ab und stellte sie in einer Kegelbahn in Los Angeles auf: 25 Cents, um Deans kaputtes Auto zu sehen; 50 Cents, um sich auf seinen Todessitz zu klemmen und das verbogene, blutverkrustete Lenkrad anzufassen. Es wurden 800 000 Tickets verkauft, bevor man das Paar zwang, die Ausstellung endgültig abzubrechen.

Und immer noch weigerte sich der Tod, zu sterben. Der Wagen wurde auseinandergenommen und Stück für Stück als Souvenir verhökert. Der kleine Porsche hätte die Ausmaße eines Schlachtschiffs gehabt haben müssen, wenn alles echt gewesen wäre, was Dean-Verehrer als „echte" Stücke kauften: verbogenes Aluminium, blutige Stoffetzen, sogar Farb- und Glassplitter.

Es wurden Ringe mit „echten Brocken" von Deans Grabstein verkauft, die wie Diamanten gefaßt waren. Lebensgroße James-Dean-Büsten kamen auf den Markt, die mit einer fluoreszierenden Kunsthaut bespannt waren. Rote Windjacken mit Reißverschluß, wie Dean sie in „Denn sie wissen nicht, was sie tun" getragen hatte, wurden in einem Laden in Hollywood verkauft und fanden so reißenden Absatz, daß sie monatelang nachbestellt werden mußten.

Deans Apartment in New York und sein Haus in San Fernando wurden geplündert. Seine Freunde konnten einiges von seiner persönlichen Habe retten. Doch jeder, von dem man wußte, daß er etwas von Dean hatte, lief Gefahr, verfolgt zu werden.

Warner Brothers ergriffen strenge Sicherheitsmaßnahmen, um die Fans daran zu hindern, in die Studios einzubrechen und Souvenirs zu stehlen. Die Kostüme, die Dean in seinen Filmen getragen hatte, wurden begehrte und hochbezahlte Sammler-Stücke.

Noch Jahre nach seinem Tod blieb Dean ein Sinnbild für Unruhe, Unzufriedenheit, Selbstmitleid oder Auflehnung gegen die Gesellschaft.

ENDE

Noch heute pilgern Fans an Deans Grab auf dem Friedhof von Fairmont

Aus dem Buch „James Dean" von John Howlett, deutsch von Jörg Fauser, Verlag Monika Nüchtern, München

'Who the gods love?'

Wen die Götter lie

Ich will herauswachsen aus dieser unbedeutenden kleinen Welt, in der wir leben. Ich will all das hinter mir lassen, all diese kleinlichen Gedanken über unwichtige Dinge, die ohnehin nach hundert Jahren vergessen sein werden.
James Dean, 1931 – 1955

Kann sein, daß James Dean in hundert Jahren vergessen sein wird. Die Original-Kopien seiner drei Filme verfallen schon langsam. Aber sein Mythos ist zäher als Zelluloid.

Bob Dylan, Jahrgang 1941, gibt offen zu, daß er Dean kopiert hat: „Ich fühlte, daß er sich in seinen Rollen selbst darstellte." Wie Dean in seinen Filmen drückte Dylan in seinen Songs später die Probleme des ewigen Außenseiters aus. Genau wie Dean: Melancholisch, höhnisch, aggressiv, gereizt, sprunghaft, unberechenbar.

Mit 21 war James Dean das jüngste Mitglied an der berühmten Theaterschule von Lee Strasberg, gegründet von dem aus der Türkei eingewanderten Regisseur Elia Kazan. Ältere Kollegen von Dean hießen Marlon Brando, Montgomery Clift, Marilyn Monroe, Paul Newman. Kontakt fand er nicht zu ihnen.

Jimmy liebte das Landleben. Auf Parties (hier mit Ursula Andress) ließ er sich nur ganz selten sehen

Clift sagte einmal: „Er war völlig undiszipliniert. Wenn man mit ihm einen Dialog auf der Bühne hatte, wußte man nie, wo er sich hinstellte. Er nuschelte seine Sätze unhörbar für seine Partner, machte spontan Sachen, die nicht im Drehbuch standen. Aber alles, was er machte, war genial."

James Dean, inzwischen finanziell gesichert durch Fernsehspots, leistete sich außer einem Motorrad, Büchern und Schallplatten keinerlei Luxus. Er mochte Elvis Presley, afrikanische Musik, Haydn, Bartok, Berlioz und Dave Brubeck.

Seine Zugeständnisse an ein „normales Leben" wurden immer geringer. Er befand sich auf dem besten Wege, sich von jeder Art gesellschaftlicher und persönlicher Zwänge zu lösen.

Er litt, obwohl inzwischen prominent, unter seinem Mangel an Bildung. Manche vermuten sogar, daß ihm das Lesen schwerfiel. Er kompensierte das mit fast lästiger Neugier. Der Schriftsteller Bill Bast: „Er leerte die Köpfe seiner Gesprächspartner so, wie ein Blutsauger aus einem nichtsahnenden Menschen die Kraft saugt."

Vertrauen und Liebe waren Gefühle, vor denen Dean sich fürchtete, denen er nicht gewachsen war, an denen er möglicherweise zerbrochen wäre. Dean-Vertraute vermuten, daß der Tod der Mutter ihm diese Fähigkeit genommen hat. Er wechselte zwar häufig seine Freundinnen, man sagte ihm sogar nach, daß er bisexuell gewesen sei, aber alle Bindungen waren nie intensiv oder dauer-

"I want to grow out of this insignificant little world in which we live. I want to leave all that behind, all those petty thoughts about unimportant things that will be forgotten after a hundred years anyway." James Dean

ben...

In „Giganten" stellte James Dean in entlarvender Weise den amerikanischen Traum dar, der zum Alptraum wird

haft. Auf jeden Fall war seine körperliche Sinnlichkeit mehr femininer Art wie der melancholische Narzißmus eines Flamenco-Tänzers.

Seine tänzerischen Fähigkeiten, die er in New York ausbilden ließ, brachten ihm einen großen Theaterauftritt im „Immoralist" ein, in dem er einen arabischen Diener spielte. Elia Kazan („Streetcar Named Desire", „Viva Zapata") sah Dean und war begeistert. Er arbeitete gerade am Drehbuch von John Steinbecks „East Of Eden". Kazan unterhielt sich ausführlich mit dem

SUPER-POSTER-STORY

JAMES DEAN:
Die letzten Min
vor seinem T

Unter tragischen Umstän
der Star, der auch
Euch ein l
BR

Gemeinsam bereiteten Jimmy und Rolf Wütherich (r.) den 6000-Dollar-Porsche auf das Rennen vor

Jimmy und Rolf bei der Abfahrt in Los Angeles. Rolf, ein Deutscher, war sein Mechaniker und Vertrauter in Auto-Angelegenheiten

In „Blackwell's Corner", an der Kreuzung der Highways 466 und 33, trafen sich Jimmy und seine Freunde zur letzten Kaffeepause. Das Café hat Firuz Askin fürs BRAVO-Super-Poster gezeichnet

Das letzte Foto: James und Rolf im Spider. Rolf starb 1981 auch bei einem Autounfall…

Die tödliche Kreuzung: James Dean fuhr auf dem Highway 466, Donald Turnupseed kam auf der Gegenfahrbahn und bog nach links ab. Er gab an, den in Dämmerlicht mit überhöhter Geschwindigkeit heranbrausenden grauen Porsche nicht gesehen zu haben

W ie ein riesiger Feuerball hängt die Sonne am Himmel; sie scheint James Dean und seinem Beifahrer Rolf Wütherich direkt ins Gesicht. Es ist noch ziemlich heiß, und die Straße zerfließt in der Ferne, vermischt sich mit dem Braun der Wüste, die den Highway 466 nach Salinas begleitet. Die Straße ist leer an diesem 30. September 1955, Freitag gegen 17.30 Uhr. Die einsetzende Dämmerung taucht den grauen Asphalt in flimmerndes Zwielicht…

Erst vier Stunden zuvor waren James Dean und sein deutscher Mechaniker Rolf Wütherich in Los Angeles aufgebrochen. Jimmy saß am Steuer seines vier Tage alten Porsche Spider 550.

Auf dem silbergrauen Lack trug der Flitzer bereits die Startnummer 130 und den Kosenamen „Der kleine Bastard", wie Jimmy ihn getauft hatte. Ihr Ziel war Salinas.

Dort wollte Dean nach längerer Rennpause – dieser gefährliche Sport war ihm während der „Giganten"-Dreharbeiten vertraglich untersagt worden – an einem Autorennen teilnehmen.

Zwei ebenfalls rennbegeisterte Freunde, Bill Hickman und Sanford Roth, hatte er überredet, ihm im Ford-Kombi mit dem Anhänger für den Porsche zu folgen.

Die beiden Wagen verließen Los Angeles im Norden über die Ridge Route (damals Highway 99), machten unterwegs eine kurze Pause, weil Wütherich die Maschine kontrollieren wollte. Sanford und Bill hielten ebenfalls und warnten Jimmy, daß er zu schnell sei. Bei ihren 100 km/h würden sie ihn kaum noch sehen, außerdem sei die Straße kurvenreich und gefährlich. Doch Jimmy winkte übermütig ab. In Bakersfield wurde er schließlich von einer Polizeistreife angehalten und bekam einen Strafzettel, weil er in der 70-Kilometer-Zone 100 gefahren war. Gegen 17 Uhr trafen sich Dean, Wütherich und die beiden anderen zu einer Kaffeepause in „Blackwell's Corner" an der Kreuzung der Highways 466 und 33. Autonarr Dean entdeckte sofort einen nagelneuen Mercedes 300 SL, zeigte dem Besitzer gleich seinen Strafzettel und meinte ärgerlich: „Und ich habe gerade einen Reklamefilm über Straßensicherheit gemacht. Irgendein Journalist wird das mit Freude auswalzen.

(Während der „Giganten"-Dreharbeiten hatte Dean sich im Jett-Rink-Kostüm filmen lassen, als er über Autos plauderte. Seine Abschiedsworte: „Denk dran, vorsichtig zu fahren – denn das Leben, das du rettest, könnte meins sein.")

Jimmy kaufte noch eine Tüte Äpfel, setzte sich zu Wütherich in den Wagen und ließ den Motor aufheulen. Im Abfahren rief er den anderen zu: „Seh'

Die Unfallstelle: Etwa zwölf Minuten saß Dean tot in seinem total zerfetzten Porsche, bis die Ambulanz eintraf. Noch in derselben Nacht identifizierte ihn sein Vater im Leichenschauhaus in Paso Robles. Rolf Wütherich (rechts, auf der Erde liegend) wurde mit Knochenbrüchen und Kopfverletzungen in die Klinik von Paso Robles gebracht

BRAVO 44

...uten ...od

...den verunglückte heute noch für viele von ...dol ist, vor 27 Jahren... AVO schildert, wie es dazu kam...

Nur einer („Jenseits von Eden") seiner drei Filme lief im Kino, als James Dean mit 24 tödlich verunglückte. Obwohl „Denn sie wissen nicht, was sie tun" und „Giganten" erst nach seinem Tod Premiere hatten, machten sie „Jimmy" zum Idol der rebellierenden Jugend auf der ganzen Welt

Jimmys Grab: Am 4. 10. 1955 wurde er in Fairmont neben seiner Mutter begraben. 3000 Fans kamen zur Trauerfeier

...such zum Abendessen in Paso Robles."

Jimmy und Rolf näherten sich der Kreuzung der Routen 466 und 41 in Cholame, als plötzlich ein Ford von der entgegenkommenden Straßenseite nach links einbog. Am Steuer der 23jährige Student Donald Turnupseed aus Kalifornien.

Jimmy schrie noch: „Der Kerl da muß anhalten; der muß uns doch sehen." Zu spät. Sekunden später – die Uhr zeigte 17.45 Uhr – bohrte sich der leichte Sportwagen in den Plymouth, wurde wie ein zerknülltes Blatt Papier in den Straßengraben geschleudert.

Als Sanford und Bill etwa zehn Minuten später die Unfallstelle erreichten, bot sich ihnen ein Bild des Grauens. Rolf Wütherich lag neben dem Wrack, bewußtlos mit gebrochenem Bein und schweren Kopfverletzungen. Am Finger den Ring, den Jimmy ihm während der Fahrt zum Zeichen seiner Freundschaft geschenkt hat.

Jimmy selbst saß noch hinter dem Steuer, sein Kopf war unnatürlich nach vorne gebeugt, wies aber auf den ersten Blick keine Verletzungen auf. Doch James Byron Dean war bereits tot. Sein Genick gebrochen, sein Oberkörper von der Lenksäule aufgespießt. Donald Turnupseed, der Todesfahrer, lief unverletzt, aber im tiefen Schock umher und stammelte immer wieder: „Ich hab' ihn nicht gesehen."

Während der Wartezeit auf den Rettungswagen machte Sanford Aufnahmen von den beiden Autos, falls sie als Beweismittel gebraucht würden. Doch die Fotos, die er von Jimmy machte, der aufgeschlitzt und mit gebrochenem Genick hinter dem Steuer saß, hat er keinem Menschen je gezeigt...

Margit Rüdiger

251

34 Jahre nach dem Tod von James Dean: Noch nie g ER L WEI

James bei Kostümproben für „Jenseits von Eden"

Einsamer Spaziergang am Hafen

Proben mit einem Stuntman für „... denn sie wissen nicht, was sie tun"

In sich gekehrt: James Dean wartet im Hotelzimmer auf die nächste Szene

James in der Garderobe

Selbst bei der Rasur rauchte James

Jan Dean

Gag am Rande: Das Messer steckt direkt in seinem Namensschild

Drehpause

Stellprobe für Zweikampf in „...denn sie wissen nicht, was sie tun"

James mit „stichfester" Weste

Ein aufgelockerter James Dean mit Fans im „Griffith Park"

Er war menschenscheu, verschlossen, verletzlich. In seinem kurzen Leben liebte er nur einmal von ganzem Herzen. Doch sie heiratete einen anderen. James Dean (geboren am 8. Februar 1931 in Marion, Indiana) drehte nur drei Filme („Jenseits von Eden," „... denn sie wissen nicht, was sie tun" und „Giganten"). Er war der jugendliche Rebell auf der Kinoleinwand mit Jeans und weißem Unterhemd. Er wurde zum Idol von Millionen auf der ganzen Welt. Heute, 34 Jahre nach seinem Tod, hält der Kult um seine Person immer noch an. James Dean war am 30. September 1955 mit seinem Porsche in einen Ford geknallt, dessen Fahrer die Vorfahrt übersehen hatte ...

Ein seltenes Dokument: Diesen Liebesbrief schrieb James Dean in seiner fast unleserlichen Handschrift am 26. April 1954 an seine New Yorker Freundin Barbara Glenn. Ein Brief eines von Selbstzweifel geplagten jungen Mannes. In großen Buchstaben schrieb er „Ich will sterben" oder „Ich habe hier mit niemandem geschlafen." Dean war ein Einzelgänger, der kaum jemand an sich heran ließ. Auch in seinen Briefen ließ er dies des öfteren durchblicken

War James Dean krankhaft ehrgeizig? War er ruhmsüchtig? Ruhelos, frustriert, arrogant, gar haßerfüllt? Liebte er nur sich selbst? Dies behauptet jedenfalls der amerikanische Schriftsteller Barney Hoskyns in der Biographie „James Dean - Der Rebell von Hollywood" (192 Seiten, 181 Bilder, 48 DM). Hoskyns hat mit Leuten gesprochen, die Dean gut kannten, hat in Archiven und Filmstudios recherchiert. Papier ist geduldig. Es wird sogar behauptet, daß James Dean Männern nicht abgeneigt war. Tote können sich nicht mehr wehren...

Es ranken sich unzählige Legenden um James Dean, der seit nunmehr 35 Jahren tot, aber doch unsterblich geblieben ist. Am 30. September 1955 raste James Dean, den alle nur Jimmy nannten, mit seinem silbergrauen Porsche Spider auf der 466. Straße nach Salinas. Der Tachometer zeigte 125 km/h, als der Porsche in einen entgegenkommenden Ford prallte. James Dean war sofort tot - gerade 24 Jahre alt.

Noch heute hat er Millionen Fans, noch heute pilgern sie an sein Grab, bis heute hat Hollywood keinen „neuen James Dean" hervorgebracht. So richtig gekannt aber hat ihn keiner. Nach außen hin cool, innen aber verletzlich und äußerst sensibel. Als er acht Jahre alt war, starb die heißgeliebte Mutter an Krebs. Ihren Tod hat Jimmy nie überwunden.

Einige Nachbarn behaupteten, Jimmy sei ein Muttersöhnchen gewesen. So soll er seiner Ma vor dem Schlafengehen stets Briefe geschrieben und sie unter ihrem Kopfkissen versteckt haben. Seine Vettern lachten ihn aus, weil er Gedichte las und Violine spielte.

Geboren wurde Jimmy am 8.2.1931. Seine Größe: 1,72 m

Als er nach Hollywood kam, kam mit ihm ein neuer Typ Schauspieler: Einer, der sich nicht anbiederte, der die allmächtigen Filmbosse nicht um Rollen anflehte, der auf seine Chance wartete.

Der Außenseiter, der Rebell war er in seinen drei unvergessenen Filmen „Jenseits von Eden" (das schwarze Schaf der Familie), „Denn sie wissen nicht, was sie tun" (Einzelgänger mit Hang zu waghalsigen Mutproben) und „Giganten" (Ranch-Angestellter wird zum Öl-Millionär).

Plötzlich wollten die Teenager so sein wie er. Sie trugen Jeans und T-Shirts, eine neue Mode-Welle war angesagt. Aber James Dean ließ keinen Menschen so richtig an sich ran. Die ganz große Liebe blieb ihm auch versagt, obwohl es natürlich zahlreiche Affären gab. Doch Jimmy war nicht fähig, sich zu binden, er wollte frei sein. Er genoß auf heißen Motorrädern und in seinem Porsche den Rausch der Geschwindigkeit.

Er war der Sohn eines Zahntechnikers und wurde der beliebteste Schauspieler aller Zeiten.

Peter Raschner

Der blonde Jimmy war nicht nur in seinen Filmen ein Außenseiter

BRAVO 68 'Was James Dean pathologically ambitious? Was he glorious? Restless, frustrated, arrogant, even hateful?'

TOT - ABER UNSTERBLICH
'Dead - But immortal'

Eigentlich sollte Jimmy Rechtsanwalt werden

Mit Pferden verstand er sich prima

James Dean rauchte täglich bis zu 50 Zigaretten

Der kurzsichtige Jimmy lachte nicht sehr oft

EO-KASSETTEN ZU GEWINNEN!

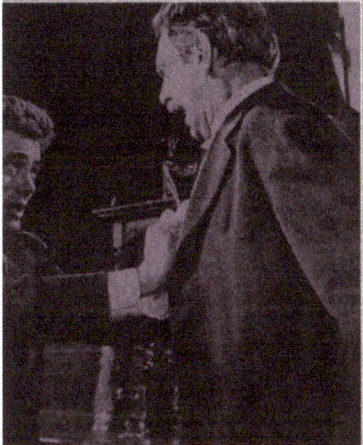
...ibt Ärger mit seinem Vater, weil dieser Geld von ...ablehnt, das Kal durch Spekulation verdient hat

Die hübsche Abra, die eigentlich Aron heiraten wollte, flüchtet sich in die Arme von Kal. Aron ist verzweifelt und meldet sich zum Militär

Der Vater erleidet einen Schlaganfall und bleibt gelähmt. Kal und Abra bleiben bei ihm

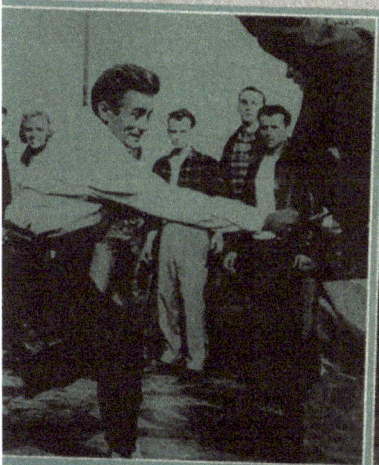
...der neuen Schule wird Jim von Buzz, dem Chef ...r Klassenbande, zum Messerduell gefordert

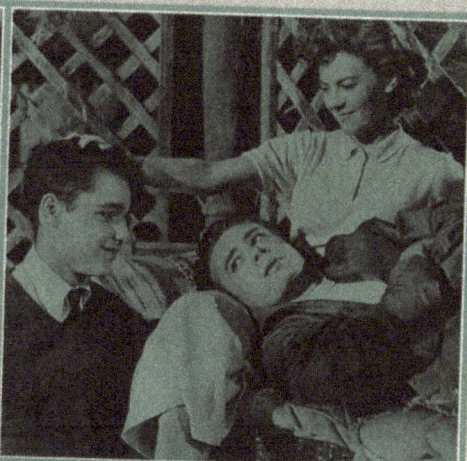
Jim, Judy (Nathalie Wood) und Plato (Sal Mineo) sind Freunde. Aber eine Auto-Mutprobe reißt sie auseinander

Bei dieser Raserei stirbt Buzz. Jim flieht zu Plato, der sich mit Buzz' Freunden schlägt. Pluto wird erschossen

...heiratet die blutjunge Leslie ...zabeth Taylor), die ihn liebt

Jett verliebt sich in Leslie. Er erzählt ihr von seinen Träumen, einem eigenen Stück Land. Leslie findet Jett sympathisch, mehr nicht

Eines Tages erbt Jett ein kleines Stück Land und findet Öl. Er wird schwerreich

Aber das Geld hat ihn nicht glücklich gemacht. Er ist allein

Jimmy meldete sich aus dem Jenseits

Diese Frau sprach mit dem toten James Dean!

BRAVO-Reporter waren dabei

James Dean
Monats-Bildkalender 1987

13 großformatige Bilder (9 schwarzweiß und 4 vierfarbig) zeigen James Dean in den unvergessenen Filmszenen. Die Bildlegenden und das Kalendarium sind zweisprachig, deutsch und englisch. Format 34,5 x 48 cm, 13 Blätter mit Klarsichtfolie.
Verlag u. Auslieferung W. Geisselbrecht/Stuttgart
Verkaufspreis DM 29,80 + Versandkosten.

--------------- (ausschneiden) ---------------

Bestellcoupon

Hiermit bestelle ich _____ Expl.
Bildkalender „James Dean", 1987
zum Verkaufspreis von DM 29,80 + Versandkosten.

Name / Vorname

Straße / PLZ und Ort

Datum / Unterschrift

Senden Sie bitte den Coupon in deutlicher Druckschrift an den **Kino-Verlag GmbH**, Milchstraße 1, 2000 Hamburg 1.

JAMES DEAN
1931 – 1955

In dieser Woche pilgern wieder viele Fans zu seinem Grab: Jimmy hatte am 8. Februar Geburtstag

Der Rebell, der nicht zur Ruhe kommt

James Dean

Auf der Inschrift des schlichten grauen Grabsteins auf dem kleinen Friedhof von Fairmont/Indiana, fehlen bereits zwei Buchstaben. Immerhin ist es 26 Jahre her, seit James Byron Dean am 4. Oktober 1955, vier Tage nach seinem tödlichen Autounfall, dort beigesetzt wurde. Doch am 8. Februar wird die Gedenkstätte wieder einem Blumenmeer gleichen. Denn an diesem Tag wäre Jimmy 51 Jahre alt geworden. Und an jedem seiner Geburtstage pilgern Jahr für Jahr seine Fans nach Fairmont, wo er einst bei Verwandten aufgewachsen ist. Sie legen Blumen am Grab nieder, zünden Kerzen an und feiern ihren eigenen Gottesdienst für ihren „ewigen Rebellen".

In der Tat ist Jimmy ein Rebell, der nie zur Ruhe kommt. Der blonde, blauäugige Typ mit der Bürstentolle, der auf Fotos nie lacht, ist ein echtes Phänomen: Er drehte nur drei Filme, starb mit 24 Jahren und ist trotzdem auch heute noch das Idol für viele Jugendliche in aller Welt.

Die meisten von ihnen kamen erst Jahre nach seinem Tod zur Welt. Und doch fühlten sie mit ihm, wenn sie seine Filme auf dem Bildschirm oder im Kino sahen. In seinen Außenseiter-Rollen entdecken sie ihre eigenen Probleme wieder. Denn Jimmy schlüpfte nicht wie andere Schauspieler in fremde Charaktere. Er gab immer ein Stück seiner eigenen Persönlichkeit preis.

In seinem ersten Film „Jenseits von Eden" (1954) war er das „schwarze Schaf", der böse Bruder und Herumtreiber Cal Trask – ein mißtrauischer, liebebedürftiger, hassender und rebellischer Junge wie Jimmy selbst.

Mit Cal wurde in Jimmy seine eigene frühe Jugend wieder wach – das Außenseitertum in Fairmont bei Onkel und Tante Winslow, wo er nach dem frühen Krebstod seiner geliebten Mutter Mildred, „abgeben" wurde, wo er wegen seiner dicken Brille, seiner Geige und seinen Gedichtbänden von den Bauernburschen als Träumer verlacht wurde.

Er hatte Schwierigkeiten mit seinem Vater, einem Zahntechniker, der mit seinem Literaturbegeisterten Sprößling wenig anfangen konnte, der ihn „zu einem richtigen Mann" machen wollte und zum Jurastudium zwang.

Seinen Vater-Sohn-Konflikt trug James Dean auch in seinen nächsten Streifen „Denn sie wissen nicht, was sie tun", der noch im selben Jahr entstand.

Im Kampf gegen seinen autoritären Vater und seine verständnislose Umwelt an der neuen Schule, schließt sich Jim Stark an zwei andere Jugendliche, Außenseiter wie er. Wie er sind sie auf der Suche nach Liebe und Geborgenheit und geraten gemeinsam im Milieu messerstechender Jugendbanden in eine Katastrophe mit tödlichem Ausgang.

Auch privat zeichnete Jimmy stets die heftige Ungeduld aus, dabei sein zu wollen. Doch ein früh entwickeltes, übersteigertes Mißtrauen verschloß ihm meist den Weg zur Gemeinschaft. Die Heftigkeit seiner Sehnsucht und seiner Angst, machte ihn den Kollegen gegenüber oft arrogant und egozentrisch, ließ ihn nicht selten einsam sein. Doch dahinter steckte dieselbe Verletzlichkeit wie bei Jim Stark.

Jimmy war sein ganzes kurzes Leben auf der Suche nach Liebe – ebenso wie der verlachte Cowboy Jett Rink in Jimmys letztem Film „Giganten", dessen Aufführung er nicht mehr erlebte. Unglücklich verliebt in die Frau seines Bosses, eines Großgrundbesitzers, arbeitet sich Jett zum Ölmagnaten empor. Doch selbst auf dem Höhepunkt seines Erfolgs erscheint ihm sein Leben leer und sinnlos.

Privat war Jimmys große unglückliche Liebe die italienische Schauspielerin Pier Angeli, die er in den Hollywood-Studios während der Dreharbeiten zu seinem zweiten Film kennengelernt hatte. Viele Mädchen hatten bis dahin seinen Weg gekreuzt – einmal wollte ihn ein sitzengelassenes Filmsternchen, das sich selbst als „Hexe" bezeichnete, mit Voodoo-Zauberriten ins Grab wünschen – doch bei keiner hielt Jimmy es länger als eine Nacht aus.

Seine Einstellung zu Mädchen änderte sich erst mit der 23jährigen Pier. Keine Stunde wollte er mehr ohne sie verbringen.

Doch Piers strenge Mutter verbot ihr den Umgang mit dem „wilden Verführer" – und hatte auch sofort einen Tröster an der Hand. Innerhalb von vier Wochen verlobte sie Pier mit dem Schlagersänger Vic Damone.

Jimmy war unterdessen nach Hollywood geflohen. Doch am Tage der Hochzeit – so erzählte man sich in Hollywood – soll er auf seinem Motorrad in der Nähe der Kirche gesessen und geweint haben.

Seinen Schmerz betäubte Jimmy von da an auf immer rasanteren Fahrten mit schnellen Wägen. Nach Abschluß der „Giganten"-Dreharbeiten – bis dahin war es ihm von der Filmfirma vertraglich untersagt gewesen – wollte er seine Teilnahme an Autorennen wieder aufleben lassen. Aus diesem Grund kaufte er sich von seiner letzten Gage einen silberfarbenen Porsche Spider. Er brachte ihm den Tod. Auf dem Weg zum Autorennen in Salinas raste er auf schnurgerader Straßen gegen einen abbiegenden Ford. Der leichte Porsche landete als zerknülltes Wrack im Straßengraben...

Text: M. Rüdiger

'The rebel who finds no rest'

One night after shooting, the director and the actor went together to see a revival of James Dean in *Giant*. Shepard is far taller, far less tenderized than Dean. But that's another great influence, I would guess, especially in Dean's darker moments: in *East of Eden*, coaxing from under the tree, and dragging his brother toward the darkness of their mother; in *Rebel Without a Cause*, an edgy mastermind in the planetarium, apparently trying to save Plato, but acting like his nemesis; in *Giant* slamming Rock Hudson in the stomach.

Maybe Shepard cherished the Dean who wanted love and understanding; maybe. But it's the instinct for authority and the violent turmoil in Dean that speak out in Shepard's plays. Phil Kaufman, though, had cast Shepard a little in the way one puts a poster on one's wall, for "His intense dedication to the manly life, rejecting New York, the taste for cowboys and rodeos—and all with the look of a man in a leather jacket on a horse meeting a jet plane in the desert."

That *is* an arresting image, and Shepard is all that Kaufman wanted in *The Right Stuff*—a creation of myth, as quaint, private and authentic as the abo-

On the making of *The Right Stuff*, *Films Illustrated*, December 1983

James Dean on the set of Giant.

Ausschneiden + sammeln!

FOTOS, DIE GESCHICHTE SCHRIEBEN

James Dean, 1955
Der einsame Rebell
'The lonely rebel'

Hinter seinem lässigen Aussehen versteckt sich ein einsames Herz: James Dean ist ein junger Mann, der Zeit seines Lebens kämpfen muss. Kämpfen gegen seinen Vater, der nie wollte, dass er Schauspieler wird. Kämpfen gegen die Einsamkeit, nachdem seine große Liebe Pier Angeli († 39) ihn verlassen und einen anderen Mann geheiratet hat. Mit dem Film „Jenseits von Eden" wird der Amerikaner 1955 zum rebellischen Idol der Jugend und **weltweiten Frauenschwarm.** Zwei weitere Filme machen ihn zur Legende. Doch er hat kaum etwas von seinem Ruhm. Am 30. September 1955 rast James Dean mit seinem offenen Porsche in ein entgegenkommendes Auto. Er stirbt sofort – im Alter von 24 Jahren.

Fotos: Imago(2)

Der Schauspieler mit seinem geliebten Porsche. Seine Vorliebe für rasante Fahrten kostet ihn das Leben

ニューヨークでは、ジミイは三年ばかり生活した。そのあいだに、バレーを習い、ボンゴをたたき、車にのって走りまわった。音楽の指導者は、作曲家のレナード・ローゼンマンであった。バレーをすゝめたのはアーサ・キットであった。こうしているうちに、エリア・カザンが「背徳者」の舞台をみて大へんほれこみ、彼の次作「エデンの東」に抜てきしたのである。こうして、ジミイはニューヨークを去り、ハリウッドに移ってきたのである。その時の彼は、ワーナー撮影所のむかいの下宿屋に入った。週給一千ドルのジミイは、ネクタイ一本位しかもっていなかった。普段着一着。外出用一着。ネクタイはエンジ色、ブルー、他一本位であった。こうして、ディーンは「エデンの東」で大成功をおさめ、使い古したオートバイでやって来た風来坊が一躍スターとなったのだ

ジェームス・ディーンは、サンタ・モニカのジュニア・カレッジを卒業した時に、既に俳優になることを志していた。カリフォルニア大学の演劇科に入ったジミイは、古典をいろいろ演じた。しかし学校だけでは不十分だとしったジミイは、ニューヨークの俳優学校へ移った。そこでリー・ストラスバーグに手をとって教えられた。ニューヨークの生活にもようやくなじんだジミイは、舞台にもよく出て、ようやく俳優としての基礎をきずいたのである。ジミイの舞台で有名なのは「ジャガーを見よ」と云う演劇だった。相手役はアーサー・ケネディであった。大へん不入りであったが、この役でテレビにひっぱられ、再び舞台にもどって、アンドレ・ジイドの「背徳者」に出演し、ジミイの俳優としての名声もようやくあがってきたのである。

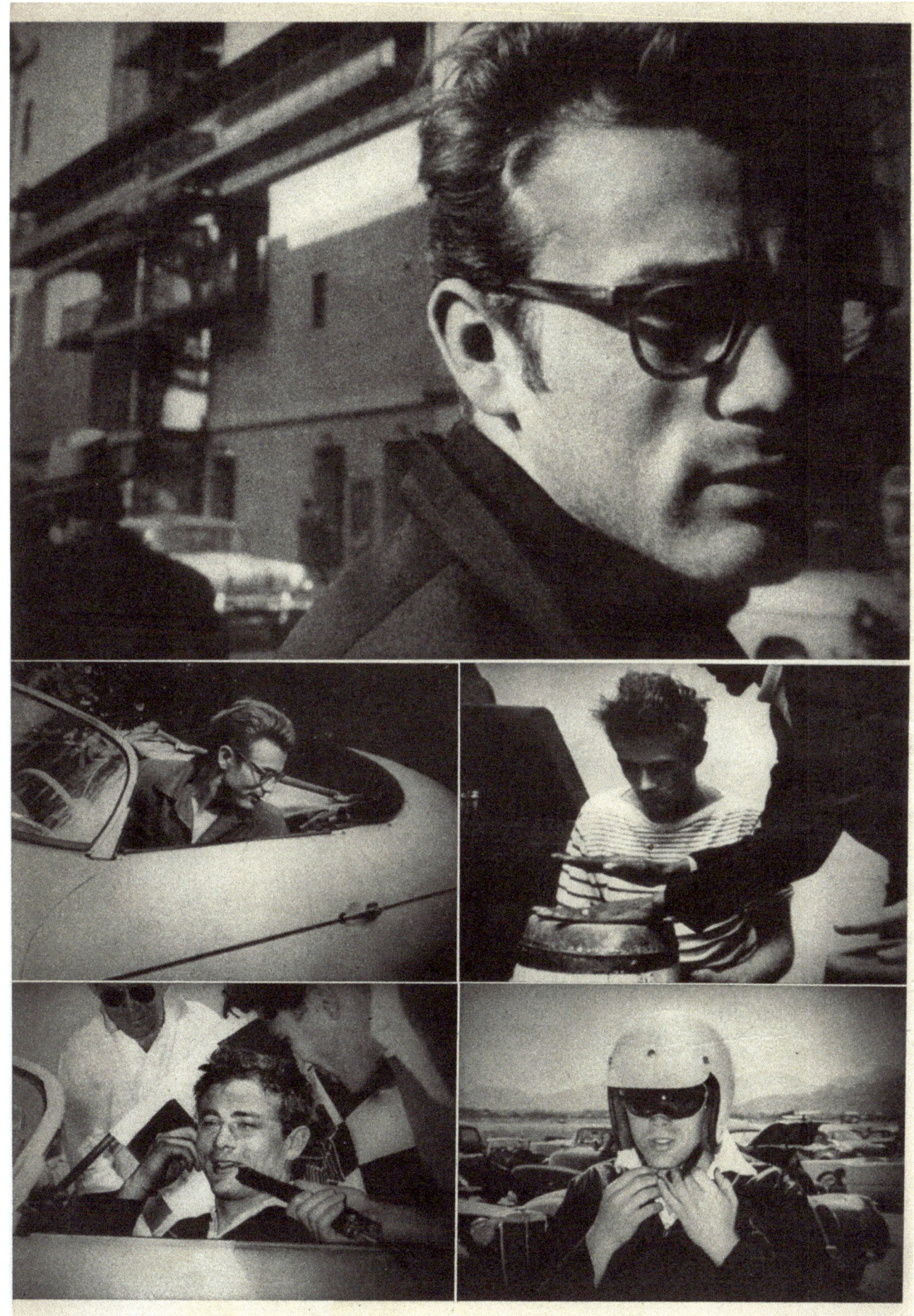

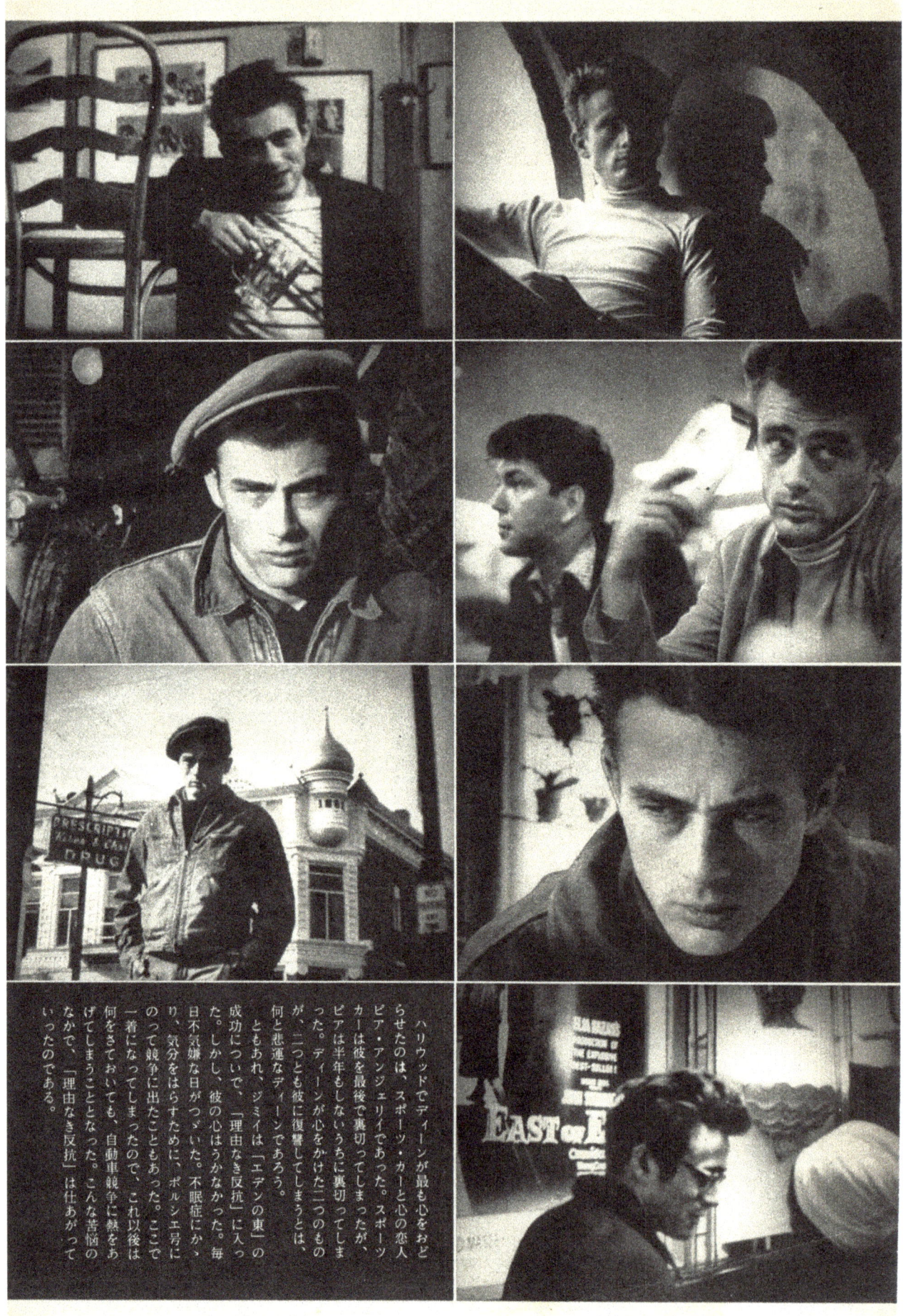

ハリウッドでディーンが最も心をおどらせたのは、スポーツ・カーと心の恋人ピア・アンジェリであった。スポーツカーは彼を半年も最後で裏切ってしまったが、ピアは半年もしないうちに裏切ってしまった。ディーンが心をかけた二つのものが、二つとも彼に復讐してしまうとは、何と悲運なディーンであろう。

ともあれ、ジミイは「エデンの東」の成功について、「理由なき反抗」に入った。しかし、彼の心はうかなかった。毎日不気嫌な目がつづいた。不眠症にかり、気分をはらすために、ポルシエ号にのって競争に熱をあげてしまうこともあった。ここで一着になってしまったので、これ以後は何をさておいても、自動車競争に出たこととなった。こんな苦悩のなかで、「理由なき反抗」は仕あがっていったのである。

DAVID CASTELL

JAMES DEAN: PUZZLE OF A DOWNFALL CHILD

"I felt that Dean's body was very graphic; it was almost writhing in pain sometimes. He was very twisted, almost like a cripple or a spastic of some kind. He couldn't do anything straight. He even walked like a crab, as if he were cringing all the time... But I also think there was a value in Dean's face. His face is so desolate and lonely and strange. And there are moments in it when you say, 'Oh, God, he's handsome—what's being lost here! What goodness is being lost here!'"

Elia Kazan, director East of Eden

Films Illustrated October 75 p2

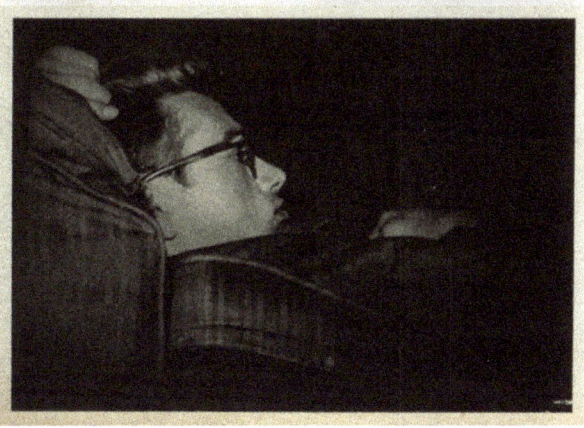

On February 1, 1954 a barely known young actor stole the applause and the notices with his award-winning performance as a homosexual Arab boy in "The Immoralist." The play brought James Dean to Broadway but, in a typically flamboyant and perverse gesture, he handed in his resignation on opening night. On September 30, 1955 they prised his body out of a tangled car wreck and laid it gently in the ambulance where he died.

Just twenty months of notoriety, scandal, celebrity and — some would say — genius. Twenty years later, interest in Dean is as keen as ever. Television repeats again and again the three major films he made (and occasionally he is to be spotted in tiny roles in *Sailor Beware, Fixed Bayonets* and *Has Anybody Seen My Gal?*) and books about him abound. Warner Brothers have just brought out an album of dialogue from *East of Eden, Rebel Without a Cause* and *Giant*, while a new documentary by Ray Connolly, *James Dean: The First American Teenager*, invites us to reassess him.

Dean, a child of Indiana farmland, was shunted off to live with relatives when cancer killed his mother. The boy was nine at the time, and there has been conjecture about how much this childhood trauma disturbed his personality, even his sexuality. His dramatic abilities became evident during his teens and he was later to quarrel with his father over the fact that he preferred acting studies to a conventional academic training.

His contemporary impact was unexceptional — insignificant radio parts, short runs in two plays and adequate performances in television programmes of unbelievable banality.

In *East of Eden* he gave a fine performance as Cal, and the sensitivity of his screen persona surprised those Los Angelites who had suffered the boorish slobbishness of his off-screen self.

With *East of Eden* he made a sizeable dent in Hollywood's reserve, but it was the coincidence of his death and the release of *Rebel Without a Cause*, the seminal Dean film, that sent the mortal shock waves round the world. A cut-out of monster proportions, a true representation of surly self, towered above Piccadilly Circus while, beneath it, queues shuffled respectfully into the London Pavilion. It was more like a lying in state than the first run of a movie.

There on the screen was Dean — arrogant, vital, erupting with the fury of living (*Le Fureur de Vivre* was the film's apposite French title). There in the press was news of his senseless end. Yet in fulfilling his own premonition of an early death Dean sowed the seeds of his legend. It has nothing at all to do with death wish, but there have always been certain personalities in the public arena, from Christ through to Kennedy, who have had a fateful instinct for the moment of exit.

Had Dean lived, he would now be forty-four. Of his contemporaries, only the admired Brando made that transition with grace. The range of Dean's playing did not look wide enough for him to sustain his initial level of success. His technique was superb, but his dependence on it was all but total. The love-craving, parent-hating rebel became his instant trademark. The confrontations with the fathers in *East of Eden* (Raymond Massey) and *Rebel Without a Cause* (Jim Backus) have distinct similarities, not really because of their dramatic context, but because of the same lapel-clutching intensity Dean brought to them.

In his last film, *Giant*, he was impressive as the rebellious ranch hand but in the latter part of the film, where the character metamorphosised into a powerful oil tycoon, he had far less strength. It is an open secret that a friend, Nick Adams, was called in to dub the drunk scene that comes towards the end of the film. Director George Stevens just did not find Dean sufficiently convincing.

Could he have continued as the perpetual teenager? At the time of his death he was cast to play boxer Rocky Graziano in *Somebody Up There Likes Me* for Robert Wise. Paul Newman, who screen-tested for *East of Eden* alongside Dean, won the role: the film also marked Steve McQueen's debut. Also in the pipeline was another project that went to Newman, a realistic look at the life and times of Billy the Kid, which Dean particularly wanted to produce. It was finally made by Arthur Penn as *The Left-Handed Gun*.

Only three films of substance, yet Dean's popularity endures unabated, forcing us back again and again to review, to search for clues to the puzzle of this downfall child. There are recurring themes, in his life as in his work, but these have been over-schematised by the media, particularly by the press that, in the years after his death, could never provide enough words on Dean to satisfy the grieving fans. Interviewed for Ray Connolly's new film Sal Mineo, who played Plato in *Rebel Without a Cause*, comes as close as is probably possible to finding the quintessence of the Dean appeal. It had to do with a specific rebellion in a specific period of time — the '50s. It was simply that he gave the teenager a status.

Dean was the mirror in which the post-war generation saw their own frustrations, their rebellion, their affluence and their unique power to form their own culture. While suffering from his own identity problems, Dean unwittingly taught a generation who it was, what it could do and where it could go.

He was the spokesman for a void that ached with loneliness rather than anger. We did not want to choke our fathers, but every one of us recognised those tensions that knotted us with growing pains.

An avalanche of material clouds the personal facts about Dean. David Dalton's biography is perhaps the most perceptive. Nevertheless conflicts abound. The importance of Pier Angeli to Dean varies from account to

> "I used to feel that he was a disturbed boy, tremendously dedicated to some intangible beacon of his own, and neither he nor anyone else might ever know what it was. I used to feel this because at times when he fell quiet and thoughtful, as if inner-bidden to dream about something, an odd and unconscious sweetness would light up his countenance. At such times, and because I knew he had been motherless since early childhood and had missed a lot of the love that makes boyhood jell, I would come to believe that he was still waiting for some lost tenderness."
>
> —George Stevens, director of Giant

account. They dated regularly and, against the wishes of her orthodox Italian-Catholic mother, hoped to marry. With little warning, she broke off the relationship and appeared at the altar on the arm of Vic Damone. In his book "Mislaid in Hollywood," Joe Hyams claims that Dean confessed tearfully that Pier Angeli was carrying his baby. Now she, too, is dead (as are so many of his contemporaries) and the truth remains a mystery.

The tiger-like Ursula Andress, then still new to Hollywood and unschooled in the ways of the film colony, was a friend and ally. They were so alike, in looks and temperament, that it was as though a narcissistic glass were between them. A meretricious American paperback, published recently, claims that Dean had a male lover who helped architect his career. Whatever these ambivalences, confusions, it was the burgeoning hurtfulness of youth that made him attractive, even in ugliness, in vileness. And when this spokesman was snatched away, a death almost heroic in its futility, the cult began.

In a bowling alley, a shrewd entrepreneur exhibited the mangled Porsche and charged fifty cents for morbid spectators to clamber through the bloodied wreck. Soon fans had stripped the pieces of torn metal away like vultures pecking at a carcass. Dean merchandising surged ahead, a bust of the actor was stolen from the cemetery days after its erection and his tombstone itself was chipped away. The small-time actors who had known Dean divided swiftly into those who wouldn't talk about him and those who would, to anyone.

The periphery of the cult was ultra-sick but young people growing up today, those who were born after Dean was buried in Indiana, recognise intuitively some quality that is still valid. Watching recently his television film, "The Unlighted Road," it came as a shock to see actresses swishing full '50s skirts, so undated is the technique of Dean's own performance.

The mourning fans who signed suicide pacts on the first anniversary of his death are not impossible to understand. At September 30, 1955 their sense of loss, of disenfranchisement, must have been acute. Rock, whose revolutionary parade Dean trailed, was to provide no single person who tweaked so contemporary a nerve-end.

As an actor, Dean was an interesting distillation of Montgomery Clift and Marlon Brando. But twenty years after his death, he has gone beyond the role of actor. As long as youth rebels against adult authority and holds that pure but angry ideal of a world-that-ought-to-be, the memory of Dean survives — a curiosity, an accident, a freak of sociology.

As a living actor, his professional decline would, I think, have been inevitable. The exquisite timing of his death fixes for all time his image and the hope it offered, like a frame of film that jams in the projector gate and remains, mysteriously unburned and unbuckled, frozen on a screen for anyone who cared to look at it.

Elizabeth Taylor and James Dean in Giant

e entertainment (1994) medienprogramm des monats

In memoriam

james dean

Vor 40 Jahren raste James Dean in den Tod. Er war gerade 24. In den Trümmern des silbergrauen Porsche 550 Spyder starb ein Junge, der mit nur drei Filmen die ganze Welt verändern sollte. Der Mythos vom sensiblen, unverstandenen Rebellen wirkt bis heute nach und hat nichts von seiner Faszination verloren. Doch was verbarg sich hinter dem Idol?

James Dean der schauspieler

James Dean the actor

„Jimmy war als Schauspieler extrem sensibel. Man konnte durch ihn hindurchsehen, direkt ablesen, was ihn bewegte. Sein Körper drückte seine Gefühle sehr plastisch aus; manchmal wandte er sich wie in großen Schmerzen, krümmte sich regelrecht, als wäre er verkrüppelt oder würde unter spastischen Anfällen leiden. Sogar seine Art zu gehen, erinnerte an einen Krebs, als wollte er beständig vor etwas ausweichen."
(Elia Kazan, Regisseur von „Jenseits von Eden")

"Jimmy was extremely sensitive as an actor. You could see through him, read directly what moved him." Elia Kazan

„Er befand sich ständig im Kampf mit seinem schauspielerischen Naturell, war hin- und hergerissen zwischen dem Wunsch, theatralisch zu sein, und dem Wunsch, wahrheitsgetreu zu spielen." (Mildred Dunnock, Schauspielerin)

James Dean der mythos

„Hätte er weitergelebt, er hätte seinem Ruf nie gerecht werden können."
(Humphrey Bogart, Mythos)

„Wir fühlten alle, daß er sich selbst spielte. Es war nicht nur eine Rolle. Die Rolle war er selbst." (Bob Dylan, Musiker)

"We all felt that he was playing himself. It was not just a role. The role was himself."

"James Dean was the model youths use to shape their image. He was, literally, the masterpiece, the mould from which sculptures are cast."

„James Dean war das Modell, nach dem die Jugend ihr Bild gestaltet hatte. Er war buchstäblich das Meisterstück, die Form, aus denen Plastiken gegossen werden. Seit Dean war Jungsein zum eigentlichen Ziel im Leben geworden. Was danach kam, schien weder vorstellbar noch erstrebenswert zu sein. Er hatte für uns die Entscheidung getroffen: Wir dürfen nie erwachsen werden." (David Dalton/Ron Coyen, James Dean – Sein Leben in Bildern)

„Wenn Brando die Art änderte, wie man schauspielert, änderte James Dean die Art, wie man lebt." (Martin Sheen, Schauspieler)

James Dean's favorite book was *The Little Prince*. It contains the sentence: "The truth is invisible."

James Deans Lieblingsbuch war „Der kleine Prinz" von Antoine de St. Exupery. Darin findet sich der Satz: „Die Wahrheit ist unsichtbar." In unzähligen Büchern, Zeitschriftenartikeln, Dokumentationen und Filmen wurde nach einer der vielen Wahrheiten über James Dean geforscht. Auf diesen und den folgenden Seiten kommen Menschen zu Wort, die ihn kannten und mit ihm zusammengearbeitet haben. Jeder von ihnen hat seine eigene Wahrheit über das Idol James Dean.

Deans Grab in Fairmount

James Dean der mensch

'He was the eternally mature hooligan'

„Er war der ewig frühreife Halbstarke, der immer gleichzeitig Aufmerksamkeit erheischte und einen zum Narren halten wollte." (Barney Hoskyns, „James Dean – Der Rebell von Hollywood")

'He had something sweet about him, even though he was some kind of bad boy.'t

„Er hatte etwas Süßes an sich, obwohl er so eine Art böser Junge war. Er kam mir vor wie ein Tom Sawyer. Er manipulierte seine Mitmenschen und wußte auch, daß er es tat." (Julie Harris, Deans Partnerin in „Jenseits von Eden")

„James Dean hatte keine Ader für Distanz oder Objektivität... das setzte eine Kompromißlosigkeit oder Arroganz voraus, die er im täglichen Leben mit fast katastrophalen Resultaten einsetzte." (Dean-Biograph John Hewlett)

„Man weiß nie, was Jimmy als nächstes tat." (Deans Onkel Marcus Winslow)

'You never know what Jimmy wtill do next.'

„Der Tod lauert überall, ich will ihn erobern." (Dean zu dem Komponisten Leonard Rosenman)

"Death lurks everywhere, I want to conquer it."

'I want to conquer death'

„ich will den Tod erobern"

„Es gibt nur eine Form von Größe für einen Mann. Wenn ein Mann den Abgrund zwischen Leben und Tod überbrücken kann – ich meine, wenn er weiterlebt nach dem Tod –, dann war er wohl ein großer Mann. Für mich liegt der einzige Erfolg, die einzige Größe in der Unsterblichkeit." (Dean 1953 in einem Brief an seinen Freund, Pastor James DeWeerd)

"If a man can bridge the abyss between life and death, if he lives on after death, then he must have been a great man."

„Er war ein verstörter Junge, der sich irgendeinem verschwommenen Leitstern verschrieben hatte, den weder er noch sonst jemand gesehen hatte." (George Stevens, Regisseur von „Giganten")

"He was a distraught boy who had committed himself to some blurry guide star that neither he nor anyone else had seen."

James Dean der liebhaber

James Dean the lover

In New York of the fifties, Jimmy would go beyond the greyness of his sexuality as he had never done before.

„Im New York der Fünfziger würde Jimmy die Grenzen seiner Sexualität so weit überschreiten, wie er es noch nie getan hatte. Mit einem jungen Tänzer hatte er eine wilde, hemmungslose Sexaffäre." (Paul Alexander in seiner Dean-Biographie „Boulevard of Broken Dreams")

He had a wild, unrestrained sex affair with a young dancer

„Pier war die einzige Frau, die ich liebte"

„Jimmy war der einzige Mann, den ich so innig geliebt habe, wie eine Frau einen Mann nur lieben kann."
(Pier Angeli, Schauspielerin)

„Sie war die einzige Frau, die ich liebte." **(Dean über Pier Angeli)**

„Jimmy war weder homosexuell noch bisexuell. Ich glaube, er war multisexuell. Er sagte einmal, daß es gar keine Bisexualität gibt. Er fühlte, daß wenn er seelische Unterstützung von einem Mann bräuchte, wäre er wahrscheinlich homosexuell, aber wenn er seelische Unterstützung von einer Frau bräuchte, wäre er mehr heterosexuell." **(Jonathan Gilmore, Schauspieler und Deans kurzzeitiger Liebhaber)**

„Man weiß nie, was er im nächsten Augenblick tun wird. Er soll die Zeilen so lesen, wie sie dastehen!" (Raymond Massey, Deans Filmvater in „Jenseits von Eden" während einer Drehpause)

"You never know what he will do in the next moment. He should say the lines as they stand!"

„Ich muß wissen, wer ich bin, ich muß wissen, wie ich bin." (James Dean als Jim Stark in „...denn sie wissen nicht, was sie tun")

„ich muß wissen, wer ich bin"

"I have to know who I am."

„Er trat nie vor die Kamera, ohne erstmal mit den Knien unterm Kinn Luftsprünge zu machen oder mit voller Geschwindigkeit um den Drehort zu rennen und dabei wie ein Raubvogel zu krächzen. Dean war schwer auszuhalten." (Rock Hudson, Deans Partner in „Giganten")

"He never stepped in front of the camera without jumping in the air with his knees under his chin or running around the set at full speed, screeching like a bird of prey."

"The guy just has to stop. He will see us soon." James Dean's last words

JAMES DEAN IN BILD UND TEXT

Wir verlosen 10 Biographien „Der einsame Rebell" von Joe und Jay Hyams (vgs; DM 44,–) und 10 Bildbände „Ein Porträt" von Roy Schatt (Schirmer/Mosel; DM 34,–)

PIN UP DEAN

Zu gewinnen gibt's jeweils zehn Riesenposter zu den drei James-Dean-Filmen (Close-Up-Posters)

REBELL AUF VIDEO

„Giganten", „...denn sie wissen nicht, was sie tun" und „Jenseits von Eden": Wir verlosen die komplette James-Dean-Edition auf Video (Warner Home Video)

Photoplay (UK)
January 1980

GOING GOING GONE

DAVE SMITH reports on a Sotheby's auction of movie posters

● WHEN *Rebel Without A Cause* was first released you could see the poster on any cinema front-of-house; on any street-corner hoarding; anywhere in fact, you cared to look. But 25 years on the posters have disappeared — into the film company vaults perhaps; onto the living room walls of people with connections; and the majority, no doubt, have just been screwed up and thrown away.

The point is, they're in scarce supply. Which goes some way to explaining why a single copy of the poster from James Dean's most famous role came under the hammer at Sotheby's recently — and was sold for £130.

That poster was the gem in a private collection of posters and stills that were auctioned by Sotheby's Belgravia, and raised in total nearly £1,000.

Attach the label "cult" to something, and you triple its value. And most of the items in this collection could be so described.

Some 50 people assembled before the auctioneer, and in a flurry of nods, winks, and gestures of hand, snapped up such goodies as *The Jolson Story* poster (£50), sets of stills from *The Graduate* and *If...* (£50), *The Prince And The Showgirl* poster (£90), a collection of stills from the Connery Bond movies (£20), and a poster advert for James Dean's *Giant* (£50).

"We expected some of the rarer items to go for higher prices," explained Hilary Kay, who conducted the sale. She had hoped to see the *Rebel Without A Cause* poster fetch nearer £250, *The Prince And The Showgirl* nearer £150.

Still, the buyers must have been happy. Four people did most of the bidding, and between them bought the majority of the lots.

Posters and stills from films appear on the Sotheby's calendar about once a year — so if you're thinking of attending the next one, you'd better start saving now.

D.S.

Bestenliste

Exklusiv in TV-SPIELFILM: Die Top- und die Flop-Liste. Wir sagen Ihnen, welche Filme Sie im Fernsehen auf keinen Fall versäumen dürfen und welche Sie sich lieber ersparen sollten. Zusätzlich finden Sie eine Bestenliste nach Filmgenres geordnet — vom Krimi bis zur Komödie, von Erotik bis zum Thriller. Die besten und die schlechtesten — übersichtlich aufbereitet auf einen Blick.

James Dean-Report

Der klassische Rebell einer jungen Generation war und ist das große Kino-Idol. Zu seinem 35. Todestag bringt TV-SPIELFILM alles über Leben, Tod und Filme des unsterblichen Kino-Rebellen

...denn sie wissen nicht, was sie tun

Mehr als jeder andere Hollywood-Film spiegelt er die Wünsche und Ängste einer ganzen Teenager-Generation wider. James Dean schuf einen Helden, der sowohl wild als auch zärtlich ist. Dieser Kultfilm um den klassischen Vater-Sohn-Konflikt läuft am Sonntag, 30.9., 22.10 Uhr.

Picturegoer (UK), December 1957

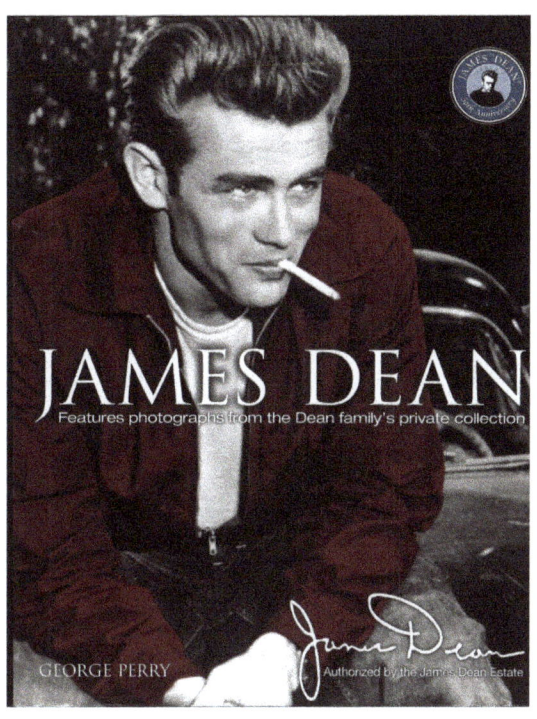

JAMES DEAN: A PORTRAIT
By Roy Schatt
Published by Sidgwick & Jackson £4.95

● Only close friends knew of James Dean's desire to become a photographer. Author/photographer Roy Schatt tells the story of a very special 'teacher and student' friendship with Dean who died in a car crash 26 years ago.

A small section at the front of the book covers personal memories and anecdotes while the rest of the book is full of photographs of James Dean or those taken by him.

November 1977

Neue „Gallery" eröffnet!
JAMES DEAN

Am 30. September 1955 raste James Dean mit seinem Porsche in den Tod. In seinem Heimatort Fairmount wurde jetzt die „James-Dean-Gallery" eröffnet.

In diesem alten Herrschaftshaus ist die „James-Dean-Gallery" untergebracht

David Loehr ist der größte Sammler von James-Dean-Erinnerungsstücken. Es gibt Hunderte von Ansteck-Buttons

Er drehte nur drei Filme („Jenseits von Eden", „...denn sie wissen nicht, was sie tun", „Giganten") und starb mit 24 Jahren. Aber der Kult um seine Person ist lebendig wie eh und je. Nun gibt es in Fairmount sogar eine „James-Dean-Gallery".

Dort ist die größte Sammlung der Welt an Erinnerungsstücken angehäuft. Zusammengetragen von dem New Yorker David Loehr, der sich selbst als größten James-Dean-Fan bezeichnet. Loehr zog mit seinen Kostbarkeiten durch die Staaten, ehe er sich zu diesem Museum entschloß. Es befindet sich in Fairmount, jenem Ort, an dem Dean geboren wurde und wo auch sein Grab ist.

Neben unzähligen Bildern, Postern, Filmplakaten in allen Sprachen, gibt es natürlich auch viel Kitsch zu sehen. Aber auch ein absolutes Highlight: Jenen Anzug, den Jimmy in „Giganten" trug. Vor vielen Jahren blätterte Loehr 2500 Dollar dafür hin.

Am 29. September werden sich in Fairmount die treuesten Fans treffen, um in einer stillen Feierstunde ihres Idols zu gedenken. Am 30. September, dem Todestag, gibt es auf dem Friedhof einen Gedenk- und Trauergottesdienst.

Ralf Brunkow

Fotos: Kaplan, FMS

Auch viel Kitsch ist im James-Dean-Museum zu sehen, wie Teller und Trinkbecher

„Direktor" David Loehr (Mitte) mit zwei Mitarbeitern vor der Postersammlung der drei Filme von James Dean

Rebel with a Shrine

In a culture that worships youth, James Dean remains one of our most potent icons—a young man for whom youth itself was a torture
By MOLLY HASKELL

Shrine of St. James: Cramming the Manhattan loft (*above*) of David Loehr, James Dean fan and archivist, are the treasures of his obsession—posters, ashtrays, hallowed relics like costumes from Dean's films. This month, Loehr—whose many Dean projects include an annual six-hour walking tour of his idol's NYC hangouts—puts his cult kitsch on permanent display. The James Dean Gallery will be located in Fairmount, Indiana—Dean's hometown, visited by thousands of faithful each year. *Left*, Dean in Warner makeup for *Giant*. *Inset*, clowning with death in L.A. apartment. —RICHARD ALLEMAN

DIE YOUNG, STAY PRETTY LUCRATIVE

He starred in just three high-profile roles, but 60 years after his death, **James Dean** has continued to infuse popular culture, and music in particular. Patrick Humphries looks back at his short life and his enduring impact

Hard to believe, but James Dean, the archetypal Rebel Without A Cause, died 60 years ago this year, on 30 September 1955. True to his "live fast, die young" philosophy, it was at the wheel of a Porsche on his way to a race meeting.

The short life of the star is well known; what fascinated me is the legend which began immediately after his death. In life, Dean was a promising newcomer; in death he became a legend – and an industry.

James Dean didn't know about rock'n'roll: he died before it came along. But rock'n'roll knew all about James Dean. His image as the archetypal rebel without a cause, the moody, misunderstood teenage outsider influenced everyone from Bob Dylan to Morrissey; from Brett Anderson to Lady GaGa.

And that incendiary, brief, bright burning flame also registered with subsequent rock'n'roll icons – the careers of Nick Drake, Jim Morrison, Jimi Hendrix, Kurt Cobain, Amy Winehouse… all blazing talents cut off in their prime.

Of course, part of the Dean legend is that incredibly short career – he only lived to attend the premiere of one of his films, *East Of Eden*. By the time *Rebel Without A Cause* and *Giant* were released, he was long gone.

The cult of James Dean began immediately after his passing. His studio was still under siege from bereft fans, who wrote letters by the sackful. Fanzines and societies commemorating him sprang into existence.

But the cult really came alive 20 years after Dean's death. In the mid-70s, in the wake of

"TOWERING OVER THAT MUSICAL LANDSCAPE WAS THE FIRST US TEENAGER"

Don McLean's American Pie, rock music and youth culture began looking over their shoulders. The success of films like *American Graffiti* and *That'll Be The Day*, John Lennon's *Rock & Roll* album, and retro groups such as Showaddywaddy and Sha Na Na all harkened to the 1950s. And towering over that landscape was the immortal figure of the first American teenager…

James Byron Dean was born on 8 February 1931. His mother died when he was only nine, which saw him raised by his aunt and uncle in rural Indiana. Dean was an average, short-sighted teenage boy, milking cows on the farm, driving tractors and roaring round town on his motorcycle (a photo of which Morrissey selected for The Smiths' Bigmouth Strikes Again). At school he excelled at baseball and basketball, but following a suggestion from his estranged father, Winton, he joined him out in California.

As a 15-year-old, Dean witnessed Marlon Brando in his film debut, *The Men*. As a result, he switched to studying drama at the University Of California, Los Angeles (UCLA). It was there he acquired an agent, landing bit parts in the movies as teenagers.

He made his film debut in the 1951 production *Fixed Bayonets*, but his one line ("It's a rear guard coming back") ended up on the cutting room floor. He can be glimpsed in the Dean Martin and Jerry Lewis comedy *Sailor Beware*.

But Dean's first on-screen utterance came in a Rock Hudson vehicle *Has Anybody Seen My Gal*. Though it hardly suggested future greatness: "Hey pops, I'll have a choc malt – heavy on the choc, plenty of milk, four spoons of malt, two scoops of vanilla, one mixed and one floating!"

With lines like that, Dean decided maybe Hollywood was not for him, and headed out East to try his luck on the stage.

New York City in 1952 was buzzing… There were the stages of Broadway or the studios where live television was broadcast. And there was jazz. Dean immersed himself in the subterranean world of the city's jazz clubs. He was fascinated by the rhythms he could pound out on his bongo drums. At one point, he even busked alongside New York street legend Moondog.

Enlisting in drama classes, Dean was pictured alongside Eartha Kitt, who gave him dance classes. Sammy Davis Jr was a friend. He dated the first Bond girl, Ursula Andress. Dean was spellbound by Charlie Parker and frequented the clubs along 52nd Street and cellars of Greenwich Village. Boppin' to Chet Baker, Miles Davis, Parker… he loved the sound of Big Maybelle singing Tweedle Dee, Big Mama Thornton's original Hound Dog, Billie Holiday, Sinatra's *Songs For Young Lovers*, African music, Bartok, blues.

Then it was back hustling for roles – the TV work was forgettable, but plentiful. He was energetic in a Pepsi commercial, was a warm-up man for *Beat The Clock*, and played "troubled" individuals in dramas such as *Death Is My Neighbor*, *A Long Time Till Dawn* and *Glory In The Flower*. He specialised in psychos, hoods and juvenile delinquents.

Short runs in Broadway plays cemented Dean's reputation for truculence: he really was a rebellious figure. Fortuitously, one night in 1954, a Hollywood director was in the audience and James Dean's career was assured. It was Elia Kazan, who had steered Brando to stardom in *A Streetcar Named Desire* and *On The Waterfront*, effectively bringing "the Method" to the movies. Brando's naturalism and animal magnetism ushered in a new era of screen acting. But Kazan was looking for a younger, edgier actor to play the troubled Cal in his next film, a lavish adaptation of John Steinbeck's novel *East Of Eden*.

The title is taken from the Bible and the name was later adopted by one-hit, several-decent-album wonders best known for the 1971 track Jig-A-Jig (Bruce Springsteen also cites it in Adam Raised A Cain), and it was the 1955 film *East Of Eden* which hurled James Dean to stardom. It was the only one of his three films he lived to see open, and it is often forgotten in any appreciation of Dean just how good he is in that breakthrough role.

Troubled and tormented, surly and rebellious, the unknown actor is compelling throughout. The antagonism with his screen father Raymond Massey is palpable. Dean brilliantly brings to life his character's willingness to be accepted in the family, but his resistance to compromise.

One of his co-stars was the folk singer Burl Ives. An under-valued chronicler of American folk music, Ives had travelled with Woody Guthrie and Pete Seeger during the 1930s Great Depression. But due to his testimony at the infamous McCarthy anti-Communist witch-hunts, where he "named names" of "known Communists", Ives was vilified.

Dean brought a naturalism to his acting in his starring debut, but it was his next role with which he is most closely identified: *Rebel Without A Cause*.

The film had begun life when the studio inexplicably purchased a 1946 psychiatric text, *Rebel Without A Cause: The Hypnoanalysis Of A Criminal Psychopath*. It had lain on the shelves for years until a rewritten script saw Dean cast as Jim Stark. It was a part in which he became the emblem of teenage 50s rebellion, an image maintained ever since.

The year the film opened also witnessed the premiere *of The Blackboard Jungle*, where the clarion call of Bill Haley's Rock Around The Clock was first heard. This was the movie which sent spasms through the establishment of cosy Eisenhower America and conservative UK. When the film finally opened in Liverpool, a teenage John Lennon was disappointed to find there were no gangs of Teddy Boys slashing the cinema seats, which he'd been led to believe would accompany every screening!

Rebel Without A Cause had the same effect, but its impact was intensified by the fact that the film's star had died months before. As well as Lennon, all the 60s idols went to see *Rebel* – Mick Jagger, Bob Dylan, Keith Richards... they all tripped to their local fleapit to pay homage.

In his red windcheater, Dean came to represent the archetypal teenager, the one whose parents couldn't comprehend him and was always going to be an outsider. Leonard Rosenman's cool jazz score underlined Jim Stark's outsider status.

Dean lived the life of an outsider too – rumours abound of his homosexuality, his bisexuality, his penchant for masochistic sex. Sifting through the gossip, it looks like Dean's true love was the actress Pier Angeli, but her strictly orthodox Catholic parents disapproved. True to his outsider chic, the day she married crooner Vic Damone, Dean lingered across the street; when the happy couple emerged from church, Dean gunned his motorcycle and disappeared for days.

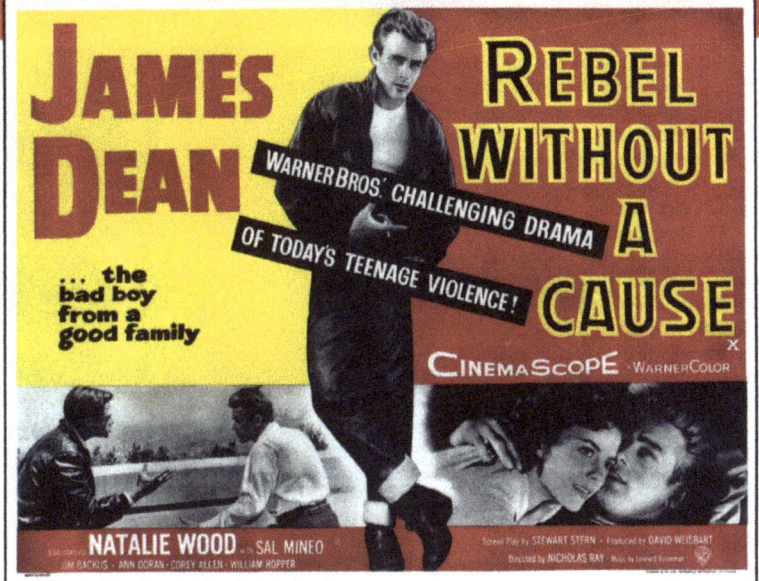

Just 10 days after he finished filming *Rebel*… Dean was in Texas to begin his final film, *Giant*. A sprawling tale of oil, it pre-empted *Dallas* by two decades. It found him acting alongside Rock Hudson (who loathed him) and Elizabeth Taylor (who loved him).

Giant is the only film which saw James Dean stretch himself as an actor. We watch his character Jett Rink age, and in the film's final scenes, as an old man, we witness James Dean disappearing before our eyes.

He probably was a better actor than was appreciated in the hysteria which accompanied his premature death. There is an edgy naturalness to his screen presence. He manages to suggest something introspective, and a fleeting thought behind his eyes. Dean conveyed a brooding, pensive presence in his starring roles. Just look at the contrast between his twitchy Jett in *Giant* and Rock Hudson's lumbering, old-school performance.

Dean was scheduled to star as boxer Rocky Graziano in *Somebody Up There Likes Me* and as Billy The Kid in *The Left-Handed Gun*. Ironically, both roles went to Paul Newman, who had unsuccessfully auditioned for the part of Dean's brother in *East Of Eden* (Morrissey chose Dick Davalos, who did play Aron Trask, for the sleeve of *Strangeways Here We Come*).

James Dean was looking to play the ultimate misunderstood rebel: Hamlet. Just prior to his death, Dean talked about Shakespeare's flawed hero: "Only a young man can play him as he was… Laurence Olivier played it safe. Something is lost when the older man plays him… This kind of Hamlet isn't the stumbling, feeling, reaching, searching boy that he really was."

But it was never to be. On his way to a race meeting in his brand new Porsche Spyder, James Dean crashed at the junction of Highways 466 and 41. He was 24 years old and the accident's only fatality.

Dean's short life is shadowed by death – one of his favourite sayings was: "Live fast, die young and leave a good-looking corpse!" Mere weeks before his death, eerily, he was filmed on the set of *Giant* for a road safety commercial. "People say racing is dangerous," Dean mutters, "but I'd rather take my chance on the race track than on the highway." The line he was meant to say was, "Take it easy

driving, the life you save may be yours," but a fortnight before his death on a California highway, what he actually said as he addressed the camera was, "Take it easy driving, the life you save may be mine."

Even Hollywood was unprepared for the hysteria which followed Dean's death. Within weeks, trash magazines appeared: "Did James Dean Really Die?"; "James Dean Speaks From Beyond The Grave!"; "James Dean Is Alive!". For years after his death, his Hollywood studio was still receiving 4,000 fan letters a week, addressed to a dead star.

And the "tribute" discs soon followed – 100 or so, including His Name Was Dean, We'll Never Forget You, Remembering James Dean, The Death Of James Dean.

In 1957 the Robert Altman film *The James Dean Story* opened. Fans slept out overnight to glimpse the dead 24-year-old icon. Actually a documentary, there were plans to feature a young up-and-coming star playing Dean in dramatised sequences.

Elvis Presley was approached to play him in the biopic, but the producers weren't willing to take a chance on such an unknown. While making his first film, *Love Me Tender*, Elvis heard director Nicholas Ray was in the studio commissary and literally knelt at his feet. Ray recalled: "He knew I was a friend of Jimmy's and had directed *Rebel*, so he got down on his knees before me and began to recite whole passages of dialogue from the script."

The singer later admitted he must have seen *Rebel Without A Cause* "a hundred times". When *Rebel* opened in late 1955, Elvis was a regional phenomenon, little known above the Mason-Dixon line. By the time Dean's final film *Giant* premiered in November 1956, Elvis was the biggest entertainment sensation in America, with five No 1 singles in the US alone that year.

Incredibly, in the short-lived world of youth culture, the James Dean cult showed no sign of diminishing. Robert Shelton opened his striking biography of Bob Dylan, *No Direction Home*, with the young Robert Zimmerman returning to his Hibbing, Minnesota, home after watching *Giant* and

going down to his basement den, the walls covered in pictures of the late movie star.

He was Bob Dylan's first idol, even before he discovered Woody Guthrie. In an early bootleg, the young Bob boasts about early photos taken on his arrival in New York: "You should see me, man, I look like Marlon Brando, James Dean…" And that cover of *Freewheelin'* carries echoes.

But Dylan's most obvious Dean identification came on the cover of his third album: while the obvious parallel on The Times They Are A-Changin' was with Woody, the angle and look of Barry Feinstein's cover photo recalled the classic "torn sweater" shot of Dean taken by Roy Schatt.

And while on his Never Ending tour in 1988, Dylan went to Fairmont, Indiana to pay homage. The James Dean Museum was opened especially for Dylan, who spent an hour roaming the artefacts and memorabilia of the actor who had influenced him so strongly as a teenager.

Another pilgrim to the small Indiana town was Morrissey, whose Suedehead video was filmed at Dean's grave. But then Dean was also the subject of young SP Morrissey's second book, *James Dean Is Not Dead*.

The Beatles' original bassist Stuart Sutcliffe was largely kept in the group not because of his musical virtuosity, but because of his resemblance to James Dean. In the *Anthology* book, Paul McCartney stated: "Stuart had got himself looking like James Dean. He would put his shades on and stand there with his bass – it was all a big pose."

Years later Lennon reflected on his teenage years: "Not only did we dress like James Dean and walk around like that, but we acted out those cinematic charades."

It was in the early 70s that Dean began to really percolate through rock culture – Don McLean included him in American Pie – he was, in fact, the only real person (aside from Lenin and Marx) named in the song. Lou Reed in 1972's Walk On The Wild Side was another to use Dean as a shorthand for cool. David Essex's 1974 breakthrough hit Rock On had Dean running through it like veins in a blue cheese.

The success of the film soundtracks of *American Graffiti* and *That'll Be The Day* testified to an audience happy to cast their minds back to the simpler, uncomplicated days of rock'n'roll. Inevitably, Dean was either referenced or became a handy visual symbol of that era.

One of the earliest tributes had come with The Beach Boys' A Young Man Is Gone, which struck an incongruously sombre note on 1963's *Little Deuce Coupe* LP. The group's voices blend beguilingly around lyrics by Bobby Troup (author of Route 66 and The Girl Can't Help It).

In song, Dean has been memorably commemorated by The Eagles (with a little help from Jackson Browne and JD Souther). James Dean (the song) became the band's sixth single, and a standout track on their third album, *On The Border*. Whether deliberately or by coincidence, The Eagles headlined what has been called "the crowning achievement… [of] the entire Southern Californian rock scene". Alongside Jackson Browne and Linda Ronstadt, they packed out Los Angeles' Anaheim Stadium – and the date chosen was 30 September 1975, the 20th anniversary of the death of James Dean.

Ray Connolly's exemplary 1975 documentary *James Dean: The First American Teenager* further cemented the links between Dean and rock'n'roll. As well as The Eagles' song, the Dean legend is explored to a background of music from Elton John and

"You'll cry, you'll dance, you'll close" – News Of The World
"F****ing great – see the f***ing thing" – Kenneth Tynan

Fairly original songs by R.Z. Immerman & Phil Ochs
Any resemblance to James Dean is purely in the minds of the stars

Johnnie Fahey   Steve Morrissey   Nicholas Heyward   Ricky Nelson

David Bowie. It's no surprise that Dean was venerated by the generation which grew up with his movies at the cinema – thus Van Morrison's Wild Children from 1973's *Hard Nose The Highway* is an epitaph for the "war children" of 1945, citing Dean and Brando. School Days, the opening track of Loudon Wainwright III's eponymous 1970 debut is a reflection on youthful promise, where he compares himself to Brando and Dean, then rather flamboyantly Keats and Blake, before concluding with, uh, Buddha and Christ.

That same year (on the ironically titled *Greatest Hits* album), Phil Ochs' worthy, but really rather tedious Jim Dean Of Indiana was further evidence of Dean's impact.

A quarter of a century after his death, Dean was still being cited: Bruce Springsteen's rambunctious Cadillac Ranch was one of the jaunty rockers on 1980's *The River* which mentions Dean, as did John Mellencamp's 1982 US No.1 Jack & Diane. Mellencamp even went as far as adopting Dean's "Little Bastard" nickname (it was the name of his last car) himself. Tom Petty's 1985 track Spike, from the *Southern Accents* album, mentions Dean. Mick Jagger testified on 1987's Primitive Cool ("Did you walk cool in the 50s daddy? Did you dress like James Dean?"); Billy Joel's shopping-list 1989 single We Didn't Start The Fire contained the obligatory Dean mention.

And on into the 90s the references continued: Madonna's Vogue was a 1990 UK No 1. John Prine's Picture Show was from 1991's *The Missing Years*. Even Suede submitted to the cult on Daddy's Speeding (from 1994's *Dog Man Star*), Brett Anderson revealing he wrote it after a dream about Dean, later reflecting: "He's become this utter cliche… and yet at the heart of him, there was something really powerful."

Sheryl Crow got in on the act with Hard To Make A Stand, from her eponymous 1996 second album. Of them all, REM's Electrolite (from *New Adventures In Hi-Fi*) included him in a touching trilogy as Michael Stipe sang: "Hollywood is under me, I'm Martin Sheen, I'm Steve McQueen, I'm Jimmy Dean…"

With all the new technology, the Dean legend now extends into the 21st Century, on DVD, Blu-ray and the internet, a testament to his "iconic" status. Daniel Bedingfield hit big with James Dean (I Wanna Know) in 2002. Then the ladies took over – Lady GaGa (Speechless, 2009), "With your James Dean glossy eyes"; Beyoncé (Rather Die Young, 2011), "Boy you'll be the death of me, You're my James Dean... You drive too fast, you smoke too much." Lana Del Rey (Blue Jeans, 2012); and of course, Taylor Swift (Style, 2014), "You got that James Dean daydream look in your eye…"

Amazing that, after more than half a century, these divas are testifying to an actor who still exemplifies cool.

The James Dean estate is overseen by his cousin, with an estimated yearly turnover of $5m. Dean's image has been licensed to more than 250 products since his death, including

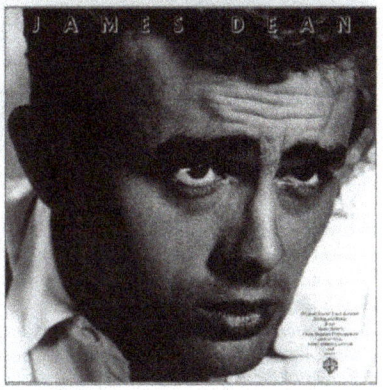

Levi's jeans, the National Westminster bank, Rebel Yell bourbon and 4711 cologne. Oh, and pillow cases, towels, lighters, coasters, trainers, designer glasses, watches, jigsaws, belt buckles… all featuring the image of an actor who only ever starred in three films and died 60 years ago.

In 2005, the 50th anniversary of Dean's death, there was an array of events across America. The most ghoulish must have been when a replica of the car Dean was driving when he died, a Porsche Spyder 550, toured the country. The original car literally disappeared as fans stole parts when it was displayed over the years, with the chassis finally vanishing in 1985!

Dean's influence on actors was manifest: Steve McQueen, Al Pacino, Robert De Niro all slouched onscreen in the style of Jimmy Dean. Martin Sheen's career began when he played a moody murderer obsessed with James Dean in the 1973 cult film *Badlands*, a tale which went on to inspire Bruce Springsteen's *Nebraska*. Over the years, Leonardo DiCaprio, Brad Pitt, Robert Pattinson and Johnny Depp have all been considered to play Dean in a biopic.

All these years later, Dean maintains his cool. Fashion journalist Peter Lyle commented: "You never see a bad photo of him… There were bad pictures of Clint before he became Clint and there are bad pictures of Warren Beatty when he looked clean cut. You never see bad pictures of Dean." That T-shirt, jeans and red windcheater look remains timeless. Oh, and he had great hair for 1953. In 2010, Tommy Hilfiger name-checked Dean for his summer collection.

There was something almost wholesome about Dean's demise – not for him the sad decline of Presley or the shattering suicide of Kurt Cobain; not Janis Joplin's solitary drug overdose or Lennon's senseless murder. The actor's friend, the sculptor Kenneth Kendall, identified part of Dean's enduring appeal: "One wonderful thing about dead movie stars – they can't disappoint you. And that's about *all* the live ones are capable of doing."

Of course, there is endless speculation about how his career would have developed, had he lived. Contemporaries such as Paul Newman enjoyed a distinguished career right up to the end, whereas Marlon Brando frittered away his considerable talent. But the idea of an 80-year-old rebel is iconoclastic.

James Dean never did find what he was searching for, and that quest probably plays a part of his ongoing appeal. And that feeling that he never quite achieved his potential, leaving a sense of what-might-have-been, is perhaps at the heart of our continuing fascination with an actor who died 60 years ago, who leaves such a slim celluloid legacy.

Forty years ago, Andy Warhol perceptively reflected on the actor: "He is not our hero because he was perfect, but because he perfectly represented the damaged but beautiful soul of our time."

You can pick up the 2CD + DVD package The James Dean Story *(Blue Moon BMCD 4104) for around a fiver – a package which includes the Altman film, music from Dean's film soundtracks, a couple of those cringe-worthy singles, trailers for the three classic films and three of Dean's TV plays.*

James Dean let out a great wail in the middle of a decorous decade, shook us all with the violence and nakedness of his need for love, and then he was gone. His death, in an automobile accident on September 30, 1955, inspired a cult as crazed as Valentino's: screamers and weepers would gather at the "site" where Dean's Porsche crashed; scavengers would ransack his apartment and dismantle his car. Now their successors, who may never have seen *East of Eden* or *Rebel Without A Cause* in Cinemascope, will have a shrine to worship at in the form of a museum in his hometown of Fairmount, Indiana.

I was never drawn to candle-burning, but the fanaticism surrounding Dean I can understand. *East of Eden* was released in 1955, just before he died, *Rebel* soon after, and *Giant* the following year. For those of us who were teenagers when we saw and were stunned by his three great performances, a new star had appeared in the firmament. Here was a young person for whom youth itself was torture; someone who was beautiful, and baffled and "bad" in ways we felt ourselves to be. As the patron saint of teenagers, he had put us on the map and altered the balance of power forever. And as an androgynous new male icon, he presided over the first slippage of sexual roles.

Teenagers are now an institution, a "market," a fifty-first state with its own language, movies, brat-pack stars, and arsenal of defenses—contempt and withering scorn against weak and ineffectual parents. But when Dean came along, families—movie families—co-existed in the relative harmony of shared values. Boys wanted to grow up to be like their fathers (and, for that matter, girls like their mothers). With postwar material success, America was ready to turn its attention inward, to the suburban *(Continued on page 752)*

James Dean

(Continued from page 686)

dream, to the Puritan ethic, and to the Oedipal underbrush on which Freud had turned his spotlight. A chasm was opening between the generations, and Dean was on the edge of it.

When he flailed against a pious, hypocritical father (Raymond Massey's righteous patriarch in *Eden*) or a henpecked dishwasher (Jim Backus in *Rebel*), raged at the mother who'd abandoned him (Jo Van Fleet in *Eden*), Dean fought in the name of emotional honesty and "authenticity" over the prevailing emphasis on appearances, on moral rectitude. His brooding face on posters, the hangdog look tell only half the story: for in articulating all that was inarticulate in teenage misery, he was fearless, mercurial, aggressive, forcing every secret mood, every smoldering resentment out into the open. His body, taut one minute, slack the next, was as eloquent as his voice. "He doesn't say much," says Sal Mineo of his idol in *Rebel Without A Cause*, "but when he does, he means it."

Dean shared with some of the greatest stars of the past—Olivier, Garbo, Gary Cooper, Dietrich, Mae West, Katharine Hepburn—an androgynous image. But Dean took it a step further, blurring the boundaries not only between male and female but between adult and child. He was a lusty twenty-four-year-old man playing a fumbling teenager, impelled by the polymorphous desires of an infant.

"Girls really run after you," Julie Harris says to him twice in *East of Eden*; and so, for the first time almost openly, did boys. Sal Mineo's Plato in *Rebel Without A Cause* idolizes him with something more than the comradely admiration with which his namesake is associated. Dean turns the same lost, yearning look on everyone because, for him, everyone is a potential mother. As with Brando, another androgynous actor, Dean's fusion of male and female qualities may have resulted from being the child of an artistic mother (Dean's died when he was eight) and a remote businessman father. Unlike Brando, however, Dean seems more at ease with his feminine side and therefore with women.

Dean seems to have defined a generation, and indeed, male "softness" has become commonplace, so much so that stoicism may be making a comeback in such refreshingly stiff-upper-lipped types as Kevin Costner and Harrison Ford. But "soft" may be the wrong word for Dean. Vulnerable, yes, but shrewd and tyrannical with his genius. He knew how to keep everyone off balance, to reach into the depths of his psyche, and to get the last word, as the actors he upstaged can tell you. Onscreen and off. Remember when his sweetheart, Pier Angeli, spurned the unstable romantic for Vic Damone? Dean came to the church, waited outside on his motorcycle, and, when the bride and groom emerged, gunned his machine noisily as they kissed. Our hearts were broken, but could it have been otherwise? Dean in Damone's shoes, embarking on a 'fifties marriage—with stardom, children, maturity, old age? Wasn't he far happier out in the streets, a Byronic figure, gunning his motorcycle, enjoying the drama of his rejection—and stealing the scene completely from his ladylove? ▽

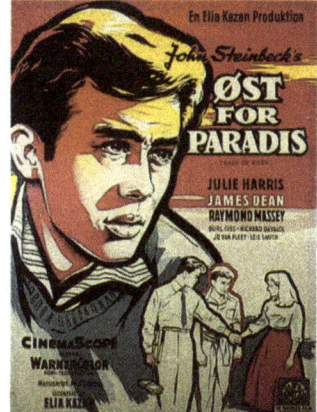

A Danish poster for *East of Eden*

> He turned the same lost, yearning look on everyone because, for him, everyone was a potential mother

Mark Sinker, *Sight & Sound* (UK), June 1998

James Dean
Before Clift and Brando, a screen persona broadcast inner immutability – and if all was confused and provisional within, the surface read as depthless flibbertigibbet. Now watch Dean (b. 1931) as Jett Rink in *Giant* (1956, above) against three interminable hours of immutable Rock Hudson. Dean's misfit Texan nobody turned mumbling racist millionaire is impossible to figure, but you can't stop thinking about what you're not seeing. Dean's gift to acting isn't 'youth' or 'rebellion', but a genius for liminal states. His death at 24 froze the subject matter of *Rebel without a Cause* (1955) into myth and he was appropriated en masse by teens bent on sentimentalising themselves (among them Dennis Hopper, who for years shoehorned a monotonous troubled teen into Westerns none the better for it). With its overlapping cast (Hopper, pretty little Sal Mineo), *Giant* hints at where Dean and Method might have gone. Some way in he finally lets fly: covered in oil, Jett's a sticky black man leering at rich white Liz Taylor; later he's winningly funny (if badly made-up) as a middle-aged success on the brink of drunken disaster. Elsewhere 50s adolescence rarely achieves such ambiguities: Natalie Wood is wide-eyed, winsome and troubled in *Rebel*, a mutely unturbulent victim in *The Searchers* (1956), virginal and magnificently frazzled in *Splendor in the Grass* (1961).

Hellraiser James Dean hogs his hometown limelight

JAMES Dean cozies up to a prize porker in his hometown, Fairmount, Ind., in 1955. It was his last visit to his old stomping grounds. Seven months later, the 24-year-old actor was dead.

As a teen growing up in the strait-laced town, Dean was every bit the hellion he portrayed in *Rebel Without a Cause*. According to classmate Sandy Hill, he was "a little off-limits — almost juvenile delinquent status."

Once during study hall he latched onto a girl's bra strap and let it snap. Another time, at a weekend dance for teens, he brought an out-of-town girl with whom he remained lip-locked for most of the night.

"The chaperones sent everyone home early and that was the last of those weekend dances," says Hill.

STAR September 1, 1998

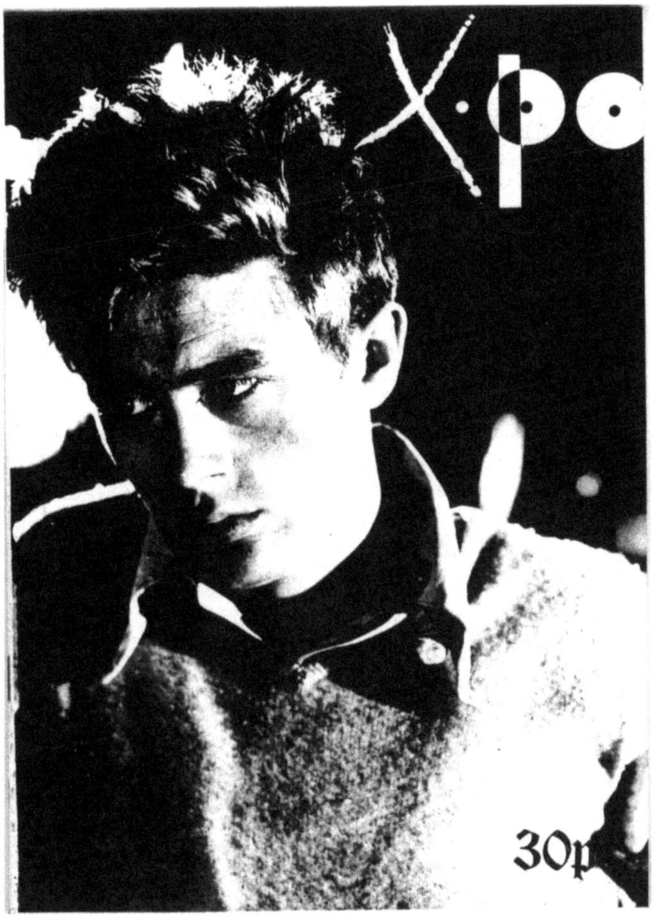

The Life and Death of James Dean

by Paul Sutton

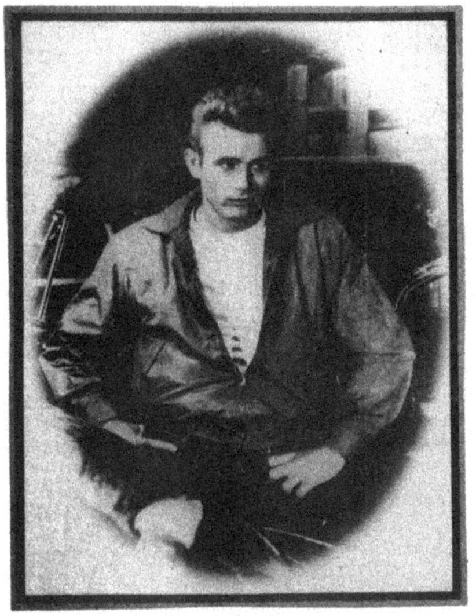

February 8th, 1931 — 30th September, 1955.

Loughborough University, January 1987

James Byron Dean was born in Marion, Indiana to a Quaker family that could be traced back to the 'Mayflower'. His mother died from breast cancer when he was nine years old, and his father in debt with medical bills, sent him to live with his Aunt Winslow in Fairmount.

"*Jimmy had a terrible anger for his mother*" said Barbara Glenn, an actress he later dated, "*she died. He was a nine-year-old child saying how can you leave me? When he talked about her, it wasn't a twenty-one or twenty-two-year old. It was a child and he was deserted . . . He loved her desperately and she left him. I think it had a profound effect on him. And he expressed it in terms of his art.*"

In high school Jimmy excelled at sport. He broke the pole vault record for Grant County despite poor eyesight and a shortage of height (5' 10"), and was a star of the *Fairmount Quakers* basketball team. He won regional public speaking competitions, and at the age of eighteen came sixth in the U.S. nationals with a rendition of *The Madman* from Charles Dicken's *The Pickwick Papers*. But attempts to develop these thetrical skills were halted by his father — in 1949 *normal* American sons didn't do 'Dramatics and the Free Arts' — Jimmy reluctantly enrolled, for a short time, at the Santa Monica college majoring in P.E. before entering U.C.L.A. to study theatre arts. He was accepted by the Sigma Nu fraternity even though he needed artificial resusitation when his swimming pool initiation stunt went wrong.

It was here , California, where Dean won his first professional acting job — a sixty second commercial for Coca cola. In the ad Jimmy handed out cokes to other kids on a merry-go-round. A simple task but what fuel it gave the elaborate theorist of the future — Jimmy (soon to become the screen image of disaffected youth) handing out Coca Cola (established symbol of free America) to happy smiling, *conforming* teenagers on a roundabout (spinning to represent the imminent turbulence of America's youth culture) — hmm.

His first television appearance came a few days later. Jimmy played John the Apostle in an Easter Holiday special *Hill Number One*. Although he had only three lines and his appearance was brief, it brought him his first fan club — The Immaculate Heart James Dean Appreciation Society, high school girls who wooed him to a party they held in his honour — and it led to his first motion picture assignment: a bit part in a Korean war film **Fixed Bayonets**. His one line "*it's a rear guard coming back*" was cut, so all that remained of Jimmy was a shot of his muddied face.

After being expelled from his fraternity for "*hitting a couple of the other guys*", Jimmy went east to New York City. Hoping to begin a career in television he was hired by *Beat The Clock*, a weekly TV show on which contestants had to attempt *impossible* stunts in order to win cash prizes. It was one of the most popular shows in America. Jimmy's job, week after week for one year, was to single-handedly solve *all* the problems, thereby justifying the *impossible*.

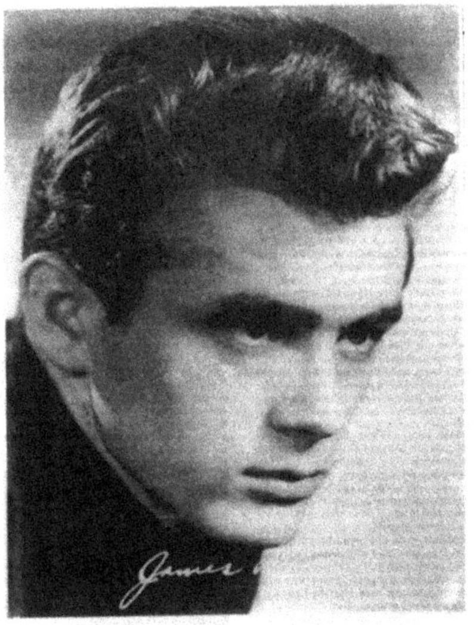

The pay was poor. Jimmy lived in near poverty in a run down apartment and often went days without food. But 1951 had been television's first year of general programming. Five hundred live dramas were to be presented in 1952 alone so there was opportunity enough for any number of budding young hopefuls to live their "*fifteen minutes of fame*".

James Dean's first New York television appearance was on May 11th, 1952. It was in an hour long drama, fittingly entitled **Prologue To Glory**. Within a year he would have the Broadway theatre on its feet, within three years he would be a star in Hollywood, and within four years he would be dead.

Major roles followed in fourteen similar television dramas, but what is left of Jimmy's TV career are mere fragments. Studios lost or destroyed his old kinescopes and films unaware. Today there exists only a few press release photographs, a bootleg LP with the complete soundtracks to a couple of his shows, and a brief scene from a television special **Teen-Age Idols** which has Jimmy screaming and being killed by machine gun fire.

James Dean first appeared on Broadway in **See The Jaguar**. The play opened on December 3rd, 1952. Jimmy played a young boy who's been locked in an ice-house all his life ("*hid from all the meanness of the world*") by a zealously over-protective mother. One critic noted that Jimmy "*played the part with sweetness and naivete that made the tortures singularly poignant*" and added "*an extraordinary performance in an almost impossible role . . .* ". But however 'sweet' the notice is the play closed after five performances.

Dean became a student of the Stanislavsky 'Method' which developed his naturalistic acting style. Students were taught to collect a repertoire of gestures and mannerisms, the material of life from which they can build a character. "*An actor*" said Dean, "*must interpret life, and to do so must be willing to accept all experiences that life has to offer. In fact, he must seek out more of life than life puts at his feet. In the short span of his lifetime an actor must learn all there is to know, experience all there is to experience – or approach that state as closely as possible.*" Jimmy studied Bach with Frank Caparo, dance with Katherine Dunham and played bongos with Cyril Jackson.

His second (and final) Broadway role was in **The Immoralist**. Dean's portrayal of Bachir — a thieving homosexual Arab houseboy — earned him two awards, the 'Tony' and the 'Daniel Blum' award, both for the most promising actor of the year.

Jimmy was touchy and uneasy about the sexual ambivalence of the role. Speculation about his sexuality is still rife though, as writes David Dalton, author of the definitive Dean book 'The Mutant King', "*the form it has taken has usually been self-conscious, using Jimmy as a libidinous mirror.*" Fictionalized homosexual incidents, written to satisfy the voyeuristic perversions of adolescent dreamers appeared in a couple of pulp biodramas — *Farewell My Slightly Tarnished Hero* by Ed Corley and *The Immortal* by Walter Ross. 'The Sun' newspaper's recent linking of Dean with AIDS tragedy Rock Hudson (Dean's co-star in **Giant**) is absurd. The two hated each other. Dean made no secret of his disrespect for Hudson's wooden acting style, and Hudson in a 1970 'Hollywood Reporter' interview said about Dean " . . . *he was always angry and full of contempt . . . He was sulky; and he had no manners. I'm not that concerned with manners – I'll take them where I find them – but Dean didn't have 'em.*"

James Dean however, did feel that he was prey to latent homosexuality. He wrote with characteristic irony to Barbara Glenn: "*I'm staying in a guy's apartment while he flies to London . . . He's been staying here with me. He also considers me a victim. I refuse to be sucked into things of that nature (pun, ha ha) Street urchin again.*"

Bill Bast made a list of all the people who claimed to have lived with James Dean, and added up the time they claimed to have spent with him. If all their claims were true, James would have been a hundred and forty seven years old when he died.

Aside from opeing up the floodgates of the future gossip columns *The Immoralist* indirectly brought Dean to the attention of Elia Kazan, one of the most highly acclaimed directors in Hollywood. After a face-to-face screen test with Paul Newman, Dean was chosen to play the pivotal role of Caleb Trask in **East Of Eden**. Kazan's film based upon the last quarter of Steinbeck's biblical allegory — Cain and Abel, the new society — was made in secret, but long before its release the Warner Brothers publicity mill was grinding out stories of Kazan's 'new genius'.

East Of Eden premiered in New York. Tickets sold at $150 a-piece and patrons were escorted to their seats by celebrity usherettes — Marlene Dietrich, Eva Marie Saint, Terry Moore — even Marilyn Monroe attended. The only star missing from what was touted "*the biggest turnout ever*" was Dean himself — he had gone home to visit his aunt in Fairmount.

For a very short time afterwards Dean played out the role of the Hollywood star — obligatorily attending film premiers dressed in a tuxedo with a 'screen goddess' of the era on his arm. One of the first women to be romantically linked with James was Vampira, a camp occultist who dressed ghoulishly in black and introduced hack horror films on late night television. She sent him a photograph of herself sat by an open grave with the words "*Darling, come and join me*" emblazoned across:

"*I have a fairly adequate knowledge of satanic forces*", said Dean, "*and I was interested to find out if this girl was obsessed by such a force. She was a subject about which I wanted to learn. I met her and engaged her in conversation. She knew absolutely nothing!*"

Vampira built an altar for Jimmy because she believed he was destroying himself and needed help. In a last, vain attempt to get his attention she shaved off her long black hair. Vampira later claimed responsibility for James Dean's death after publicly putting a curse on him on national television:

"*O, Ye powers of Mwuetzi Moon Men, come to my aid!*"

His one real Hollywood romance was with Pier Angeli who starred alongside Paul Newman in **The Silver Chalice**. The couple often escaped to a secret hideaway along the Pacific coast. "*Sometimes we would just go for a walk along the beach, not actually speaking, but communicating our love silently to each other. We were like Romeo and Juliet, together and inseperable*".

However, Pier's mother strongly disapproved (James Dean was not Catholic) and to the world's surprise Pier announced her engagement to singer Vic Damone, the wedding would be in two weeks. "*The day of the wedding, Jimmy sat on his motorcycle across the street from St Timothy's Catholic Church and gunned his motor as the bride and groom emerged*". (David Dalton)

Five years later she was divorced. Pier remarried in 1962 but again divorce soon followed. She died in 1971 from a drugs overdose reported 'accidental' — "*I tried to love my husbands but it never lasted. I would wake up in the night and find that I had been dreaming of Jimmy. I would lie awake in the same bed as my husband, think of my love for Jimmy and wish it was Jimmy and not my husband who was next to me.*"

Rumours suggest that Pier was pregnant by Jimmy when she became engaged to Damone, and that she aborted the child soon after the marriage.

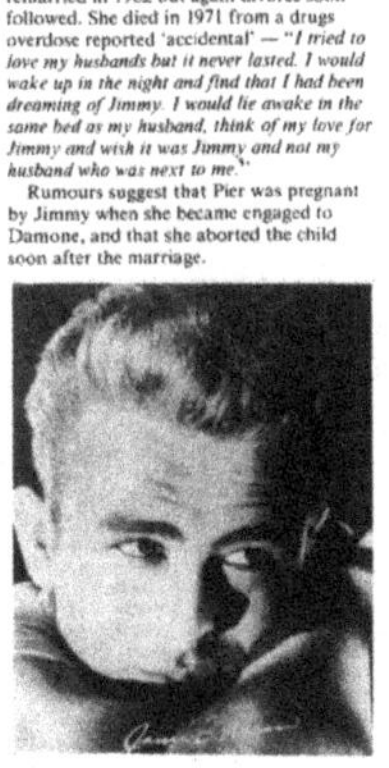

Two final television films — **I Am A Fool** and **The Unlighted Road** — were made and screened before work began on **Rebel Without A Cause** and **Giant**. Dean completed the films and signed a new contract with Warner Brothers that gave him "nearly a million dollars for nine films over the next six years". He was cast immediately as Billy the Kid in **The Left-Handed Gun** and as Rocky Graziano in **Somebody Up There Likes Me**. He celebrated by buying himself a Porsche 'Spyder'. A $6000 sports car with a top speed of over 150 miles per hour. He used the car in a commercial for safe driving: "*People say racing is dangerous, but I'd rather take my chances on the track any day than on the highway . . . drive safely . . . because the life you safe may be – mine.*" Words of tragic irony.

Dean had entered the Porsche in a race at Salinas. The car had only 150 miles on the clock, and since it needed at least 1000 to be in peak racing condition Jimmy took the decision to drive it there.

30th September, 1955 — Jimmy began the journey at 1.30 pm. His mechanic friend Rolf Wutheridge sat in the passenger seat.

3.30 pm — Dean received a ticket for speeding. He was doing 65 miles per hour in a 45 miles per hour zone.

5.15 pm — They made a fifteen minute stop at Blackwell's Corner before pressing on "non-stop to Paso Robles". It was twilight as the car approached the intersection of Routes 41 and 466 in Chalame. A Ford Sedan going in the opposite direction, along Route 466, began to turn left: "*That guy up there's got to stop; he'll see us.*"

5.45 pm — James Dean was dead.

His body was taken home to Fairmount and buried beside his mother.

Dean received the first posthumous Academy Award nomination for the work on **East Of Eden**. Fans went hysterical; distraught masses held frenzied pilgrimages in attempts to 'contact' the dead star. They bought jewellery made from fragments of the Porsche's smashed windscreen and ransacked the studios where he had worked. Stars who die at their peak always receive adulation far beyond what could have been achieved had they lived out their natural career, for example Marilyn Monroe and Buddy Holly. The public (in sympathy) tends to remember then only for their 'genius' and the fans, now deprived of further developments in their star's career, can only speculate on what-would-have-been. And in most cases such speculation can lead only to even higher regard.

James Dean was different from the other posthumous stars; his popularity peaked *after* his death. Of the three films he had made only **East Of Eden** had been released; and that was after a huge promotional drive by Warners that had made him the idol of millions before anyone had even seen the film. This fanatical enthusiasm was then cannoned out of all proportions by the young star's tragic and untimely death. Only when this delirious worship was at its height did Warner Brothers release **Rebel Without A Cause** that established Dean as the patron saint of misunderstood youth. The following year Dean's *final* film **Giant** was unveiled to a begging public; it co-starred Elizabeth Taylor, the Queen of the movies and was directed by Hollywood legend George Stevens; it's not difficult to imagine the hype it received and the pandemonium it caused. James Dean was no longer just an all-American country boy turned superstar; he was above all that; he had become a religion.

FOTOS: J. D. FOUND/CURTIS MANAGEMENT GROUP

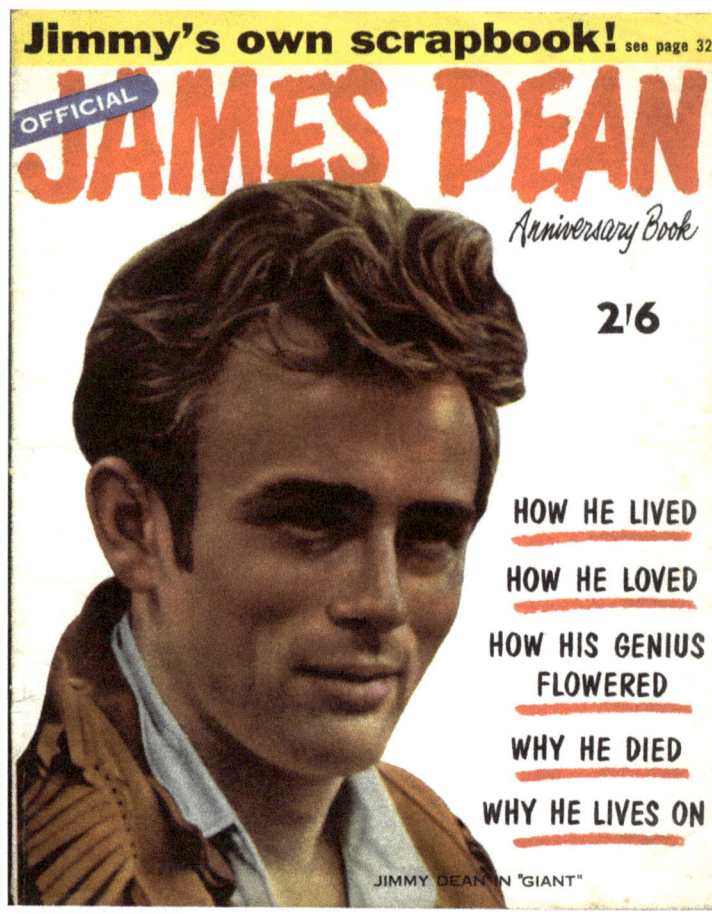

BRAVO
Deutschlands
größte Zeitschrift
für junge Leute

James Dean
Jimmy beim Studieren
seiner Rolle: Dieses Foto
von ihm habt Ihr noch nie
gesehen. Obwohl er seit
über 28 Jahren tot ist,
bleibt James Dean
unvergessen...

www.ingramcontent.com/pod-product-compliance
Lightning Source LLC
Chambersburg PA
CBHW041232240426
43673CB00010B/321